Regional Pathways to Complexity

AMSTERDAM ARCHAEOLOGICAL STUDIES 15

Editorial Board:
Prof. dr. E.M. Moormann
Prof. dr. P.A.J. Attema
Prof. dr. N. Roymans
Prof. dr. F. Theuws

Other titles in the series:

N. Roymans (ed.): *From the Sword to the Plough*
Three Studies on the Earliest Romanisation of Northern Gaul
ISBN 90 5356 237 0

T. Derks: *Gods, Temples and Ritual Practices*
The Transformation of Religious Ideas and Values in Roman Gaul
ISBN 90 5356 254 0

A. Verhoeven: *Middeleeuws gebruiksaardewerk in Nederland (8e – 13e eeuw)*
ISBN 90 5356 267 2

F. Theuws / N. Roymans (eds): *Land and Ancestors*
Cultural Dynamics in the Urnfield Period and the Middle Ages in the Southern Netherlands
ISBN 90 5356 278 8

J. Bazelmans: *By Weapons made Worthy*
Lords, Retainers and Their Relationship in Beowulf
ISBN 90 5356 325 3

R. Corbey / W. Roebroeks (eds): *Studying Human Origins*
Disciplinary History and Epistemology
ISBN 90 5356 464 0

M. Diepeveen-Jansen: *People, Ideas and Goods*
New Perspectives on 'Celtic barbarians' in Western and Central Europe (500-250 BC)
ISBN 90 5356 481 0

G. J. van Wijngaarden: *Use and Appreciation of Mycenean Pottery in the Levant, Cyprus and Italy (ca. 1600-1200 BC)*
The Significance of Context
ISBN 90 5356 482 9

F.A. Gerritsen: *Local Identities*
Landscape and community in the late prehistoric Meuse-Demer-Scheldt region
ISBN 90 5356 588 4

N. Roymans: *Ethnic Identity and Imperial Power*
The Batavians in the Early Roman Empire
ISBN 90 5356 705 4

J.A.W. Nicolay: *Armed Batavians*
Use and significance of weaponry and horse gear from non-military contexts in the Rhine delta (50 bc to ad 450)
ISBN 978 90 5356 253 6

M. Groot: *Animals in ritual and economy in a Roman frontier community*
Excavations in Tiel-Passewaaij
ISBN 978 90 8964 0 222

T. Derks & N. Roymans: *Ethnic Constructs in Antiquity*
The role of power and tradition
ISBN 978 90 8964 078 9

Tesse D. Stek: *Cult places and cultural change in Republican Italy*
A contextual approach to religious aspects of rural society after the Roman conquest
ISBN 978 90 8964 177 9

Regional Pathways to Complexity

SETTLEMENT AND LAND-USE DYNAMICS IN EARLY ITALY FROM
THE BRONZE AGE TO THE REPUBLICAN PERIOD

AUTHORS

PETER A.J. ATTEMA, GERT-JAN L.M. BURGERS
& P. MARTIJN VAN LEUSEN

AMSTERDAM UNIVERSITY PRESS

This book meets the requirements of ISO 9706: 1994, Information and documentation – Paper for documents – Requirements for permanence.

Cover illustration: Stele from the Archaic necropolis of L'Amastuola (Crispiano, TA),
photo Bert Brouwenstijn.
Cover design: Kok Korpershoek, Amsterdam
Lay-out: Bert Brouwenstijn, ACVU Amsterdam

ISBN 978 90 8964 276 9
e-ISBN 978 90 4851 344 4
NUR 682
© Amsterdam University Press, Amsterdam, 2010

All rights reserved. Without limiting the rights under copyright reserved above, no part of this book may be reproduced, stored in or introduced into a retrieval system, or transmitted, in any form or by any means (electronic, mechanical, photocopying, recording, or otherwise), without the written permission of both the copyright owner and the editors of this book.

CONTENTS

PREFACE	I
1. INTRODUCTION	1
1.1 Background	3
1.2 Approaches	11
1.3 Issues in regional landscape archaeology	19
Box 1.1 Case study: fabric analysis in southern Lazio	17
Box 1.2 Case study: visibility and other bias factors in the surface archaeological record of the Sibaritide	21
Box 1.3 Modelling settlement hierarchy and territories	26
2. REGIONAL SETTLEMENT DYNAMICS OF THE PONTINE REGION	31
2.1 Introduction	31
2.2 Environmental studies	32
2.3 Land systems and the archaeological record	40
2.4 Concluding discussion	57
Box 2.1 Pollen studies in the Pontine region	36
Box 2.2 Colluviation and alluviation in the Pontine Plain	41
3. REGIONAL SETTLEMENT DYNAMICS OF THE SALENTO ISTHMUS	59
3.1 Introduction	59
3.2 Environmental studies: sedimentation, climate and anthropogenic impact	60
3.3 Land systems and the archaeological record	62
3.4 Concluding discussion	79
4. SETTLEMENT DYNAMICS OF THE SIBARITIDE AND ITS HINTERLAND	81
4.1 Introduction	81
4.2 Environment and historic land use	82
4.3 Settlement and land use in the coastal plain	89
4.4 Protohistorical centralization in the foothills	91
4.5 The contribution of field survey: the Raganello Archaeological Project	100
4.6 Conclusion	103
Box 4.1 Pollen evidence for Bronze Age pastoralism	85
Box 4.2 Research and visibility biases of the Sibaritide hinterland	102
5. CENTRALIZATION AND PROTO-URBANIZATION IN THE BRONZE AND IRON AGES	107
5.1 Introduction	107
5.2 Differing regional pathways to complexity in protohistory	108
5.3 Conclusion	117
Box 5.1 Indicators of socio-economic complexity in the Sibaritide	114

6. RETHINKING EARLY GREEK – INDIGENOUS ENCOUNTERS
   IN SOUTHERN ITALY   119
   6.1 Introduction   119
   6.2 The hegemony of Sybaris   120
   6.3 Iron Age indigenous settlement expansion and early indigenous – Greek encounters 122
   6.4 A colonial enclave and its wider context: Taras and the Salento peninsula 124
   6.5 Questioning early Greek colonial impact   01
        Box 6.1 Greeks and natives at L'Amastuola   129

7. INDIGENOUS URBANIZATION IN THE ARCHAIC PERIOD   135
   7.1 Introduction   135
   7.2 Archaic urbanization in the Salento peninsula   135
   7.3 Urbanization and early Roman colonization in the Pontine region   140
   7.4 Conclusion   145

8. RURAL INFILL, URBANIZATION AND ROMAN EXPANSION   147
   8.1 Roman conquest and colonization   147
   8.2 Rural settlement   149
   8.3 Urban development   150
   8.4 Rural infill and the expansion of agriculture   152
   8.5 Local variability in rural trends   155
   8.6 Comparing rural settlement patterns in Central and South Italy   160
   8.7 Exploring a macro-regional explanation   164
   8.8 Epilogue: late Republican agriculture and the city of Rome   166

9. A SUPRA-REGIONAL COMPARATIVE PERSPECTIVE   171
   9.1 Introduction   171
   9.2 Methodological advances   171
   9.3 Interpretations   176
   9.4 Final remarks   179

Bibliographic references   181

Index   199

Colour plates   205

PREFACE

This volume synthesizes the results of a Dutch landscape-archaeological project in central and southern Italy, called *Regional Pathways to Complexity* (RPC). Although the project itself started in 1997 and formally ended in 2001, it is correctly viewed as only the latest in a long series of archaeological research projects by the Groningen Institute of Archaeology (GIA) and the Archaeological Centre of the Free University of Amsterdam (ACVU) in Italy. Accordingly, this volume synthesizes studies undertaken since the early 1980s as well as others conducted in the years since the RPC project ended.[1]

A study of central and southern Italy between the end of the Bronze Age and the end of the Roman Republican period presents several major challenges: the size of the region, the length of the period under investigation, and especially the difficulty to investigate effectively the long-term processes operating at this time in this area, processes that involved the growing complexity of indigenous societies, and the transformation of traditional rural and pastoral ways of life into urbanism during the period of 'external' Greek and Roman colonization.

Our purpose was not only to synthesize the results of the fieldwork, but also to present interpretations of and reflections on these processes, the approaches we used to investigate them, as well as the strengths and weaknesses of the theoretical models applied by ourselves and others to explain our findings. This is why the introductory and concluding chapters contain extensive discussions of methodology. It is hoped that the RPC experience, once published, will be of interest to others pursuing similar studies.

STRUCTURE OF THIS BOOK

Chapter 1 introduces the RPC project itself and provides an outline of its methodology. The chapter discusses, firstly, the integration of settlement archaeology, environmental research, ethnography and ceramics studies; and, secondly, the problems presented by, on the one hand, systematic biases in the archaeological record and, on the other, by our attempt to compare differently constituted regional archaeological records. The remainder of the volume is organised into two parts, the first (chapters 2 to 4) being arranged chronologically by region, the second (chapters 5 to 8) chronologically by theme. A final chapter pulls together the main threads and conclusions of our argument.

The first few chapters deal with each of the three RPC regions in turn (chapter 2: Pontine region, chapter 3: Salento isthmus, chapter 4: Sibaritide). Each chapter begins with a reconstruction of the principal geographical and environmental factors that influenced the forms of human habitation and land use. This is followed by a chronologically ordered discussion of actual settlement configurations and land use patterns, based on comparisons of the various field surveys and other settlement data. Each chapter sets out to describe the intra-regional differentiation in settlement and land use in relation to geography and environment. Together, these chapters provide a general context for the thematic and chronological comparison of the three RPC study regions in part II.

The later chapters deal with the major changes that occurred in our three regions between the Bronze Age and the Roman Imperial period. Chapter 5 is dedicated to the protohistorical phases, with a particular focus on the formation of proto-urban centres and 'rural infill' of the landscape prior to Greek

---

[1] All Dutch research up to 2005 in the three study areas has been included in the current study, as well as important publications up to 2008.

or Roman colonization. Chapter 6 looks more closely at the earliest colonizations, investigating the impact of Greek colonization on indigenous settlement and society and questioning the presumed political and cultural dominance of the Greek colonial city-states. Chapter 7 focuses on Archaic urbanisation processes in Salento and the Pontine region. Chapter 8 explores the phenomenon of rural expansion that accompanied the process of urbanization in Italy in the Hellenistic (or Roman Republican) period, and in particular in the late 4th-3rd centuries BC; it closes with an epilogue dedicated to further transformations during the late Republican period.

ACKNOWLEDGEMENTS

The RPC project was one of three large archaeological projects that received funding from the Netherlands Organization for Scientific Research in 1997, in the context of the programme 'Settlement and Landscape in Archaeology' (NWO grant no. 250-09-100). We are extremely grateful to have been given the opportunity to pursue this line of research, as well as for NWO's patience when this final synthetic volume was delayed.

Likewise, the Royal Netherlands Institute in Rome (KNIR) has steadfastly supported RPC project staff and students of the participating institutions over the years by hosting meetings and study visits. We are especially grateful for the Institute's sponsorship of this publication, which together with smaller subsidies by GIA and ACVU made possible both proper editing of the English text, and the use of colour for the maps and photographs.

Several colleagues from both participating institutions have been closely involved in the research for many years, and we wish to acknowledge our debt to their work, enthusiasm and expertise: Dr. Bert Nijboer for sharing with us his extensive knowledge of protohistoric Italy, Prof. Douwe Yntema for his expertise on Apulian archaeology and supervision of the dissertations of Veenman and Mater, Prof. em. Marianne Kleibrink for first directing the excavation programs at Satricum and Francavilla and then sharing her profound knowledge of the archaeology of Latium and the Sibaritide, Dr. Jan Sevink for his supervision of Van Joolen's dissertation, and Dr. Jan Delvigne for his supervision of students and especially for the enjoyable and insightful field trips at which we learned a lot about the past and present landscapes of the Pontine Region and the Sibaritide. Other colleagues contributed toward the success of the RPC project through their participation in a 3-day conference organised by the RPC team in 2002 at Groningen University:[2] Dr Maria Beatrice Annis (Rome), Dr Arnold Beijer † (Groningen), Professor John Bintliff (Leiden), Mr Bastiaan Bijl (Assen), Dr Gabriele Cifani (Rome), Professor Francesco D'Andria (Lecce), Dr Helga Di Giuseppe (Rome), Professor Abbas Farshad (Enschede), Mr Hendrik Feiken (Groningen), Professor Gaetano Forni (Milan), Professor Maurizio Gualtieri (Perugia), Dr Gerard Heuvelink (Amsterdam), Dr Helle Horsnaes (Copenhagen), Dr Kees Koot (Amsterdam), Professor Clive Orton (London), Dr Helen Patterson (Rome), Dr Grazia Semeraro (Lecce), Prof Alastair Small (Edinburgh), Dr Steve Thompson (Austin), Professor Jean-Pierre Vallat (Paris), Dr Piet van der Velde (Leiden), Dr Elisabeth van 't Lindenhout (Groningen), Dr Gert-Jan van Wijngaarden (Amsterdam), Dr Alessandro Vanzetti (Rome), Dr Philip Verhagen (Amsterdam), Professor Frank Vermeulen (Gent), Dr Juanita Vroom (Leiden), Dr Rob Witcher (Durham), and Dr Andrea Zifferero (Siena). For their help in discussing, defining and refining research questions, we thank them again.

The PhD research of our three colleagues in the RPC project, Benoît Mater, Froukje Veenman and Ester van Joolen, figures prominently in this volume. We hope that we have done justice to it, and that our readers will be enticed to sample the original publications!

[2] Published in Attema *et al.* 2002.

Beside the authors themselves, several other people have been involved in the production of this book. Bert Brouwenstijn, draughtsman at ACVU, was responsible for most of the work on the maps and figures, and for the entire layout; Jaap Fokkema and Martijn van Leusen assisted in the production of the maps. The correction of the text was professionally handled by Gerre van der Kleij at GrondTaal Vertaalbureau.

Finally, much of the research on which this book was based took place in Italy. Thanks are due first of all to the student participants, who are too numerous to be mentioned here by name, and in particular to the team leaders, both those of our field surveys of the period 1997-2000, and those of the later surveys and excavations that we continue to direct in the RPC regions. For many, this was their first encounter with archaeological fieldwork in Italy, and we hope they have enjoyed it as much as we have.

Of course, no foreign archaeological mission in Italy could be successful without the help and participation of local authorities and Italian colleagues active in the study and management of the regional archaeological heritage. We acknowledge their contributions here by region:

The GIA research programme directed by Kleibrink in the Sibaritide, entitled 'Dominant versus non-dominant, Greeks and Oenotrians on the Timpone della Motta', started in 1993 while the regional Raganello Archaeological Project, directed by Attema and Van Leusen, started in 2002.[3] This latter project studies the catchment area of the Timpone della Motta and the up- and highlands of the upper and middle Raganello watershed area. Both programmes were financed by the Netherlands Organisation for Scientific Research and the Groningen Institute of Archaeology, and are now supported by and developed together with the Italian *Direzione Generale per i Beni Archeologici* and the *Soprintendenza per i beni archeologici della Calabria*. We sincerely thank our Italian colleagues and especially the then *soprintendente* dott.ssa Elena Lattanzi, the inspector dott.ssa Silvana Luppino, Prof. Renato Peroni † and Dr Alessandro Vanzetti for their kind cooperation.

The ACVU research programme in the Salento isthmus is being financed by the Vrije Universiteit Amsterdam and the Netherlands Organisation for Scientific Research. It was developed in close collaboration with the *Scuola di Specializzazione di Archeologia Classica e Medioevale 'Dinu Adamesteanu'* of the University of Salento (*Progetto Strategico no. 25100* of the *Consiglio Nazionale per le Ricerche*), and the *Soprintendenza per i beni archeologici della Puglia*. We sincerely thank our colleagues for their cooperation, and especially Prof. Francesco D'Andria, Prof. Mario Lombardo, Prof. Grazia Semeraro and dott. Girolamo Fiorentino (University of Salento) and dott. Giuseppe Andreassi, dott.ssa Assunta Cocchiaro, dott.ssa Antonietta dell'Aglio and dott.ssa Grazia Angela Maruggi † (*Soprintendenza*). The data from this programme are gradually being published in a number of monographs (Boersma 1990; 1995; Yntema 1993a; Burgers 1998. Interim reports are being presented in the *Bulletin Antieke Beschaving*).

The GIA research programme in the Pontine region, 'Roman colonization south of Rome, a comparative survey of three early Romanized landscapes', was financed by the Dutch Royal Academy of Sciences (KNAW) in the period 1994-1997. The surveys were published in Attema and Van Leusen 2004 and in the form of various papers in the annual GIA source publication *Palaeohistoria*. Thanks are due to dott.ssa Nicoletta Cassieri, dott.ssa S. Ghini and dott.ssa A. Zarattini and dott. F. di Mario and dott. G. Cassatella of the *Soprintendenza per il Lazio, Roma*, prof. P. Chiarucci of the *Museo Civico di Albano Laziale*, dott. F. Zaccheo of the *Antiquarium Comunale di Sezze* and dott. A. Lutazzi of the *Antiquarium Comunale di Colleferro* for their support. Earlier surveys of the Pontine Region Project were subsidized by the Netherlands Organization for Scientific Research (NWO) and were published in Attema 1993. Key publications on the Groningen excavations at Satricum are Maaskant-Kleibrink 1987 and 1992a; a monograph on the Pontine region by Attema is in preparation.

---

[3] Kleibrink 2002.

1 Introduction

'Regional Pathways to Complexity' was the short title for a project covering the long-term archaeology of three regions in Italy. It began in late 1997 and is now, more than a decade later, completed with the publication of this synthetic volume. The full title of the project was *Regional Pathways to Complexity, Landscape and Settlement Dynamics in early Italy*, and its primary aim was a multidisciplinary and comparative assessment of processes of centralization and urbanization in three Italian landscapes during, roughly, the 1st millennium BC.[1] Particular attention was paid to the internal social dynamics of the regions investigated and, correspondingly, to local responses to and interaction with the process of Greek and Roman colonialization.

In the archaeology of Italy from the Bronze Age to the Roman period, the study of the internal development of indigenous Italic societies and landscapes has remained a relatively underdeveloped area. This is due to the emphasis on explanations relying on external factors (the influence of non-Italic cultures), dominant historical processes (the Greek and Roman colonizations), and a traditional culture-historical view of society (stages of growth, flowering and decline). Much attention has been lavished on the influence on regional Italic cultures of foreign artefacts and manufacturing techniques during the 'Mycenaean' and Graeco-Roman periods, when contacts of trade and exchange ranged throughout the Mediterranean. Similarly, interest in Greek and Roman colonization, mainly based on historical sources, has dominated over the study of the role of native cultures. This one-sided approach has led to the view that the early urbanization of central and southern Italy has been a relatively homogeneous process, in which the role of international impulses and colonization movements has been paramount.

Accordingly, the aim of the RPC project has been to demonstrate both the more complex nature of the archaeological reality, and the significant perspective offered by regional archaeological landscape studies. This was done by comparing the development of indigenous societies in central and southern Italy through the 1st millennium BC until and including their incorporation into the Roman state.

The regional perspective of the RPC project fits in with a well-established tradition of regional projects in Dutch archaeology. In 1996 this interest gave rise to a new research programme of the Netherlands Organization for Scientific Research (NWO), on 'Settlement and Landscape in Archaeology'. Ours was one of the three projects subsidized under this programme, which is an acknowledgement of the quality of existing Dutch research in Italy. It was a joint undertaking by the Groningen Institute of Archaeology (GIA) and the Archaeological Institute of the *Vrije Universiteit of Amsterdam* (AIVU[2]), and it employed six researchers specializing in settlement and landscape archaeology, environmental reconstruction, artefact analysis and spatial analysis. Four PhD students carried out the primary research on interrelated topics: Esther van Joolen and Martijn van Leusen at the GIA, and Froukje Veenman and Benoit Mater at the ACVU. Dr Peter Attema of the GIA, and Dr Gert-Jan Burgers on behalf of the ACVU, were responsible for the day-to-day management of the project and for the final integration of the various studies. Other senior scholars involved in the project were Prof. Marianne Kleibrink and Dr Bert Nijboer of the GIA, and Prof. Douwe Yntema of the ACVU.

---

[1] As our fieldwork turned up more and more significant remains dating to the Bronze Age, this period was increasingly included in our studies as well.

[2] Now renamed Archaeological Centre, we will refer to this institute by its current acronym ACVU in the remainder of this volume.

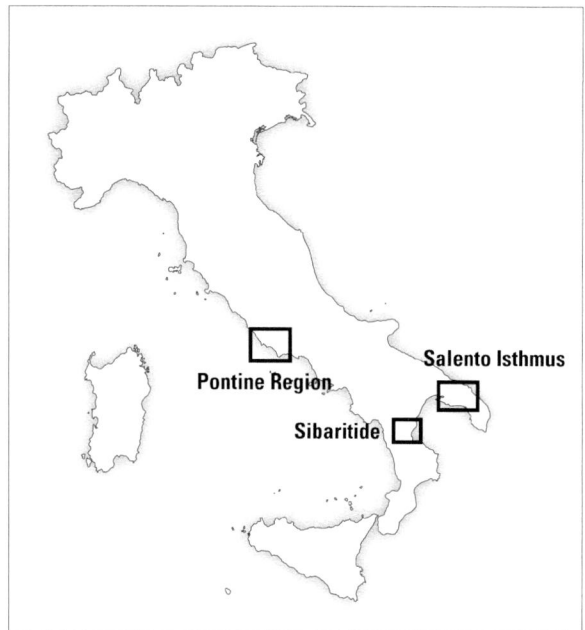

Fig. 1.1. Locations of the three core research areas of the RPC project in Italy.

The research was organized around two main themes, each comprising two complementary topics: on the one hand settlement and land use studies based on archaeological and ethnographical research, and on the other landscape and technology evaluation founded on paleo-environmental research and technological studies. Each of the four interrelated topics required a specialist study, and each had by 2005 resulted in a PhD dissertation[3].

Central to the RPC project was a study of spatial patterning in the archaeological record (by Martijn van Leusen). Regional site records have been inventoried in a single site database, and mapped for the purpose of analysis in a Geographical Information System. Using information on settlement distributions and land use potential provided by other project members, this research aimed to develop and use spatial modelling techniques derived from catchment and visibility analysis, and to model the processes of colonization and urbanization in the study areas.

A second study, by Esther van Joolen, focused on past potential land use, and was carried out in the form of a land evaluation analysis using a system adapted from that of the FAO.[4] This model was tested using pollen cores collected before and during the project (see chapter 2). The project employed the so-called Automated Land Evaluation System (ALES),[5] as well as GIS software in order to produce land suitability maps. It also used information on past actual land use and agricultural technology.

The third research theme focused on the reconstruction of actual (as opposed to potential) land use (by Froukje Veenman). Different types of pastoral land use were reconstructed on the basis of data from off-site find patterns, ethnographic parallels, and archaeozoological analysis. Changes in land use were interpreted in the light of contemporary processes of urbanization and colonization.

The fourth study concerned the scale, organization and technological development of pottery production (by Benoît Mater). Ceramic analysis was used to attempt the reconstruction of local pottery production and consumption systems through time. The primary goal here was to distinguish between 'internal' progress and external stimuli in pottery technology and production – which of these speeded up or slowed down technological improvement in pottery production, or possibly even led to a decline.

The four studies discussed above were integrated with the analyses of the settlement data available for the three regions, and with new fieldwork carried out by the team in the form of intensive field surveys in each region. The latter were intended to compensate for gaps in the regional archaeological records, gaps which were especially apparent in marginal or extensive exploitation areas such as those that were wetlands and highlands in antiquity. The areas investigated were the lagoonal *Fogliano* area near Latina in the Pontine region, the *Murge* plateau near Ostuni in the Salento isthmus region, and the foothills and terraces in the vicinity of Francavilla Marittima in the Sybaris region.

[3] Van Leusen 2002; Veenman 2002; Van Joolen 2003; Mater 2005.

[4] United Nations Food and Agricultural Organization.

[5] Developed by the International Institute for Geo-Information Science and Earth Observation (ITC) at Enschede (Netherlands).

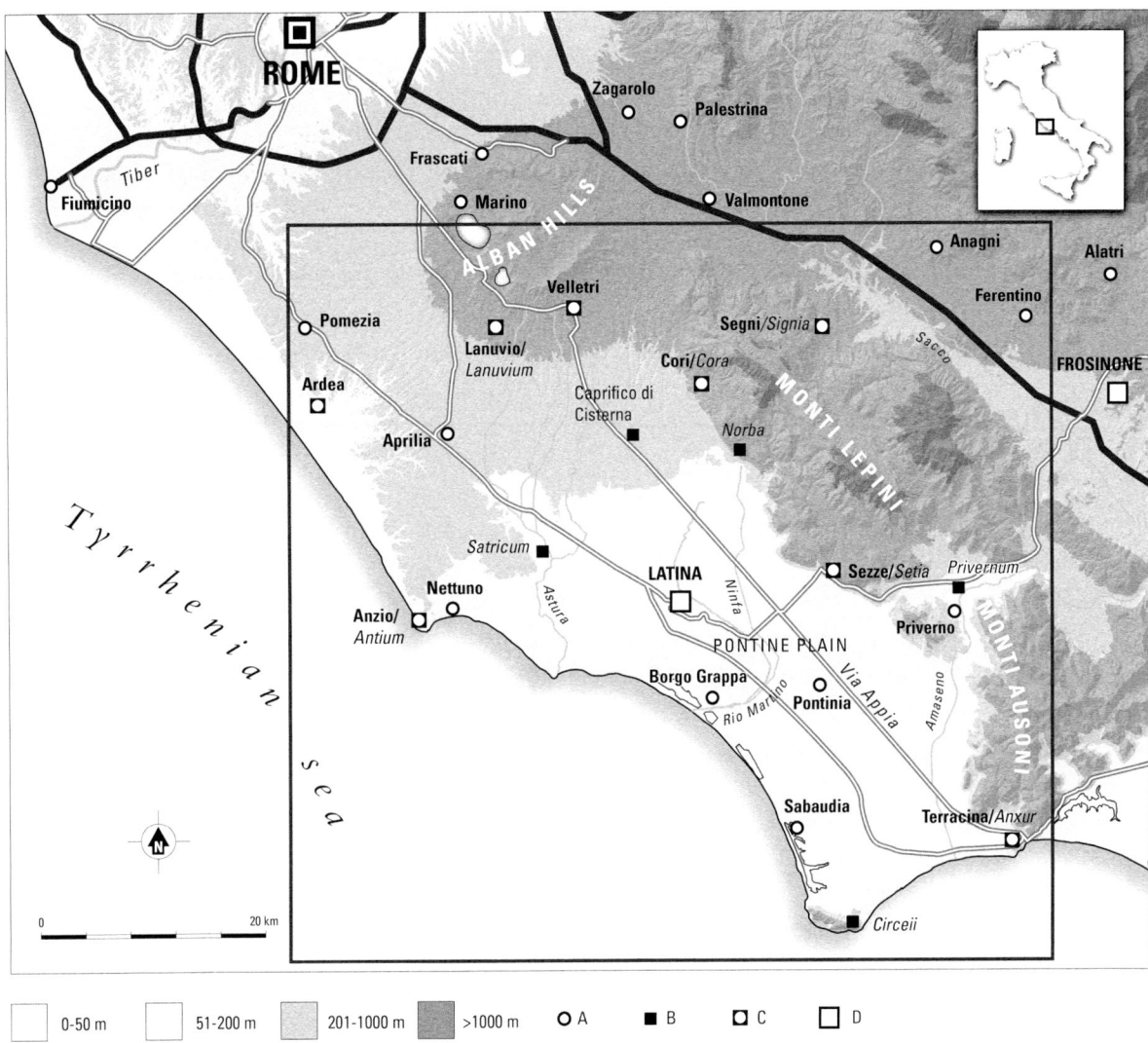

Fig. 1.2. Geography and topography of the Pontine region. A modern town; B ancient town; C ancient and modern town; D modern provincial capital. The RPC study area is indicated by a box. For a colour version of this figure, see page 205.

1.1 BACKGROUND

1.1.1 GEOGRAPHICAL AND CHRONOLOGICAL SETTING

Figure 1.1 shows the three regions constituting the core research areas of the RPC project: the Pontine region in Lazio, the Salento isthmus in Apulia and the Sibaritide in Calabria. There is a rich and ongoing tradition of Dutch archaeological fieldwork in all three regions, which provided the datasets constituting the starting point for the RPC research.[6] These projects were funded by the participating universities, by the Netherlands Organization for Scientific Research (NWO) and by the Royal Netherlands Academy of Arts and Sciences (KNAW), and they were developed in collaboration with the Italian *Soprintendenze* of Lazio, Calabria and Apulia and the *Scuola di Specializzazione in Archeologia Classica e Medievale* of the university of Lecce.

---

[6] Summarized in Attema *et al.* 1998a and 1998b.

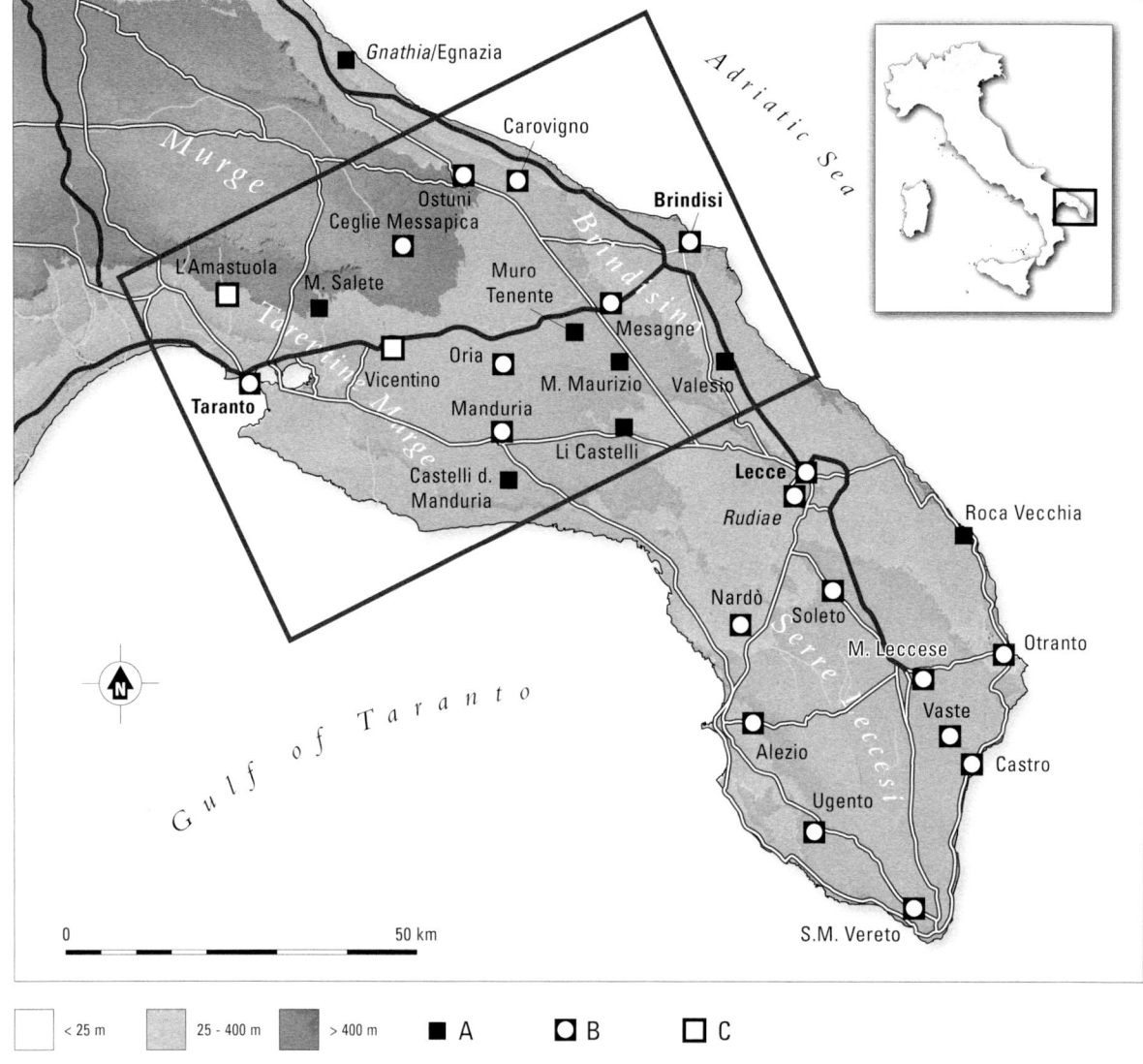

Fig. 1.3. Geography and topography of the Salento peninsula. A ancient town; B ancient and modern town; C named archaeological site. The Salento Isthmus is outlined. For a colour version of this figure, see page 206.

Figure 1.2 shows the digital elevation model of the Pontine region, which has been surveyed over the past decade in the context of the Pontine Region Project directed by Prof. Peter Attema. The project includes transect surveys, urban surveys and surveys of the rural catchment areas of ancient settlements, and with the help of these data analyzes settlement patterns and land use in the Pontine region between the Late Bronze Age and late Antiquity. By these means the project attempted to create a context for the study of urbanization and Roman colonization in this region. The study area, which lies between 60 and 80 km south of Rome, can be divided into three main physiographic units. The first is that of the Pontine plain, an almost flat coastal area with ancient beach ridges. Towards the north-west this plain is bordered by the volcanic area of the Alban hills, and towards the north-east by the limestone mountain range of the Monti Lepini. The settlement data available for these areas are, broadly speaking, of four different types. A first dataset consists of inventories of incidental finds reported to the archaeological *Soprintendenza*; a second set consists of controlled sets of topographical data mapped by Italian topographers and published in the so-called *Forma Italiae* series.[7] A third and major dataset for the region is

[7] Lugli 1926; 1928; Vittucci 1968; Piccarreta 1977.

formed by the reported results of excavations, notably those at Satricum carried out by the GIA and the University of Amsterdam, directed by Prof. Marianne Kleibrink and Prof. Marijke Gnade respectively.[8] Long-term excavation and documentary research into the protohistoric site of Satricum have resulted in invaluable insight into the development of an early Latin settlement, within the framework of regional socio-economic and religious dynamics. Our fourth and final dataset derives from the systematic surveys carried out by the Pontine Region Project and the Agro Pontino Survey of the University of Amsterdam.[9] The Pontine Region Project surveys by 2005 covered an estimated area of 13 sq.km, from sample areas on the lower slopes of the volcanic Alban hills (e.g. at Lanuvium), the alluvial parts of the Pontine plain (e.g. near Valvisciolo and Sezze) and the slopes and uplands of the Monti Lepini.[10] In the context of the RPC project these were supplemented by intensive surveys of the beach ridge/lagoonal landscape along the coast near Borgo Grappa in 1998-9.[11] The latter was combined with geomorphological and sedimentological research and vegetation studies as well as with land evaluation. In the period 2003-2006 further surveys, covering 9 sq.km were carried out in the coastal area between Anzio and the mouth of the Astura river.[12] The data collected so far in the various landscape units give us a fair idea of the major transformations in settlement and land use in the Alban hills and the Pontine plain.

Figure 1.3 shows the digital elevation model of the second of the three regions central to the RPC project. The Salento isthmus is a ca. 80 km-wide stretch of land between Taranto and Brindisi in Apulia, connecting the Salento peninsula to the mainland of Italy. Here, the RPC project has drawn largely on databases created in the context of the ongoing Brindisino project of the Archaeological Centre of the Vrije Universiteit of Amsterdam (ACVU, led by prof. Douwe Yntema, dr. Gert-Jan Burgers and, formerly, by em. prof. Johannes Boersma. The Brindisino forms the eastern half of the Salento isthmus. The larger part of this area is formed by a slightly undulating plain which from the Adriatic rises very gradually to approximately 60 m above sea level and consists mainly of light arable soils. By contrast, in the immediate coastal zone one finds a landscape alternating between dunes, low cliffs, and lagoons. Toward the south the plain merges into the hillier, calcareous landscape of the Serre Leccesi. To the west and north the Brindisi district encompasses some of the hard limestone spurs of the Murge uplands, a plateau which gradually rises up to the Apennine mountain chain.

The general theme of the Brindisino project is Romanization, a process that is studied from a long-term diachronic perspective with ample research devoted to the social dynamics of pre-Roman indigenous groups back to the Late Bronze Age. A major aim of the project is to study the relationship between social dynamics and the organization of settlement and landscape. To discover the latter, various teams carried out a series of intensive field surveys in the 1980s and 1990s, complemented by environmental research. The fieldwalking carried out up to 2008 (shown in figure 1.3) covers a total surface area of some 110 sq.km and incorporates environmental zones throughout the Salento isthmus. Approaches have ranged from total coverage surveys of major urban catchment areas, as at Oria and Valesio,[13] to urban surveys like those at Muro Tenente and Muro Maurizio and transect surveys crosscutting various physiographic units such as the Murge area near Ostuni.[14] These latter surveys were conducted in the context of the RPC project, and were supplemented by the archaeological data extracted from archival and museum research and from publications of sporadic find reports and incidental forms of field walking, such as those inventoried by Lorenzo and Stefania Quilici Gigli in the Brindisino.[15] Both our own surveys and the reports of sporadic finds were frequently tested by augering and by excavation of well-

---

[8] see Maaskant-Kleibrink 1987; 1992; Gnade 1992; 2002.
[9] see especially Voorrips et al. 1991; Attema 1993.
[10] Area estimate based on De Haas 2005.
[11] The Fogliano survey, which covered another 3 sq.km; Attema et al. 2001; Attema et al. 2005.
[12] For the Astura and Nettuno surveys: Attema et al. 2008; Attema et al. 2009.
[13] Yntema 1993a; 1993b.
[14] Burgers 1998; Burgers et al. 1998 [published 2004].
[15] Quilici / Quilici Gigli 1975.

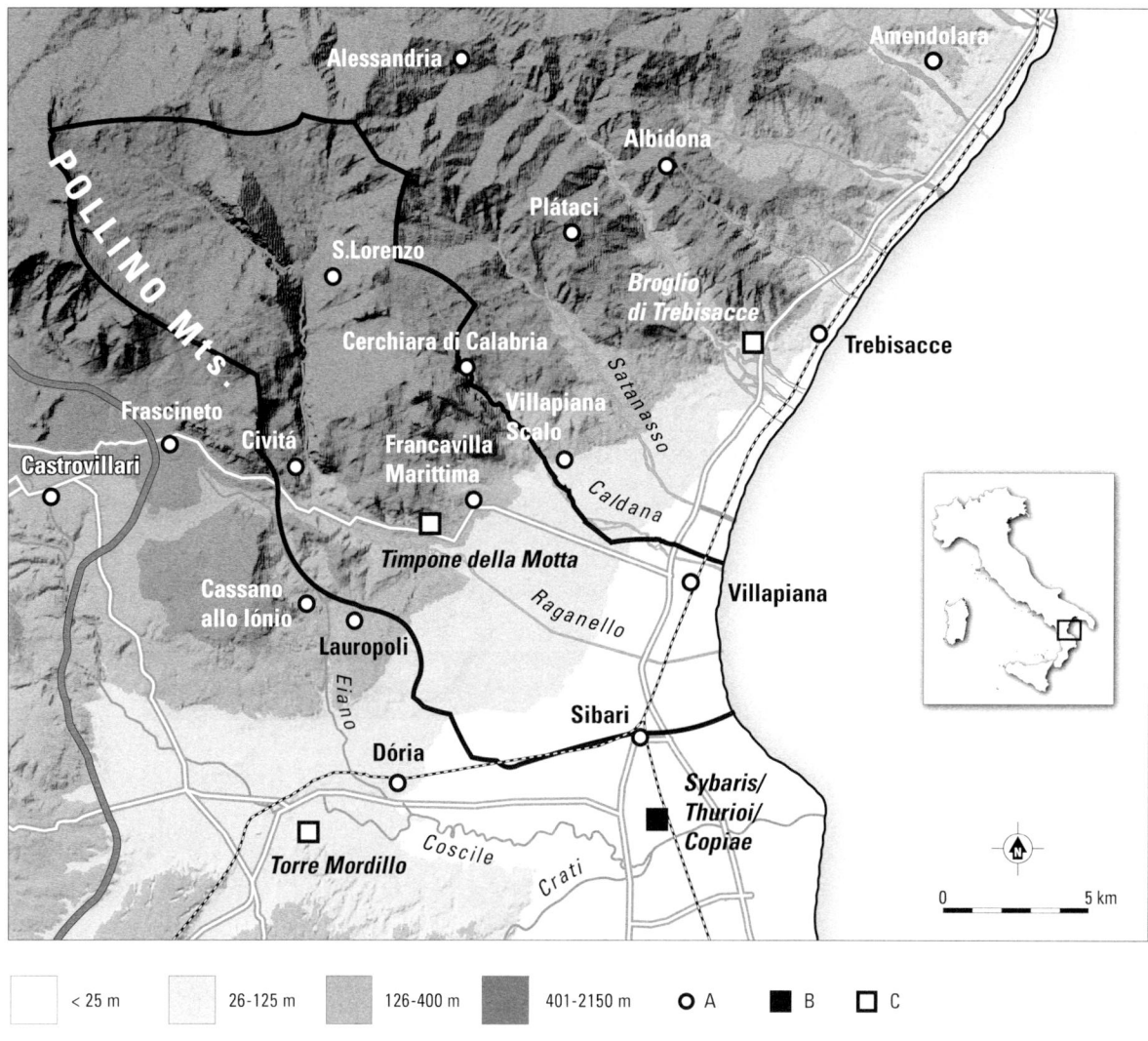

Fig. 1.4. Geography and topography of north-eastern Calabria. A modern town; B ancient town; C major archaeological site. The RPC study area is outlined. For a colour version of this figure, see page 207.

preserved stratigraphies. Furthermore, in the context of the Brindisino project large-scale excavations were carried out after the surveys at fortified sites such as Valesio and Muro Tenente.[16] These excavations provide the necessary chronological, functional and spatial refinements.

Figure 1.4 shows the digital elevation model of the third study area of the RPC project, a region known as the Sibaritide in Cosenza province, Calabria, south Italy. The model shows a quite different landscape than that in the two other regions, for it largely consists of a crescent-shaped alluvial plain. Toward the north this plain is delimited by a mountain range, with access routes to the hinterland largely restricted to the wide beds of the streams entering the plain. The Sibaritide has been the subject of research by the GIA since 1990. The primary problem that is being studied is the comparison of indigenous colonization in the Bronze Age and Early Iron Ages with Greek colonization movements

[16] Boersma / Yntema 1987; Boersma 1995; van Alberda et al. 1999; Burgers / Yntema 1999, Maruggi / Burgers 2001, Yntema 2001.

in the Sybaris plain. In line with the 'Regional Pathways to Complexity'-theme, the general aim of the project was to shift attention away from the dominant archaeology of Greek colonization, and to focus instead on the non-dominant archaeological history of the native societies. The database we worked with in this region is again derived from a variety of sources. Initially, the main study object was a system of Bronze-Age hilltop sites, one of which - on the *Timpone della Motta* near Francavilla Marittima - would develop into a hilltop sanctuary in the Iron Age, with settlements of huts and houses occupying three lower plateaus. Following earlier excavations in the 1960s and early 1970s by P. Stoop of Leiden University, the site has been excavated since 1991 by Prof. Marianne Kleibrink.[17] Beside the records of these excavations, our dataset includes an inventory of several hundreds of sites and find scatters compiled by Italian topographers in the 1960s as well as an inventory of protohistoric sites collated by the team of Prof. Renato Peroni in the early 1990s.[18] To this we may add a number of field surveys carried out by the GIA in the vicinity of the excavations on the hill Timpone della Motta. In 2000 the RPC team carried out intensive surveys on the landscape of ancient marine terraces in the transitional zone between the plain and the foothills, and this has since been followed by regular intensive and extensive surveys of the foothills and inland mountainous zone.[19]

I.1.2 A COMPARATIVE REGIONAL APPROACH

As will be clear from this brief overview of RPC project data sources, systematic and intensive field surveys constitute the principal point of departure for our analyses. Since the pioneering work of Sir John Ward Perkins in southern Etruria fieldwalking surveys have come of age, particularly in Italy. Just a few decades ago the technique of intensive field survey still needed strong justification even among archaeological field workers, but now it is generally recognized as a basic tool for the study of regional landscapes. In Italy, this acknowledgement has been accompanied by a wave of survey projects, covering plains, plateaus, valleys and, though to a lesser extent, mountains. At the same time, issues ranging from methodological details to problems of data analysis and interpretation are continuously and fervently debated - a critical attitude which demonstrates the health of the discipline. However, macro-regional interpretative schemes have not yet been widely employed: regional archaeological projects are all too often inward-looking. Projects may therefore evaluate basically similar dynamics from different perspectives and, consequently, explain them in rather different terms. This is an unhappy incongruence, and it precludes the analysis of patterns and dynamics in a supra-regional framework.[20]

One must conclude that, although regional surveys have contributed much to the breakdown of traditional generalizations about the Italian landscape, and have proved to be a rich source of new data, few attempts have yet been made to formulate new questions about historically known developments, or to create supra-regional syntheses. Rather, the regionalization inherent in recent fieldwork programmes has led to an overemphasis on internal factors - from environmental constraints to elite social strategies - as stimuli for regional change. Factors relating to the integration of local societies into interregional networks of exchange or power, or to shared mentalities, were somewhat neglected. This seems especially odd in the case of Italian urbanization studies, since with urbanization - and growing social and economic complexity in general - the scale of integration tends to increase and supra-regional processes are therefore likely to increasingly determine intra-regional dynamics.

Of course, this does not exclude the possibility that developments in some regions may have fol-

---

[17] Maaskant Kleibrink 1993; Kleibrink / Sangineto 1998; 2006.

[18] De Rossi *et al.* 1969; Peroni / Trucco 1994.

[19] Van Leusen / Attema 2003; Attema *et al.* 2004; Attema *et al.* 2006.

[20] Bintliff 1997.

lowed a unique trajectory. On the contrary, specific regions might, in particular phases of their history, demonstrate phenomena completely unique and unlike any supra-regional patterns. Still, we can only establish whether this is the case if we first follow the comparative regional approach. Such research is a prerequisite also if we wish to move away from the traditional perception of Italian urbanization as a rather homogeneous process, triggered in particular by dominant Greek and Roman colonial and urban institutions. Fortunately, the range of regional projects carried out in the last decades allows us to approach urbanization in ancient Italy as a spatially differentiated phenomenon and to acknowledge that there existed a range of variations in regional trajectories towards complexity.

1.1.3 DEFINING THE CONCEPTS

Complexity

In a recent publication Robert Chapman looked critically at the use of the term complexity in archaeology,[21] noting that, although the term is widely used, it is often poorly or only implicitly defined. Whilst acknowledging the critique of various scholars that the simple-versus-complex duality is a creation of modernity, Chapman is of the opinion that, if one turns to the long-term record of archaeology, there is 'no doubt that the human societies which inhabit this planet have become more complex (in the sense of interconnectedness) and more unequal, both within individual societies and at the level of global relations. [This is] a gross trend, superimposed on shorter-term records of evolution and devolution, of 'rise' and 'fall' of more complex societies such as the earliest states, of change at different rates and scales, or to put it more grandly, of history. There have been many different forms of society, as there are today and complexity should not be conceived of as the ultimate goal of social evolution'.[22] In line with this, Shennan observes that recent theories of complexity do indeed 'direct us to a comparative approach that attempts to explain the similarities and differences between local trajectories of change.[23]

We too believe that it cannot be denied that the societies in the regions we have studied became more complex in the *longue durée* from the Bronze Age to the Roman period. This happened both in terms of social and administrative 'interconnectedness' (as their organizational forms developed from tribes to chiefdoms and from early states to the incorporation in the Roman Empire) and in terms of geographical 'interconnectedness' (as exchange and trade systems in the Mediterranean became more intricate).[24] To define complexity in practical terms, archaeologists have concentrated on its material expressions, such as the growth of a settlement hierarchy, the emergence of fortifications, the birth of cities, social stratification, technological innovations, the introduction of writing, and long-distance trade. As will be clear from the chapters that follow, many of these traits can indeed be identified in the archaeological record of the regions studied in this book. In what follows, these traits will often be implicitly assumed to mean that the societies we study did indeed become more complex in the long run. At the same time, however, we will see that the trajectories of change were far from uniform, culturally and socially as well as in time and space.

Urbanism and urbanization

The concept of urbanization, and therefore also that of urbanism, is central to the RPC project. Perceptions of urbanism are manifold, ranging from positive associations with 'civilization', to negative, moralist

[21] Chapman 2003.
[22] Chapman 2003, 7.
[23] Shennan 2001.
[24] One definition of *complexity* would be 'things complex have more parts and more connections between parts' (Chapman 2003, 82, referring to Price 1995).

correlations with despotic power and centralized economy and ideology.[25] Such notions also underlie archaeological studies of the ancient town, although most of them are outspokenly positive, mirroring the classical view of the proper organization of society. It is above all the success of the Roman town and the Greek polis that has attracted major attention from classical archaeologists to urbanism and urbanization. Traditionally they focused on physical aspects, in particular on the development of an urban lay-out and of public buildings and city walls. However, in the last three decades research perspectives have widened considerably, due in large part to the introduction of the technique of field survey alongside the excavation of urban sites in the tradition of the 'big dig'. The regional scope of surveys made it possible to focus on the relationship between town and countryside, including the wider landscape in urbanism studies. Questions could now be asked about the town's role as economic centre and the spread of market exchange, about the town's consumer role versus the supply role of the countryside, and about the political and religious relationship between town and countryside. These questions have long been central to the debate on urbanism among historians, and as field surveys are able to monitor long-term trends in the occupational history of a region, archaeology was now finally able to contribute to this debate.[26] Diachronic regional archaeological surveys have made it possible to study such questions from a developmental perspective, and to give ample attention to the less visible centralization processes occurring before the spread of urbanism. Field surveyors' focus on regional landscapes also encouraged an interest in social processes in areas that were previously considered marginal to the study of ancient urbanism. In the RPC regions, indications of such processes have long been treated merely as signs of the diffusive strength of the Greek and Roman experience, with colonization generally being regarded as a 'prime mover'.

The RPC team closely adheres to the approaches discussed above. Central to its definition of ancient urbanism is the existence of a town-country split and the close social, political and economic interdependence between the two.[27] The nature and intensity of this relationship define the specific character of urbanism at any particular stage in a region's history. Indeed, the concept of urbanism only makes sense if it is contextualized by developments in the wider regional landscape,[28] including even the marginal areas beyond the settled landscape of town and country. Moreover, studying urbanism within a wider, formative perspective can uncover more detail. For example, it allows one to study urbanization as a process of regional transformation from a relatively undifferentiated landscape of hamlets and villages into a settlement network dominated by central population agglomerations that incorporate non-agricultural specialists and are supported by agricultural hinterlands.[29] Urbanization defined in this way does not refer only to the emergence of urban centres; it also refers to a transformation process involving large parts of the landscape. The urban centres may be conceived of as epiphenomena, emerging from and expressing the underlying transformation of both society and landscape.

Ian Morris provided a powerful example of a study of ancient urbanization, concluding that in the Greek case it was in essence a relatively slow process.[30] Significantly, and typically for Greek urbanization studies, he cast his analysis in terms of the process of polis formation, that is, as an internally driven process. By contrast, the emergence of urbanism in Italy is generally conceptualized from a diffusionist perspective, as having been enhanced by the pervasive strength of Greek and, subsequently, Roman urban culture.[31] In comparison with the urban core models of *Megale Hellas* and of Rome, traditional settlement forms in the larger part of Italy are generally considered at best as lagging behind, at worst as chronically underdeveloped. Mario Torelli, for example, explicitly contrasts the Ionian and Tyrrhenian coastal areas of

---

[25] McIntosh 1991; Wallace Hadrill 1992.

[26] cf. Wallace Hadrill 1992, xi.

[27] cf. Wallace Hadrill 1992; Morris 1992; Andersen *et al.* 1997.

[28] Andersen *et al.* 1997; Osborne 2005, 4; Iacovou 2005, 16.

[29] cf. McIntosh 1991, 208.

[30] Morris 1992.

[31] cf. Whitehouse / Wilkins 1989; Burgers 1998.

economic growth with underdevelopment in other regions, notably the entire mountainous backbone of Italy from Sabina to Bruttium.[32] According to Torelli the limited economic potential of the latter areas inhibited the emergence of urban centres, allowing only for a *vicatim* (village based) settlement type.[33] This is not to say that Torelli denies all development: contact with the Greek world is considered to have brought some urban aspects, such as fortifications. However, it is only with the subsequent integration into the Roman state that the 'backward' regions went through a rather sudden leap into complexity. In these perspectives of 'Hellenization' and 'Romanization', the indigenous groups of most Italic regions were denied a significant role in the contemporary social processes.

Colonization, Hellenization and Romanization
It was (and sometimes still is) held that the Greek and Roman cultures were inherently superior and therefore eagerly awaited by indigenous peoples; its diffusion supposedly took place notably through colonization. Greek and Roman colonization, indeed, were perceived as natural and benevolent civilizing enterprises. Although research conducted along these traditional lines has produced important results, from the 1960s onwards dissatisfaction with these concepts, incited by the debate on Romanization in north-western Europe, has grown vocal. A major point of critique that has been advanced is that the classical archaeological perception of Greek and Roman colonization as 'civilizing' ventures was influenced by, and at the same time legitimised, the idea of a western civilizing mission current in nineteenth- and twentieth-century colonialist concepts.[34] The 'New Archaeology' is seen by many as the force that finally put native populations on a cultural par with the conquering military and administrative population.[35] Both in north-western Europe and in Italy, ongoing research has now largely disassociated itself from such traditional classicist concepts, introducing alternative social-science-based theories which approach colonization and urbanization as social processes, and employing theories and models ranging from acculturation and integration to centre-periphery and peer-polity.[36] In their narratives, modern classical archaeologists no longer approach the Graeco-Roman world as an ideal society, but from a cultural-relativist perspective, as one of many civilizations in world history. Likewise, Greek and Roman colonization are no longer considered as instruments of Graeco-Roman 'High Culture', but as historical migration movements that need to be studied in their specific historical contexts. Attention is no longer limited to specific groups of colonists and their motives and background, but now includes indigenous groups in the regions studied. Greek or Roman dominance is no longer assumed; the nature of the relationship between colonizers/migrants and indigenous people is now a major research question in itself.

Landscape and longue durée
We approach the concept of landscape in a similarly open manner. In Mediterranean landscape archaeology, the most popular current perspective on landscape studies is one inspired by the *Annales* historian Fernand Braudel.[37] Braudel's theory regards historical change as being articulated in three different time

---

[32] Torelli 1988, 53 ff. and 1999, 5.

[33] To Italian historians criticizing him for the modernist tendencies implicit in the application of the developed - underdeveloped concept, Torelli replied that both quantitative and qualitative aspects of the material culture of the various Italian regions clearly allow for such a distinction. In the underdeveloped regions climate was much worse and food and luxuries much scarser than in the developed regions. As a final test of his arguments, he invites his critics 'to try to live just one month in conditions similar to those of the regions I describe as underdeveloped and to prove to have enjoyed them more than the conditions of my 'developed' regions' (Torelli 1999, note 26).

[34] cf. Mattingly 1997; van Dommelen 1997; Morris 1994.

[35] e.g., Trigger 1989, 294-303.

[36] e.g., Brandt / Slofstra 1983; Whitehouse / Wilkins 1989; Herring 1991.

[37] Bintliff 1991; Knapp 1992; Delano Smith 1992; Malone / Stoddart 1994; Barker 1995.

scales: the long-term change of 'structures' and the landscape, the medium-term change of demographic and economic cycles, and the short-term change of human actions and the world of events. Braudel's long-term *structures* and medium-term *conjonctures* offer particularly suitable scales at which to describe the processes investigated by us in the context of the Italian landscape. However, this perspective is very much embedded in the processualist school of thought, and is therefore not shared by postprocessualists. Later generations of *Annales* historians and postprocessual archaeologists alike have criticized Braudel's structural determinism, trying instead to restore a dialectic relationship between landscape, structures and events and questioning the fundamental primacy of landscape and social structures over individual human actions on the grounds that human actions also create, reproduce and transform the structures. As Ian Morris put it, social structures have no independent, extra-human existence and therefore cannot determine human behaviour.[38] Everything people do is informed by learned social structure, but the structure itself is only transmitted through the actions or reactions of those very same people. From this perspective, the archaeologist's main field of study, material culture, should not be investigated solely as the passive reflection of all determinant social structures.

Whether, and how, these ideas are reflected in the models, narratives and explanations generated by the archaeologist depends to a large extent on the academic tradition prevailing within individual research departments, and on the inclinations of the individual archaeologist. At the Groningen Institute of Archaeology, the processual perspective on landscape archaeology has been prevalent, whereas the Archaeological Centre of the Vrije Universiteit of Amsterdam stresses postprocessual aspects. Consequently, the RPC project uses both processual and postprocessual perspectives on the landscape. This volume contains sections describing large-scale patterns in space and time, explaining them in terms of constraints and opportunities provided by the landscape, climate change, and economic forces, but it also contains sections focusing on the historical role of groups of people in effecting changes in the landscape (e.g. chapters 6 and 7).

1.2 APPROACHES

Regional settlement models built by archaeologists are typically based upon both a review and assessment of all the available archaeological information for the region, and on theoretical models of the structure and development of past societies. The RPC project team is no exception: it has sought to integrate archaeological settlement studies, environmental, palaeotechnological and ethnographical research, and ceramics studies for the three regions, with the aim of constructing and testing dynamic settlement models. It has been rather more unusual in its concern with interregional comparison, and it has had to develop approaches to allow such comparison. This section presents a short overview of the methods and techniques that we have employed to further this goal: land evaluation, historical geography, palaeo-geographical reconstruction, ceramic fabric analysis, and various forms of fieldwalking survey. This is followed in section 1.3 by a brief discussion of the theory and methodology of constructing and comparing regional settlement models on the basis of collected records of archaeological observations.

1.2.1 LANDSCAPE AND LAND-USE STUDIES

It has long been recognised by archaeologists that studying the landscape and its (potential) past use can help inform the study of the archaeological remains present in that landscape. The RPC project

---

[38] Morris 1992, 6.

has aimed to reconstruct the ancient landscapes of protohistorical to Roman central and southern Italy (including their settlement and off-site patterns) both in space and through time. Not only are parts of the physical landscape reconstructed through palaeogeographical studies, but the subsistence and economical value and occasionally even the ancient perception of that landscape is evaluated.

Palaeogeographical reconstructions

The palaeogeographical landscape reconstructions of the RPC project are based on a combination of geomorphological and sedimentological studies, and pollen analysis. Study of sediments in deep cores (up to 10 m) taken in several campaigns since the mid-1990s has resulted in the description of depositional regimes through time and space, and some of its stages were dated through radiocarbon analysis of organic sediments and cross-correlation with archaeological remains. The late Holocene climate and vegetation history of central Italy can to some extent be reconstructed from palynological studies of cores obtained from wet environments; and indeed cores collected and studied since the mid-1990s have been used to sketch broad and local changes in the vegetation of the Pontine region, as well as the level and type of human influence on the natural environment and agricultural activities that can be deduced.

Sedimentological studies have concentrated on the relatively dynamic environment of the Pontine graben (a geologically subsiding zone), where processes of alluviation and colluviation have changed the landscape throughout history and prehistory. Attempting to date the progression of these processes, we radiocarbon dated organic sediments at the top of the lagoonal sediments and the base of the alluvial-colluvial cover.[39] Attema and Delvigne were able to show that streams emerging from the Monti Lepini and from the adjoining part of the Alban hills began depositing alluvium in the centre of the graben near Sezze before 2000 BC. Stream beds and the accompanying alluvial sheet progressed towards the southeast, with deposits with a thickness from 1 to over 4 m laid down between approximately 1000 BC and AD 0. This process mostly predates the start of significant human impact in the 6th century BC, and certainly by the time of the Roman colonization in the 4th century BC the alluvium was available for agricultural allocation. Sedimentation after the Republican period was much less, amounting to only 40 cm. Van Joolen carried out a similar study of fluvio-colluvial sedimentation further to the east, in the basin of the Amaseno river.[40] The progressive sedimentation of this originally lagoonal environment can be followed through a first phase when the shifting beds of the Amaseno wound their way through a marshy landscape, and a second phase from about 1000 BC in which, possibly as a result of deforestation in the hinterland around Priverno, the Amaseno alluvial fan began to extend to the south. This fan reached approximately halfway to the sea by the late Imperial period. From about AD 500, colluvium emanating from the Ausoni began to cover part of the southern peaty area as well, while the Amaseno alluvium covered the remaining distance to the sea, impeding drainage of the Pontine graben along the way. Box 2.2 provides further details on these sedimentological studies.

To place these developments in a supraregional context, the climate and vegetation history of the period between roughly 3000 BC and AD 0 as reflected in pollen studies for central Italy were reviewed by Van Joolen.[41] These show that the earliest human influence, with evidence for forest clearance and pastoral and agricultural activities in the craters of the Alban caldera, can be dated to the Early Bronze Age. Somewhat later, but still in the Subboreal, such activities were extended to the lower slopes of the Alban hills, around the coastal lagoons, and on the footslopes of the Monti Lepini. Certainly the archaeological evidence for Iron Age habitation in the higher parts of the Pontine plain supports the pollen evidence for farming practices. Deliberate deforestation in the Alban hills and the higher parts of the Pontine plain becomes much more likely in the Archaic to Roman Republican periods (600 BC – AD 0), when it is

---

[39] Attema / Delvigne 2000; Van Joolen 2003; see also Feiken, forthcoming.

[40] Van Joolen 2003, 68-84.

[41] Van Joolen 2003, 153-177.

accompanied by an increase in chestnut, walnut, and olive tree pollen. The lower parts of the plain were probably used for extensive grazing.

Environmental research in the two southern Italian regions is less developed than in the sedimentary environment of the Pontine region, but limited sedimentological research and pollen analysis have recently taken place both in the Sibaritide and the Salento.[42] It was demonstrated that substantial sedimentation (several meters) took place in some parts of the Sibaritide plain during and after the Roman period, deeply covering all potential archaeological evidence from earlier periods. Further environmental studies will be needed to reconstruct palaeogeographical landscapes for both regions.

Land evaluation
The RPC project uses the method of land evaluation to assess the agricultural potential of the landscape in its three study regions, and the way it has changed over time under the influence of climate change, the availability of new types of crop, and developments in agricultural technology. Whilst agricultural yield studies based on experimental and historical evidence have long been a tool of the archaeologists' trade, land evaluation as a formal technique was borrowed much more recently from the field of soil science. Widely used in the 1970s and 1980s by soil scientists at the Food and Agriculture Organization of the United Nations (FAO) for estimating the economic potential of alternative land uses in third world countries, land evaluation is defined as 'the process of collating and interpreting basic inventories of soil, vegetation, climate and other aspects of land in order to identify and make a first comparison of promising land use alternatives in simple socioeconomic terms'.[43] The core feature of land evaluation is its comparison of the requirements of land use with the resources offered by the land. Land evaluation requires information from three sources: land, land use, and economics.[44]

Land evaluation was first introduced to archaeology to serve as a framework for integrating palaeoecological and archaeological data, in an effort to understand the relation between past populations and their natural environments.[45] Archaeological land evaluation has been used to construct models of land use for different time periods on the basis of ecological and socio-economic data. These models present the economic potential of the landscape and can be confronted with the archaeological evidence in order to identify, or predict, activity areas.[46] Within the RPC project, Van Joolen has applied the technique to assess the agricultural potential of the different land systems in all three regions, for up to eight different land use types in three periods differentiated by palaeotechnological criteria (Bronze Age, Iron Age, and Archaic to Roman periods).[47] Field studies were undertaken to determine appropriate criteria for the mapping of land systems and landforms, whilst information about land use requirements (LURs) and land use types (LUTs) was gathered from the literature and from visits to experimental farms in Italy. The full Pontine and Salento study regions were evaluated at a scale of ca. 1:100,000 (individual units often measuring tens or hundreds of sq.km).[48] Generally speaking, the agricultural options open to the inhabitants of our regions have become wider as time progresses, due to the spreading of technological advances and (in the Pontine region) natural and man-made improvements to sediments and drainage.

The application of land evaluation takes place in several stages. First, an inventory of the natural environment, collected by field surveys and literature reviews, forms the basis for a reconstruction of the natural environment at different times in the past. Socioeconomic models for early forms of land use are constructed using ethnographic, historic and archaeological data. The study area is classified into land units

---

[42] For the Sibaritide, see chapter 4; Attema, Delvigne / Van Leusen 2004. For the Salento, see chapter 3; Bijlsma / Verhagen 1989; Foeken / Gietema 2000.
[43] Brinkman / Smyth 1973, 7.
[44] Dent / Young 1981.
[45] Kamermans *et al.* 1985.
[46] Kamermans 1993.
[47] Van Joolen 2003.
[48] In the Sibaritide, only a small-scale study was completed.

[land systems, landforms] on the basis of physical factors. These units are described in terms of their properties to provide a qualitative land classification. A semiquantitative measurement of the suitability of the area for a certain type of land use on the basis of the requirements for that type of land use then follows. An *expected* form of land use may then be constructed for every chosen socioeconomic model based on these results. Finally, a comparison of this expected form of land use with the archaeologically observed land use provides a basis for further modification of the model. The use of land evaluation techniques in archaeology does, however, require some important modifications to be made. Since it is impossible to measure prehistoric land qualities directly, they must be *reconstructed* from data obtained by surveys of modern land characteristics and from palaeogeographical reconstructions. Equally, direct economic and social analysis of contemporary society has to be replaced by *models* of prehistoric socioeconomic situations, for which information on the ecological and technical requirements of different kinds of land use as well as data on the economic and social context has to be generated from ethnographic, archaeological, and historical sources.

The degree to which past societies could have realised the agricultural potential of the various land systems depends, among other things, on their knowledge and use of agricultural techniques. Among the relevant technological advances would have been the development of depth-regulated plough-shares, scythes and other tools of bronze and iron, fallowing and crop rotation, haymaking, hydrological interventions, and the combination of grain and olive culture. The introduction of new types of cultivated plants (grapes, chestnuts, olives) and the effects of changing agricultural technologies would of course also have increased the number of potential land use types to be considered. Information on ancient agricultural technology in Italy was derived from archaeological (e.g. excavated tools), literary (especially the ancient agronomers), and iconographic sources, as well as from modern experimental research.[49] The detailed results of the evaluation by region, period and cultivation type are provided by Van Joolen.[50] In summary, in the Bronze Age the Salento isthmus landforms *Murge* and *Brindisi undulating land* were only suitable for olive cultivation, whereas the *Mottola* landform was suitable for all other kinds of cultivation, and the suitability of all other landforms varied according to the intended land-use type. The region as a whole in this period was best suited for a combination of olive cultivation and subsistence farming. In the Iron Age, the Brindisi and Mottola landforms became marginally suitable for all cultivation types of that period, and in the Archaic and Roman periods the Murge became marginally suitable for cultivation of barley, cereals and olives. Polyculture of olives and cereals other than emmer wheat remained possible almost everywhere. In the Pontine region, most landforms were unsuitable for any kind of agriculture in the Bronze Age, with the exception of the *Latina alluvial fans* and the aeolian part of the *Borgo Grappa plain*, which were marginally or wholly suitable for most land use types. In the Iron Age the Amaseno area, by then covered by alluvial sediments, joined these exceptions. By the Roman period, most landforms were marginally or wholly suitable for all contemporary land use types, especially the cultivation of wheat, barley and millet.

To repeat, the purpose of land evaluation in archaeology is to evaluate the socio-economic models based on our expectations about past land use, by comparing the expected form of land use with the archaeologically observed form of land use. In chapter 9 we will assess whether it has indeed served this purpose. Besides land evaluation, other types of research may also shed light on ancient land use. One of the PhD projects within the RPC project focused on a review of ethnographical studies of traditional pastoralist societies, a comparative assessment of archaeo-zoological material from excavation contexts, and the use of historical maps.[51] Veenman's review of ethnographical studies allows us to compare our archaeological data and reconstructions to recent descriptions of a range of traditional societies. Her work suggests how isolated observations supplied by environmental archaeological studies can be understood

[49] Van Joolen 2003, 101-128 with references.
[50] Van Joolen 2003, 137-152.
[51] Veenman 2002.

in terms of integral 'strategies', employed by societies to cope with the opportunities and restrictions afforded by their environment. Historical cartography is obviously helpful in the reconstruction of palaeo-environments, in the modelling of traditional patterns of land use, and in understanding past perceptions of the landscape.[52] Sixteenth-century historical maps of the Pontine region record for example traditional territorial divisions (indicating which *macchia* belongs to which town), the approximate lines of major streams and roads, and the long drawn-out process of draining the Pontine marshes. More recent cartography for the same region helps us to understand how the land reclamations of the 1930s have altered the traditional landscape, and provides us with high resolution environmental data.

1.2.2 FIELD SURVEYS

Archaeological field survey is a prospection technique that is typically used when undertaking an inventory of archaeological remains within a defined study area. Surveys can be, and have been, conducted with all manner of aims and approaches, but broad historical trends can still be discerned for them, at least in Italy. Most relevant here is the 'topographic' phase (1920 – 1980) which itself originated in the preceding 'antiquarian' phase.[53] It is characterised by inventories of relatively obtrusive (mainly classical) remains made through a combination of archive studies and field checks, and epitomised by the *Forma Italiae* series which uses the 1:25,000 scaled topographic map series as its organizational principle. Since about 1980 these have slowly given way to more intensive and systematic landscape-oriented surveying techniques.

Surveys of this latter phase were all more or less influenced by the ideas and ideals of the New Archaeology, and they can be classified in three groups, according to their purpose.[54] *Sampling* surveys are designed to estimate archaeological parameters of the sampling universe, such as the overall density of the various site types in the various periods covered by the survey. This type of survey can also be used to test specific statistical hypotheses and to create predictive models. A second group of surveys is designed to *detect spatial structure* and in general does not use a sampling approach but attempts to cover a block of land, for example the catchment area of some (usually excavated) site. Third, *prospective* or 'purposive' surveys are intended to find particular targets or types of targets, to test specific predictions, or to ensure that the previous two types of surveys have been thorough enough to achieve their goals.

Within Italy, if not within Europe in general, surveys of the first type enjoyed a brief popularity with the emergence of the New Archaeology during the late 1970s, but were unable to fulfil their original promise before archaeological theory took a more post-modern turn in the mid-1980s. Surveys of the second type have become increasingly popular especially since the 1980s, and have tended to become more intensive (as measured by the amount of time or effort spent per unit area) over time. The RPC surveys are almost all of this type. They were either aimed at mapping the spatial structure within and around urban or proto-urban settlements, or at providing systematic and detailed information about the archaeological history of areas that are regarded as (geographically and socio-economically) marginal to the processes of urbanization and colonization. The main impact of those processes took place at the urban or proto-urban settlements. Purposive surveys (the third type) as a group have the oldest roots, and still occur alongside 'mapping' surveys of the second type.

The campaigns conducted by the RPC project have tried to detect spatial structure in the archaeological record by conducting intensive and systematic field-by-field surveys within specific landscape units that were defined using geomorphological (e.g., the Lepine footslopes) or socio-economical criteria

---

[52] Attema 1993 and 1996.
[53] Cambi / Terrenato 1995.
[54] Banning 2002, 341.

(e.g., the Oria catchment area). The details of the methodology have evolved much since the early 1980s, with a trend towards greater intensity and greater attention to non-diagnostic, unobtrusive, and 'off-site' materials. The general purpose has however remained the same: to trace the patterns and dynamics of settlement and land use from the earliest Bronze Age down to the end of the classical period. But this methodological development came at a price. As the RPC surveys intensified their coverage decreased until a typical three-week field campaign by two teams could cover no more than 3 sq.km. Throughout the campaign and including time spent in find processing and administration, coverage was on average only one hectare per person per day. It therefore became important to find ways to increase the efficiency of the surveys, and since 2000 we therefore experimented with methods and technologies to make surveys more efficient and accurate. The later surveys have achieved much greater mapping accuracy through the use of direct GPS-based registration methods in the field, with increasingly high resolution mapping of rural non-site areas (generally in 50 by 50m-units, with a maximum error of 5 meters).

The greater intensity with which the RPC surveys have been conducted, resulted in the detection of higher umbers of small 'sites' and ceramic surface scatters, with an increased chronological and (probably) functional range. Typically, landscapes that were previously known only for their above-ground classical remains now acquire a pre- and protohistorical dimension as well. The degree of observable settlement continuity increases as more sites yield materials from more periods, and it becomes increasingly difficult to maintain a clear concept of what constitutes 'marginality' in the use of the landscape.

1.2.3 DATING AND POTTERY STUDIES

Pottery studies are essential not only for the dating and functional assignment of sites and surface scatters, but also for our understanding of past production modes and the functioning of the ancient economy in a broader sense. Various, often complementary, approaches to pottery studies were used in the research projects on which the RPC project was based. Whilst traditional typo-chronological studies still form the backbone of our pottery research, new approaches including fabric analysis and other technological studies were added over time.

Yntema's much-cited 1990 volume on the matt-painted pottery of south Italy and his 1998 study of Apulian Grey Gloss wares are examples of the type of fundamental pottery studies conducted in the context of ACVU's Brindisino project. Yntema further published influential articles on pottery-related themes in the Dutch journal *Bulletin Antieke Beschaving* (Babesch), and edited pottery catalogues for ACVU's Brindisino surveys and excavations.[55] Equally fundamental typochronological publications on pottery for the Pontine region and the Sibaritide were produced by Kleibrink,[56] but in the early 1990s GIA also began to explore the research potential of pottery technology. One of the objectives of the pottery research at the GIA has been to trace the development of ceramic craft technology in central Italy. In 1998 Nijboer published an account of the transition, between 800 and 400BC, from household production to pottery workshops on the basis of pottery and kiln debris excavated at Satricum and other relevant sites in central Italy. A detailed study and classification of impasto and coarse-ware fabrics by GIA researchers was by then underway, which used pottery from Satricum and other sites in the Pontine region and highlighted technological changes in pottery production during the Iron Age to Roman period (for details, see Box 1.1).[57]

---

[55] e.g., Yntema 1993a on the Oria surveys and, more recently, Yntema 2001 on pre-Roman Valesio.

[56] e.g., Maaskant Kleibrink 1987 and 1992; and most recently Kleibrink 2006 with references to earlier publications.

[57] Attema *et al.* 2003a.

Box 1.1 Case study: fabric analysis in southern Lazio

In the absence of decoration or substantial typological development in Latial pottery of the 1st millennium BC, the criteria used by the GIA for the classification are: fabric colour (on a fresh break) and presence, type, and quantity of various mineral inclusions. Three large colour *families* (red, orange, and pale) were distinguished after refiring a sample of shards under controlled conditions (this greatly reduces the colour variation of a fabric), and then described using Munsell colour ranges. Within these families, fabric groups and individual fabrics are distinguished on the basis of their natural and added inclusions, as determined by macroscopic and microscopic inspection and petrographic analysis. Fabric *groups* are characterised by the dominance of specific minerals, e.g. ferromanganese (FeMn) nodules, augite, lava, tuff, or quartz/feldspar. The size, sorting, quantity and relative proportions of the minerals and the hardness of the fabric are determined and classified. A typical red-firing fabric from Lanuvio in the Alban hills area of the Pontine region, for example, contains 5-20% by volume of a temper dominated by augite (moderately to poorly sorted, coarse to very fine grains) and is identified by the code *LAV I E.ms-ps(1-4).bc*. This fabric is known from the excavations at Satricum to have been used for roof tiles and large storage vessels of the 6th-5th century BC, hence even the non-diagnostic shards of this fabric that are typically picked up during surveys can be used for dating and (limited) functional classification of on-site and off-site materials. The fabrics from the Satricum excavations form a physical reference collection for the wider Pontine region; Attema and colleagues (2003a) provide a discussion of the fabrics from Satricum, Sezze, Segni, and Lanuvium.

A fabric or fabric group can become a dating tool once the fabric typology is augmented with vessel types derived from closed contexts (tombs, deposits, and stratigraphic excavations). Usually the fabric is a less precise dating tool than the vessel type because potters tend to be conservative in their use of material resources, but individual fabrics may have been used briefly enough to become useful dating tools. The combination of fabric and vessel type, or fabric and ware, can also result in a fairly precise dating. During the Iron Age and Orientalizing period (9th – 7th centuries BC), a limited number of fabrics were used in the Pontine region for a variety of vessels. By contrast, the Archaic pottery tradition uses distinct fabrics for architectural terracotta's and large vessels (red and orange impastos, *impasto chiaro*), table wares (depurated fabrics) and cooking vessels (coarse fabrics). One particular fabric was used only for 6th-century terracottas. In the 6th century BC specialised potter's workshops were established in the major urban centres of central Italy, corresponding to the larger process of urbanization in Etruria and Latium.

Are the fabrics of southern Lazio related to those at Satricum, and if so, in what way? These questions are answered by comparing and correlating independently constructed regional fabric classifications (currently available for Lanuvio, Segni, and Sezze, all within 30 km of Satricum) to that of Satricum. The highest level of classification into red-, orange- and pale-firing fabric families turns out to be identical for all four sites. A study of the vessel forms suggests that the technological change from red- to pale- and (slightly later) orange-firing fabrics occurred in the late 6th century BC throughout the region, so this phenomenon can be used as a crude but convenient dating criterion. The emergence of standardised forms from the 5th century BC onwards reflects workshop conditions and a changed mode of production that can be related to the process of Romanization. The second level of classification, that of fabric groups based on temper and surface treatment, also shows broad regional concordance. The emergence of FeMn-, augite- and quartz/feldspar-dominant groups in the advanced Iron Age can be followed at all four sites. The large-scale adoption, in the 5th and 4th century BC, of orange- or pale-firing, augite-dominated fabrics with a powdery surface for large vessels and tiles means that the previously largely 'invisible' post-Archaic period can now be identified with relative ease in the field. At the lowest level of classification, that of individual fabrics, differences have emerged between the samples of the red-firing family that appear to be based on differences in local geology. We must presume that similar differences will also emerge on further study of

> the orange- and pale-firing families. In general the fabrics from Lanuvio, Segni and Sezze do not precisely match those from Satricum, hence probably derive from different production centres. They do, however, display common characteristics that point to regional trends distinct from those in Etruria: notably the lack of 7th-century *figulina*, painted *impasto rosso*, and imitation-Greek ceramics, whereas unpainted red-slipped wares are common.
>
> The three systems of classification (by vessel form, ware, and fabric) are complementary, and together provide a practical typology for fieldwork. For futher examples, see the LCM website at www.lcm.nl

This research was extended by Mater in her PhD study on the changes in the systems of pottery production in the context of colonization and urbanization processes in the three RPC regions during the first millennium BC.[58] Mater particularly studied those changes in pottery technology that suggest an upscaling of pottery production in the context of Archaic urbanization and Greek and Roman colonization. She selected case studies from each region, highlighting social and technological changes over a broad time span from the Bronze Age to the Roman period. These case studies subsequently formed the basis for a comparative study of developments in the three RPC regions. The question if, and how, pottery can be used as a source of information on the organization and change of society was the topic of a workshop organized by her at Groningen University in 2000.[59] This workshop highlighted current problems in interpreting pottery distribution patterns and in establishing typochronologies for local plain wares.

Mater took the *theory of practice*, which studies pottery technology as a process involving both social and material factors that are structured by the interaction of individuals and groups in time, space, and cultural context, and made it the theoretical framework of her study. Material remains reflect, and therefore enable us to study, such processes. As the pottery data had been collected by different research groups in different ways and with different research questions in mind, it quickly proved impossible to make direct comparisons between these datasets. However, the answers produced for each of the three RPC regions to a new question – the organization of pottery production – did prove to be comparable. The data analyzed for this study were derived from studies of the pottery itself, excavations of pottery production sites, ethnographic studies of pottery production and social organization, and visits to modern potters in south Italy.

Ethno-archaeological models for pottery production were used to throw light on the potential organization of pottery production in the past. Although knowledge of pottery production processes does not automatically lead to a definition of useful archaeological correlates, we are constrained to follow this approach 'in reverse' if we want to reconstruct past production processes. Both material and social aspects of ethnographically studied pottery production provide handles for the analysis of archaeological pottery, not least because they help move our focus from production towards distribution and consumption of pottery.

The low functional and chronological resolution typically obtainable from surface pottery has been one of the main obstacles to a more detailed archaeological understanding of regional dynamics of settlement and land use. Perhaps 90 % or more of the finds picked up during an intensive fieldwalking survey are non-diagnostic, so such finds tend to have been discarded in the field or even not to have been picked up at all. Yet the unintended effect of such policies is that many smaller or poorer sites would be entirely absent from our distribution maps, and long-lived sites might end up lacking certain phases that are characterised by non-diagnostic ceramics. It would therefore be much better to include this

[58] Mater 2005.   [59] Mater / Annis 2002.

material in our analyses, and indeed analysis and classification of the fabrics of worn and non-diagnostic shards can help to link this plentiful but difficult material to well-defined pottery groups and well-dated contexts. Starting in 1994, researchers at the GIA developed a fabric classification method that relates surface pottery that was collected during fieldwalking surveys in the Pontine region to a securely dated typology of Latial settlement pottery that has been established on the basis of the Institute's stratigraphical excavations at the protohistoric site of Satricum.[60] A dating tool based on fabric seemed fundamental for the pottery from the survey, since other distinguishing characteristics such as surface treatment and/or form characteristics are mostly absent. The identification therefore hinges on the fabric and the construction method of the pot rather than on surface treatment, form and style of decoration.[61] At present the ceramics from surveys near Lanuvio (1995), Segni (1997), and Sezze (1994) have been fully classified in this manner. The method of fabrics analysis and classification is explained in several recent articles,[62] and details are provided in Box 1.1.

1.3   ISSUES IN REGIONAL LANDSCAPE ARCHAEOLOGY

If we want to study the *whole* of the archaeological record within a given region, we must be prepared to face certain issues relating to the quality of our primary data and our interpretations. Major problems with primary-data quality stem from the fact that regional archaeological datasets always consist of a historically accumulated set of reported accidental observations, plus one or more sets of systematic and professional observations whose limitations vary with the goals and methods employed by the archaeologists involved. The idiosyncratic nature of the individual studies, combined with typically severe limitations on the amount of primary data that can be published, mean that regional landscape archaeologists have little choice but to rely on the *interpreted* results of each study. The comparison of *primary* results (that is, archaeological field data within their environmental contexts) emerging from each of the three RPC projects must, therefore, be separated from the comparison of *interpretations* (that is, the diachronic narratives that have emerged for each region separately). The diachronic comparison between the three RPC regions in chapters 5 to 8 of this volume necessarily takes place at an interpretative level. The following sections discuss, respectively, the systematic biases in our primary data, the uneven content of regional 'site' databases, the inextricable mix of observations and interpretations in many older publications of regional site inventories, and the use of models to summarise, predict and explain aspects of the regional archaeological record.

1.3.1   SYSTEMATIC BIASES

Modern surveys, like those of the RPC project, attempt to achieve the unbiased collection of data on surface remains of all periods within the survey area, within the limits of achievable accuracy and precision set by the available time and resources. Accordingly, the methods chosen tend to be formal (following set procedures) and systematic. However, it was clear early on that data collection by field survey teams would have to contend with a whole series of biases, some of which would prove very difficult to avoid or even to

---

[60] Based on Adams / Adams 1991; the resulting typology is concordant with existing typologies by Carafa (1995) and Betelli (1997).

[61] Fabric was defined by Adams and Adams (1991, 266) as 'a collective term for the internal constituents used in making pottery. These include the basic clay, marl, or mud which is the primary constituent, and any other material (temper, levigation, etc.) which is mixed into the clay, marl or mud to facilitate firing or to impart hardness, porosity, or other characteristics to the vessel walls'.

[62] Attema, *et al.* 1997; Attema / Van Oortmerssen 2000; and most extensively Attema *et al.* 2003a.

quantify.[63] *Post-depositional* biases occur because surface (plough-soil) archaeology is rarely an accurate reflection of the history of settlement and land use within the survey area. Deposited materials tend to degrade and/or become hidden by subsequent sedimentation or eroded away at different rates, with the earliest periods and weakest materials suffering the most. Further major biases occur in the *design stages* of a survey, for example when decisions are taken to target arable fields only, or to collect 'diagnostic' material only. Once a survey is underway, a third set of *visibility and research* biases further complicates matters. Visibility biases involve factors that limit the ability of surveyors to discover material on the surface, for example vegetation cover, admixture of stones or recent material, mud, dust, excessive sunlight or shade. Research biases relate to surveyors' limitations, e.g. their limited survey experience, limited knowledge of the archaeological materials encountered, limited vision/concentration span, and the tendency to concentrate on specific material types (e.g., flint). A fourth and final set of biases occurs during the processing of the finds collected in the survey. These might be termed *classification* biases, since they include the creation of mutually exclusive find classes or 'bins', the ignoring of fuzziness, and the further exclusion of 'non-diagnostic' materials. Box 1.2 presents a case study of such biases in operation in one of our study regions, the Sibaritide.

In view of the above, much attention should be paid to the evaluation of, and correction for, these biases before the archaeological results of a survey can be interpreted. Ideally, the effects of each bias factor should be modelled,[64] but such ideas have for the most part not yet been put into practise.[65] Quantitative bias correction methods, often applied during the GIS processing of survey results, are limited to corrections for the factor 'visibility', the effect of which is typically 'guesstimated' in the field by the survey team leader. However, the resulting corrected find density maps are not generally trusted by the academic community, and the tendency is to insist on publication of the 'raw' data (if such a thing exists).[66] We believe, however, that use of the term 'raw data' presupposes a degree of objectivity at the collection and description stages that simply does not exist in reality. Hence, the question of which data to publish remains to be settled.

1.3.2 REGIONAL 'SITE' DATABASES

The modelling of regional settlement trends requires that we create a regional database of settlement sites, before applying models in order to explain observed structure in that database. A regional database of archaeological sites must be created from existing published or otherwise accessible site records, and from newly collected field data. Both present problems. Existing site records are often extremely limited in scope, providing little more than the fact that ceramics of a particular – often very broad – period were observed in a particular location. Many of these records are also quite old and of unknown origin, so that the quality of the information as well as the significance of the wording are doubtful. Most importantly, it is no longer possible to separate what was actually observed from what has been interpreted – we must simply trust that the record is correct in essentials. The situation is rather different with newly collected field data, where we typically have excellent information on what has been observed, but have a hard time deciding what it means. This is mostly due to the ephemeral nature of the large majority of ceramic surface scatters: does a particular scatter of shards represent habitation, burial, discard, or temporary use of a particular location? How many shards do we need before we have a 'site', and what is the significance of the 'off-site' material? No internationally agreed rules have yet emerged for answering this kind of question, nor has the RPC team been able to decide on a common standard.

All this means that typical regional site databases are 'mixed bags' with highly uneven spatial coverage and site records of varying completeness and reliability. Clearly, a comparative project such as the RPC must find ways of dealing with these problems. The purpose of the RPC site database originally was

[63] Ammerman 1981 and 1985.
[64] Van Leusen 1996.
[65] Banning 2002.
[66] See Millett 2000, 93-94.

Box 1.2 Case study: visibility and other bias factors in the surface archaeological record of the Sibaritide

The importance of bias factors in our interpretation of regional archaeological records may be illustrated by looking in some detail at the case of the Sibaritide, where different factors affect the record in each of the three landscape zones - plain, foothills, and hinterland.

The alluvial plain of the Sibaritide hides an extensive buried archaeological landscape, as was first demonstrated in 1960 –1965 by a team from the University of Pennsylvania in collaboration with the Italian Lerici foundation in the famous 'Search for Sybaris' programme.[A] To find Sybaris, famous from ancient sources, various types of magnetometer surveys were carried out in the Crati plain in combination with mechanical

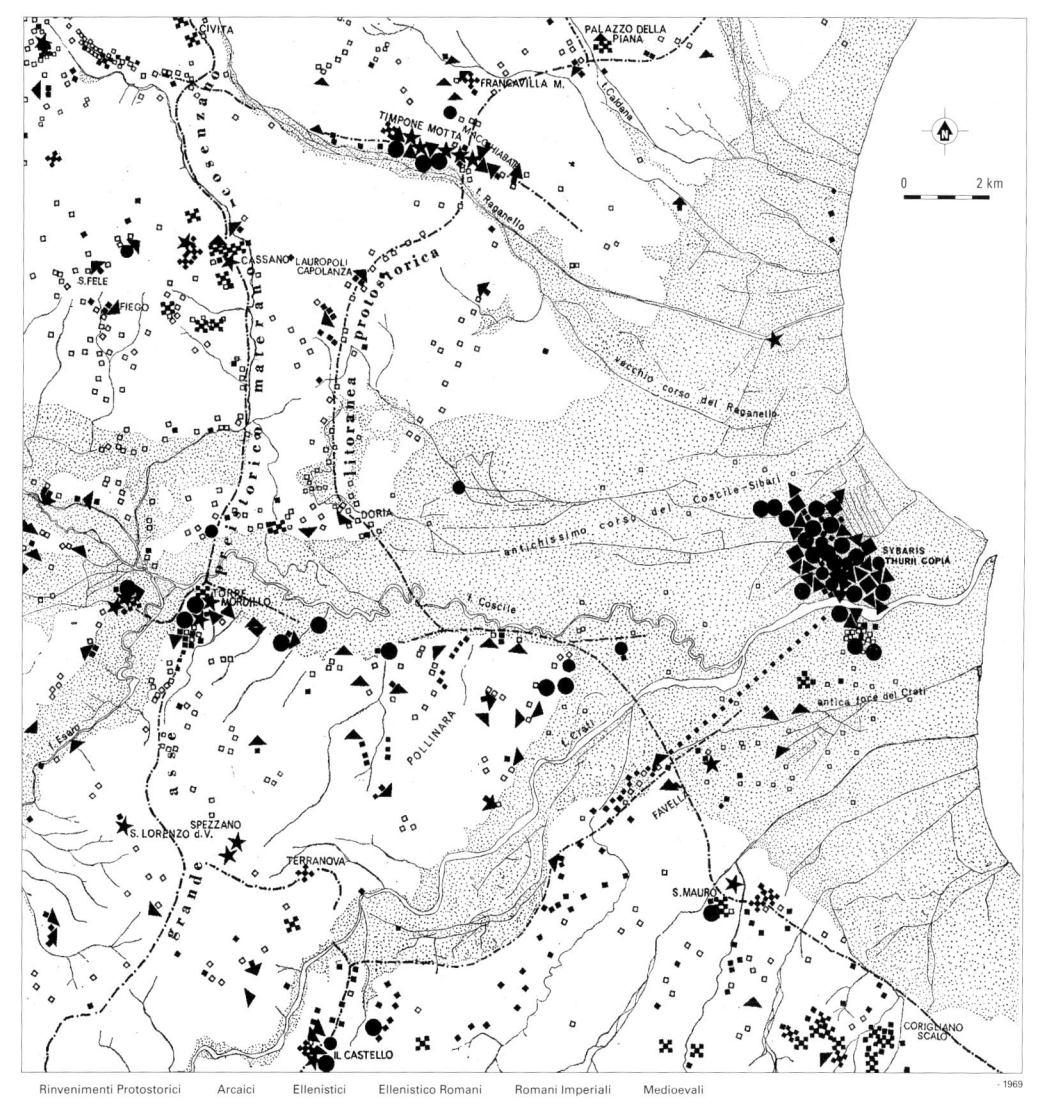

Fig. 1.5. Site index map for the extensive archaeological inventory of the Sibaritide undertaken in the mid 1960s (source: De Rossi et al. 1969).

[A] Rainey / Lerici 1967.

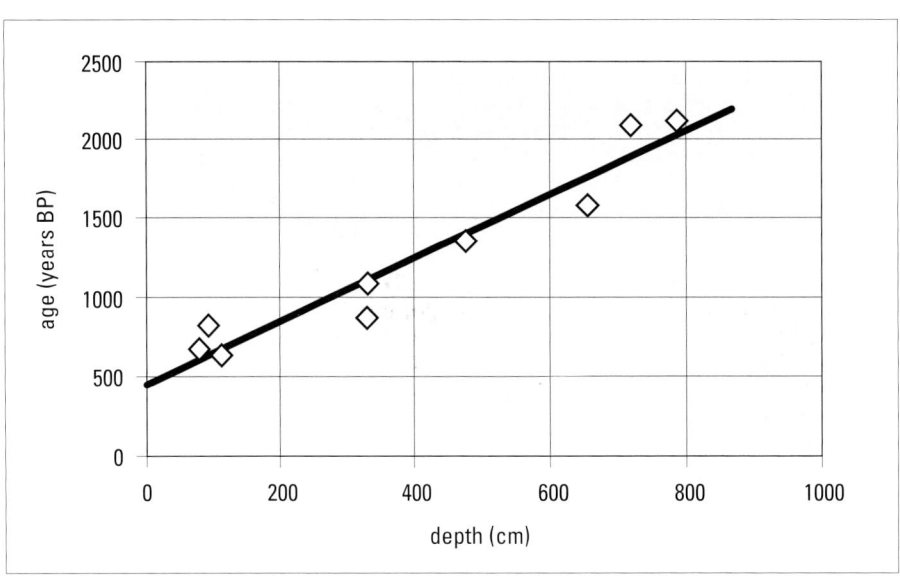

Core ID	Core depth (cm)	Sample depth (cm)	^{14}C-date (cal. BP)	composition
01-6	810	785-790	2120 ± 35	Clayey peat
01-8	885	115	640 ± 50	Peat
01-9A	665	80	675 ± 25	Peat
01-9B	665	95	825 ± 25	Peat
01-17	560	330-332	870 ± 70	Peat
01-22B	780	650-660	1580 ± 30	Humic clay with pebbles
01-22C	780	715-725	2090 ± 30	Peat
01-24A	670	320-340	1090 ± 50	Loam with plant remains and shell fragments
01-24B	670	470-485	1360 ± 30	Loam with plant remains

Fig. 1.6. The regression line based on sample depths and radiocarbon dates from the 2001 GIA augering cores in the Coscile floodplain indicates an average sedimentation rate of 0.5 cm/year for the Roman and Medieval periods.

augering at over 1500 locations. The augering depth was mostly from 6 to 12 meters, and the distribution of cores with archaeological materials was by far the densest in the area of what later proved to be the urban site of Sybaris and its successors Thurioi and Copiae. However, datable archaeological layers were occasionally hit upon elsewhere in the plain as well. Layers with identifiable Archaic, Classical, Hellenistic or Roman archaeological materials were generally found at depths between 3 and 6 meters, far below the level reached by modern deep-ploughing, but occasionally as deep as 12 meters.[8] These observations (some of them well outside the supposed perimeter of Sybaris, especially south of the Crati river) suggest

[8] cf. the list of augering locations in Rainey / Lerici 1967, 135-249.

that a process of rural infill had already begun by the 6th century BC and that the plain remained in use until at least Roman times. Yet hardly any of this is visible at the surface, as is shown clearly by the results of the fieldwalking surveys conducted parallel to the coring programme by a team of archaeologists from the University of Rome 'La Sapienza' (see fig. 1.5). Archaeological landscapes predating the 6th century BC are buried even more deeply, of course, and are even less accessible today.

Continual alluviation in the central Crati plain has therefore rendered surface survey a useless exercise, and recent augering by the Groningen University has confirmed that this is also the case for the northern part of the plain, in the basin of the Raganello river. To reconstruct the landscape of the coastal plain in prehistoric and early historic times, hand augering up to a depth of 8.5 m was carried out, and peat layers suitable for radiocarbon dating were identified. The fine-textured soils in front of recent alluvial fans and in the floodplain of the Coscile river were chosen as augering locations. Sediment types proved to be remarkably uniform at all depths, indicating no big shifts in river patterns in this area. In six of the cores, a total of nine samples from thin peaty layers were collected (see fig. 1.6).

Fig. 1.7. Addition of the paved and unpaved roads and the 25m elevation contour (dashed line) shows the 1960s site pattern to be heavily influenced by the researchers' ability to visit agricultural areas, and (in the plain) by the plough's ability to reach buried archaeological sites.

> Surprisingly, even at a depth of over 7 m radiocarbon dates were not older than 2150 years BP. The regression line of radiocarbon dates plotted against depth indicates an average sedimentation speed of 0.5 cm/year over the period 2100 to 450 BP, and suggests that sedimentation stopped at about 450 BP. The derived sedimentation speed for the Raganello alluvium agrees very well with that of the neighbouring Crati river basin, which was calculated as 0.49 cm/year for the period from 500 BC up to the present.[c] Naturally, we cannot contribute the immense accumulation of sediment solely to erosion in the hinterland; continuing geological subsidence also plays an important role. A correlation in space and time between, on the one hand, erosion in the hinterland as a result of climate and human impact and, on the other, sedimentation in the plain can, however, not be attempted on the basis of the data presently available.
>
> Field survey as a method for mapping the regional archaeological record of the alluvial and coastal plains can therefore only operate effectively in areas where the ancient living surfaces are within regular – or at least occasional - reach of the plough, i.e. where ancient landforms such as dunes breach the modern surface. A detailed mapping of alluviation depths across the plain would also help to establish more precisely the line (approximately at the 25 m contour, see fig 1.6) along which the more ancient and stable landforms of the foothill zone dip beneath the alluvium of the plain.
>
> [c] Cotecchia / Pagliarulo 1996, Cherubini *et al.* 1994.

to collect all of the available data on archaeological remains within the three study regions, and to use these in an interpreted form for archaeological landscape analysis. More specifically, we wanted to create a database in order to:

- collect available site-oriented information from published and unpublished sources, assess and document that information;
- reorganise it if necessary (e.g., by applying a systematic terminology or by splitting or merging observations); and
- interpret it in terms of meaningful archaeological entities.

We felt it important that the database should contain the data as presented by the original source in unaltered form, keeping them separate (and separable) from any additional or transformed data and from our own interpretations. The provision of *metadata* (data describing data properties) was considered to be equally important, because low-quality data had to be prevented from inadvertently 'polluting' our analyses. Given the problems discussed above with interpreting existing archaeological records, it was thought essential that the database framework should keep the 'information trail' intact and thus allow the researcher to access and check all data-transformation steps between raw data input and high-level interpretation. Finally, the RPC database design called for two more interrelated properties: it should be able to hold off-site records, and it should be independent of scale. The first requirement allows the inclusion of landscape- rather than site-oriented data, such as finds densities per survey unit, including the observed *absence* of finds. The second requirement means that data can be included irrespective of its level of spatial or chronological detail (size, duration). Whilst we must admit that we have in fact only been able to take the very first steps towards this 'ideal' regional archaeological database, the work on the database did allow us to investigate some important aspects of data quality and interpretative problems relevant to future regional archaeological databases and their comparison.

1.3.3 DATA QUALITY

Regional projects such as the RPC must, to a large extent, work from pre-existing archaeological records. This dependence, on a patchy and uncontrolled recording process stretching back decades, means that records must go through an assessment process, or 'source criticism'. Put simply, we want to know if the descriptive information in the records contains any serious errors of fact or omissions, and if the interpretative information in the records is useful and reliable. Checking factual errors involves an assessment of the source's reliability, field checks (picking out *incidental* errors such as mistakenly identifying a Roman agricultural terrace wall as a road revetment), and general knowledge of the history of archaeology (to detect *pervasive* errors, such as field workers' general failure to identify late-Roman site phases until Hayes published his typological study of African Red Slip ware in the 1970s).

Since regional settlement models and their comparison are based on *interpreted* data, we should also look at how those interpretations are arrived at and if they are sufficiently well-defined. When combining information from many sources and collected over a long time, we cannot assume that all interpretations by these sources were correct at the time, or have remained so since. In an ideal world we would be able to separate these interpretations from the *observations* that they were based on, but this is unrealistic, for two reasons. Firstly, no clear distinction exists in reality between 'observations' (a term suggesting value-free data) and 'interpretations' (a term which acknowledges the changeable nature of what we consider to be the significance of archaeological remains). Hence it may be better to regard all observations as interpretations.[67] Secondly, many sources record little, if any, of the descriptive information on which their interpretations are based, and we will therefore never be able to evaluate the nature of most historical primary (or even secondary) records. What we *can* attempt to do is to separate such records into descriptive elements and interpretative elements; this would allow us then to ignore previous interpretations and attach our own interpretations to the compiled descriptive information instead.

If we are to interpret what the published sources tell us, we must also find ways of dealing with the 'fuzziness' of their descriptions. Fuzziness can take any of several guises: overlap or lack of clarity in the definitions and scopes of descriptive terms; lack of distinction between observations and interpretations; and measurement errors and uncertainties. Many of the terms used to describe archaeological field observations and the interpretations based upon them are not precisely defined, have been used differently by different authors or by the same author over time, and/or have been used to describe overlapping sets of archaeological observations. This lack of formal definition of the terms used when describing the results of regional inventories or surveys precludes a direct comparison. An example of using different terms to describe broadly similar phenomena is Perkins' preference for 'village' over the terms 'hamlet', 'nucleated settlement', and 'proto-urban settlement' that were variously employed by us.[68] Is a 'village' identical to a 'nucleated settlement', or is it more like a 'hamlet' or 'proto-urban settlement'? It may have properties of both, but may also lack properties of either. Whilst clearly attempting to describe similar phenomena, this one example already implies that it is impossible to compare settlement distribution maps produced by these authors directly, because neither provides precise criteria by which to distinguish the settlement classes. This and related unresolved issues were the topic of a workshop held at the University of Michigan in 2002.[69]

---

[67] e.g., Scollar 1992, 98.
[68] Perkins 1999; Burgers 1998; Attema 1993.
[69] Published as Alcock / Cherry 2004.

Box 1.3 Modelling settlement hierarchy and territories

Peer polity interaction models play an important role in our understanding of the organization of Italian society on regional and supra-regional scales throughout most of the periods studied in this volume, at least until the start of the Roman period. These models are supported by rank-size studies into the degree and type of hierarchization of the settlement structure, and territorial divisions are visualised using cartographic techniques including Thiessen polygons and Renfrew and Level's (1979) XTENT model.

Peer Polity Interaction

Edward Herring, when discussing peer polity interaction in the South Italian Iron Age and Classical period, aimed 'to show how communications (on all levels) between the different communities could have been a major dynamic to socio-political change'.[A] He argued that the Greek colonies were themselves tribal societies and therefore peer polities to the native tribes, and attempted to fit the available archaeological evidence into Renfrew's six characteristics of peer polity interaction. Herring concluded that the peer polity model 'works well between the late 8th century to sometime in the 6th century', while for the later period he sees two systems of peer polity interaction (one indigenous, one colonial Greek) co-existing in southern Italy, with the change being brought about by exogenous factors. Herring struggled to avoid reverting to the old Hellenization idea when he discussed the later period. While new ideas and products from Greece reached the natives via the Greek colonists, he argued that this was an exchange between equals rather than one between a dominant and a weaker partner. Peer polity models for the organization of pre- and protohistoric societies have enjoyed a growing popularity with students of Bronze Age and Iron Age hillforts, especially those working with GIS, because the underlying assumption of equality between hillforts belonging to the same system allows the application of a number of spatial analytical techniques. Hillforts probably formed the top of the settlement hierarchy in the tribal societies of the Bronze Age and Early Iron Age in large parts of Europe, but very little is known about the living systems they were a part of. Since many of them have only been investigated from a topographic point of view and the few available dates are only based on diagnostic surface finds, their contemporaneity must be assumed in order to be able to treat them as the foci of interacting peer polities. The polities themselves might best be viewed as tribal subdivisions or 'cantons' with a population ranging from a few hundred to a few thousand people.

Rank-size analysis

It has been established empirically, and supported by theory, that societies of a certain level of complexity must have a hierarchical organization.[B] This hierarchy is expressed by, among other things, differentiation in the size of, and functions performed at, its settlements. Therefore the degree of integration (complexity) of a society can be derived from the rank-size distribution of its settlements. Zipf's (1949) rank-size rule states that the population size of the nth ranked settlement equals the population size of the largest settlement multiplied by the inverse of its rank. This empirical finding has been used and modified by archaeologists to model expected rank-size relationships for several types of settlement hierarchy.[C] Several types of non-random rank-size graphs have been defined. In general, more steeply curved relationships indicate a larger degree of organization of society; ideally, the curve should also be stepped to reflect each hierarchical level in classical central place theory. Berry distinguished *rank-size* relationships, which display an exponential continuum of sizes, and *primate* relationships where there are a large number of small settlements with one or a few very large ones; intermediate relationships can also exist.[D] Societies are thought to move from primate to rank-size patterns, and this is what archaeologists are looking for in rank-size graphs.

[A] Herring 1991, 35-36 and 42-49.
[B] Johnson 1985.
[C] Hodder 1979, 118-120.
[D] Berry 1961.

If we display the rank-size relationship in a graph using logarithmic scales on both the rank and the size axes, it becomes a straight line and we can describe other graphs by their type and degree of curvature. A concave graph is produced when the differences in size between the largest settlements and the rest of the settlement system are larger than expected; a convex one when they are smaller. Both types of graphs supposedly indicate low levels of settlement-system integration; as societies 'mature', the graphs approach the ideal log-log graph.

Such models are derived from human geography and they are not easily transposed to archaeological datasets, since reliable information about site size and chronology is not always available. If we want to describe and interpret rank-size patterns within the RPC study regions, we must first examine the theoretical and methodological problems involved with this technique. In a thorough discussion of the subject, Hodder examined twelve archaeological datasets not only with regard to their rank-size interpretation, but also looking at their intrinsic quality. Archaeological rank-size graphs are constructed on the basis of site sizes, as a proxy measure for population figures. Site size is normally estimated or measured either on the basis of the area covered by (a certain minimum density of) surface pottery in surveys, or on the basis of the area enclosed by defences; in the case of proto-urban settlements in Italy, the geomorphologically defined available space is used (i.e. 'plateau size'). Whilst there are significant problems with the first two approaches, proponents of the latter approach in Italy in particular have recently re-examined their assumptions.[E] A more reliable approach to the determination of site rank would be one that is based on the combination of size and other, qualitative criteria, viz. the presence or absence of indicators such as defensive structures, civic or cultic monumental architecture, and formal cemeteries.

XTENT modelling

If a region such as the Salento was at some time divided into polities, then the size and shape of these polities can to some extent be predicted on the basis of properties of their putative centres and of the physical landscape. In its simplest form, a model of the polities can be constructed using only the criterion of horizontal distance – resulting in the classical Thiessen polygons. Although this approach can be refined by adding 'weights' to the central places and by taking into account variations in the ease of communication across the landscape, it remains limited to sets of sites of equal rank. If the existence of a site hierarchy is suspected, more sophisticated approaches are needed to construct realistic models of territorial organization. Below, one specific model (Renfrew and Level's XTENT model, 1979) will be applied to settlement data provided in Burgers (1998, 1999) and D'Andria (1999).

Renfrew (1978) suggested that the effective polity (the highest-order social unit) may be identified by the scale and distribution of central places; this idea was developed into the XTENT model by Renfrew and Level.[F] Their approach is based on four assumptions: 1) territories consist of one continuous polygon, 2) they fall under a single authority *or none*, 3) normally the largest settlements are the capitals, and 4) larger capitals have larger territories. Not all settlements above a certain size need to be capitals. These assumptions lead to a different model (and result) than do those underlying (weighted or unweighted) Thiessen polygons, because they enable the modelling of a political or administrative hierarchy of settlements within polities without requiring any information on rank.

The XTENT model implements this idea by assuming the 'influence' of any centre to be proportional to a function of its size and declining linearly with distance. If, at the location of a second centre, the influence of the first, larger, centre is larger than that of the second centre itself, then this second centre is subordinate; if not, then the second centre is independent. Because a linear decline with distance is being used, areas of 'unclaimed land' can exist as well. Territorial boundaries can be of two kinds: they are either the lines of

---

[E] See especially Vanzetti 2002; Guidi 1985.   [F] Renfrew / Level 1979, 149-152.

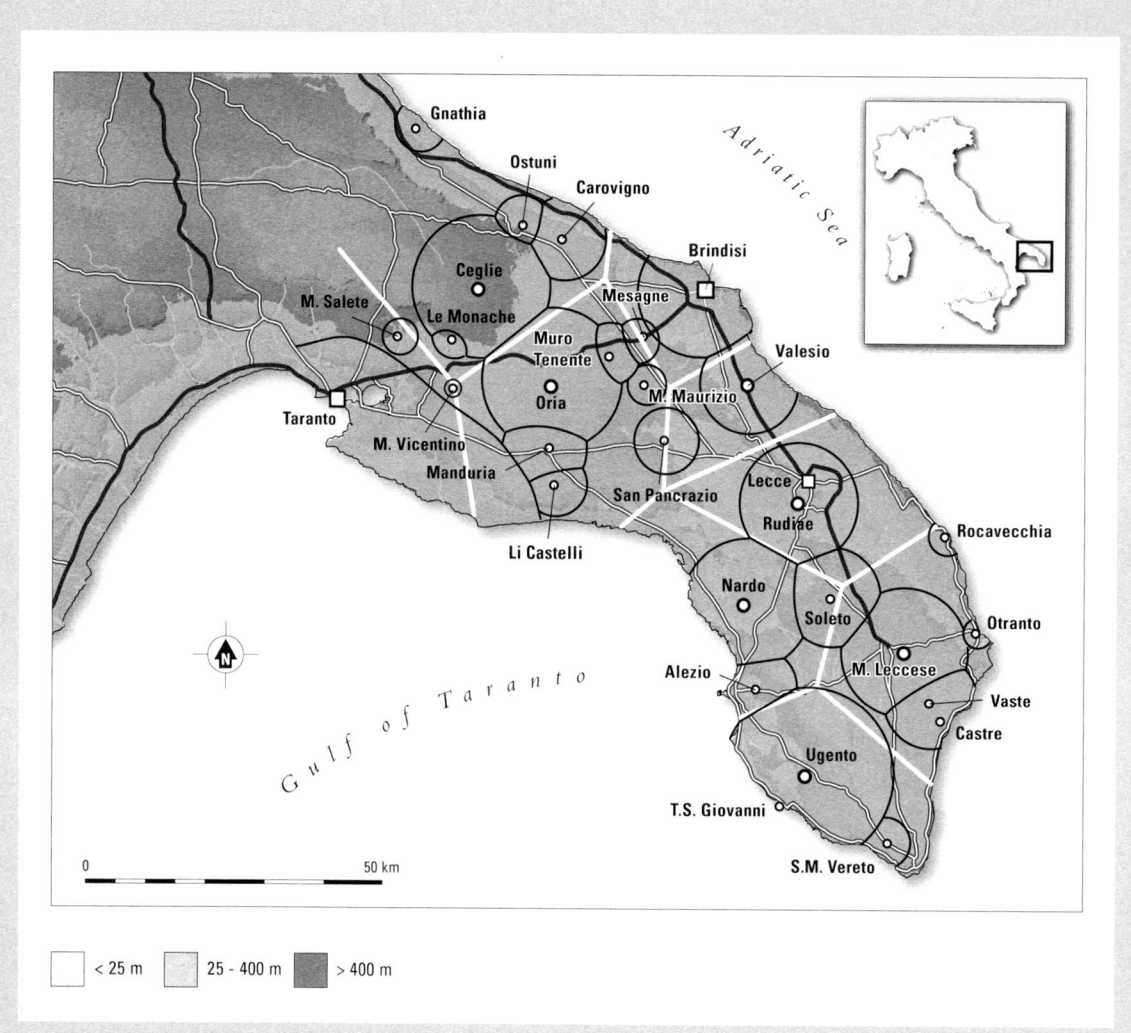

Fig. 1.8. Modelling early Hellenistic territorial organization of the Salento peninsula using Thiessen polygons for the largest sites (white) and XTENT 'bubbles' for all sites (black) (after Burgers 1999, 26-27). For a colour version of this figure, see page 208.

equal influence between two centres, or the lines where influence drops to zero. The three variables to be determined within this model are the degree of influence at each centre (e.g. based on settlement size), the unit of distance (e.g. travel costs), and the geometrical function of the decline of influence. The latter should be determined empirically and obviously depends on the effectiveness of the available means of communication: a slowly declining function tends to lead to the dominance of a single centre over the entire region, while a fast decline leads to 'local autonomy' for all centres. Renfrew and Level experimentally applied the XTENT model to Maltese Neolithic temples, modern European cities and late Uruk settlement in Mesopotamia, varying the slope and the size-influence function to arrive at an acceptable value of .5 for the latter (i.e. site area is proportional to population, which is in turn proportional to territorial area). Alteration of the last remaining variable, slope, was found to mimic the passage of time in some respects.

In the case of the Salento isthmus, settlement ranks have been defined on the basis of size alone (see section 7.2.2), and both Thiessen polygons and XTENT 'bubbles' have been used to model the appropriate territories (figure 1.8). During the early Hellenistic period the central settlements of the Salento expanded in size and in degree of hierarchization, as can be inferred from the intra-mural areas of walled settlements

> provided by D'Andria.[6] The Thiessen polygons in figure 1.8 are based on the sites with the largest fortified areas, which are assumed to form a separate site class. By contrast the 'bubbles' created by the XTENT model are based on the fortified areas of *all* sites (in this example a relatively steep decline function has been used, resulting in large 'unclaimed zones' and a relatively small number of sites that fall under their neighbour's sway).
>
> [6] D'Andria 1991, 445; discussed in Burgers 1998, 227-231.

1.3.4 SCOPE AND LIMITATIONS OF REGIONAL SETTLEMENT MODELS

The regional settlement distribution maps produced by the RPC project can be used to generate and evaluate settlement and territorial models at various spatial and chronological scales. Such models are derived from the general literature on human geography and Italian archaeology; alternatively they were developed to explain specific local or regional settlement patterns when aspects of the palaeogeography and palaeo-environment, historical sources, or ethnographic parallels gave cause to do so. The models occasionally presented throughout this volume are mainly concerned with explaining the *longue durée* geographical distribution of the various settlement types for the pre-classical period; see, for example, Box 1.3 and the use of Thiessen polygons for both the Pontine region (chapter 2) and the Sibaritide (chapter 4).

At the broadest of spatial scales and the longest of *durées*, the combination of demographic growth and technological change presumably drove many of the processes of change in early Italy. However, we shall see that explanatory models of socio-political change tend to concentrate on more immediate causes. Among these, quantitative/geographical models went out of favour in the mid-1980s, and were replaced by sociological models conforming more to the humanistic outlook of most archaeologists. Nonetheless, at coarser resolutions of time and space, physical parameters such as climate, the presence or absence of geographical boundaries or the availability of natural resources may well have conditioned the historical outcome of the processes we study.[70] For example, bio-geographical similarities might explain why crops, animals, and lifestyles could be communicated across the Mediterranean basin with relative ease.

In the archaeological literature on the structure of protohistoric and early historic societies of southern Italy (and generally of Europe), two types of explanatory models were advanced in the mid-1980s to replace the earlier 'advance of classical civilization' model. The Peer Polity Interaction model, introduced by Renfrew and Cherry in 1986, states that change is initiated by the interaction and competition between a large number of independent and - at first - equally powerful polities. The Core-Periphery model, advanced at almost the same time by Rowlands, describes change as being driven by unequal interacting parts of single systems.[71] It is not our intention here to argue for or against either. Instead, these models act as a backdrop against which hypotheses about the reasons for the occurrence of patterns in the archaeological record in our three study regions may be developed. The value of explanatory models lies in how well they are able to predict certain types of archaeological phenomena. In chapter 9 we will return to this topic, and see how these models have been applied within the RPC project. In the following three chapters we will explain how the approaches introduced in the present chapter have been used in each of the three RPC study regions.

[70] cf. Diamond 1998.

[71] Renfrew / Cherry 1986; Rowlands *et al.* 1987.

2 Regional Settlement Dynamics of the Pontine Region

2.1 INTRODUCTION

The aim of this chapter is to delineate the long-term settlement history of the Pontine region from the Bronze Age to the Roman Imperial period, in the context of its natural environment. We will first describe the variations in the landscape that conditioned the development of patterns of settlement and landscape exploitation. To this end the results of various pollen cores and sedimentation studies are used that were carried out in the course of the Pontine Region and RPC projects. We will then delineate and evaluate the various land systems that can be discerned in the Pontine region, in order to establish relations between specific environments (mountains, marshlands, river valleys, coastal dunes) and the archaeological record. These relations will then be considered in the overarching framework of core processes studied in the RPC project, highlighting any micro-regional differentiation. We will discuss the socio-economic responses of the Pontine protohistorical communities in the Alban Hills to the process of centralization that started in the Middle Bronze Age, as well as the early urbanization of the volcanic areas during the Late Iron Age and Archaic periods. We will furthermore discuss the Roman colonization that, in an area this close to Rome, possibly started already in the early 5th century BC. The land systems approach that we have adopted here accentuates the fact that these core processes affected each part of the landscape at different times and in different ways. This allows some cautious observations on issues such as continuity and discontinuity, core and periphery relations, micro-regional differentiation in social and economic structures, and changing perceptions of the landscape. We will present the archaeological data in chronological order for each land system, starting with the Bronze Age and ending with the Roman Imperial period. A thematic recapitulation of the dynamics of settlement and landscape in the Pontine region in comparison with the Salento isthmus and the Sibaritide will be presented in chapters five to eight.

Middle Bronze Age	MBA	1700	- 1350	BC
Late Bronze Age (Recent and Final)	LBA	1350	- 1020	BC
Early Iron Age	EIA	1020	- 780	BC
Late Iron Age (including Orientalizing period)	LIA	780	- 580	BC
Archaic period	-	580	- 480	BC
Post-Archaic period	-	480	- 350	BC
Republican period	-	350	- 30	BC
Early Imperial period	-	30 BC	- AD 100	
Mid Imperial period	-	AD 100	- 300	

Table 2.1. Chronological scheme for the Pontine Region, with abbreviations used in the text.

2.2 ENVIRONMENTAL STUDIES

The study area referred to here as the Pontine region comprises the southern part of the volcanic formation of the Alban hills down to the Tyrrhenian coast, the south-western and western slopes of the limestone massif of the Monti Lepini and Ausoni, and the Pontine plain itself. The region as a whole is situated in the southern part of the present-day province of Lazio in Central Italy (fig. 2.1). The toponym 'Pontine region' is no longer used for this area, but in the 19th century it indicated the vast territory south-east of the river Astura, to the point where the Ausoni mountains reach the Tyrrhenian sea near the ancient town of Terracina.[1] Although we will consider developments in the Alban Hills, which form an important point of reference for the Pontine region proper, the main focus of attention throughout this chapter will be in this latter area.

There are three major physico-geographical units in the Pontine region. These are the undulating volcanic landscape with its deeply incised river valleys, the limestone mountain range with its steep slopes and alluvial fans, and the low Pontine plain with its heavy fluvio-colluvial clay sediments, its former marshes and its slightly elevated sandy coastal area. These three units form a complex of land systems that, in the *longue durée* of the Pontine region, were used differently and with varying intensity. Archaeology, history and ethnography reveal that these land systems have been socio-politically interlinked in various ways through time. In order to describe and evaluate the settlement and land-use dynamics of the Pontine region for the major proto- and early historical periods, we must therefore take into account any environmental changes that would have had a significant impact on the physical landscape, regardless of whether their causes were natural or human. The landscape of the Pontine region as we perceive it today is very different from how it looked in antiquity. What changes can we detect, and how can we reconstruct the ancient environment? Below, we will look at some of the changes that took place in the physical landscape of the Pontine region since the beginning of the Holocene.

2.2.1 CHANGES IN THE PHYSICAL LANDSCAPE

We will begin our discussion of landscape change by describing human interventions in the landscape during and after the periods under discussion. One of the most significant effects of these interventions was the almost total elimination of wet areas in the Pontine landscape. Since the period of early urbanization wetlands were perceived as unproductive by urban and rural dwellers alike, an attitude which led, for example, to the reduction of the extent of seasonal inundation of valleys in the volcanic area by the construction of underground drainage channels (the so-called *cuniculi*) as early as the first half of the first millennium BC. Powerful examples of the negative attitude of external authorities to the Pontine wetlands can be found in the many historical attempts to drain the famous Pontine marshes, and to regulate the variable water level of the coastal lagoons.[2] However, pre-20th-century attempts at reclamation were generally restricted to only parts of the plain. The total elimination of the marshes only succeeded under the fascist regime during the 1930s. This so-called *bonifica integrale* continued after the second World War with agricultural reform programmes implemented all over the region from the 1960s onwards, and together with the more recent impact of modern urbanization these have wrought changes to the landscape on an unprecedented scale. These changes must be taken into account in any archaeological reconstruction of the ways in which the Pontine land systems were interlinked in antiquity. For an image of the pre-industrial landscape of the Pontine region, we refer here to a map drawn up in 1851 by surveyors of the Military Cartographic Institute of the then Austrian-Hungarian Empire. This map shows land-use

---

[1] Attema 1993, 14.

[2] Attema 1993, 27-53 with references.

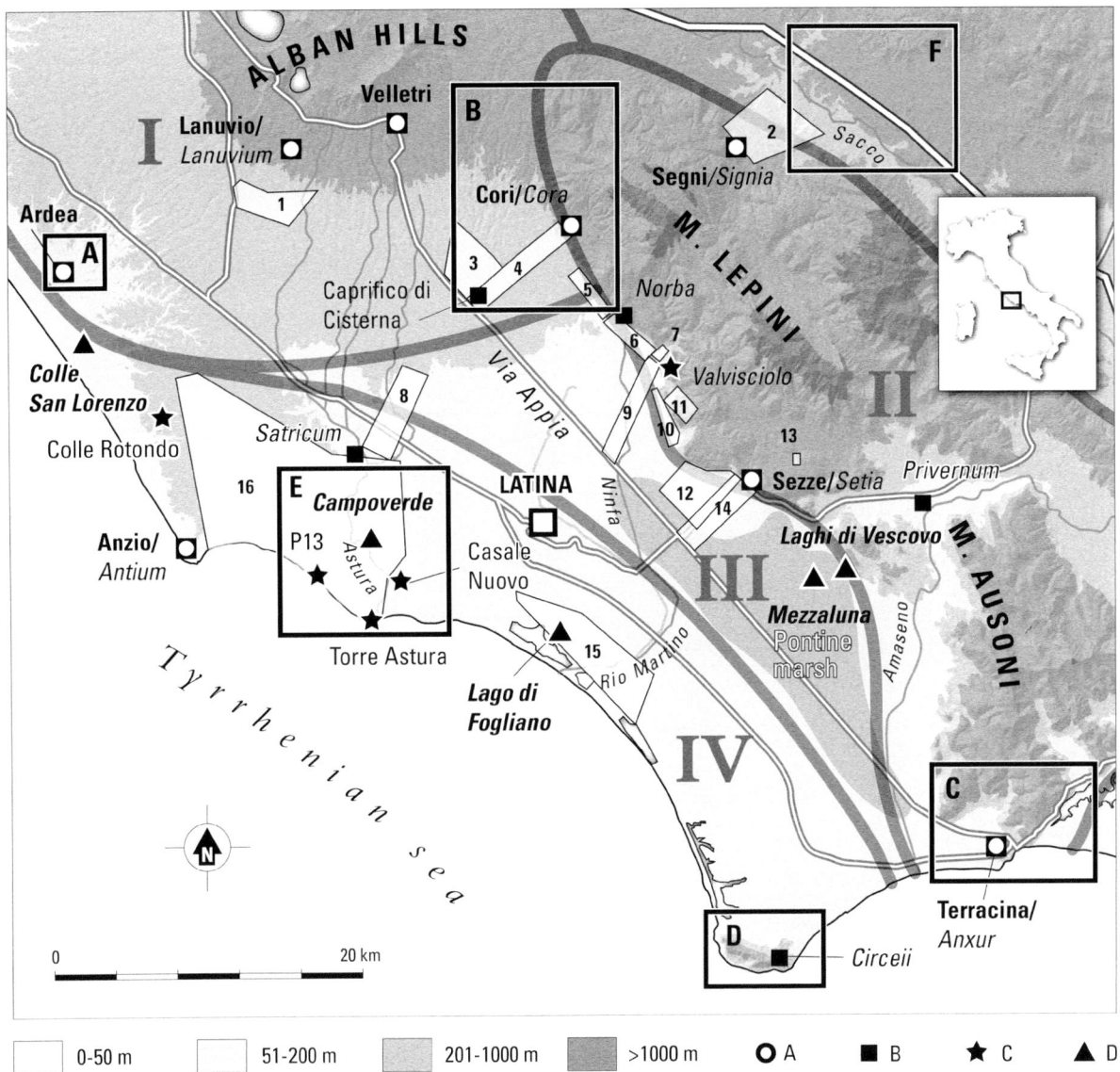

Fig. 2.1. The main land systems of the Pontine region (I - IV), with areas investigated for the *Forma Italiae* series (A - F), areas investigated by the GIA (1 - 16), and pollen locations mentioned in the text. Legend: A modern town, B ancient town; C named archaeological site; D pollen location. For a colour version of this figure, see page 209.

patterns and infrastructure of the mid-19th century and highlights the differences that existed between the various landscape units (fig. 2.2). Although it cannot serve as a direct parallel for the situation in antiquity, the map shows that the landscape can be divided into intensively cultivated areas (the volcanic hills and slopes of the Monti Lepini), extensively used areas (the coastal areas with its many fens and lagoons) and the reclaimed, and therefore formerly marginal areas (the Pontine marshes). Of particular note is the close spatial relationship that apparently existed between land use, towns, and infrastructure, a relationship that will have been equally close or closer in antiquity given the more limited means of transport.

Whilst the 1851 map suggests both the potential and the constraints of the Pontine region for dwelling and cultivation, it cannot be taken at face value in a reconstruction of the ancient landscape. The physico-geographical characteristics of some of the landscape units represented on the map were changed, and we must also take into account subsequent changes in the vegetation pattern and hydrography. This brings us to a second set of factors of landscape change, which involve climatic change (espe-

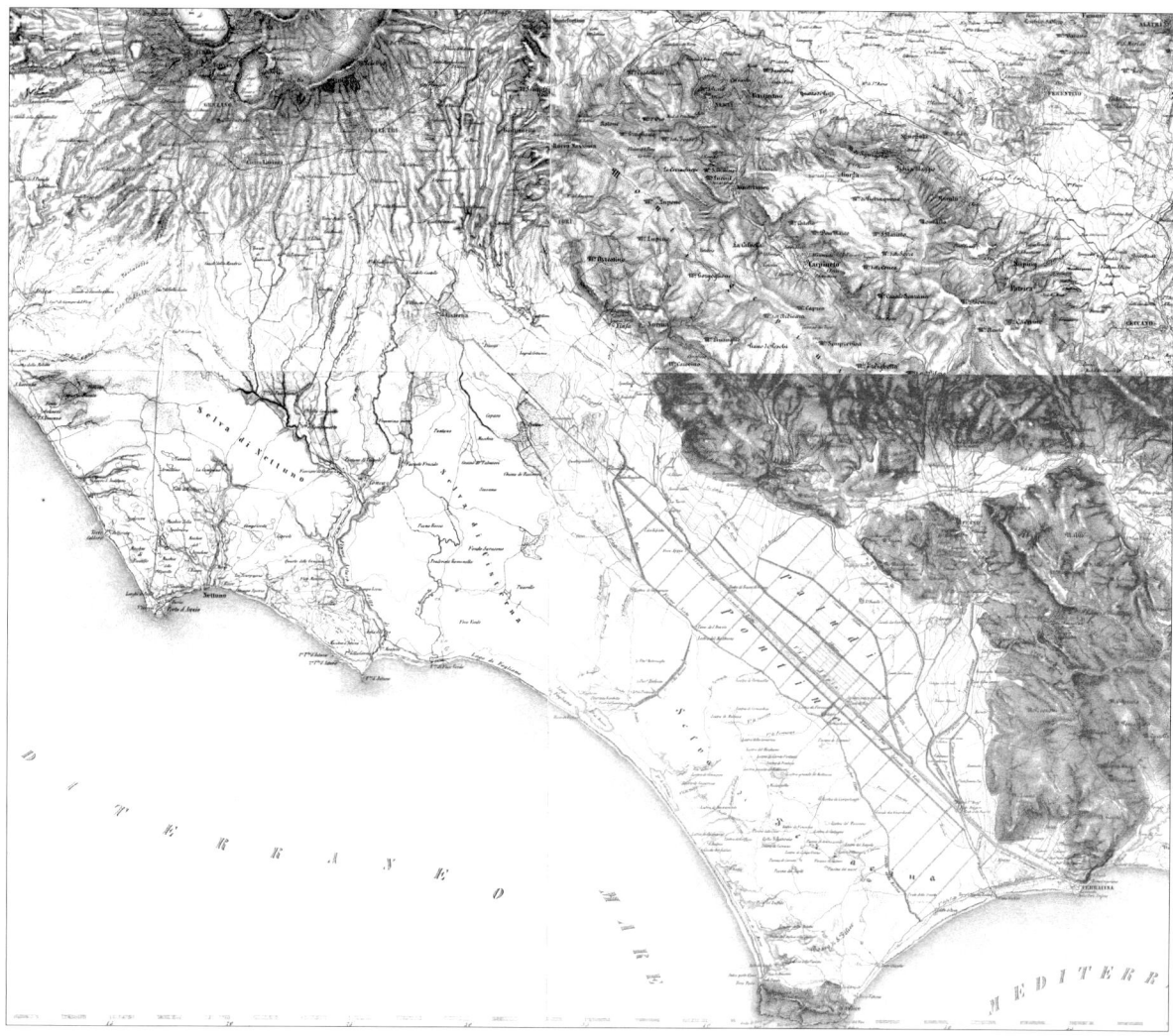

Fig. 2.2. Extract of the 1851 topographical map for the Pontine region, produced by the Military Geographic Institute in Vienna (Austria).

cially fluctuations in precipitation) and changes caused by human and animal interference (e.g. woodland clearance for agriculture, and pastoral activities). Both climate change and human and animal interference in the landscape are expressed in the pollen record of the region, and in its regime of erosion and sedimentation. A decrease in arboreal pollen in combination with increased sedimentation in the coastal plain may indicate the increasing impact of humans. Many studies have shown how human impact changed the appearance and potential of the landscape from the Neolithic onwards to the extent that we can no longer accept the idea of the ancient landscape as a static backdrop to settlement development and land use. Pollen analysis and sedimentation studies show that this is especially true of the Pontine region. Natural processes and human interference combined there to change the conditions of settlement and cultivation during proto- and early history. Below, we will elaborate on this aspect of change.

2.2.2 CLIMATE AND HUMAN IMPACT: EVIDENCE FROM THE POLLEN RECORD OF CENTRAL ITALY

Quite a number of pollen cores from lake sediments and lagoon environments in Lazio, both north and south of the Tiber, have been analyzed.[3] In combination, these pollen records allow for some cautious observations on later Holocene climate change and its effects on the natural vegetation and land use potential of the Pontine region. In northern Lazio and the Alban Hills near Rome, most cores were taken from volcanic crater lakes or basins, while in the Pontine plain cores were mostly taken in former lagoons. On the basis of the pollen diagrams for northern Lazio, Barker has stated that the shift towards Holocene climatic conditions began some 12,000 years ago, and around 6000 BC the increased rainfall and temperature resulted in a dense forest cover of the uplands of the Italian peninsula. Between ca. 2000 and 1000 BC a decline in woodland occurred that some palynologists attribute to human clearance, but others mainly to drier conditions during this period resulting from climatic change.[4] One fact that suggests climate was a factor responsible for landscape change is the widespread evidence for the falling of lake water levels in the later Bronze Age. The available data seems to point to climate as an agent in the developments that led to a more open landscape but we agree with Barker that this does not rule out a contribution of early farmers to the process. Indicators for arable farming and pasture are present in Latial pollen diagrams north of the Tiber from the Neolithic onwards, as well as in the pollen diagrams of cores from the Pontine region. It is therefore plausible that a combination of climatological and human factors in the later Holocene led to the more open landscape that characterized central Italy during the protohistorical and early historical periods. Archaeological evidence for human activity during the Neolithic in the Pontine region is almost absent despite the pollen record. This demonstrates the limitations of archaeological survey and excavation as well as the importance of palynological research. In the following section we will focus on the impact of man on the natural landscape of the Pontine region as observed in pollen diagrams (see Boxes 2.1 and 2.2 for a detailed discussion).

2.2.3 HUMAN IMPACT ON THE PONTINE REGION AS OBSERVED IN POLLEN DIAGRAMS

The general picture obtained from the pollen cores of central Italy also holds for the Pontine region. During the Neolithic and Early Bronze Age the landscape gradually opened up, and indicators of arable farming and grazing in the pollen record suggest an increasing human impact.[5] The diagram from the Mezzaluna pollen core in the north-eastern part of the plain shows the appearance of a *macchia*-like vegetation after 4500 BP, but vegetation development in the uplands remains unclear, and more research is required there.[6] At the beginning of the first millennium BC, the vegetation of the north-eastern part of the Pontine plain consisted of alder carr and some willow, with oak, elm and hornbeam forest on the nearby Lepine footslopes.

The details of the PRP and RPC cores in Box 2.1 suggest that the Pontine pollen record from the later Neolithic to Roman periods without exception reflects the gradual decline of forest cover on the Alban hills and in the Monti Lepini, and the resulting gradual opening up of the landscape. Drier conditions in the plain seem, however, to have depended on the silting up of the marshy areas and lagoons through improved drainage of the graben near Terracina, rather than on climatic change. All cores indicate an intensification of farming, but the evidence is more consistent for the Alban hills than for the

---

[3] Summarized, respectively, in Barker / Rasmussen 1998, 38-41 and Van Joolen 2003, 156.

[4] See also the discussion in Van Joolen 2003, ch. 6.

[5] See van Joolen 2003, ch. 6; Eisner / Kamermans 2004.

[6] Cf. Barker / Rasmussen 1998, 39.

Box 2.1 Pollen studies in the Pontine region

Analysis of pollen cores taken in the course of the Pontine Region and RPC projects in formerly wet areas of the Pontine region contributed to a reconstruction of the vegetation sequences in the land systems as defined by us, and revealed changing local circumstances throughout the period under study. Pollen data were also used to test our land evaluation model for the Pontine region (fig. 2.3).[A] Analyses focused on the pollen zones that cover the Neolithic to Roman periods, and they were especially useful in tracing the introduction of cultivars such as wheat, olive and sweet chestnut. The pollen evidence for human impact on the landscape is especially consistent for the north-western part of the Pontine region from the advanced Bronze Age onwards. In the lagoonal milieu along the coast human impact was probably more episodic, and on the slopes of the Monti Lepini it appears to have arrived only later in the second half of the first millennium BC. Here, we present an overview of the main results for these three areas.

The north-western part of the Pontine region

On the micro-regional level, the *Colle San Lorenzo* core provides evidence for a continuous decline of the Holocene forest between the late Neolithic and Roman period. It shows a general change from a pine-oak dominated forest to the characteristic open landscape of classical antiquity. The first clear signs of cereal cultivation appear in the pollen diagram around 3000 BC (i.e. in the late Neolithic) and continue into the second millennium BC (Middle Bronze Age). Substantial human impact on the landscape becomes evident only in the later phases of the Bronze Age, with a significant increase of *cerealia* (wheat) and a dramatic decrease of tree pollen. Van Joolen supposes that as more land was needed for farming trees were cut, which resulted in a less dense oak-beech forest. The lithology of the pollen core shows a transition from a low-energetic environment with peat development to a dynamic environment in which coarser sediments were deposited. This, too, indicates erosion caused by forest clearance and more intensive cultivation of the volcanic soils in the Alban hills. This phase has not been precisely dated, but it began somewhere in the Recent or Final Bronze Age, and the decline in tree pollen (with the exception of common oak [*quercus robur*]) continued into the Early Iron Age. Signs of agricultural practices remain present in the pollen sequence until the end of reliable pollen data around AD 0, but the local environment around Colle San Lorenzo was in all periods characterized by more or less wet conditions.

The *Campoverde* core supports the case for cereal cultivation since the later Bronze Age.[B] This 4.25 m-deep pollen core was taken from sediments of the former lake of Campoverde (or 'Lago di Monsignore'), located on the fringes of the Pontine plain some 20 km from the Alban hills. Little remains today of this spring-fed lake after the land reforms of the late 1970s, but it is well-known for the many archaeological finds that suggest the presence of an open-air sanctuary of protohistorical date.[C] The pollen core was radiocarbon dated at depths of 95 and 385 cm to AD 720 – 1026 and 2920 - 3790 BC respectively, and it contained clear indications for an agricultural phase which was dated between 2460 – 1889 BC and again between 2026 – 1528 BC. Since the older date appears higher in the core than the younger one and additional C^{14} dates showed the same inversion, this suggests that the core contains an inverted sediment. This could only have been caused by lateral erosion of the lake shores causing younger sediments to become buried by older sediments. A likely explanation for this, supported by the presence of *Liguliflorae* pollen, is denudation of the lake's surroundings. Pollen could then have ended up in the core in either of two ways, by direct deposition or by lateral erosion, resulting in the observed mixture of well-preserved and corroded pollen.

[A] See the concluding chapter of Van Joolen 2003 on the testing of the land evaluation model.

[B] Veenman 1997.

[C] In late 2008, illegal excavations destroyed much of the site while confirming its great significance by uncovering a large number of votive objects.

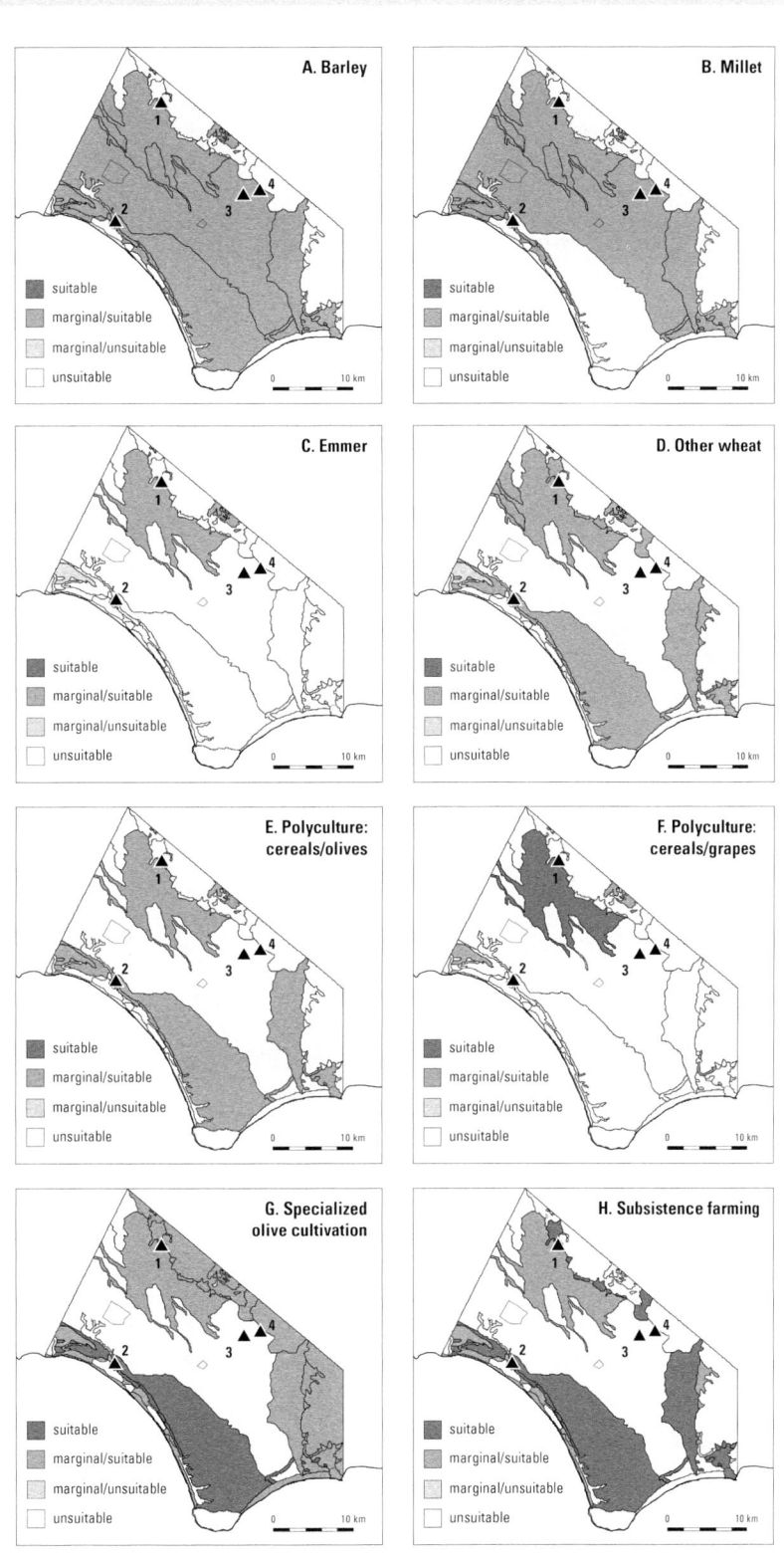

Fig. 2.3. Land evaluation models for four grain types and four cultivation types in the Pontine region (after Van Joolen 2003, figs 5.8 and 6.2). Locations of relevant pollen cores: 1. *Monticchio*, 2. *Lago di Fogliano*, 3. *Mezzaluna*, 4. *Laghi di Vescovo*. For a colour version of this figure, see page 210.

Remarkably, the highest scores of *Liguliflorae* occurred in combination with *cerealia*, which would indicate that the lateral erosion was caused by denudation of the surroundings of the lake for cereal cultivation. Denudation would have begun between 1500 and 1200 BC, that is at the end of the Middle Bronze Age or in the Recent Bronze Age.

The south-eastern part of the Pontine region

The *Lago di Fogliano* core was taken in the south-eastern part of the Pontine region, in the clayey/peaty sediments adjacent to lake Fogliano. The Fogliano lagoon lies between the narrow line of younger dunes of the Terracina level and the older and much broader beach-ridge system of the Borgo Ermada complex. The latter is characterized by an undulating landscape of sandy soils alternating with lagoonal clayey deposits in low-lying positions. Unfortunately the radiocarbon dates of the Lago di Fogliano core have a low resolution, impeding a close match between vegetation change and settlement history.

Van Joolen draws two main conclusions from the Fogliano pollen diagram. Her first conclusion is that it shows unmistakable, albeit modest, agricultural activities in the area surrounding the lake from at least the Early Bronze Age onwards, and probably even since the Neolithic. Farming intensified at some stage between the Late Iron Age and the middle Republican period, but van Joolen cautions that the evidence suggests that the area within 5 km of the coring location (maximum airborne travel distance of wheat) was used only marginally. Her second important observation is that the pollen sequence indicates that the water-body of lake Fogliano was drying out from the end of the Bronze Age or the start of the Iron Age, as can be concluded from the disappearance of aquatic plants, the poor conservation of the pollen, and the low pollen percentages.[D]

Locally, the Lago di Fogliano-core indicates wet conditions for the Early and Middle Bronze Age. On the regional scale, a gradual reduction of the oak forest along with beech, hornbeam, and hop hornbeam that had begun already in the Neolithic is continuing. The reduction of the oak forest may have to do with human interference, but more research is needed. Olive and vine, probably not domesticated, appear throughout the period in small quantities. Grasses and heather dominate the non-arboreal pollen. Evidence for cereal farming in the form of *triticum* wheat is present in the later part of this period. Other indicators of human exploitation of the higher grounds near the lagoon are provided by plantain, knapweed and nettle. Aquatic plants and green algae characterize the local vegetation, indicating the presence of deep water.

In the next pollen zone, which presumably coincides with the Recent Bronze Age and the Iron Age, tree pollen continue to dominate with species such as the common oak, ash tree and willow. Olive and vine (now perhaps domesticated) and indicators of agricultural activity appear and disappear in the sequence, indicating occasional and small-scale land use. Aquatics disappear, indicating a drier phase that may have been caused by a natural, partial silting-up of the lagoon.

The final pollen zone, incorporating the Roman period, shows an intensification of farming activities in an increasingly dry environment, as aquatics significantly decrease throughout. The alder-willow forest surrounding the lagoon is replaced by an open landscape of myrtle, grasses, heather and sedges. Regionally, the common oak/hornbeam/hazel forest regenerates, but the number of tree species is diminished. Van Joolen suggests that deforestation accompanying the preparation of fields for olive cultivation may have caused this phenomenon. The percentage of olive pollen increases towards the top of the pollen zone, and may reflect the increased numbers of Roman Republican farmsteads noted in the field surveys. The lithology of the core also indicates a locally increasingly dynamic environment in terms of sediment supply.

[D] Van Joolen 2003, chapter 6.

The Pontine graben and Lepine foothills[E]

The *Laghi di Vescovo* core was taken close to the location of the *Mezzaluna* core in the clayey/peaty deposits east of Sezze, near the slopes of the Monti Lepini.[F] Chronologically this core, which starts roughly around 800 BC, follows after that of Mezzaluna which ends around 2000 BC. This leaves us with a hiatus of more than a millennium which is still awaiting detailed study. The core from Laghi di Vescovo shows that the Monti Lepini were covered by a mixed oak forest in the period around 2500 BP, but there is also evidence for the presence of vines and olive trees on the footslopes of the Lepini around this time. The presence of colonizing species of cultivated soils would indicate that these vines and olives were domesticated. Increased human influence is clear from the appearance of a wide variety of anthropogenic factors pointing to a phase of substantial deforestation. At a slightly later stage around 2300 BP, and presumably from the Roman Republican period onwards, sweet chestnut was cultivated on the Lepine slopes besides olives, but evidence for viticulture is lacking. That olive cultivation became widespread at this time on the footslopes of the Lepini is also indicated by the *Monticchio* core that was taken in a small depression in the plain near the Lepine footslopes close to Sermoneta. Both cores thus give a good indication of the type of specialized exploitation taking place at the Roman 'platform' villas discussed in section 2.3.2. The absence of fully aquatic species in the plain immediately around the Laghi di Vescovo indicates that the local environment around 2500 BP was characterized by shallow water or moist conditions. Van Joolen therefore concludes that the surroundings of the Vescovo lakes were unsuitable for agriculture. However, it seems that the lake from which the core was taken dried out around 2300 BP, since there is severe corrosion of all organic material. Aquatic plants and most non-arboreal pollen disappear, while *dryopteris* (wood fern) increases significantly. The plain must have become progressively dry in this period, as corroborated by sedimentation studies carried out nearby (see Box 2.2).

[E] The published radiocarbon dates for the pollen cores in this area must be treated with caution, as recent research suggests that they may have been contaminated by ancient dissolved carbon.

[F] The Mezzaluna core was taken as part of the Agro Pontino Project (Hunt / Eisner 1991; Eisner / Kamermans 2004).

Pontine plain. Both the San Lorenzo core and the Campoverde core in the volcanic area show evidence for cereal farming in the Early (3000 BC) and Recent Bronze Age (mid-second millennium BC) respectively. In combination with the evidence from cores taken in the crater lakes this suggests the widespread introduction of wheat cultivation in the volcanic area.[7] That wheat cultivation in the Bronze Age was also practiced in the coastal margins, is evident from the presence of cereal pollen in the Fogliano core. The evidence for agriculture continues into the Iron Age, with indications of barley and wheat/rye cultivation in the volcanic area and farming activities in the coastal area. For the Roman period, evidence for cereal cultivation and an expansion of chestnut, walnut and olive in the area of the volcanic lakes is supported by the Colle San Lorenzo core, taken near Ardea on the coast of southern Lazio. Evidence for olive cultivation on the footslopes of the Monti Lepini from the 4th and 3rd centuries BC onwards is consistently present in pollen cores. Both the Monticchio and the Laghi di Vescovo cores show the introduction of olive trees on a substantial scale on the Lepini slopes. As we will see later on, this evidence can be connected to farmsteads that were established along the Lepine margins in the Republican period, and that are believed to have been involved in the production of olive oil. We may conclude that cereal cultivation was practised in the Pontine region as early as the late Neolithic/Early Bronze Age. In our discussion of the individual land systems we will return to the use of pollen data as indicators of land use.

[7] Lowe *et al.* 1996.

2.2.4 EROSION AND SEDIMENTATION AS AGENTS OF LANDSCAPE CHANGE

We will continue our discussion of evidence for human impact on the landscape of the Pontine region with some results of recent research into Holocene erosion and sedimentation. The main case studies presented here consider sedimentation phases in the north-eastern part of the Pontine plain, in the area of Sezze and the Amaseno basin respectively, but we will also discuss examples of colluviation in the volcanic area.

The soil map that was compiled in the early 1980s by physical geographers at the University of Amsterdam reveals that recently formed fluvio-colluvial sediments occur in two parts of the Pontine plain.[8] However, it is only since the augering programme carried out in the course of the PRP that a more precise date for their formation could be established,[9] using radiocarbon dates obtained from the top of peaty layers underneath the fluvio-colluvial cover that provide reliable post quem dates for various sedimentation phases. The work demonstrates how the environmental characteristics and agricultural potential of parts of the landscape were subjected to considerable change. In Box 2.2 we discuss the alluvial deposits in the plain below the Roman colony Setia, present-day Sezze, and we will demonstrate that the silting-up of parts of the plain between the later Bronze Age and the Middle Ages affected the living conditions and the agricultural potential of these areas. Whereas we must essentially envisage the protohistorical landscape in this part of the plain as a wetland, by Roman times it had become dry cultivatable land.[10] That such changes have a very local impact is demonstrated by a sedimentation study along the Amaseno river,[11] which revealed a sedimentation regime different both in nature and in chronology from that near Sezze. In general, marshy conditions lasted longer in the Amaseno area than in the Sezze area, and this will have influenced the possibilities for land use accordingly.

Sedimentation studies were also carried out as part of the PRP in the western part of the Pontine plain. In the volcanic hills at Cisterna di Latina augering was carried out to map slope wash,[12] while valley infill due to colluviation was mapped and radiocarbon dated in the Astura valley between Borgo Le Ferriere (ancient Satricum) and Borgo Montello.[13] These latter studies indicated that the more stable landscape in the western part of the Pontine region had also undergone considerable environmental change which had affected both the land-use potential in the past and the visibility of the archaeological record in the present. At Contrada Trentossa near the protohistorical settlement of Caracupa-Valvisciolo, evidence for a more catastrophic sedimentation event in the form of a mud flow can still be seen as an elongated ridge in the landscape to the south of that settlement. Ceramic finds within the sediment indicate that mud flows occurred between the 7th century BC and the Roman period.[14]

These studies show that any reconstruction of land use in the hills of the volcanic area and the slopes and uplands of the Lepini and Ausoni mountains must take into account substantial erosion, just as sedimentation was a major agent of landscape change in the lower parts of the Pontine plain.

2.3 LAND SYSTEMS AND THE ARCHAEOLOGICAL RECORD

In this section we will describe and evaluate the land systems of the Pontine region using the environmental data presented above, and we will provide an overview of archaeologically attested settlement patterns in each land system. A *land system* is an area or group of areas with a recurring pattern of landforms, soils and vegetation. Van Joolen formalised the description of a number of land systems in

---

[8] Sevink et al. 1984.
[9] Attema / Delvigne 2000.
[10] Attema et al. 1999, 111-116.
[11] Van Joolen 2003, ch. 3.
[12] Attema 1993, 181-196.
[13] Bouma et al. 1995.
[14] Attema et al. 1999, 105-111.

Box 2.2 Colluviation and alluviation in the Pontine Plain

The Sezze alluvial fan

The plain below Sezze consists of a gently sloping alluvial fan that emanates from the valley opening of the Fosso Briolco and gradually merges into an alluvial sheet. Working backwards from the edge of the alluvial deposits, hand augering was carried out to collect radiocarbon samples from the top of the underlying peaty layer. The results are here summarised in fig. 2.4.[6] Among the conclusions reached by Attema and Delvigne was the observation that the top of the peaty layers below the alluvial cover represents a roughly horizontal surface that is continuous with the filled-up lagoon of the former Pontine marshes. The peat deposits they found were not very thick, and from many augering cores only peaty clay could be collected. This led to the conclusion that when the lowland territory of Setia silted up, marshy conditions continued or returned locally, as is demonstrated by samples from core 5, wich indicate that one meter of clay was deposited between ca. 3000 BP and 2000 BP. Later conditions were such that peat could form again. The samples also demonstrate that the peaty layers underlying the southern alluvial sheet are slightly older than those underneath the northern alluvial fan. This suggests that sediment transported by streams coming from the north-west covered the edge of the marsh at a slightly earlier date (just over 4000 years BP) than did sediments from the local fan being formed by the Fosso Briolco. Attema and Delvigne referred to the older sediments as 'fingers' because of their elongated shape which suggests that the sediment supply came from the north-west, in the longitudinal direction of the plain. However, sedimentation in a lateral direction by the Fosso Briolco must have caught up rapidly, since peaty deposits dated ca. 3900 BP were found underneath no less than five meters of alluvial clay. The contour lines in fig. 2.4 highlight the fan shape of the Briolco deposits. Attema and Delvigne were thus able to distinguish two sedimentation mechanisms that were active in this part of the Pontine plain during the Bronze Age and Iron Age, each with its own source area and dynamics: the Alban Hills and the Monti Lepini. Together, these sediments slowly silted up the wetland environment that characterized the plain below Setia in protohistorical times and that can only have been sparsely settled then. That the area was not completely uninhabited at this time appears from a study of the ceramic surface finds produced by a field survey of 1995. These revealed several areas with a thin scatter of protohistorical material (see section 2.2 for details). Judging from the surface pottery record, settlement density peaked in Roman times. Evidently the Roman colonists that had been sent to this remote part of the Pontine region used the, by then, silted-up area to their advantage. From the 4th/3rd century BC onward, the plain below Sezze became densely settled and intensively cultivated, and it was to remain the productive *ager* of the colony of Setia throughout the Roman period.

This example illustrates the interaction between landscape dynamics and settlement and land use patterns. Having started out, in or before the early Holocene, at the footslopes of the Alban hills, the alluvial sheet only began to cover the lagoonal deposits in the Pontine plain in the Bronze Age, and so gradually improved the possibilities for settlement and arable farming.

Sedimentation in the Amaseno basin

A second example of landscape change affecting the Pontine plain comes from the river Amaseno area. Research conducted within the framework of the RPC project followed essentially the same method as was used in the Sezze area. Hand augering was used to obtain radiocarbon samples from peaty layers for the purpose of reconstructing the chronology of sedimentation. Physical geographers of the University of Amsterdam had already mapped the soils in the area in detail by shallow augering up to ca. 2 m depth at a large number of locations, and Van Joolen supplemented these by augering much deeper at another 30

---

[6] Attema / Delvigne 2000.

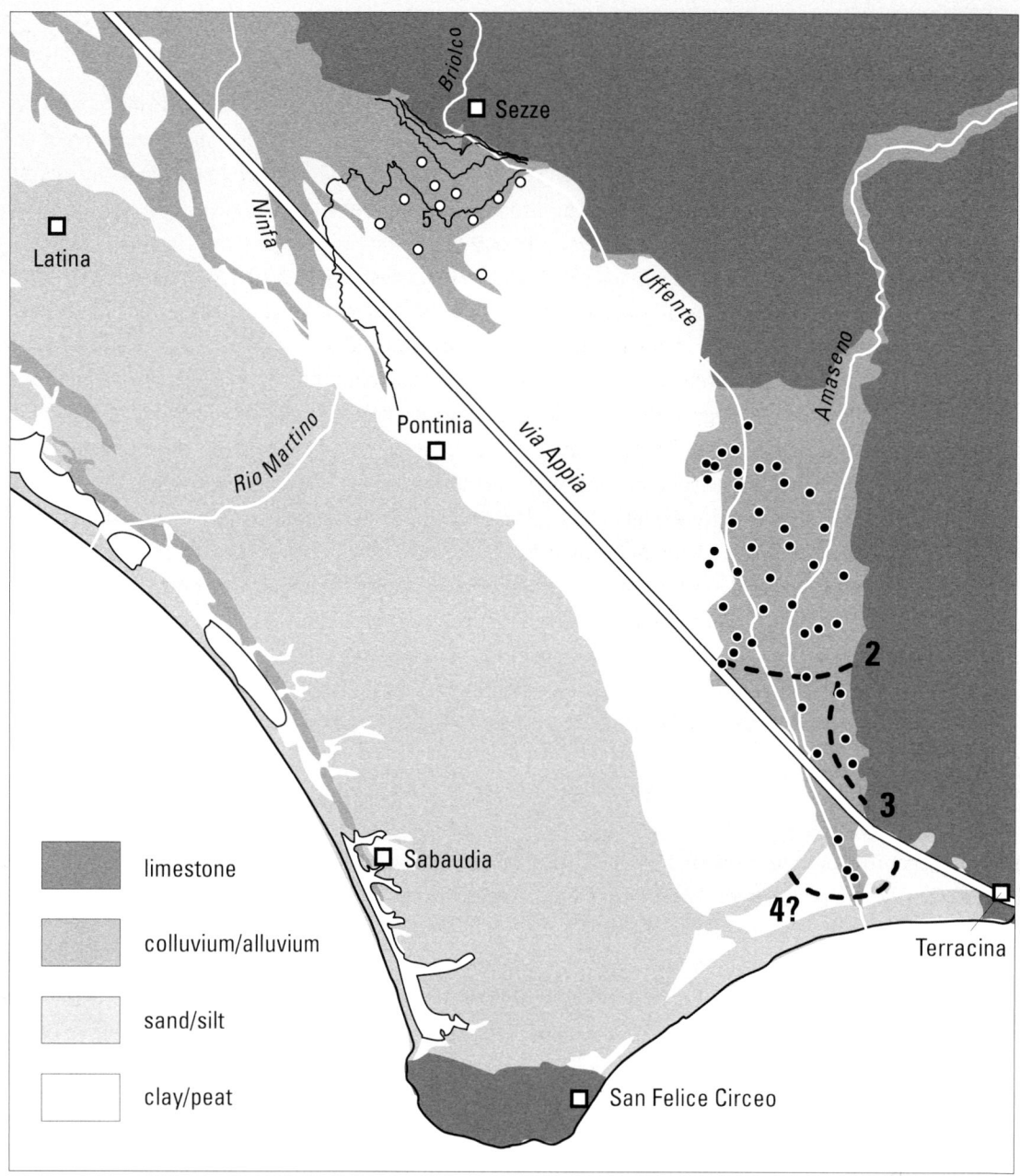

Fig. 2.4. Results of the geo-archaeological work conducted on the Sezze and Amaseno alluvial fans up to 2002 (compiled from Attema / Delvigne 2000, fig. 4 and Van Joolen 2003, fig. 3.32). Sediment corings and geomorphology both indicate complex and phased palaeogeographical development development; for the Amaseno alluvium, phases 2 - 4 are indicated.

locations.[11] Almost all cores have a top layer of fluvio-colluvial deposits, which decreases in thickness from circa 4 m in the north to only a few cm in the south, where it covers mainly lagoonal deposits. On the basis of the sedimentological information obtained from the 30 deeper augering holes, and the ten radiocarbon dates of clayey/peaty layers with a date range between 1618-1410 BC and AD 600–772, Van Joolen was able to reconstruct four phases of (fluvio-) colluvial deposition in the Amaseno basin. These she related to

[11] Attema / Delvigne 2000.

erosion caused by human activities in the foothills of the Monti Lepini and Ausoni. As in the Sezze area, the radiocarbon dates show how marshes and lagoons in the Amaseno basin became covered with sediments during the later Holocene, which increased the area's suitability for ancient agriculture. However, the dates of the peat layers suggest that marshy conditions in this part of the plain lasted longer than in the Sezze area. Van Joolen describes the situation before 1000 BC as one in which the river Amaseno meandered south through a dried-up lagoonal environment. In the north, vegetation would have grown between its tributaries, and in the south it would have bordered the lagoon and have formed peat. By the end of the first millennium BC the northern area would already have been covered by the alluvial fan built up by the Amaseno. This fan gradually extended southwards until, by late Roman times, it had covered the entire lagoonal environment. The supply of sediments needed for this gradual transformation may be attributed to an increasing human impact on the landscape of the Monti Lepini and Ausoni, causing soil instability and consequent erosion. The lithology of the Laghi di Vescovo pollen core (Box 2.1) indicates a disturbance of the lake environment in the Roman Republican period during which the lakes occasionally dried up. Since these lakes are fed by perennial springs it is improbable that this drying-up can be explained by a diminished water supply. An alternative explanation might be that the Romans drained the lakes as part of their efforts to improve the agricultural potential of the area.

Van Joolen found evidence for a renewed phase of colluviation in the late and post-antique period, between AD 400 and 800, when coarse material covered the older and finer alluvium in the plain. Since the archaeological evidence for this period points to a contemporary decrease in the exploitation of the Lepini and Ausoni mountains, the increased erosion may be tentatively attributed to a shift from agriculture to animal husbandry in combination with the abandonment of cultivated plots.

the Pontine region on the basis of fieldwork in the area between lake Fogliano and the Monti Lepini (table 2.2).[15] For the purpose of this chapter we have expanded these land systems to include areas with comparable physical-geographical characteristics, and we have added systems not covered in her study. We have also combined some systems where van Joolen's classification was too detailed for our purposes. Since the southern slopes and the caldera of the Volcano Laziale are an important geological as well as cultural point of reference for the landscape and the archaeological record of the Pontine region, we have included a discussion of this area as well. We will discuss the following areas and land systems (see figure 2.1 and table 2.2):
a) the Alban hills and the surrounding landscape of tuff-based soils
b) the margins and uplands of the Monti Lepini
c) the coastal land systems, including the Astura valley
d) the Latina land system, including the *graben*.

Using this approach we will next describe the archaeological record of the Pontine region for each of the areas mentioned.

2.3.1 THE ALBAN HILLS AND SURROUNDING LANDSCAPE

Bronze Age and Early Iron Age
The volcanic complex of the Alban Hills with Monte Cavo as its highest peak is an important landmark for the Roman Campagna as far away as Rome, and for the Pontine region as far as Terracina. It consists

---

[15] Van Joolen 2003, 62-92.

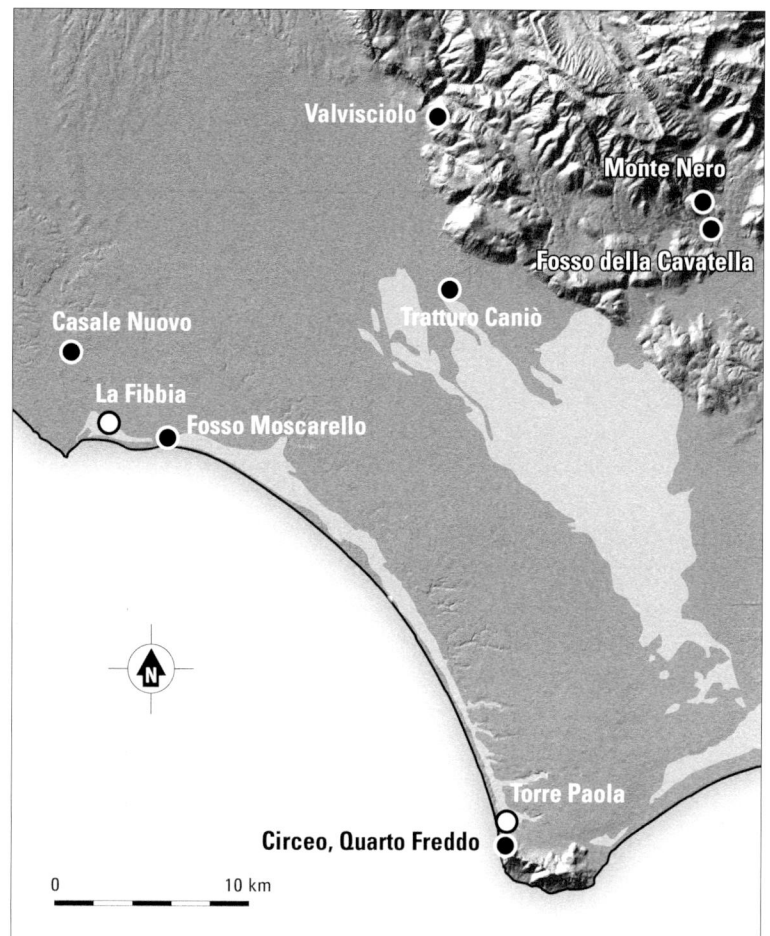

Fig. 2.5. Late Bronze Age (bronzo finale) settlements in the south-eastern part of the Pontine plain and the adjacent foothills. Closed symbols: certain sites; open symbols: probable sites (source: L. Alessandri, GIA).

of steep outer slopes covered by dense vegetation, the crater rims themselves with internal slopes that are also covered by dense vegetation, and crater lakes of which the larger ones are lakes Albano, Nemi, and the now dry lake of Ariccia. Further down the outer slopes of the Alban Hills, the obvious volcanic morphology makes way for a landscape composed of smaller or larger volcanic hills separated by often narrow and deeply incised valleys. This landscape extends in a southerly direction towards the sea but is separated from it by a wide coastal strip with dunes and lagoons. To the south-east it borders directly on the Pontine plain. This volcanic land system offers excellent settlement locations with ample access to surface water provided by many rivulets. The landscape is characterized by its highly fertile but poorly drained soils, which will have conditioned arable farming and the possibilities for pasturing.

For the protohistorical archaeological record of the Bronze Age and Early Iron Ages, most information on occupation patterns in this part of southern Lazio came from the area of the Alban caldera itself and the steep outer slopes.[16] This reinforced the idea that the Alban Hills form the core area of the Latin Iron Age culture, an idea based originally on the distinct material culture of the many Iron Age tombs that dot the slopes of the Alban Hills.[17] According to the evidence currently available, substantial permanent settlement started in the Middle Bronze Age in the caldera itself with the *villaggio delle macine* or 'village of the grinding stones', found partially submerged in lake Albano. The size of this site and the nature of the finds indicate that by the Middle Bronze Age a process of centralization may have started of which this village is at present the earliest example.[18] Although the precise dimensions of the site are unknown, it is assumed to have been large, judging from the extent of the finds on the lake bottom. Moreover, series of wooden palisades were recently excavated on the lakeshore, which form the tangible remains of the Bronze Age settlement.[19] The finds include storage pottery and table ware, bronze axes and other metal tools, as well as a great number of unused grinding stones, which suggests that these were traded. This indicates that the settlement fulfilled an economic role for the wider area. We have little direct evidence

[16] Angle *et al.* 1987.
[17] Gierow 1964.
[18] Chiarucci 1985; Angle *et al.* 2002; Angle 2003.
[19] Angle *et al.* 2002; Zarattini 2003.

Land systems and land forms	Morphology	Soils
Fogliano coastal land system	**holocene mobile dunes with a maximum elevation of 15 m and beach sands, in front of lagoons with marshy areas (peats, black earths and muds).**	
dune	irregular positive relief < 20 m including small flats, and beaches	arenosols; very loose, well-drained, calcareous sands
lagoon	a water-filled bay inshore, lying parallel to the coast	-
Borgo grappa land system	**upper pleistocene level to rolling beach ridges ('old dunes') composed of reddish aeolian sands, alternating with narrow valleys and broader floodplains.**	
undulating land	sequence of relatively low ridges and valleys, 2 – 13 m above sea level, consisting of sandy loam to sandy clay loam	luvisols
plain	minor or no relief; soils may be shallow; overlain by at least 50 cm well-sorted calcareous sands in aeolian areas; poorly drained lagoonal sandy clay	most commonly solodic planosols but also luvisols, vertisols and fluvisols
floodplain	area of subdued relief formed by deposits of flooding rivers; minimum width 100 m	-
Latina land system	**large flat area characterised by a wide variety of soil types and sediments; geological faulting has produced a relatively depressed zone (graben) near the monti lepini.**	
circum-lagoonal plain	poorly drained lagoonal deposits (peats; the former Pontine marshes), partly covered by the well-drained loams of the sezze alluvial sheet (very stony vertic gleyic cambisols) and amaseno fluvio-colluvium (chromic luvisols, no stones); minor or no relief	non-calcareous histosols, gleysols
floodplain	area of subdued relief formed by deposits of flooding rivers; minimum width 100 m	-
Monti lepini land system	**steep and dissected limestone and dolomite formation, characterised by weathering phenomena (karst) especially in the east, and flanked by holocene slope deposits.**	
undulating slopes	unconsolidated slope deposits	very stony lithosols, cambisols and luvisols
alluvial fans	undulating slopes and gently sloping, cone-shaped alluvial fans radiating from a point on the mountain front	very stony soils (phaeozems to luvisols), well-drained
mountains	steep to very steep peaks surrounded by sloping to moderately steep areas	thin, excessively drained, dark brown to black loams; very stony lithosols, rock outcrops
river valley	relatively deep (> 20 m) valley incised by a seasonal stream, at least 100 m wide; deep, non-calcareous, well-drained loamy fluvio-colluvial fills	luvisols, no stones

Table 2.2 Summary land system and land form characteristics of the Pontine region (after Van Joolen 2003, 84-92). The Alban hills land system is not covered.

as yet of rural infill in the wider region that can be dated to the Middle Bronze Age, but we recall here the pollen evidence from Campoverde (Box 2.1), which indicated that cereal farming was practiced in this period and also, through indications for erosion, that humans had an impact on the local tree cover.

This growing human impact on the Bronze Age landscape is reflected in a growing settlement density as shown on the map of Late Bronze Age settlement distribution (Fig. 2.5). This shows a relatively dense distribution of Recent and Final Bronze Age sites on the steep slopes of the Alban caldera itself and in the land system of the volcanic hills to the south. Current research therefore supports the idea that the Alban caldera and its slopes were the core area of Bronze Age protohistorical settlement. Unfortunately, excavated settlement contexts dating to this period are few. Around the caldera, Middle Bronze Age to Final Bronze Age settlement continued uninterrupted into the Early Iron Age, when the funerary record indicates an increasing population.[20] The earliest grave assemblages in the Iron Age represent the first manifestation of the later Latial culture. This distinct material culture is characteristic for the Latins who in the course of the Iron Age developed a proto-urban society in the Alban Hills and adjacent volcanic areas. This process is known in Italian scholarship as the *Formazione della città*,[21] a concept that was initially based on the funerary evidence alone and therefore was studied solely as a social phenomenon (see chapter 5). Thanks to recent settlement excavations and field surveys we are now able to rephrase it in terms of the growth of central places and the development of the countryside. This process becomes archaeologically visible during the advanced Iron Age and the Archaic period. The results of field surveys carried out around the protohistorical settlement of Lanuvium and in the land system of the tuff hills confirm this. So far these surveys have not revealed any archaeological materials predating the later Iron Age, having mostly produced data on proto-urban settlement and rural infill from the Orientalizing period and afterwards (see below).[22] The land system of the volcanic hills played a prominent role in this development, since it provided ample space and fertile soils, abundant streams and excellent settlement locations.

The Late Iron Age and Archaic period

In the Late Iron Age and Archaic period a large number of settlements such as Ariccia, Lanuvium and Velletri, all of them presumably of protohistorical origin, became central places in the land system of the volcanic hills and on the slopes of the volcano Laziale. In combination with sites along the coast to the north-west, such as Ardea, Lavinium and Satricum, and inland sites such as Cisterna di Latina and Caracupa-Valvisciolo, these form a consistent pattern covering the landscape south of the Tiber. This pattern is generally interpreted as indicating independent towns, each controlling its own territory.[23] In the next section we will discuss three such sites. Two of these are located on the margins of the volcanic land system overlooking the Pontine plain: Satricum and Caprifico di Cisterna di Latina (perhaps ancient Pometia). A third site, Lanuvium, is located on a prominent ridge in the Alban hills and overlooks the volcanic land system as well as the Pontine plain. All three sites are well studied through archaeological excavations, topographical research and/or intensive site surveys.

Satricum

Particularly the extensive and ongoing excavations carried out at the protohistorical settlement of Satricum provide an insight into the formation of the Archaic town, for they have produced Iron Age remains dating to the late 9th and 8th centuries BC.[24] These were small features dug out in the virgin soil, the smallest of which have been interpreted as rubbish pits in which the remains of meals were deposited,

---

[20] Angle *et al.* 1987.

[21] Dialoghi di Archeologia 1980.

[22] Attema 1993; Attema / Van Leusen 2004, 180ff.

[23] See, for example, Bouma / Van 't Lindenhout 1996-1997.

[24] Maaskant Kleibrink 1987 and 1992 for detailed discussions; Gnade 2002 and, most recently, 2008.

and the larger ones as proper huts to live in. Whether these huts indicate year-round habitation and as such constitute a proper village, or if they were semi-permanent structures 'in which meals were consumed during religious ceremonies', as the excavator is inclined to believe, is a matter of debate.[25] Huts and rubbish pits were certainly grouped around a water basin connected with a cult that may be dated to this period. These modest structures precede a more substantial 7th-century BC phase during which larger timber structures partly covered by thin red roofing tiles were erected. On the basis of the finds these timber buildings should certainly be interpreted as permanent dwellings, most probably of the elite who buried their dead in the rich 7th-century BC tombs that are also known from Satricum.

The 6th-century BC urban phase at Satricum was characterized by the adoption of monumental architecture within a planned settlement layout. Satricum boasted a Greek-style temple dedicated to the goddess Mater Matuta, courtyard houses and, in the late Archaic phase, a number of *stoai*. It had therefore already by the mid-6th century BC grown into a prestigious and self-conscious proto-urban community headed by a probably wealthy elite that was in charge of the religious and political institutions. This development towards an urban way of life was the result of the increasingly complex structure of Latial society from the 7th century BC, by which time local aristocracies had developed. A conspicuous feature of Archaic Satricum was its demarcation by an *agger*, a defensive earthwork in combination with a ditch. Pre-Roman fortifications of this type are known also from the protohistoric coastal site of Antium (present-day Anzio) and from the sub-coastal site of Ardea. Although their date is often disputed this type of fortification belongs either to the 7th century BC or, as seems to be the case at Satricum, to the Archaic period.

There is evidence at Satricum for social stratification from the 7th century BC, and monumental ritual and domestic architecture as well as fortifications are found within a proto-urban plan from the 6th century BC. These features are characteristic for all the larger settlements in the area between Rome and the Pontine plain. We may add to this the evidence for craft specialization (in Satricum pottery production and metal working) and for participation in a widespread exchange system.[26] Especially burials and ritual were exceptionally rich in Satricum, but these characteristics are to some degree shared by other Latin settlements on the margins of the Pontine plain, such as the protohistorical settlement at Cisterna di Latina.

Caprifico di Cisterna di Latina
Fieldwork at the site of Caprifico di Cisterna di Latina has demonstrated that a transformation comparable to that at Satricum had taken place: an Iron Age settlement of huts was turned in the Archaic period into one characterized by domestic and monumental architecture.[27] The settlement area of Caprifico di Cisterna di Latina, which according to some scholars should be identified with ancient Pometia, probably occupied a now levelled plateau on the eastern rim of the volcanic zone some 10 km to the northeast of Satricum. No excavations were ever carried out, but topographical investigations by the Italian archaeologists Quilici Gigli and Melis, and intensive field surveys by the Pontine Region Project, have provided data on the chronology and extent of the settlement area. Recently a convincing reconstruction of the morphology and extent of the site has been proposed by Lorenzo Quilici on the basis of the very detailed 1:5000 maps made for the *Opera Nazionale per i Combattenti* of 1927.[28] As no funerary evidence is known from the site, its Iron Age phases cannot yet be closely dated. The pottery indicates, however, that it probably started out as a modest nucleus in the Iron Age (ca. 800 BC, as at Satricum). In the Orientalizing and Archaic periods it grew into a sizeable town occupying an estimated area of 37 ha,[29] and perhaps larger if we include adjacent areas that were possibly also settled.[30] The reconstruction of habitation in the periphery of the site is, however, made impossible by the large-scale movement of soil that has taken place from the 1960s onwards. According to Quilici and Melis the site of Caprifico di

---

[25] Maaskant Kleibrink 1992, 123.
[26] Nijboer 1998.
[27] Quilici Gigli / Melis 1972; Attema 1993.
[28] Quilici 2004.
[29] Quilici 2004, 257.
[30] Attema 1993, 223.

Cisterna also had a defensive system, probably an *agger*, and the find of a number of terracotta revetment plaques depicting ceremonial processions indicates the presence of monumental architecture during the later Archaic period. The relatively large amount of bucchero found in the survey corresponds to quantities of bucchero known from private collections, and confirms the importance of the settlement. It may have been a ceramic production site in its own right, and a node within the regional exchange network.

The extent of its settled surface indicates that Caprifico di Cisterna di Latina was among the larger settlements in the contemporary Latin settlement system. Small-scale field surveys carried out by the Pontine Region Project in 1992 and 1996 near Olmobello, between Cisterna di Latina and Satricum, provide some evidence, in the form of small shard scatters, for 6th-century rural infill. In these surveys a number of sites were found that probably represent (clusters of) modest farmsteads located along the incised streams of the volcanic land system.[31]

Rural infill in the Alban Hills: Lanuvium and the Lanuvium survey
To the north-west of Satricum, a test area in the territory of the Latin settlement of Lanuvium was investigated as part of the Pontine Region Project. Lanuvium itself lies on a prominent spur of the Alban slopes at 324 m above sea level. Like Satricum and Cisterna di Latina, it probably started out as a modest Iron-Age settlement in the 9th century BC, which by the Archaic period had developed into a sizeable town boasting a temple dedicated to Juno. Chiarucci has described the development of the protohistorical phase of this settlement,[32] whilst the surveys of the PRP have established that the origins of the surrounding rural landscape on the Alban slopes must be sought in the 7th century BC.[33] We will briefly discuss the results of the survey here.

In the 1995 survey by the Pontine Region Project fields totalling 407 ha, and located between 1.5 and 3.5 km from Lanuvium itself, were systematically investigated. A total of 51 sites were recorded, 39 of which had an Iron Age and/or an Early Archaic component. Of the latter, 20 sites or just over half were interpreted as habitation sites, while the remainder was tentatively placed into the protohistorical off-site category. Subsequent pottery studies have led us to believe that rural infill, in the form of dispersed habitations in the territory of Lanuvium, had begun by the 7th century BC. This is earlier than was the case in comparable areas of *Latium Vetus* surveyed by the Pontine Region Project, such as at Segni in the Sacco valley and around Sezze in the Pontine plain, and underlines the leading role of the Alban Hills area with regard to this aspect of early urbanization.[34]

The post-Archaic period
The study of continuity and change in the landscape of the Alban hills and the volcanic land system during the transition from the Archaic period to the Roman Republican period in the 5th and 4th centuries BC is still neglected. This is the period of the Volscan wars, and according to the historian Livy the Latial towns and countryside suffered much from raiding and warfare.[35] Although historians label this as the early Republican period, we prefer to adopt the more neutral term 'post-Archaic period', as introduced by one of us for the 5th and 4th centuries BC in the Pontine region.[36] From an archaeological point of view at least, Roman influence in the Pontine region only becomes visible in the settlement pattern and material record by the second half of the 4th century BC. The period of the 5th and 4th centuries BC is characterized rather by the dissolution of existing central settlements, with their inhabitants seemingly moving to the countryside, and the general poverty of its material remains. Satricum is a case in point: a flourishing 6th-century town, its spatial and functional organization was substantially degraded in the 5th

---

[31] Drost 1996, fig. 3.
[32] E.g., Chiarucci 1983.
[33] Attema 2005b.
[34] Attema / Van Leusen 2004, 189.
[35] Cf. Attema 2000.
[36] Attema 1993.

and 4th centuries BC.[37] Its monumental Archaic acropolis was no longer maintained, while only a few of the Archaic houses continued to be inhabited or re-used. A particularly significant functional change during the post-Archaic was the re-use of a part of the hill, just to the southeast of the remains of the Archaic temple, for burials. Satricum did however remain an active cult place, judging by the contemporaneous votive deposit unearthed by the Groningen Institute of Archaeology west of the temple. Whereas few, if any, graves are known from the Archaic period, most of the graves belonging to the post-Archaic community living at Satricum were located in the north-western part of the site, in the so-called south-west necropolis. This cemetery was excavated by a team from the University of Amsterdam that characterized the buried people as Volsci.[38] The socio-economic, political, and possibly ethnic changes observed in the archaeological record of this period turned Satricum during the post-Archaic period into a rather insignificant town that continued, in an even more reduced form, into Roman times.

The results of the field survey at Caprifico di Cisterna di Latina also indicate profound changes in its development, including the abandonment of the principal settlement area in favour of more dispersed habitation some time towards the end of the Archaic period. Unfortunately, much less is known about the development of the settlements in the Alban Hills, as continuous occupation from protohistorical times till the present precludes archaeological observations. However, the PRP survey of the rural territory of Lanuvium did show a substantial increase in the number of sites from the Archaic to the post-Archaic period. It also indicated a high degree of continuity of site locations, only two of which were abandoned. This continuity and flourishing of the countryside may be explained by the fact that Lanuvium already in 493 BC concluded a pact with Rome, and went on to acquire the status of *municipium* in the course of the 4th century BC. In any case, the settlement pattern around Lanuvium suggests a larger degree of continuity than was the case at either Satricum or Cisterna.

The Roman Republican period

In general we may state that the Roman Republican period is well documented on the slopes of the Alban hills and in the volcanic land system. Many villas and farmsteads are known from Italian topographical studies in both areas. It is therefore significant that, whilst large and luxurious villas appear amongst the rural site types on the slopes of the Alban hills, the volcanic land system extending down to the coast remains characterized by modest farmsteads. The flourishing of the towns on the Alban hill slopes and the investments in rural villa architecture can be explained mainly by the position of the area along the Via Appia. This guaranteed good connections with Rome, which gave the area in the late Republican period a suburban character. Its pleasant climate and scenery made it especially popular with the Roman elite. The Lanuvium survey indicates that the post-Archaic rural settlement pattern may have contracted in favour of fewer but more complex villa sites, each possibly dominating a single ridge in this dissected landscape.

While formerly important Latin settlements like Satricum and Cisterna had dwindled to insignificant villages by the Roman Republican period, towns such as Lanuvium in the Alban Hills, Antium on the coast and Norba in the Monti Lepini flourished. Recent research has shown that the acropolis of Satricum in this period was reduced to a handful of simple farms that may not even have been distinguishable from the more general rural settlement surrounding the Archaic acropolis. The area around Cisterna was only revitalized by the establishment of the nearby road station of Tres Tabernae at the time of the construction of the Via Appia. However, not all former Archaic Latin urban settlements shared this ignominious fate: those situated towards the north-west (Ardea, Castel di Decima and Lavinium) show a more continuous development into the Roman Republican period. It seems therefore that former Latin towns that were in a good location with respect to the new infrastructure could profit from Roman

---

[37] Attema *et al.* 1992; Gnade 2002.   [38] Gnade 1992.

rule, while those that were peripheral to it were less well off. Sites on the Via Appia in the Alban Hills, as well as those on the coast such as Antium, flourished in the Roman period while less well-connected sites such as Satricum contracted into mere rural hamlets. As far as we can tell, many rural sites (hamlets and farmsteads) show continuity well into the Imperial period, but so far we have found no significant evidence of a transition to exploitation by means of *latifundiae*.

2.3.2 THE MARGINS AND UPLANDS OF THE MONTI LEPINI

The Monti Lepini are connected to the Colli Albani by the Lariano saddle, and fertile but heavy soils of volcanic origin are found on its footslopes as far south as the medieval settlement of Ninfa. The steepness and ruggedness of the Monti Lepini form a contrast to the gentler and richly forested Alban Hills. Van Joolen describes the Monti Lepini land system as a complex of steep to very steep mountains with gently sloping foothills, dissected by a few valleys running north-west to south-east. Landforms include the mountainous area of the Lepini range itself with its peaks and intermontane basins, the river valleys that give out onto the Pontine plain, the undulating, gently sloping alluvial fans and the slope deposits of the footslopes. A large part of the mountain area proper is forested or in use for pasture. The alluvial fans and slope deposits are mainly in use for olive culture.

The Bronze Age and Early Iron Age

Settlement evidence for Bronze Age occupation in the Monti Lepini is still scarce and limited to the Middle Bronze Age cave necropolis of Vittorio Vecchi.[39] Its associated settlement has perhaps been identified during the Contrada Suso survey of the Pontine Region Project.[40] Both the settlement site of Suso and the funerary site of Vittorio Vecchi are located in the Sezze uplands, but indications for Bronze Age settlement can also be found in the plain below Sezze. A field survey by the Pontine Region Project in 1994 found a thin scatter of protohistorical shards on the surface that was almost entirely restricted to the elevated parts of the landscape where the recent alluvial cover described in Box 2.2 is absent or thinner.[41] The protohistorical landscape in the plain of Sezze therefore remains largely invisible, at least on the surface, but ongoing research confirms its presence nonetheless. In the early 1980s a Bronze Age stratum containing large quantities of animal bones and potshards was found at nearly 2 m depth beneath the remains of an extra-urban Republican temple dedicated to the goddess Juno. These finds are in the course of publication, but preliminary work indicates a date range from the Early Bronze Age to the advanced Iron Age.[42]

The locations and dates of a number of protohistorical upland sites from around Sezze and Priverno are now also known.[43] Some of these sites occupy strategic locations and may be economically linked to animal husbandry and short transhumance. Finds of a more sporadic nature from various Lepine upland areas indicate that the scarcity of evidence for Bronze Age occupation may be an artefact of the limited research that has been carried out in the land systems of the Monti Lepini; recent GIA surveys, however, are beginning to increase the number of such protohistoric sites.

The Late Iron Age and Archaic period

It is only from the later Iron Age onwards that we find evidence for the expansion of settlement along the Lepine margins. The key sites for this period are the Iron Age and Archaic settlement and cemeteries of Caracupa-Valvisciolo. The tombs of the Caracupa cemetery were excavated and published at the start

---

[39] Pascucci 1996; Rosini 1996.

[40] Attema 1998; Zaccheo / Pasquali 1972.

[41] Attema / Van Leusen 2004, 176.

[42] Anastasia 2002-2003; Feiken forthcoming.

[43] Anastasia 2002-2003.

of the 20th century by the Italian archaeologists Mengarelli and Savignoni and subsequently analysed by Angle and Gianni in an article published in 1985.[44] The earliest tombs date to the period 830 – 770 BC. Most of these were situated in the Caracupa cemetery on the alluvial cone, while a few were located on the Valvisciolo spur of the Monte Carbolino. In a later phase, the local community built a system of heavy walls in polygonal masonry to defend the settlement on this spur. After intensive surveying by the Pontine Region Project the settlement area of Caracupa-Valvisciolo and the nearby smaller protohistorical settlement Contrada Casali produced the first indication for the development of a site hierarchy in the later Iron Age and Archaic period. Ongoing field studies by the PRP and RPC projects have subsequently covered a section of the Lepine margins between Valvisciolo and Cori. This has resulted in the recording of the smaller Late Iron Age and Archaic sites that had been missing in earlier studies.

In order to provide a basis for comparison of the Lepine settlement pattern with those in adjacent land systems, we restudied, catalogued and classified all published and unpublished sites known to us in the section of the Lepine margins near the protohistorical settlement of Caracupa-Valvisciolo.[45] In this classification Caracupa-Valvisciolo stands at the top of the local settlement hierarchy on account of its size (estimated at 48 ha),[46] its substantial Iron Age cemetery containing a number of relatively rich 7th-century BC graves, and the presence of monumental defensive structures dating to the 6th century BC. Further down the hierarchy we place hilltop sites such as Contrada Casali and the various hamlets that were identified in the surveys. At the lowest level, small scatters of protohistorical pottery may be interpreted as farmsteads. A number of these are found in locations that were also occupied by farmsteads during the post-Archaic and early Roman Republican periods. This means that we may situate the start of the development of urban-rural relationships in the Monti Lepini in the late 7th and 6th centuries BC.

The post-Archaic period

The 5th and 4th centuries BC saw the abandonment of the Archaic settlement area at Caracupa-Valvisciolo, which eventually became the site of a Republican villa. Meanwhile the Roman colony of Norba arose in an impregnable location on a high and steep cliff nearby, overlooking the entire Pontine plain. Whether this displacement was a gradual, spontaneous retreat by the community living at Caracupa-Valvisciolo, or a process forced by external Roman power, we cannot tell from the archaeological sources. Historical sources, however, suggest that the latter was the case. The 5th and 4th centuries BC saw a struggle for power between Rome and its allies and the Volsci, centring on the Pontine region and the Sacco valley. Ancient texts depict Norba, like its counterpart Signia on the northern rim of the Monti Lepini, as an early Roman stronghold (*arx*) guarding the Pontine plain. The traditional foundation date of Norba according to Livy is 492 BC. In order to maintain its control over the Pontine plain Rome founded other colonies along its margins, such as Setia (present-day Sezze) and Circeii. Although the foundation dates of these early strategic colonies are a matter of debate among historians and archaeologists, they certainly were the strongholds from which the Romanization of the Pontine region was initiated. Romanization, here described as a military, political as well as a socio-economic process, was to change the Pontine region locally into a densely settled and intensively cultivated landscape. The results of the Pontine Region Project field survey carried out in 1995 in the plain below Sezze bear this out. They show how during the later Archaic and post-Archaic periods pottery densities increased relative to the preceding period.[47] Building activity increases especially in the post-Archaic period, and we interpret this as evidence of a general infill of the plain with rural sites due to a sudden demographic increase caused by the founding of the colony of Setia in 382 BC. No traces of structures have been found at any of these sites, only two of which demonstrate continuity of occupation into the Roman Republican

[44] Angle / Gianni 1985.
[45] Van Leusen *et al.* 2005.
[46] Attema 1993, 180.
[47] Attema / Van Leusen 2004, 173-180.

period.⁴⁸ They are therefore interpreted as simple hamlets and isolated farmsteads. As we saw earlier the presence of similar post-Archaic farmsteads was also established on the Lepine margin to the north-west of Sezze in the Norba/Ninfa surveys,⁴⁹ although here the continuity with the preceding Late Iron Age and Archaic site patterns is much stronger.

The Roman period

The PRP and RPC field surveys on the Lepine margins below Sezze, Norba and near Ninfa have shown that, from the 3rd century BC onwards, the lower slopes of the Monti Lepini became dotted with villas of the platform type. These are farmsteads built on terraces constructed in polygonal masonry, which we tentatively connect with the increasing specialization in olive culture which is demonstrated by the pollen data (see Box 2.1) as well as by the presence of olive-press beds on some of these sites. The labour that was invested in the erection of these platform villas, their regular spacing over the landscape, and their similar appearance in the archaeological record suggest the actions of an agricultural investment economy that was perhaps in part based on slave labour and economically tied to the growing local markets of the Roman colonies and/or the regional market of Rome and surroundings. As was mentioned before, the survey data suggest that some of these villas had a 5th and 4th-century predecessor, thus closing the gap between the Archaic and Roman Republican periods, at least for the rural landscape. The *ager* of the Roman colony of Sezze seems to have been particularly thriving during the Roman Republican period, as indicated by high densities of shards and sites. The reduced number of terra sigillata fragments compared to black glaze shards in the survey transects suggests a contraction of the settlement pattern by the Imperial period. Recent work on the pottery collected from Roman villa sites on the margins of the Lepini has, however, shown that many rural sites continued into the 3rd century AD.⁵⁰ A closer study of the changes that took place from the late Republican to the late Imperial period is now underway in all land systems. We conclude that the archaeological evidence suggests that the Lepine margins had a flourishing rural economy during the middle- and late Republican period. By the Late Republican period the settlements may have contracted to some degree, but the system of modest *villae rusticae* certainly wasn't completely replaced by large villa estates (*latifundiae*). In fact, no examples of such a replacement are known in the land system of the Lepine margins. If a contraction in the settlement pattern took place, it was perhaps rather forced by the sacking and abandonment of Norba in 81 BC as a result of the civil war.

2.3.3 THE COASTAL LAND SYSTEMS

The coastal land system is described by Van Joolen as an area with beaches, dunes and large lagoons, extending all the way along the Tyrrhenian coast from the Tiber delta down to Terracina. Towards the south, lagoons such as the Lago di Fogliano and the Lago di Sabaudia still exist and reflect to a degree the situation in antiquity, although the coastal strip is today much affected by tourism. One particularly characteristic landmark is Monte Circeo, on which the Roman colony of Circeii was established. From the mouth of the river Astura to the outskirts of the seaside resort of Nettuno, the coastal landscape and its archaeology have been well-preserved since the Second World War as part of a military basis. Further north, the lagoons have been filled in as part of coastal development but they can be reconstructed on the basis of historical maps.⁵¹ The modern coastal dunes have an average maximum elevation of 15 m

---

⁴⁸ Attema / Van Leusen 2004, 178.

⁴⁹ Van Leusen *et al.* 2005.

⁵⁰ Attema / De Haas 2005.

⁵¹ Cf. Alessandri's (2000-2001) study of the coastal occupation in protohistory.

above sea level, while the lagoonal areas, which in antiquity were deep-water bodies, are at sea level.[52] Until fairly recently the dunes impeded drainage of parts of the landscape and were the cause of marshy conditions around the lagoons. Van Joolen evaluated the area as unsuitable for any kind of arable farming, and indeed such farming was limited in the recent past as well according to historical maps. The pollen record indicates that this was the case in antiquity in the area of the southern lagoons (see the discussion of the Fogliano pollen core in Box 2.1). The sea, the marshy environment around the lagoons, and the lagoons themselves could, however, be put to various non-agricultural uses. Of these, fishing will have been the most profitable, but as recent evidence has made clear, we must also consider salt production as a significant ancient economic activity.[53] Other forms of less intensive exploitation of the area will have included hunting, winter grazing, collection of fuel and, historically, the production of charcoal. All of this adds up to a marginal coastal economy that we know to some degree from the ethnographical literature and recent historical documentation. The image of a marginal landscape does, however, not hold true for the Late Roman Republican and Early Imperial periods, during which the Roman elite built their large *villae maritimae* right on the coast and this certainly was an incentive to the local economy.[54]

The elevated sandy zone that lies landward of the lagoons of Fogliano, Monaci, Caprolace, and Sabaudia, is described by van Joolen as a cultivated landscape of fossil upper-Pleistocene beach ridges separated by narrow valleys and broad plains. Field observations carried out in the course of the 1998 RPC fieldwork campaign in this zone were restricted to an area around the village of Borgo Grappa.[55] Here, the beach ridges (between 2 and 13 m above sea level) are mainly covered in reddish aeolian sands, while the flat areas are characterized by a variety of sediments of marshy and alluvial origin. Between Borgo Grappa and Circeo there extends a large area of aeolian sands on former beach ridges. Present-day land use demonstrates that these beach ridges are suitable for arable farming and haymaking, while the flat areas and valleys between the beach ridges are attractive for grazing.[56] In sub-recent times the more elevated areas were mainly used for grazing in a short transhumance economy involving semi-permanent settlements called *lestre*.[57] Before the land reclamations of the 1930s these areas where known as 'Selva', largely uncultivated terrain given over to *macchia*.[58]

To the north-west of Borgo Grappa lies the Astura river valley that, though relevant for the present study, was not described by Van Joolen as it was outside her study area. The sandy slopes adjoining this valley have been subjected to intensive surveying during field campaigns of the Pontine Region Project in the period 2003 to 2005. The Astura river drains the south-eastern part of the volcanic land system into the Tyrrhenian Sea and, according to some scholars, may have been navigable in antiquity. This would explain the successful foundation of the already mentioned protohistorical settlement of Satricum where the Astura valley cuts through a gently undulating landscape of relatively fertile, sand-covered tuff plateaus. Parts of this area nowadays consist of intensively cultivated vineyards.

The Bronze Age and Early Iron Age
In recent decades the settlement developments in the Recent and Final Bronze Age in the coastal land system of the Pontine region have slowly come into focus. The Italian archaeologist Alessandro Guidi already pointed out the potentially complementary role of the lagoonal environment in the Bronze Age economy of the Pontine region for the inland economy of the Alban hills.[59] To this we would like to add the Monti Lepini and Ausoni as a third environmental zone. Our own research has indeed stressed the importance of marine exploitation at sites located on the seaboard itself. Site P13 for example, located near

---

[52] Van Joolen 2003, 84-85 and fig. 3.33.
[53] Attema *et al.* 2003b.
[54] Attema *et al.* 2009.
[55] Attema *et al.* 2001.
[56] Van Joolen 2003, 86-87 and fig. 3.34.
[57] Veenman 2002, 115-126.
[58] See, for example, the late 18th-century map by Serafino Salvati reproduced in Attema 1993, 39.
[59] Guidi 1986.

the mouth of the river Astura and excavated by the Groningen Institute of Archaeology in 2001 and 2002, was demonstrated to be a salt production site dating to about 1200 BC.[60] Salt was produced by means of the *briquetage* method, which means that brine was boiled in ceramic containers until salt crystals would form. Quite a few sites of this type have been recorded.[61] They are characterized by huge quantities of friable reddish potshards as the salt crystals had to be broken out of their ceramic containers. The large number of sites that specialized in pottery and/or salt production, and the fact that salt is a necessary commodity for inland communities, both suggest that this activity probably was of regional economic importance, and that connections must have existed between the inland and coastal communities. In apparent support of this idea, Alessandri recognized a second group of Bronze Age and Early Iron Age settlements located at some distance inland, to which the coastal sites may have been directly connected.[62] One of these is the Recent Bronze Age site of Casale Nuovo just to the east of the Astura valley, where excavation by the Italian *Soprintendenza* has yielded evidence of metalworking and contacts with Aegean traders.[63] While other inland sites further to the north-east such as Colle Rotondo have not been excavated nor surveyed systematically, their presence indicates that a complex settlement system had developed in the coastal and adjacent areas of the Pontine region by the Late Bronze Age. We found for instance evidence for the existence of a small coastal community at Colle Rotondo to the west of the Astura valley that buried its dead in a cemetery known in the literature as Cavallo Morto. The tombs are dated to the Recent Bronze Age.[64] A third group of smaller sites was detected for the first time in the already mentioned 1998 RPC Fogliano survey campaign around Borgo Grappa. This group perhaps had socio-economical ties with inland sites such as Colle Rotondo as well as with the 'industrial' sites involved in salt- and pottery production. However, the thin scatters of protohistorical material found in that survey are difficult to interpret in spatial, chronological and functional terms. More research is needed to clarify this pattern and tie it to well-dated features in the landscape. As far as we can tell at present all of them may well postdate the Early Iron Age. The only well-dated features from the Final Bronze Age or the Early Iron Age in the coastal area are the tombs that are exclusively found in the territory of ancient Antium. Their presence suggests the existence of an Early Iron Age phase of this settlement that later was defended by an earthwork (*agger*).[65] Antium may therefore be considered as a proto-urban element in the coastal settlement pattern and compared to sites such as Satricum, Caprifico di Cisterna di Latina, Caracupa-Valvisciolo and other Latial polity centres. Recent research by the PRP in the area between Anzio and the Astura river in the context of the project *Carta Archeologica del Comune di Nettuno* has resulted in the identification of a number of small Bronze Age and Iron Age sites, confirming the importance of this area in the protohistorical period.[66]

The Late Iron Age and Archaic period

The archaeological record for the coastal land system suggests that early urbanization in the Iron Age was restricted to the area west of the Astura valley. The most important proto-urban coastal settlement would have been Antium, the extent of which is known from the defensive earthworks that its inhabitants erected around their site in the Late Iron Age or Early Archaic period.[67] Thanks to recent fieldwork and the study of a collection of archaeological materials from the area in the *Antiquarium* of Nettuno, we know now of a second coastal protohistoric settlement near Nettuno, slightly to the east of Antium.[68] Materials from this site, named 'Depuratore' because of its location near a water purification installation, are exposed in a long eroding coastal cliff section and these date the site to the Late Iron Age and Archaic

[60] Attema *et al.* 2003b; Nijboer *et al.* 2006; Attema / Nijboer 2007.
[61] Attema *et al.* 2003b.
[62] Alessandri 2000-2001.
[63] Angle / Zarattini 1987; Angle *et al.* 1987.
[64] Alessandri 2000-2001, 30 ff; Alessandri forthcoming, 118-121.
[65] Alessandri forthcoming, 111-117.
[66] Attema *et al.* 2009.
[67] Alessandri 2000-2001, 33 ff.
[68] Attema *et al.* 2009.

period, although earlier shards are also present. The shard-bearing layers in the section are, however, not in situ and the precise location of the original site is still unknown.

Intensive field survey of the territory of Nettuno in 2004-5 has moreover revealed a fair number of Archaic rural sites which may have been socio-economically related to the proto-urban settlement at Anzio. However, so far we lack sufficient data to reconstruct the settlement patterns on this part of the coast. Nonetheless we may already state with some confidence that the Borgo Grappa coastal area was less densely settled and exploited than the coastal area between Anzio and Nettuno. It is less clear whether the area immediately to the west and east of the Astura river valley resembled the former area or the latter. Fabio Piccarreta recorded many archaeological sites both in- and outside the restricted military zone in his *Forma Italiae* sheet 'Astura'.[69] Although he dates most of these sites to the Roman Republican period, revisits to sites outside the restricted zone show that a substantial percentage of them have Archaic and post-Archaic components. Whether this is also the case for the sites within the zone we can't say, as its military status precludes direct field observations. The settlement and land use patterns further to the south-east seem to suggest some exploitation of the lagoonal environment in the later protohistorical period, but whether this is a continuous pattern from the Recent Bronze Age to the Archaic period is not certain due to dating problems of the ceramics. A site classification based on the results of the Fogliano survey suggests the existence of small Iron Age and Orientalizing (7th century BC) sites that we interpret as modest farmsteads. An increase in sites was noted for the Archaic period, and size estimates indicate that we are still dealing with isolated modest farmsteads and perhaps also tiny hamlets.[70] The nearest proto-urban settlements to which these sites could relate would have been the coastal site at Anzio and the inland site of Satricum.

The post-Archaic period

According to Livy, Antium (modern Anzio) played a significant role as a Volscan stronghold in the conflicts with Rome and the Latins, and therefore it must have continued in some form into the early Republican period. Unfortunately we know next to nothing of the archaeology of the settlement area of Antium in the post-Archaic period, although it is suggested that its *agger* was extended to the sea at this time by the Volscan conquerors.[71] Our only sources for the west bank of the Astura are the already mentioned body of rural archaeological sites in Piccarreta's *Forma Italiae* inventory, the revisits to these sites conducted by the PRP, and its recent field surveys in the territory of Nettuno. A fairly large number of sites seem to continue from the Archaic into the post-Archaic period, and thence into the Roman Republican period. For the east bank of the Astura we again have the Piccarreta sites and the dataset collected in the course of the Fogliano survey.

This information and the results of the more recent surveys of the Pontine Region Project in the valley of the Astura indicate that the dispersed pattern of small Archaic sites continued into the post-Archaic period. At the present state of our knowledge it is, however, too early to comment in detail on the changes in the settlement pattern in the coastal land system, as the elaboration of these recent surveys is still in progress.[72]

In the post-Archaic period the Romans adopted the isolated limestone outcrop of Monte Circeo, located on the southern extremity of the Pontine region, as a strategic point to guard and protect the plain and the stretches of the sea shore that extend towards the north-west and east. The colony was supposedly founded in 361 BC, and its archaeological remains were long believed to consist of a vast circuit of polygonal walls located on the summit of the Monte Circeo. The area demarcated by polygonal masonry was, however, not inhabited and has recently (and plausibly) been reinterpreted as a ritual site of late Republican origin.[73]

---

[69] Piccarreta 1977.
[70] Attema *et al.* 2005.
[71] Alessandri 2000-2001, 34 with references.
[72] But see the recent work published in Attema *et al.* 2008.
[73] Quilici / Quilici Gigli 2005.

The Roman period

The actual Roman colony of Circeo was located at present-day San Felice Circeii. Far to the northwest the colony of Antium was also planted on the coast. Together, these colonial enterprises show how the Romans in the Republican period developed an interest in the coast for strategic reasons and for sea trade. Antium itself has recently been the subject of a topographical study by Vittucci,[74] whilst the PRP research and earlier topographical studies have shown that the coastal land system near the Roman colonies became dotted with Republican farmsteads, some of which show evidence of continuity from 5th and 4th-century BC predecessors. Other rural sites have been shown to continue well into the 3rd century AD. In the late Republican and early Imperial period the Pontine coast from Antium down to Terracina became favoured by the Roman elite, who built luxurious *villae maritimae* either on the lagoons or directly on the coast. Some of these belonged to emperors, such as the villa of Nero at Antium and the villa of Domitianus at Sabaudia, while others belonged to people such as Cicero, who may have owned the villa at Torre Astura. A number of these maritime villas were provided with fishponds (*piscinae*) built into the sea. Quite a few fishponds are found between Antium and Torre Astura, and some may have been of commercial significance as is suggested, for example, by the amphora debris deposited prior to the erection of the late Republican / early Imperial maritime villa complex of Le Grottacce.[75]

2.3.4 THE LATINA LAND SYSTEM

Van Joolen describes the land system of the 'Latina' plain as a vast, flat area between the Monti Lepini to the north-east and the beach ridges to the south-west, with a wide variety of soil types and sediments (fig. 2.6).[76] It consists of a depressed area (former Pontine marshes), and fluvio-colluvial areas (the fluvio-colluvial plain of the Amaseno river and the alluvial sheet and ridges in the plain below Sezze). Land use in the Latina land system is diverse due to the varying micro-relief and soil conditions and the complex hydrography. Before the fascist era the depressed area was regularly unsuitable for cultivation because of waterlogging. A discussion of Bronze Age and Iron Age occupation of this land system suffers from strong research biases, as no intensive survey has taken place here and settlement in this formerly marshy and marginal area has seemed to many researchers a priori unlikely. Nor are any proto-urban centres from the Archaic period known from this area, although one Archaic site has been reported near Latina and a number of Archaic finds were located in various soil units by the Agro Pontino Survey.[77] This suggests that by the Archaic period settlement extended into formerly marginally settled land systems.

The available data indicate that substantial exploitation of the Latina land system only began with the Roman colonization of the 5th and 4th centuries BC. Slightly later, but before the construction of the Via Appia in 312 BC, the central part of the Pontine plain, away from the Roman colonies, also became more intensively exploited, as centuriation patterns recorded by M. Cancellieri along the Via Appia seem to indicate.[78] We must realize, however, that archaeological research into the pre-Roman periods in large parts of the Latina land system is much impeded by Holocene sedimentation as is demonstrated by the sedimentation studies carried out south of Sezze and in the Amaseno valley (see Box 2.2 for a detailed discussion). Archaeological survey in this area within the framework of the PRP will be carried out in the period 2005-2009.[79]

---

[74] Vittucci 2000.
[75] Attema *et al.* 2003b.
[76] Van Joolen 2003, 88.
[77] Quilici 1971; Voorrips *et al.* 1991.
[78] Cancellieri 1990.
[79] Now partly published in De Haas 2008.

Fig. 2.6. View south from the Monti Lepini across the Pontine plain towards the Tyrrhenian Sea and the Monte Circeo (photo W. de Neef, GIA 2009). For a colour version of this figure, see page 211.

2.4 CONCLUDING DISCUSSION

In this chapter we have discussed the general patterns of settlement and land use in the Pontine region within the framework of a land systems classification of the Pontine landscape. A land system was defined as an area or group of areas with a recurring pattern of landforms, soils and vegetation. For clarity's sake we chose to combine some land systems into larger units. This provided a more concise overview of the regional settlement dynamics between the Bronze Age and the Imperial period than would be possible in a separate discussion of each individual land system. We successively discussed the land system of the Alban hills and the volcanic hills to the south, the land system of the Lepine margins including the uplands, the coastal land system including the Astura valley, and the Latina land system including the graben. On the basis of differences in the chronology and intensity of the mainly rural settlement development in these landscape units, we arrived at conclusions regarding the core areas of proto-urbanization, the varying influence of Roman colonial policies, and the development of the Roman villa landscape.

The archaeological record and the pollen evidence presented in this chapter indicate that proto-urbanization and rural infill in the advanced Iron Age and the Archaic period were particularly strong in the Alban hills and adjacent volcanic areas, with their excellent settlement locations, fertile soils and large crater lakes. A similar process of infill and proto-urbanization, although much less evident for the Bronze Age than for the Iron Age, has also been attested for the foothills and slopes of the Monti Lepini near the site of Caracupa-Valvisciolo. Increasing settlement density and pressure on the available agricultural land in the volcanic land system may have triggered proto-urban settlement in the Monti Lepini. A provisional dividing line between this proto-urban landscape and the remaining less developed landscape may be drawn at the edges of the low-lying Pontine plain. This plain was especially suitable for grazing flocks of cattle and sheep in short transhumance between the nearby Lepine uplands and the plain. Near the coastal lagoons and on the coast itself, most of the recorded protohistorical sites may be connected with the exploitation of lake- and marine resources as well as with the inland (salt) trade. We noted that the Astura valley may have functioned as a corridor linking the elevated areas of the hinterland to the coast, and how proto-urban settlement also occurred in the coastal area around present-day Anzio.

In the Archaic period we may reconstruct the Pontine region as having been carved up in small territories around urban settlements of more or less equal rank. In this period the Pontine plain proper and the southern coastal area remained marginal relative to the main settlement developments. It is only with the advent of Roman colonization that the Pontine plain became part of the 'urban' infrastructure that had already developed in the proto-urban landscape of the Archaic polities. This was the outcome of a long process of Roman interference in the Pontine region, in a transitional period (the 5th and 4th century BC) referred to as the post-Archaic. This period is historically characterized by the protracted power struggle between Romans, Latins and Volsci. It is reflected in the archaeological record by the destabilization of the Archaic polity system, the general impoverishment of material culture, and the first signs of Roman colonization on the Lepine margins at Norba, Setia and Circeii. These early Roman colonial towns stimulated the growth of an agricultural economy that by the late 4th century BC extended over most of the Pontine region, with the exception of the marshy areas that were to remain a marginal element in the Roman agricultural economy. Although the colonies were mostly established on previously settled locations, they were essentially new towns planted with a population sent in by the Roman administration. Intensive survey of Roman platform villas in the surrounding landscape has started to reveal that most of these farms were built on land that had already been farmed before, and in many cases will have continued pre-existing Archaic farms. After ca. 300 BC, a villa landscape developed in the already proto-urban part of the Pontine region and spread into those parts of the Pontine plain that appear to have been only marginally settled previously. This would have been made possible primarily by the new Roman infrastructure of roads and drainage works, of which the Via Appia must have been the centre piece.

We are aware that the validity of our reconstruction of these patterns of settlement and land use is hampered by problems relating to the question of whether our archaeological dataset is representative. We have stressed the various processes by which natural and human-induced changes in the landscape (erosion and sedimentation, land use, land cover), field methodology (generic topographical research versus highly intensive survey), intensity of research, and the variable diagnostic nature of artefacts for different periods all result in significant biases in this dataset. We know as yet very little about the archaeology of two of our land systems: the Monti Lepini, and the low-lying parts of the Pontine plain. The broad patterns derived from the archaeological record that were discussed in this chapter should therefore be understood within the context of these limitations.

3 Regional Settlement Dynamics of the Salento Isthmus

3.1 INTRODUCTION

The Salento Isthmus is located in the south of modern Apulia; it is the common name for the stretch of land between Taranto and Brindisi that connects the Salento peninsula to the rest of Italy. Its highest part is the Murge plateau, an undulating tableland which averages about 400 m above sea level. The other major physio-geographical units of the isthmus comprise the much dissected marine terraces near Taranto in the south-west, and the gently undulating coastal plain near Brindisi in the south-east, which is part of the larger so-called *piana messapica*.

In the present chapter we will first discuss environmental studies that shed light on landscape formation processes in Salento in general and on the impact of human interference on them. We will focus on the human factor as our main theme. To that purpose we will evaluate the relevant archaeological data, and in particular the various systematic surveys and topographic prospections carried out on the Salento isthmus. In the last decades, the isthmus has witnessed an increase of surface prospection, ranging from judgmental site-oriented topographic research in the *Forma Italiae* tradition to systematic intensive line-walking of specific sample areas. Of these, central to the RPC project are the intensive surveys carried out in the context of the ongoing research program of the Archaeological Centre of the Vrije Universiteit of Amsterdam (ACVU). This project started in the early 1980s with the aim of studying the process of Romanization and was later extended to analyse Greek colonization and subsequent urbanization processes as well. The survey results have been published in monographs and preliminary reports. They offer not only the possibility of verifying the data provided by less systematic prospections, but also of building working hypotheses regarding the relation between regional settlement dynamics and social processes relevant to the present study.

The archaeological field work of the ACVU on the Salento isthmus has been closely integrated with geographical research, carried out first by the Faculty of Earth and Life Sciences of the Vrije Universiteit, and subsequently as part of the RPC project (fig. 3.1).[1] Besides studying the evolution of the physical landscape, a major goal of this research was to define the characteristics of the principal land systems of the Salento isthmus (on land systems in general see section 1.2.1). This research forms the basis for an investigation into the relations between specific land systems and the archaeological record, particularly the data yielded by the intensive field surveys. It allows us to highlight micro-regional variation in the main societal trajectories we study. As will become clear from our discussions, Greek colonization and urbanization as well as Romanization had an unequal impact on different parts of the regional landscape. To highlight this, the field survey data will be evaluated in section 3.3 within the framework of the major land systems of the region.

---

[1] Van Joolen 2003.

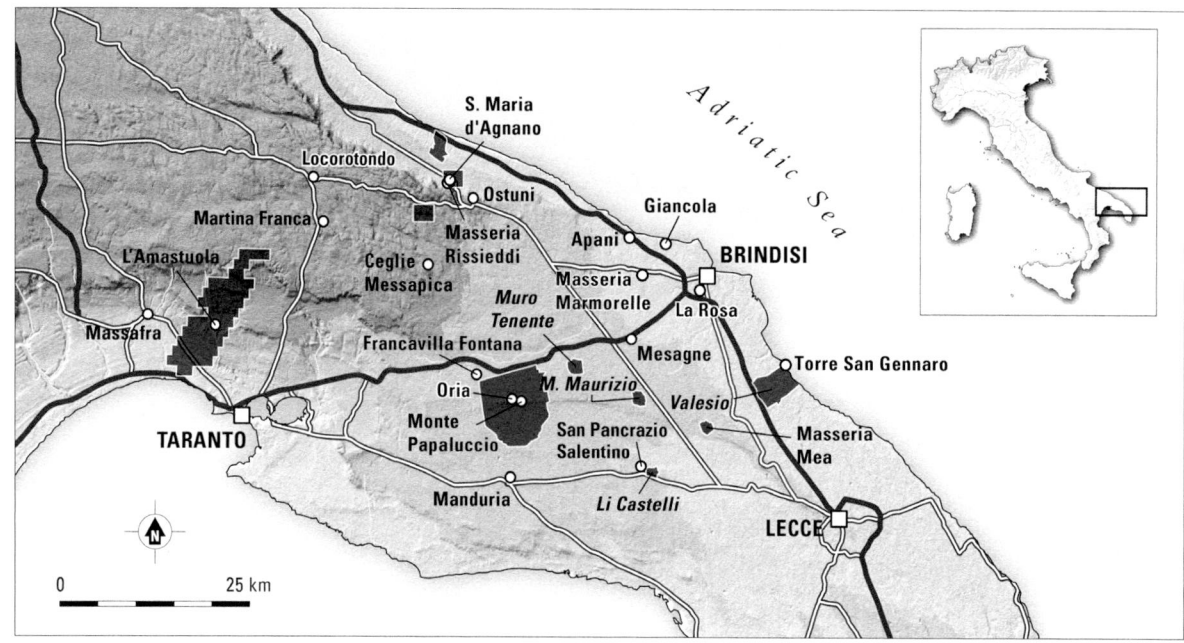

Fig. 3.1. The Salento Isthmus study area, with modern topography, archaeological sites mentioned in the text, and ACVU survey areas (areas outlined in white). For a colour version of this figure, see page 212.

3.2 ENVIRONMENTAL STUDIES: SEDIMENTATION, CLIMATE AND ANTHROPOGENIC IMPACT

Geologically, the Salento region is situated on the south-western part of the Adriatic tectonic plate. It forms a peninsula which separates the Adriatic from the Ionian Sea. Pleistocene calcareous sands, clayey sands and blue marls cover the surface in the central part of the area. Moreover, Pleistocene formations also outcrop in the north-eastern part of the *piana messapica,* whereas the oldest deposits, dating from the Cretaceous, outcrop in the Murge region. It is particularly in the latter unit that karst phenomena, such as dolines, occur. Here one also finds impressive canyon-like valleys reaching depths of 50 m. Gentler valleys with seasonal streams drain the area in a northerly and southerly direction. Net precipitation also percolates into the relatively soft limestone and consequently water flows also through underground channels.

Middle Bronze Age		1700 – 1350 BC
Late Bronze Age	Recent Bronze Age	1350 – 1200 BC
	Final Bronze Age	1200 – 1000 BC
Iron Age	(Greek colonies)	1000 – 750 BC
	(indigenous world)	1000 – 600 BC
Archaic	(Greek colonies)	750 – 480 BC
	(indigenous world)	600 – 480 BC
Classical		480 – 325 BC
Early Hellenistic		325 – 200 BC
Late Hellenistic / late Republican		200 – 30 BC

Table 3.1. Simplified chronological scheme for South Italy.

Notwithstanding the relative abundance of potential water sources, in recent decades water shortage has become a serious problem. This is mainly the result of the introduction of ever more intensive agriculture, with large-scale irrigation as a major burden. The same process of agricultural intensification has also had dramatic consequences for the landscape in general. As in many other Mediterranean regions, it is one of the most dominant factors inducing landscape change in Salento in modern times, and is accompanied by extensive woodland clearance. Especially from the 19th century onwards, woodland has gradually diminished through large-scale deforestation projects, opening up the landscape for agrarian purposes. Today, only 5 percent of the region is covered by forest. Agricultural reforms introduced from the 1950s onwards accelerated this landscape transformation; the post-war period witnessed the advent of intensive arboriculture and the cultivation of cash-crops at the cost of the remaining woodland areas, as well as of previously dominant cereal cultivation (at present, olive groves and vineyards make up ca. 65 percent of the total land use).

The ACVU fieldwork in Salento has made it patently clear that deforestation and agricultural intensification have been and still are being accompanied by serious erosion.[2] Both phenomena are generally also argued to have been a major cause of the progradation of the southern Italian coastline and the formation of its most recent Holocene dune belts, which in the Salento research area reach up to 17 m in height.[3] Similar transformations are attested for the various phases that are the subject of the present study. The issue is a classical topic since Claudio Vita-Finzi published his findings on successive phases of valley aggradation in the Mediterranean in *The Mediterranean Valleys*.[4] Whilst Vita-Finzi held that climatic changes were responsible for the formation of the successive valley sediments, others have subsequently argued that it was above all the widespread agricultural use of plains and clearance of the forests that caused a significant increase in soil erosion and subsequent filling of major valleys and coastal plains.[5] Unfortunately, in Apulia our understanding of this issue is severely limited by the scarcity of sedimentological research and radiocarbon dates. This is the case for environmental and climatic transformations in general. A welcome exception in this regard is the recent analysis of relic dune belts along the Apulian coasts, carried out by Mastronuzzi and Sansò.

Mainly on the basis of a series of radiocarbon dates of fossil shells collected at a range of localities, Mastronuzzi and Sansò identified three major Holocene dune belts. The oldest, dated roughly to the Neolithic/Early Bronze Age, is preserved only in small eroded remnants, such as those along the Adriatic coast near Ostuni at 280 m altitude. The most recent aeolian deposits, formed during the medieval period, constitute a well-preserved dune belt found along various sections of both the Adriatic and Ionian coasts. The intervening and most widespread aeolian cover in the Apulian region is generally dated to the Greek/Roman period. Evaluating all the available data, Mastronuzzi and Sansò conclude that dune development was most likely promoted by the rapid progradation of the main coastal plains, a process induced by frequent flooding and filling-in of the major river valleys, and accompanied by the development of wide coastal swamps. Mastronuzzi and Sansò hold that these processes resulted from the combined effects of human pressure on the landscape, sea-level rise and a progressively humid climate.[6] Following Neboit and Brückner, they argue that the formation of the second aeolian cover corresponds to agricultural intensification and deforestation in the Late Iron Age and 'Greek-Roman' phases.[7]

Similar phenomena have been investigated for the neighbouring Basilicata region and in particular for the territory of Greek Metapontion, immediately to the west of the Salento isthmus. The Metaponto *chora* has been the subject of landscape archaeological research by the University of Texas at Austin for

---

[2] Bijlsma / Verhagen 1989.

[3] Mastronuzzi / Sansò 2002; Abbott 1997.

[4] Vita-Finzi 1969.

[5] E.g. Delano-Smith 1981; Barker / Hunt 1995; in the case of southern Italy: Neboit 1983; Brückner 1983.

[6] Mastronuzzi / Sansò 2002, 149-150.

[7] Neboit 1983; Brückner 1983.

several decades. This research includes excavations and field surveys throughout the Metaponto landscape, integrated with detailed geomorphological analyses carried out by Abbott.[8] A major aim of the latter field-work based study was to produce a chronological model of late-quaternary landscape evolution in the Metapontino. With regard to the phases relevant to the present study, Abbott identified processes of progradation of the coastal area in the Late Neolithic/Early Bronze Age phase and the Iron Age/Classical period. Both were succeeded by phases of relative stability and soil formation in respectively the later Bronze Age and, roughly, the late Roman/Medieval period. Abbott also recognized significant human impact during these two phases of dynamism in the sedimentary record of the Metapontino, particularly woodland clearance and agricultural activity on the uplands, valley slopes and lower watersheds. According to Abbott, these phenomena were in the first phase linked to the advent of sedentism, and in the second to urbanization, demographic growth and market exchange.

Mastronuzzi and Sansò, as well as Abbott, caution against overemphasizing either anthropogenic pressure or climatic change, and consider a series of interacting processes, including not only human impact and climate but also (amongst others) tectonics, hydrology and lithology. In the following section we will focus on the human factor, evaluating the archaeological record and in particular field survey data in relation to the major land systems of the Salento isthmus.

3.3 LAND SYSTEMS AND THE ARCHAEOLOGICAL RECORD

In her PhD dissertation Van Joolen distinguished five land systems on the Salento isthmus, principally on the basis of their different morphology.[9] In figure 3.2 we provide a map of these landscapes, and in table 3.2 we list the main aspects of their land-use potential as modelled by Van Joolen. The ACVU fieldwork has focused mainly on the first two land systems, the Brindisi plain and the Murge tableland. More recently, transect surveys were started that crosscut also the latter three landscapes, but only preliminary results are available. We will therefore focus here on the first two land systems.

3.3.1 THE CENTRAL BRINDISI PLAIN

The Brindisino land system as defined by Van Joolen is marked by an almost flat landscape, sloping at a gradient of at most 2 percent, and showing no or relatively minor relief in general; it is intersected by river valleys and depressions.[10] Narrow strips of gently sloping land separate 'terraces' at different elevations. These terraces represent former sea levels. This land system covers almost the entire eastern part of the research area, including the central Brindisi plain or *piana messapica* and areas to the north-east, east and south-east of Taranto (fig. 3.3). However, the latter have not yet been systematically surveyed; the ACVU field surveys have been particularly intense in the central Brindisi plain. Therefore, in the present context we will limit discussion to this area.

The Brindisi plain has a slightly undulating topography which makes a very gradual downward slope towards the Adriatic in the east. In contrast, in the immediate coastal zones one finds a landscape alternating between dunes, lagoons and low cliffs, rising up to 20 m above sea level. The plain rises very gradually from two meters above sea level behind the dunes to 60 m inland. South of Brindisi the *piana messapica* extends all the way to the limestone range of the Serre Leccesi. North of Brindisi, the coastal plain gradually narrows to a ca. 10 km-wide strip enclosed by the Adriatic and the Murge. This strip is

[8] Abbott 1997; Abbott, in press.
[9] Van Joolen 2003, 44-62.
[10] Van Joolen 2003, 51-54.

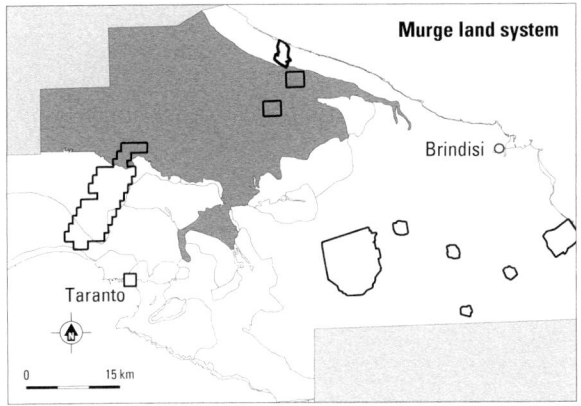
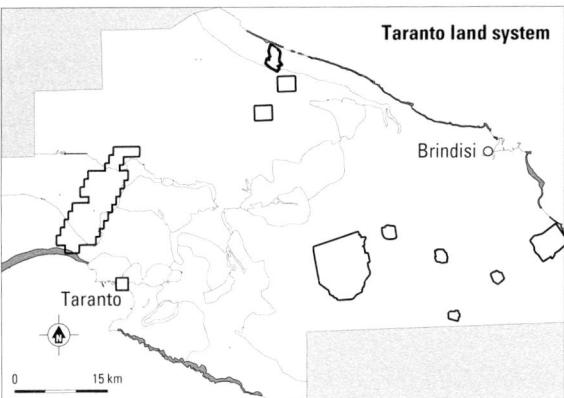
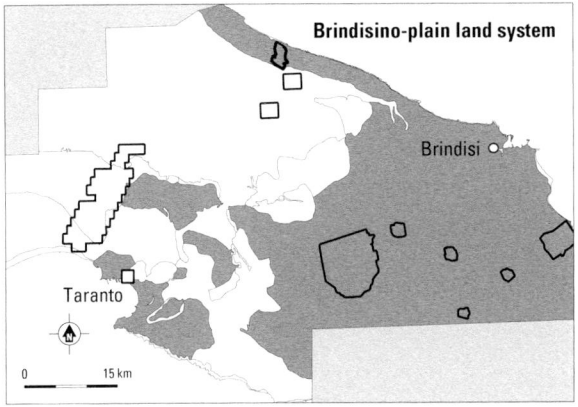
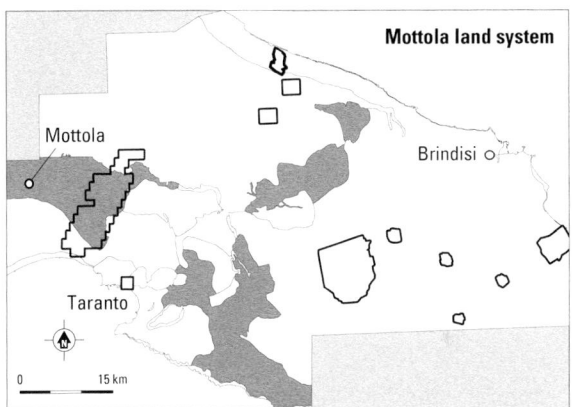
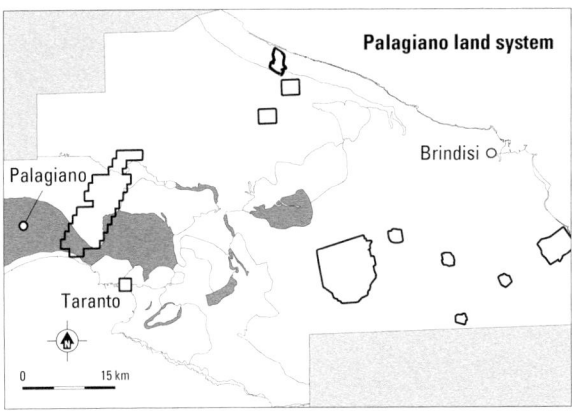

Fig. 3.2. Land systems of the Salento Isthmus, with areas surveyed by the ACVU. See Table 3.2 for land system characteristics.

incised, at intervals of 1 to 2 km, by deep, canyon-like river valleys (*lame*) which originate in the Murge upland. By contrast, in the immediate hinterland of Brindisi the plain is cross-cut by surface streams or *canali*. The width of these riverbeds hardly exceeds 100 meters. They were perennial until quite recently (on recent water shortage see section 3.1).

According to Van Joolen's land evaluation of the Salento isthmus at large, the Brindisi plain and particularly its depressions are among the most suitable land systems for ancient agriculture.[11] The deeper soils of the plain are considered suitable for a range of ancient land use types, from the typical Mediterranean polycultural system to monoculture of cereals, olives or grapes, from subsistence to market-oriented farming. As we will discuss below, the archaeological evidence regarding the Brindisi plain does indeed indicate intensive ancient agricultural use.

[11] Van Joolen 2003, 129-141.

Land system and land form	Characteristics
Brindisino land system 1760 sq.km	An almost flat area covering the eastern half of the study area, with a variety of soil depths and soil types, and predominantly cultivated with cereals and olives. Narrow strips of straight gently sloping land separate ancient marine terraces of different elevations. Olives and grapes are cultivated on thin soils, cereals and grapes on thicker soils. Fruits and vegetables are cultivated on valley floors and depressions.
Plain 1600 sq.km	A micro-relief is formed by local rock outcrops and small incised rivers. Very shallow soils on and around hills are ploughed for olive cultivation.
Undulating land 115 sq.km	An area comprising several small hills and valleys, with thin very rocky soils based on limestone, chalk and calcareous sands. Vegetation consists of shrubs.
Murge land system 900 sq.km	A landscape of alternating stony hills and ridges at up to 500 m above sea level, based on gently dipping limestones, and relatively fertile valleys dissected by (steeply) incised rivers and shallow depressions of karstic origin. Steep and concave slopes mark the southern and northern boundaries of this system.
Rolling land 730 sq.km	Elevations between 180 and 270 m above sea level. Slopes and peaks with shallow and very stony soils are sometimes cultivated with olives and almonds but are mostly *macchia* or rough grazing land. Soils in the valleys and depressions (chromic luvisols) are cultivated for fruit, olives, nuts and wheat.
Steep to concavely sloping land 130 sq.km	Singular steep slopes (25 to 55 percent) with very stony and thin soils mark the northern and southern borders of the unit, and turn into broad concavely sloping land especially along the northern borders. Rocky outcrops characterise the steep slopes that are vegetated with *macchia* and some pine and olive trees.
Taranto land system 35 sq.km	A very narrow landscape unit, present on almost all coasts and consisting of Holocene dunes and Pleistocene/Holocene lagoons. Soils in the dunes are calcaric arenosols used only for rough grazing and pine plantations; the flat lagoonal area has loamy, salty fluvisols and a marsh vegetation. Formerly active lagoons (now drained) were used for (shell-) fishing. The modern coastline has receded somewhat since Roman times. A cliff-coast occurs south-east of Taranto.
Mottola land system 500 sq.km	An undulating landscape of relatively small hills and valleys, sloping at one gradient, and traversed by canyon-like river valleys. A wide variety of rock formations and sediments (from clayey sands and gravels to breccias and limestone) occurs. Holocene alluvial and colluvial sediments occur near the southern coast. In the valleys, olives, citrus, fruits, legumes and oats are cultivated; some slopes are cultivated for grapes and olives. Occasional residual hills and peaks with very thin soils (leptosols) occur; these tend to be uncultivated.
Undulating gently sloping land 450 sq.km	The tops and slopes of the relatively small hills and valleys (slopes less than 8 percent) have a mostly shallow reddish-brown non-calcareous loamy soil, with regular rocky outcrops. Valley bottoms have a variable but generally sandy loamy soil, to which limestone fragments are often added artificially by farmers. Pine forests, low garrigue and maquis grow on top of the hills.
Palagiano land system 250 sq.km	Situated in the south-west around Taranto, this land system is composed of calcarenites and limestones. A major part is formed by gently sloping deposits of Pleistocene coastal origin, intersected by three major valleys with floodplains. Cereals, olives, grapes and watermelons are cultivated. Valley floors have thick, dark brown to black sandy clays and are more intensively cultivated with these crops, including cereals.
Straight gently sloping land 245 sq.km	No or only minor relief, slopes between 2 and 8 percent. Areas with very shallow soils to the north and north-east of Taranto are part of an uncultivated *cuesta* landscape. Areas with deeper soils of fluvial origin consist of mixed silts and sands with pebbles, and are still very stony; these are generally ploughed and rocks may have been stacked into partition walls. The vegetation consists mostly of maquis, and is used for rough grazing.

Table 3.2 Summary of land system and land form characteristics of the Salento Isthmus (simplified from Van Joolen 2003, 44–62).

Fig. 3.3. View of the Brindisi plain, part of the Brindisino land system (photo: G.-J. Burgers, ACVU). For a colour version of this figure, see page 213.

The central part of the Brindisi plain has been the object of topographic surveys in the *Forma Italiae* tradition from as early as the 1960s, when the introduction of modern agricultural techniques started to affect the buried archaeological record on an unprecedented scale. These prospections mainly focused on the detection of relatively obtrusive sites, like robbed necropoleis and Roman villas. The data resulting from this fieldwork was systematically inventoried in a number of publications. A large number of articles are dedicated to specific sites, but of particular interest is the catalogue of sites compiled by Quilici and Quilici Gigli in the early 1970s that comprises all major archaeological finds hitherto reported in the Brindisi region.[12] Unfortunately, some entries in this catalogue lack quantitative and qualitative data on the sites inventoried. In order to be able to evaluate the topographic research we have to depend on the modern intensive surveys introduced in the 1980s. Systematic surveys have been carried out in various landscape units throughout the region by the ACVU and by the University of Siena.

Of interest among the topographic research carried out are above all the prospections of Marangio, which focused notably on the Pleistocene clayey sands surrounding the modern town of Mesagne. This has resulted in a relatively high density of rural sites, which are distributed fairly evenly over the flat and fertile lands of this part of the Brindisi plain, at intervals averaging between 1-2 km.[13] The focus of Marangio's fieldwalking was on Roman period sites. The aim of his reconnaissance around Mesagne was to show that the supposedly Roman *vicus* underlying the modern town had been the centre of a densely inhabited countryside. He demonstrated the prosperity of agriculture in the Roman Brindisi region and challenged traditional theories that depicted the south-Italian countryside of the Roman period as largely abandoned.

---

[12] Quilici / Quilici Gigli 1975.

[13] Marangio 1971-1973 and 1975.

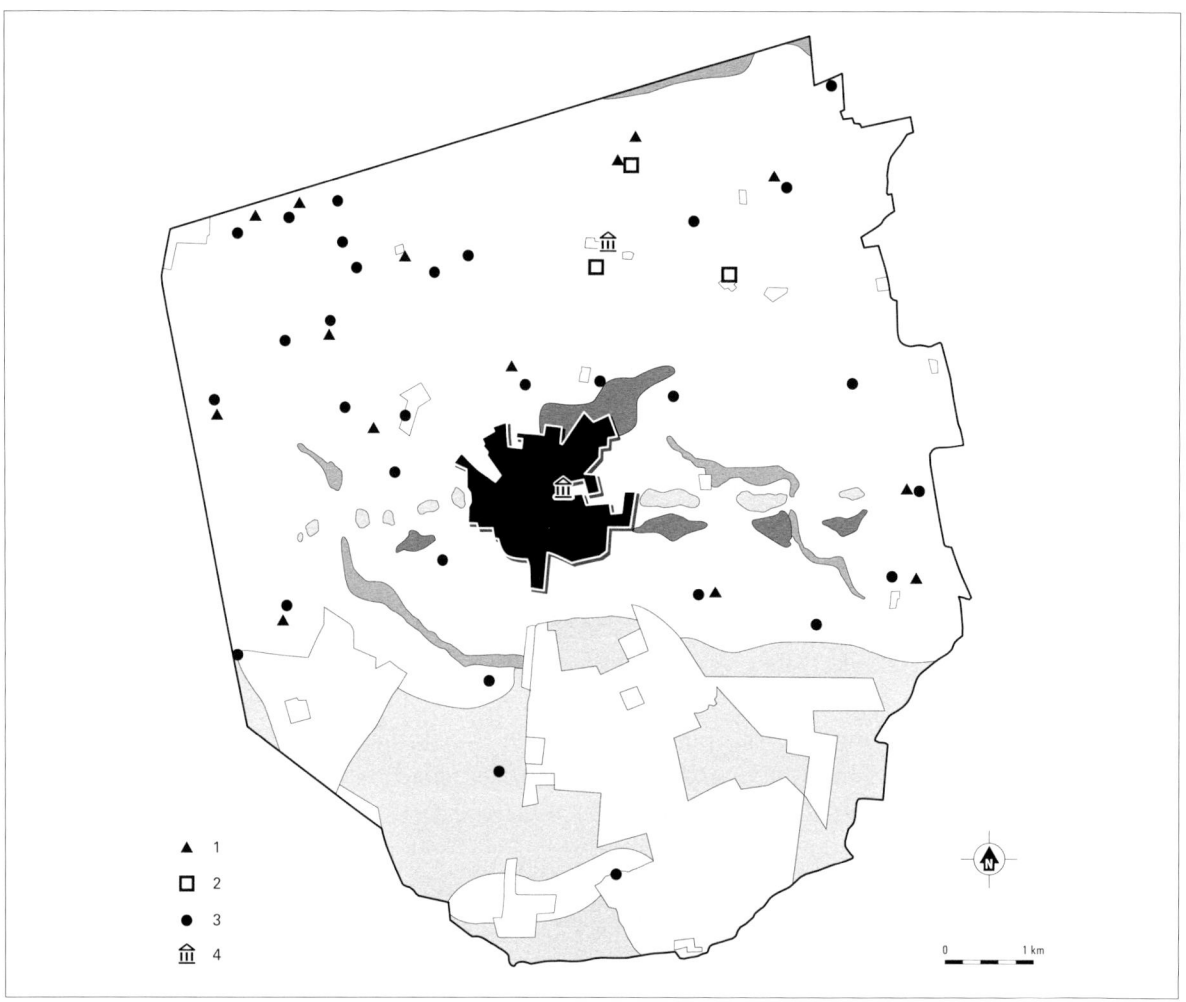

Fig. 3.4. Distribution of early Hellenistic sites in the Oria survey area. 1 necropolis; 2 hamlet; 3 isolated farmstead; 4 sanctuary. Gray shades represent different geophysical units (after Yntema 1993, fig. 74). For a colour version of this figure, see page 214.

In a similar vein, Marangio discussed the territory of the municipality of Oria, adjoining that of Mesagne and still in the Brindisi plain.[14] Oria is thought to have acquired municipal status by the early Imperial period.[15] In the light arable soils in a 10 km-wide radius around the site, a density and distribution of Roman villa sites has been documented similar to that at Mesagne. This density should not come as a surprise, considering the land evaluation carried out in the context of the RPC project. As has been emphasized by Van Joolen, the central Brindisi plain was well suited for various ancient types of land use.[16] The question is rather to what degree this land system was exploited in previous phases, a point on which topographic prospections are virtually silent.

As one of the first scholars to dedicate himself to the rural archaeological record, Marangio has contributed much to the ancient settlement history of the Brindisi region, especially that of the Roman period. His findings were further elaborated in the context of the systematic ACVU Brindisino surveys. The first of these is the Oria field survey which between 1981 and 1984 almost totally covered the area ca. 5 km around Oria in a systematic and intensive way (figs. 3.1 and 3.4).[17] The Oria survey was diachronic in nature, aiming to document even diffuse scatters of unobtrusive pre- and protohistoric

[14] Marangio 1980.
[15] Marangio 1980, 228-232.
[16] Van Joolen 2003, 141.
[17] Yntema 1993a.

impasto wares. A total of 96 sites were recorded in a surveyed area of 62.4 sq.km. With regard to the Roman period, the Oria field survey broadly confirmed the prior thesis of a relatively dense pattern of rural sites. However, the more refined survey methodology and artefact analysis allowed Yntema to detect diachronic variability. Thus, for the later Imperial phases it could be established that site numbers decrease gradually in the Oria area while the remaining sites increase in size, which is interpreted as an indication of the concentration of landholdings. Most sites were demonstrably already occupied in the - previously hardly considered - late Republican period, for which the total number of sites turned out to be even higher than is the case for any of the Imperial phases.

Equally new for southern Italy was the delineation of dense patterns of pre-Roman scatters, which allowed the identification of various phases of settlement expansion and landscape infill. The most remarkable of these can be dated to the early Hellenistic period, i.e. the late 4th/mid-3rd century BC. To begin with the surveys allowed an estimation of the expansion of the nucleated site of Oria from circa 40-50 ha in the Archaic/Classical period to just over 100 ha in the early Hellenistic period. On the basis of information from robbed necropoleis and from surface debris encountered during the surveys, Yntema established that the already inhabited zones became much more densely occupied in the early Hellenistic period. Furthermore, whereas habitation in the Archaic/Classical period turned out to have been concentrated mostly at the site of Oria, some 47 additional sites were recorded for the early Hellenistic period over large parts of the survey area. On the basis of differences in site size, artefact density and assemblages, three types of early Hellenistic rural sites were identified: isolated farmsteads (30), hamlets (3, each made up of three to five rural dwellings) and small graveyards (14). Moreover, the presence of votive material at one of the hamlets probably indicates the presence of a rural sanctuary. These data suggest a thorough reorganization of large parts of the central Brindisi plain that had previously been characterized by a strongly nucleated settlement pattern. In the course of the early Hellenistic period a sizeable portion of the population took permanent residence in the countryside.

The density of pre-Roman rural sites conforms to the land evaluation results that predict a relatively intensive agricultural use of the Brindisi plain, at least in the classical phases. However, the distribution of the new rural sites suggests that the rural infill did not affect all local landforms equally. Most of the sites were detected in the northern half of the Oria landscape, which has light, slightly clayey arable soils and is well-watered. In contrast, the southern expanses of thin soils on calcarenites and limestone were much less favoured for rural settlement. The hypothesis seems justified that the latter zone contained large areas of forest and pasture land throughout antiquity, as it did in subrecent periods.

Further analysis of the scale of the early Hellenistic settlement expansion and rural infill is made possible by the results of a range of intensive judgmental surveys carried out throughout the central Brindisi plain after the Oria study. These results invariably indicate that in the early Hellenistic period existing sites expanded considerably and simultaneously with the rural infill. The sites of Muro Tenente, Muro Maurizio and Li Castelli, for example, were shown to have more or less doubled in extent in this phase, reaching sizes of 52, 35 and 57 ha respectively. At Muro Tenente the large-scale open-area excavations carried out by the ACVU between 1995 and 2002 provided further confirmation of the site's expansion, in the form of the foundations of an early Hellenistic, newly-constructed domestic quarter in the northern periphery of the site.

The results of the surveys at masseria Mea indicate the scale of the rural infill. They brought to light a newly established, early Hellenistic hamlet (6 ha) similar to those encountered in the Oria countryside. In this case, however, the hamlet lies at a considerable distance (7-8 km) from the nearest central places, in what was probably marginal land. The area is now characterized by wide extensions of very thin, relatively infertile leptosols, with frequently surfacing bedrock. The total absence of pre-Hellenistic sites in the survey area at Masseria Mea and in the larger unit between San Pancrazio Salentino and Valesio suggests that this landscape was not favoured for permanent settlement, if it was exploited at all. In view of this, the purpose of the foundation of the hamlet may have been to initiate exploitation of this land.

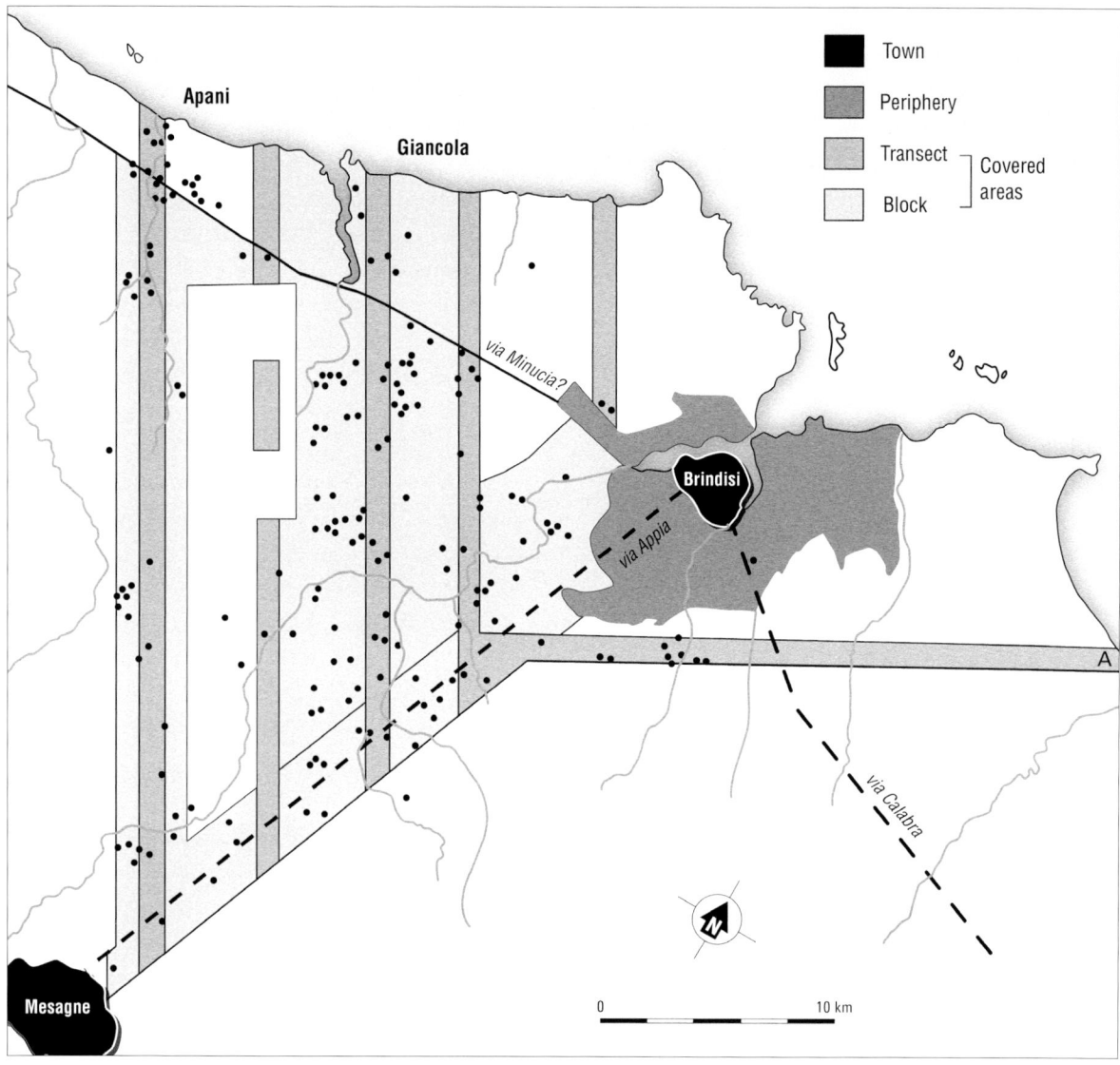

Fig. 3.5. Areas surveyed and sites recorded in the early 1990s by the University of Siena in the Brindisino (after: Cambi 2000, fig. 18.1). For a colour version of this figure, see page 215.

Although the early Hellenistic period can indeed be regarded as one of major landscape transformation, the various surveys in the Brindisi plain also demonstrate that the area was densely settled already in the Archaic/Classical period, with major settlements being distributed evenly at an average distance of 10-12 km. The available evidence from survey, excavation and incidental finds all suggest that the lay-out of these sites was relatively dispersed, with habitation nuclei being separated by open spaces. Site sizes vary considerably, pointing towards the existence of a settlement hierarchy, an impression that is accentuated by the presence of fortification walls and other monumental architecture, at least at the larger sites like Oria. This settlement configuration can be traced back to the Early Iron Age, when most of the extant Archaic/Classical sites came into existence. It is especially the surveys that identified the Early Iron Age phases of these settlements, which can be recognized in the field as scatters of matt-painted and impasto wares, generally spaced some 100 m apart. Occasionally, such scatters also occur in relatively isolated positions without any previous occupation phases.[18] Indeed, the Early Iron Age can be characterized as another major phase of settlement expansion and landscape infill, as will be discussed in more detail below.

The Adriatic coast north of Brindisi
The coastal plain immediately north of Brindisi is also part of the Brindisino land system. This has been systematically investigated between 1990 and 1994 by a team of archaeologists of the *Università degli Studi* of Siena, led by Daniele Manacorda and Franco Cambi (fig. 3.5). Initial intensive site-oriented surveys in a series of randomly selected transects were followed by judgmental artefact-surveys of specific sample areas. Whereas the former aimed to provide a general, diachronic picture of site distributions, the latter served to investigate specific questions that had come up during the transect surveys. The results of both types of survey have so far been discussed in preliminary reports only.[19] The aim of the surveys was to study the territorial and social-economic organization of the *ager Brundisinus*, the territory of the Latin colony of Brindisi which was founded ca. 245 BC. Chronologically, their focus is on the late Republican period, and notably the 1st century BC, a period which in the ager Brundisinus saw the rise of intensive, export-oriented production of olive oil, and the emergence of Brindisi as a major harbour for traffic to markets overseas.

The preliminary publications indicate that part of the northern coastline of rural Brindisi was only marginally involved in these new developments. Cambi, for example, notes when discussing late Republican settlement that this included wide stretches of marginal, 'if not completely uncultivated', land.[20] One of these is the area around the Canale Reale, a major water course some 10 km north-west of Brindisi. The lack of Roman sites and off-site scatters led the surveyors to assume that this part of the Brindisi territory was probably characterized by wide expanses of *silva* and pasture. Because the area has a very low site and off-site density in general, a similar hypothesis can be put forward for the early Hellenistic period. Like the bare limestone expanses south of Oria, the lagoonal landscape north of Brindisi was apparently passed over for reclamation in the early Hellenistic period, as well as in the ensuing Roman era.

The late Republican site patterns discussed in the preliminary reports of the Siena surveys are difficult to interpret, particularly those representing the large villages mentioned earlier, which are reportedly measuring up to 4 ha. Such large sites were also encountered in the ACVU-Brindisino surveys, but the surface assemblages there overwhelmingly consist of late Imperial artefacts, as was also observed by Marangio.[21] Late Republican diagnostic finds such as amphoras, *ceramica a pasta grigia* (Apulian Grey-gloss) and Black-gloss fine wares generally occur in much smaller quantities, which suggests a significantly more modest form of occupation for that period in the Brindisino. To be able to evaluate the significance of these differences we would need to know to what extent the large sites found on the Adriatic coast by the Siena surveys also contained artefacts of Imperial date. Similarly, more information on the nature, density and distribution of late Republican artefacts at these sites would be welcome, especially since it is explicitly stated that diagnostic fine wares from the late Republican period were also found in very small quantities.[22]

On the other hand, the idea that large late-Republican villages existed along the Adriatic coast north of Brindisi is by no means improbable, since there is also ample evidence to suggest that agriculture became increasingly market-oriented in this area (see above). These villages may have performed a market role subsidiary to the harbour of Brindisi, which - as was stated above - functioned in the late Republican period as a major port for the export of agricultural products from the Brindisi region, notably of olive oil.

Beside these villages, the surveys documented isolated farms for the early Roman period (mid 3rd/2nd centuries BC) throughout the survey areas. These farms were mostly quite small, and they were probably

---

[18] Yntema 1993a; Burgers 1998, 61.

[19] Aprosio / Cambi 1997; Cambi 2000. The full publication by Aprosio (2008) unfortunately came to our attention too late for inclusion in the present volume.

[20] Cambi 2000, 177.

[21] Marangio 1975.

[22] Cambi 2000, 176.

occupied by one or two families. This corresponds to the results of the surveys in the wider Brindisi plain. However, specific for the hinterland of Brindisi is the presence of a series of late-Republican coastal factories producing the so-called 'Brindisi amphoras'. Amphora kilns have been discovered at the sites of Apani, Giancola, Masseria Marmorelle and La Rosa.[23] Reports of amphora deposits at other sites in the vicinity of Brindisi suggest that more such production centres existed at the periphery of the town.[24] Although an exhaustive study of the distribution patterns of these olive oil containers has not yet been made, amphora specialists have identified them in many late-Republican archaeological contexts around the Mediterranean basin, testifying to the extent of the export of olive oil from the Brindisino.[25] Thus, both the production sites and the distribution of the Brindisi amphoras clearly indicate the scale of the expansion and intensification of olive cultivation in the late Republican Brindisino. Study of the stamp impressions commonly found on the handles of the Brindisi amphoras reveals that wealthy, powerful Romans had become engaged in this oleoculture boom. Among the names of the estate owners producing amphoras is that of the senator Visellius, identified by the Siena team as the owner of various properties in the Giancola area. Amphoras containing the oil produced by Visellius' estates generally have two stamps, one identifying Visellius himself as the owner, the other identifying one of his slaves in charge of a production sector.[26] There is also ample evidence for the large-scale employment of slaves on the Brindisino estates and it is in this context that one must view the emergence, from the early 1st century BC, of a system of large rural villas recorded by the Siena surveys alongside the smaller farms, villages and amphora production sites. These villas are thought to be the centres of slave-run, market-oriented estates, producing both olive oil and the amphoras for its transport overseas. Although the Siena survey team provided no details, it appears that these villas are very similar in their size and lack of luxury items to the late Republican sites recorded around Oria.

The Adriatic coast south of Brindisi
The coastal plain south of Brindisi, another part of the Brindisino land system, has long seemed to hold little of archaeological interest. The only known large site was that of the fortified pre-Roman settlement of Valesio, 15 km south-east of Brindisi and 5 km from the Adriatic coast. The ca. 83 ha-large fortified area was surveyed in 1985 to complement the ACVU excavations in the centre of the site.[27] In the early 1990s this survey was extended to the Adriatic coast, creating a ca. 3.5-by-5.5 km transect through the coastal land system (fig. 3.6).[28]

The transect has been investigated in detail by geographers of the VU, who distinguished three units of Holocene sediments in the area: coastal, fluvial and aeolian.[29] The coastal deposits comprise a lagoon-dune-beach system; the fluvial deposits, confined to the narrow beds of small rivulets, have proved to be important in dating Holocene erosion phases. In one section, layered fluvial deposits were found, containing only Iron Age ceramics, indicating an erosion phase at around 700 BC. Other, possibly related forms of erosion are indicated by the presence of thin layers of aeolian sands to the north-east and south of Valesio; these deposits probably originated as a result of agricultural activities which left the bare soil exposed to wind action. As wind action in southern Italy is not particularly strong, it is not probable that the transported material travelled over long distances. Archaeological evidence for agricultural activities probably responsible for the erosion is abundantly provided by the ACVU field surveys in this transect; these have discovered high densities of small rural settlement sites distributed fairly evenly throughout the area. Moreover, in between these sites the surveys have detected a continuum of low density surface spread, suggesting that the area was indeed intensively used.

[23] Palazzo 1988; 1994; Marangio 1974.
[24] Manacorda 1988, 97.
[25] Cipriano 1985, 192; Cipriano / Carre 1989, 72; Désy 1989 and 1993; Volpe 1990, 226-227.
[26] Manacorda 1990; Cambi 2000, 183.
[27] Yntema 1993b.
[28] Boersma *et al.* 1990 / 1991.
[29] Bijlsma / Verhagen 1989.

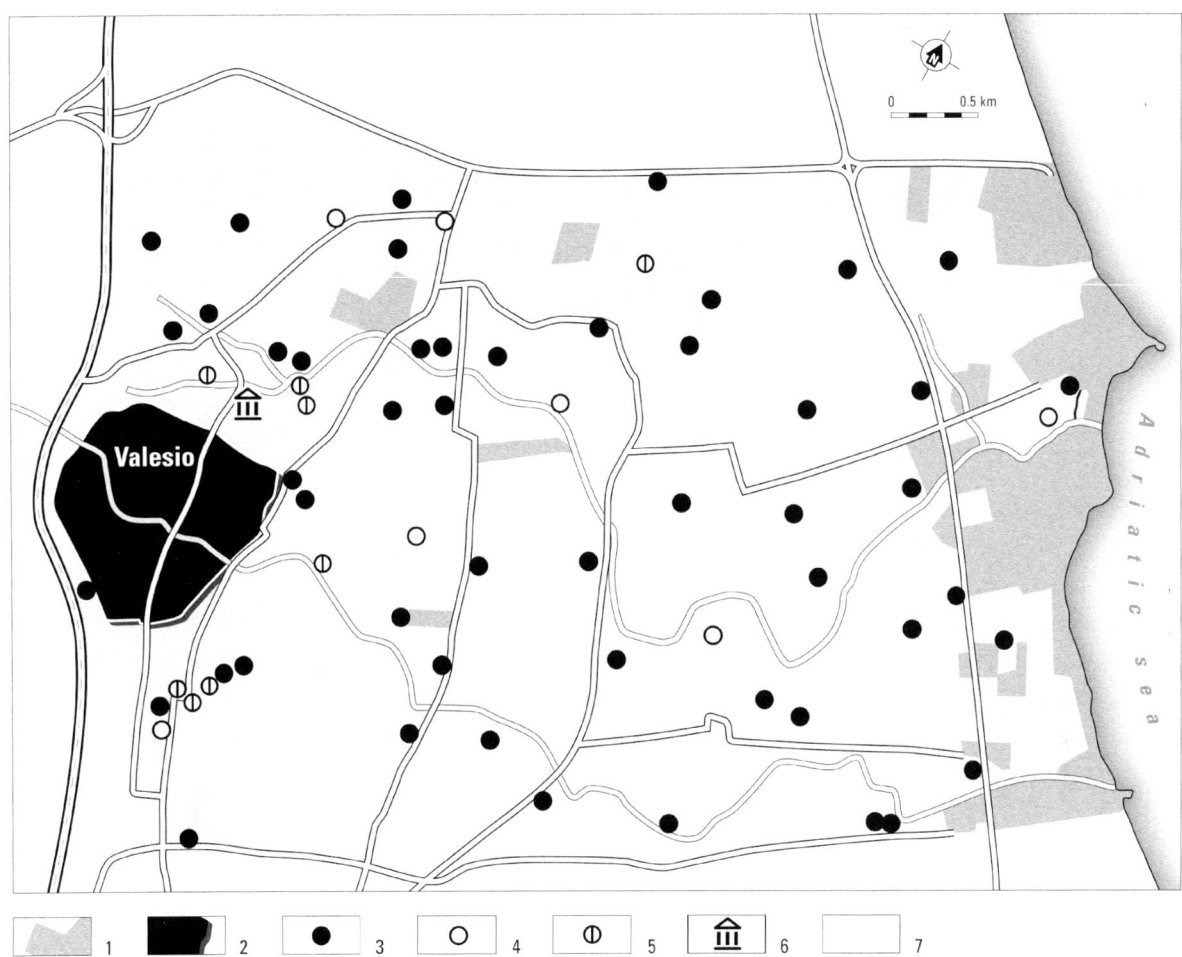

Fig. 3.6. Distribution of sites in the Valesio field survey area with artefacts dating between the late 4th century and the middle of the 2nd century BC. 1 inaccessible areas, 2 walled site of Valesio, 3 farm sites, 4 probable farm sites, 5 scatters consisting of tile and amphora only, 6 sanctuary site, 7 surveyed area. For a colour version of this figure, see page 216.

As with the Oria research, the Valesio surveys were diachronic in nature, employing a crew that had experience with artefacts from protohistoric to Roman times. Although not as familiar with Bronze Age materials, the team managed to record not only a fair number of definite Bronze Age sites, but also isolated Bronze Age impasto shards. Taken together these testify to a relatively dispersed occupational pattern, spread out notably along the two rivulets of the Infocacciuci and Pilella. Almost all of this material could generically be dated to the later phase of the Early Bronze Age or to the Middle Bronze Age. No Late Bronze Age artefacts were discovered; so far, there is no indication that the coastal area south of Brindisi was exploited at all in the Late Bronze Age. By contrast, the Early Iron Age can be characterized as one of major expansion; in the course of the 8th century BC a series of small settlement nuclei were founded in the western part of the transect, in the area in which subsequently the fortified site of Valesio developed.[30] The ACVU excavations in the centre of Valesio have uncovered part of one such Iron Age nucleus.[31] Relating stratigraphical data to the survey results at Valesio, Yntema estimated an average of some three to five Iron Age huts per hectare for this site.[32] With an estimated 5 persons per hut, he arrived at an occupation density of 15 to 25 persons per ha, and a total resident population of 45 to 90 people; this number more or less remains the same throughout the rest of the Iron Age.

[30] Yntema 1993b.
[31] Boersma / Yntema 1987.

As may be clear from the discussion of the central Brindisi plain, the 8th-century BC reclamation of this part of the Adriatic coast and the foundation of the settlement at Valesio were not isolated phenomena. Whilst incidental finds of local Geometric pottery, though unsystematically collected, already suggested an increase in sites for Salento as a whole,[33] the ACVU surveys in the northern part of the peninsula that were discussed above testify to a process of reclamation of the inland plains and hills of the Brindisi region, the larger part of which seems to have been only marginally exploited throughout the preceding late Bronze Age phases. This internal colonization movement transformed the landscape, with villages being distributed at an average distance of some 10-12 km. In some areas these villages grew exceptionally large. A major example in the Brindisi region is the site of Oria, which is estimated to have covered a total area of between 70 and 90 ha in the Early Iron Age.[34] Most other surveyed Iron Age sites are smaller, Li Castelli di San Pancrazio measuring some 28 ha, Muro Maurizio 20-25 ha, and Muro Tenente 15 ha, the latter equalling more or less the site of Valesio.[35] This differentiation in settlement sizes points to the emergence of a settlement hierarchy.

Transformations are again evident for the ensuing centuries, when the site of Valesio grew to be one of the largest of the Brindisi region, up to 83 ha in its phase of maximum expansion in the early Hellenistic period. Moreover, the surveys have discovered an extensive sanctuary site at a distance of only 400 m north of Valesio, the origins of which can be traced back to the 6th century BC.[36] The nearest parallel to the Valesio sanctuary is found at the hill of Monte Papaluccio, some 500 m east of the centre of Oria, which stands at the apex of the regional settlement hierarchy.[37] Since such sanctuary sites were absent in the countryside of the minor settlements investigated, it must be assumed that they were not merely intended to serve the local inhabitants but played a central religious role for other nearby communities as well.

The only other Archaic/Classical site that was reported in the Valesio survey transect is the one at Torre San Gennaro, where the Pilella rivulet runs into the Adriatic Sea. The finds closely resemble those from other coastal sites in Salento, where the more abundant evidence has been interpreted as indicative of the existence of local harbours.[38] These are thought to have functioned as ports of trade for ships from the opposite side of the Adriatic, and to have been administered by the nearest larger inland settlement, in this case Valesio itself.

The relationship between Valesio and the immediate coastal zone was further strengthened in the subsequent early Hellenistic period. The surveys indicate that, as in the central Brindisi plain, the entire 5 km-stretch of land between the town and the sea was dotted with farm sites during this phase (fig. 3.6).[39] An initial wave of rural sites spread out over the coastal area in the later 4th century BC, accelerating further in the mid-3rd century BC. The sites are very similar, resembling the isolated rural farms discovered in the central Brindisi plain; they measure some 500 sq.m and are mostly made up of tiles. Limited amounts of fine table wares like black gloss pottery are found, as well as coarse and plain utilitarian wares, amphoras, grinding stones and loom weights. A few scatters of similar extent have been interpreted as barns for the storage of agricultural products, because the finds consisted only of rooftiles and amphoras.

While these storage sites were limited to Valesio itself and to an area within about 1 km of its fortifications, the distribution of isolated farms is much less restricted. Some of these farms are likely to have been constructed on land that was already cultivated by people living at Valesio. Moving from the

[32] Yntema 1993b, 53.
[33] D'Andria 1991, 405.
[34] Yntema 1993a, 157.
[35] Burgers 1998, 177.
[36] Boersma et al. 1991; Burgers 1998, 204-207.
[37] The Monte Papaluccio sanctuary has been excavated by the University of Lecce. See in particular D'Andria 1990, 239-306.
[38] See in particular D'Andria 1988, 660; Lombardo 1991, 39; Pagliara 1989 and 1991.
[39] Boersma et al. 1991; Burgers 1998.

main settlement to live in the fields themselves will have allowed the rural dwellers to work these fields more intensively. However, the scale of the transformation suggests that previously untilled land was also brought under cultivation. Although we do not know the total extent of the fields that were cultivated in pre-Hellenistic times, it is unlikely to have equalled to the maximum of available land, as seems to have been the case at least from the mid-3rd century BC, when farm sites covered the entire survey area at regular intervals of about 500 m.[40] In this respect the results of the Valesio survey differ from those obtained in the central Brindisi plain at Oria, where early Hellenistic farms seem to have clustered along roads radiating from the central settlement.[41] A regular distribution pattern has also been observed in the nearby Greek *chora* of Metapontion, for which the existence of an orthogonal system of division lines is attested.[42] Another regular system of territorial division that should be considered in evaluating the Hellenistic site distribution at Valesio is that of Roman centuriation, since the area is thought to have been incorporated into the territory of the Latin colony of Brundisium shortly after the mid-3rd century BC.[43] Although no evidence for centuriation has so far been found in the Brindisino or in the Valesio area, the regularity of the site distribution pattern and the uniformity of the sites themselves suggest that the farms were arranged in some formal grid of plots of land which, moreover, were of more or less uniform size.

In contrast to the middle Republican period, when Valesio itself was at its largest and had its countryside densely settled, the site is thought to have been largely abandoned and to have dwindled into a hamlet in the course of the 2nd century BC. At the same time, approximately half of the farm sites in the transect between Valesio and the Adriatic seem to have been abandoned. The apparent general depopulation of the Valesio area contrasts with the contemporary booming of Brindisi, as well as with the relative continuity of occupation in the coastal area north of Brindisi and in the Oria survey area. Continuity of occupation has also been established for such major sites as Mesagne and Muro Tenente, between Brindisi and Oria, whilst surveys in the more peripheral areas of the Brindisi plain, as at San Pancrazio Salentino and Muro Maurizio again paint a picture of decline for this phase. Taken together this suggests that, whereas in the preceding centuries the larger part of the Brindisino was more or less equally favoured, in the late Republican period settlement concentrated in the northern periphery of the Brindisino and along the axis Oria-Brindisi, on which at least as early as the 2nd century BC the Romans constructed the Via Appia.

3.3.2 THE MURGE LAND SYSTEM

In 1999 the ACVU surveys were extended to include the Murge tableland. This karstic plateau runs from the Bari district in the north-west to the Salento peninsula in the south-east. To the south-east it gradually descends into the *piana messapica*. At its eastern edge, it drops abruptly towards the coastal plain bordering the Adriatic (fig. 3.7), whereas in the south-west it slopes more gradually towards the Gulf of Taranto. In the west it gradually merges into the Apennine mountain chain. Until recently, intensive surveys in the Murge area were limited to its north-western edge, between Apulia and Basilicata.[44] The ACVU field surveys focused instead on the southernmost part of the plateau, an area barely known as far as protohistorical and classical phases are concerned. The three main physiographic units surveyed here are, from the interior to the Adriatic coast, (1) the rolling land on the Murge plateau, (2) the concavely sloping land, and (3) the coastal plain. According to Van Joolen's research, the suitability of most of the table-

[40] Boersma *et al.* 1991, 127.
[41] Yntema 1993a.
[42] On which most recently De Siena 2001; Carter 2001 and 2006, 91-132.
[43] Marangio 1975; Cambi 2000.
[44] Vinson 1972; Small 1991; Small *et al.* 1998.

Fig. 3.7. View across the Adriatic coastal plain towards the Murge tableland near Ostuni (photo: G.-J. Burgers, ACVU). For a colour version of this figure, see page 217.

land, and in particular of the Murge, was rather limited or marginal, except for the lower parts of the slopes and the river valley floors on the plateau; these were suitable for wheat cultivation, even without the use of ards. The major factors of influence here are the relative flatness, ample nutrient availability and workability. This is also the case for the lowland units, which are (marginally) suitable for vine and olive cultivation.

Because of the potential marginality of the tableland itself, initially a survey method was designed specifically to document the low-density and low-visibility artefact scatters that are characteristic of low-intensity settlement and land use. Although we did in fact detect very diffuse and low-density ceramic scatters, it has also become clear that such scatters are not the norm in the landscape units investigated. Large and dense sites dating to the Middle Bronze Age, and settlements from the Hellenistic and Roman periods were also discovered, suggesting a more intensive human exploitation in these phases.

The level of detail at which the survey in the Murge was conducted proved successful in locating even small, low-density and low-visibility artefact scatters from the Middle Bronze Age. In all three survey areas many such ephemeral scatters were found alongside a series of larger and denser concentrations, suggestive of an extensive human exploitation of both up- and lowland areas in this phase of the Bronze Age. The major Bronze Age scatters on the Murge plateau cluster on the lower terraces at the interface between hill slopes and valley floors. This locational preference can be explained by reference to the classification of the lower parts of the slopes and the valley floors as suitable for wheat farming, due to their relative flatness, nutrient availability and workability. This is also the case for the concavely sloping land and the lowland plain proper, where sites from the Middle Bronze Age abound as well. The sheer abundance of Middle Bronze Age material in all areas makes it likely that the settlements were not all permanently occupied at the same time, which may be explained in the context of group mobility related to the practice of shifting cultivation that was made necessary by the short-term fallowing system of the Bronze Age. Nonetheless the homogeneity of the material argues for a relatively short period of use. Unfortunately, the non-diagnostic nature of the finds makes it impossible to assign this settlement period to any particular phase within the Middle Bronze Age.

The highly dispersed settlement pattern of the Middle Bronze Age established by the Ostuni survey contrasts with that of the Late Bronze Age. No definite Late Bronze Age material was found in the survey areas. However, this does not mean that the Murge area was abandoned in this phase. While Late Bronze Age sites in the Salento region as a whole are mainly concentrated along the coast line, in the Murge they are also found at the top of the steep slopes at the interface of the coastal area and the upland. A good example is the site of Rissieddi, which stretches out on one of the promontories along this edge, immediately north of the second survey area. Now largely built over, sections of a stone fortification circuit could until recently be seen to enclose a densely occupied area of some 2-3 ha.[45] The Rissieddi promontory visually dominates the surrounding landscape, as do similar Late Bronze Age sites in the Murge. On the basis of the available data it can be concluded that a strongly centralized settlement pattern had emerged by the Late Bronze Age, very different from the highly diffuse one of the Middle Bronze Age.

Much less is known about the Final Bronze Age and the Early Iron Age (11th-9th centuries BC). For the Salento peninsula as a whole, sites from this phase are still situated predominantly on the coast. In the Ostuni survey areas only one or two contemporary sites were identified, both located on terraces facing caves cut into one of the ravines near the coast. However, to conclude from this that people in the Murge land system had withdrawn to cave settlements would be to ignore the lack of archaeological research that has taken place into these phases. Future field work is indeed likely to add considerably to our knowledge. Nevertheless it is safe to conclude that further significant change occurred in the course of the 8th century BC. In the study area a shift in locational preferences can be observed in this phase, since the Rissieddi plateau and the cave sites are being abandoned in favour of a new settlement on the more accessible nearby hilltop at Ostuni.[46] This agrees with the observed general shift, mentioned above, in site locations in the 8th century BC Brindisino and elsewhere in Salento, a phenomenon that was accompanied by an increase in the number of sites. In addition to Ostuni itself, a whole series of new sites illustrates this for the Murge area, such as Locorotondo, Masseria San Pietro, Ceglie Messapica, Carovigno and Castello di San Vito dei Normanni.[47] As is the case in the other Brindisino landscapes, these Murge sites are situated on average some 10-12 km apart, suggesting that a considerable part of the land in between was now brought under cultivation.

There is strong evidence for settlement continuity at all these sites throughout the Archaic period. Although not many systematic investigations were carried out for this phase, we can point to the excavations at Castello di San Vito dei Normanni and Grotta di Santa Maria d'Agnano. Of particular interest are the excavations by the *Scuola di Specializzazione in Archeologia Classica e Medievale* of Lecce University of the fortifications at the hilltop site of Castello di San Vito dei Normanni, some 13 km south-east of Ostuni. The excavations indicate that the hillfort was monumentalized in the Archaic period, when a circuit wall was erected to defend it and a palatial structure was built in its centre.[48] In this respect the settlement resembles contemporary sites elsewhere in Salento, such as Oria and Cavallino. Since the Lecce excavations at San Vito were the first systematic ones carried out at a major Murge site, the phenomenon is possibly more widespread also in the Murge. A similar argument can be applied to the Grotta di Santa Maria d'Agnano, which is located some 4 km north of Ostuni, just below the cliff top on which lies the site of Rissieddi. The cave was excavated by Donato Coppola, who demonstrated that it became the location of a formal cult dedicated to a female divinity from the 6th century onwards.[49] The Agnano cave sanctuary is frequently compared to that on Monte Papalucio, near Oria. More such sanctuaries can be expected elsewhere in the Murge area.

---

[45] Coppola 1983, 208-213.

[46] Coppola 1983, 235-254.

[47] Fusco 1964; Coppola 1977, 304; De Michele 1986; Cocchiaro 1997 and 1998; Semeraro 1998a and 1998b.

[48] Semeraro 1998a

[49] Coppola 1983, 249-252.

Another new phenomenon, namely dispersed rural settlement, appears in the early Hellenistic period and is well documented in the Brindisino, where it seems to have been related to a process of agricultural expansion and intensification (see above). It is also manifest in the sample areas surveyed near Ostuni. In a similar situation to the one at Oria, rural sites were located in a line running just beneath and parallel to the Murge edge, suggestive of the presence of a *pedemontana* road. Also similar to the rural sites at Oria and at Valesio are the ceramic repertoires of the Ostuni sites. Besides local coarse kitchen and plain wares, these include non-local wares such as Apulian Black-gloss, Gnathia ware and Apulian Red Figure, suggesting incorporation within a market system. However, unlike similar farm sites in the Brindisino some of the Ostuni sites lack identifiable tile, which suggests that a much simpler construction method was used for the farm buildings. Nevertheless, it is possible to conclude that the Ostuni area participated in the regional trend of rural expansion. The fact that contemporary rural sites are also attested in upland survey areas in the Murge, far from any urban centre, suggests that this regional trend extended to the cultivation of even the most isolated, previously untilled lands outside the urban catchment areas.

Not only rural territories but the central places too were rearranged in the early Hellenistic period, obvious signs of urban development being present at many of them. Since only cemetery evidence is available from Murge sites, a parallel must once again be drawn with the other Brindisino sites where excavations have documented the emergence of large nucleated *insulae* with a fairly regular lay-out.[50] Besides these domestic quarters, specific urban spaces were arranged for public buildings, cult places, cemeteries, warehouses and for intensive horticulture. Fortifications were built to enclose entire settlement areas, as was the case at Ostuni and Ceglie Messapico in the Murge.[51] These urban transformations demonstrably occurred simultaneously at sites throughout the Salento peninsula. Parallel to the rural infill of the landscape surrounding these major sites, the emergence of pronounced local settlement hierarchies can be observed throughout the region.[52] On the basis of the Ostuni surveys the Murge area can be considered one such micro-region, with isolated farmsteads even appearing on the rolling land of the high plateau. We can conclude that, with the rearrangement of the wider landscape, the Murge towns also became central places serving extensive rural hinterlands in the early Hellenistic period.

The lack of systematic research at towns in the Murge that was mentioned above also impedes any definite conclusions about their development in the Roman period. However, the scarcity of Roman finds so far suggests that they contracted considerably. On the other hand, neither in the Murge upland nor in the concavely sloping land can any significant changes be observed in the number or locations of rural sites of the late Republican and early Imperial periods. Moreover, the presence of considerable amounts of fine wares on the recorded sites suggests that the area as a whole still had access to a wider market system. In fact, a basic continuity seems to exist for these phases, suggesting that rural occupation was not much affected when the centre of power in the region shifted towards the Brindisi plain as the direct hinterland of the Latin colony of Brundisium (see above).

Rural continuity is only partially attested for the later Imperial phases. For example, later Imperial fine wares are absent in the upland zone. Other contemporary diagnostic wares are lacking as well, which suggests that the area was abandoned in the 2nd century AD and that the Murge upland now became peripheral to the wider region. In contrast, African Red Slip wares are amply attested in the lowland survey area. Here there is even some evidence of site expansion, possibly reflecting a process of concentration of small, dispersed land holdings into larger, more centrally managed estates.

---

[50] Monte Sannace: Scarfì 1961 and 1962; Vaste: D'Andria 1991; Muro Tenente: Van Alberda *et al.* 1999.

[51] D'Andria 1991, 445; Coppola 1983, 269-275.

[52] As discussed in more detail in Burgers 1998, 226-263.

3.3.3 RECENT TRANSECT SURVEYS ON THE SOUTH-WESTERN SIDE OF THE SALENTO ISTHMUS

In 2003 the ACVU surveys were once more extended, this time to cover Salento landscapes that until then had not been systematically investigated, on the south-western, Taranto half of the isthmus. This microregion is generally considered to have been part of the territory or *chora* of the Greek colonial roman polis of Taras. The formation and organization of this territory is therefore one of the major issues the field surveys in this area will hopefully shed light on. Because of the preliminary state of our research in the Tarantino, we will not discuss these issues in detail here but limit ourselves to those survey results that are already available. Unfortunately, few other systematic line-walking surveys have been undertaken in the Tarantino to compare ours with, although extensive topographic prospections in the chora were launched by Cocchiaro as early as the 1970s.[53] Intensive, systematic explorations other than our own were initiated only recently in the context of a project by the *Laboratorio di Topografia Antica* of the University of Lecce and the Italian *Consiglio Nazionale delle Ricerche*.[54] Nonetheless, information on landscape organization is still largely limited to detailed inventories of the *Soprintendenza*'s archival registrations of incidental finds and small-scale excavations.[55]

To investigate the possibility of differentiation in the human arrangement of this landscape, it was decided to concentrate the field surveys initially on a 1 km-wide transect that crosscut all major land systems defined in this area.[56] In each of these land systems a sample area of ca. 1 sq.km was to be surveyed, and three have in fact been investigated so far. The most western one (the Palagiano land system) covers the lower marine terraces just behind the ancient dunes and lagoons of the Ionian coast. The easternmost sample area is situated on the Murge plateau itself, just beyond the cliff-like interface with the highest marine terraces. The third land system investigated so far (the Mottola sloping land) is situated just underneath this same cliff-like ridge and covers the fertile soils of the highest marine terraces. These recent ACVU surveys have used the methods that were developed and successfully employed in the context of the RPC project. Since most of the field survey data are still being analysed, we can here present only some preliminary results.

The Mottola land system
The Mottola land system, as defined by Van Joolen (table 3.2),[57] is an undulating, gently sloping land system, traversed by canyon-like river valleys that are sometimes very steeply incised and at least 20 m deep. According to Van Joolen, the results of the archaeological land evaluation show that most of the Mottola landforms were fairly suitable for ancient agriculture. Together with the depressions in the Brindisi plain they were even among the most suitable, compared to the other explored land systems. As is the case in the Brindisi plain, this seems to agree with the field survey data, which suggest a more intensive agricultural use here than in most other land systems of the Taranto area.

Whilst the Bronze Age sites detected during the field surveys are awaiting more precise dating, Early Iron Age occupation can already be dated with relative precision. Our survey data suggest that at least one of the sample areas in the Mottola landscape was reclaimed for human occupation in the course of the 8th century BC after a long phase of marginality. Sometime in the middle of that century one local community founded a settlement *ex novo* on the hill site of L'Amastuola, some 18 km north of Taranto.

---

[53] Cocchiaro 1981.
[54] Guaitoli 2002.
[55] Cocchiaro 1981; Alessio / Guzzo 1989-1990; Lo Porto 1990; Osanna 1992. Cf. also Alessio 2001, Dell'Aglio 2001, Maruggi 2001 and Schojer 2001. For early extensive surveys, see Cocchiaro 1981. Cf. also Greco 1981 and 2001 and Osanna 2001.
[56] Burgers / Crielaard 2007.
[57] Van Joolen 2003, 55-58 and 137-141.

The site is on one of the visually most dominant hill tops in the entire Taranto region. Besides its controlling location, the new settlement seems to have been selected also with a view to exploiting several resource zones; its catchment area offers both fertile soils for cereal cultivation and a coastal lagoonal climate suitable for animal husbandry. The foundation of the new settlement at L'Amastuola closely recalls the 8th-century BC reclamation of other areas on the Salento isthmus that was discussed above. In this respect the Mottola land system seems to conform to a more general pattern.

Another issue that the preliminary analysis of the survey data allows to elaborate on is that of the infill of the landscape with small rural settlements. In the Mottola land system this took place towards the late 4th century BC, with a modest start in the late Classical phase.

The Palagiano land system
The landscape immediately to the north, north-west and north-east of Taranto, called the Palagiano land system by Van Joolen (table 3.2),[58] mainly consists of straight gently sloping land intersected by river valleys with relatively wide floors and terraces. A uniformly steep slope, stretching north of Taranto towards the west and east, connects two areas of different elevations. Within the Palagiano land system a relatively small area was explored in 2003 and 2004. Compared to the other survey areas this yielded low artefact densities and only two definite habitation sites, at which Roman-period material was the most evident, with only a few early Hellenistic shards. However, the low site density in this coastal area must be viewed with caution, because of the recent large-scale agricultural transformations it has undergone. Many fields have been reworked, the surface bulldozed and new irrigation systems installed. Test surveys elsewhere have demonstrated that surface scatters tend to disappear under such conditions.[59]

The Murge land system
The landscape of the Murge Basse has already been discussed above with regard to the 1999 and 2001 field surveys on the Adriatic side of the plateau. In 2003 we began to study the southern side of the Murge tableland, surveying a limited area in small pockets of open fields amongst the typical *macchia* of this part of the Murge.[60] The survey method used here was the same as that employed in the other sample areas, yet the contrast with the Adriatic side of the Murge and with the Mottola land system could not have been more pronounced. Whilst especially in the latter area we detected relatively high artefact densities and high numbers of sites and scatters, hardly any archaeological artefacts were found in the southern Murge. This cannot be explained by reference to sediment cover or to other visibility bias factors such as intensive mechanized agriculture, since the fields surveyed here were open, without significant relief or vegetation cover, and have very thin soils which were never treated as the soils of the Palagiano land system have been. There is in fact every reason to conclude that this sample area was really completely void of ancient settlement. Future study will determine if it was used or frequented at all by the inhabitants of nearby nucleated settlements not yet discovered, but it already seems clear that the area can have been used only marginally.

[58] Van Joolen 2003, 59-62.
[59] E.g., Thompson 2004.
[60] Burgers / Crielaard 2007.

3.4 CONCLUDING DISCUSSION

In the present chapter we have presented and discussed the main land systems of the Salento isthmus region in relation to the results of field surveys and other archaeological datasets. Our aim was to highlight intra-regional differences and similarities in the dynamics of the ancient human organization of the landscape. We first presented environmental studies which demonstrate that in the late Neolithic/Early Bronze Age and in the 1st millennium BC humans must have been instrumental in bringing about major changes in the landscape. Contemporary processes of upland erosion and related sedimentation in valleys and (coastal) plains are generally believed to have been caused by the expansion of agriculture and the corresponding woodland clearance. Focusing on the 1st millennium BC, we turned to the individual land systems of the Salento isthmus and the relevant archaeological datasets. We have mostly drawn on the ACVU field survey datasets, which represent well-studied sample areas within specific land systems and which focus on the central Brindisi plain, the coastal areas north and south of Brindisi, and the Adriatic side of the Murge tableland. We concluded our review with a brief discussion of the results of the most recent ACVU field surveys in the Tarantino.

With the exception of the Taranto Murge, all of these landscapes have produced evidence to suggest that the local communities have, to various degrees, been involved in processes of centralization and urbanization. If for example the systematic excavations and surveys discussed above are representative of the many accidentally discovered Iron Age sites on the Salento isthmus, we must conclude that during the 8th century BC local communities engaged in settlement expansion, rural infill and reclamation of previously non-exploited or only marginally exploited landscapes. This applies to almost all major Salento landscapes, from the Brindisi plain and the Murge tableland to the Taranto area. It therefore appears that the groups of Greek immigrants that according to the literary sources settled on the Ionian shores were only some of the many actors in a regional context of great ferment; in chapter 6 we will develop this theme. In chapter 7 we will propose that during the subsequent centuries processes such as urbanization, socio-economic differentiation and political centralization were *not* mainly confined to the polis of Taras. Instead the indigenous communities of the Salento isthmus continued to play a prominent and active role in changes that affected all parts of the peninsula in the Archaic period.

We have shown that urbanization became particularly intense in the early Hellenistic period, but it affected the land systems discussed here to various degrees. Among the least affected was the Murge tableland, particularly its western part which has so far yielded only a few contemporary village sites and no rural infill at all. We can contrast this with the adjacent, gently sloping terraces of the Mottola land system, where in the early Hellenistic period exploitation appears to have reached its maximum with isolated rural sites and small villages that were distributed throughout the landscape. The emergence of this intensively cultivated landscape can only be explained by the contemporary growth in political and economic power of the polis of Taras. Significantly, an equally intense town-country relationship emerged at the same time on the eastern side of the Salento isthmus, in the Brindisi plain. Here, even marginal areas demonstrably turned into rural territories and became filled with isolated farms and small hamlets. During this large-scale settlement of the countryside existing local villages became central places, each with its own flourishing hinterland. In chapter 8 this phenomenon will be put at the centre of a comparative macro-regional analysis.

Finally, the integration of the Salento isthmus into the Roman orbit (to be discussed in section 8.8) brought about a different but equally diversified landscape. Some areas, such as the Mottola landscape, the coastal area south of Brindisi and the southern expanses of the *piana messapica,* seem to have been mostly abandoned. Others demonstrably flourished, with specialized rural sites producing for an external market. Examples are the northern periphery of the Brindisino and the zone along the central axis of the Salento isthmus, where the Romans constructed the Via Appia at least as early as the 2nd century BC. The Roman colony of Brundisium became the undisputed centre of this hinterland.

4 Settlement Dynamics of the Sibaritide and its Hinterland

4.1 INTRODUCTION

In this chapter we discuss settlement dynamics in the RPC study area in the Sibaritide and its hinterland with a special focus on the catchment area and hinterland of the protohistorical settlement of Timpone della Motta. The site of Timpone della Motta has been excavated by the Groningen Institute of Archaeology (GIA) since 1991 under the direction of Prof. Marianne Kleibrink, who continued and extended the earlier Italian excavations of the late 1960s and 1970s.[1] Systematic surveys in a 5 km- radius around the site started in 2000 as part of the third and last campaign that was carried out within the RPC scheme. It continued earlier topographical work carried out by members of the excavation team in the surroundings of Timpone della Motta. Since then the excavations at Timpone della Motta and the surveys in its catchment area have continued on an annual basis. In 2003 the surveys were incorporated in the Raganello Archaeological Project (RAP) under the direction of Attema and Van Leusen. Present knowledge of the patterns of protohistorical settlement in the Sibaritide (Bronze Age and Early Iron Age) owes much to the settlement models elaborated by Renato Peroni and his team on the basis of their excavations at Broglio di Trebisacce and the topographical surveys they carried out in the foothills of the Sibaritide. For the Archaic and Hellenistic settlement patterns we have used the sites that were recorded by Lorenzo Quilici and colleagues as a point of reference. The latter sites were recorded during a large-scale archaeological inventory of the Sibaritide plain, foothills and – to some extent - uplands. The studies that were mentioned above will be used to provide the general framework to which we will relate the results of GIA fieldwork on the Timpone della Motta. Some of the new landscape archaeological data of the Raganello Archaeological Project (RAP) have also been incorporated in the present chapter, as an example of how the current settlement models may be refined on the local scale.

This chapter is structured as follows. We will chronologically discuss settlement patterns according to a division of the study area in three physio-geographical units: coastal plain, foothills and hinterland, for which we will use the periods set out in table 4.1. However, we will first take a look at environmental change and historic land use.

Middle Bronze Age		1700 – 1350 BC
Late Bronze Age	Recent Bronze Age	1350 – 1200 BC
	Final Bronze Age	1200 – 1000 BC
Iron Age		1000 – 750 BC
Archaic		750 – 480 BC
Classical		480 – 325 BC
Early Hellenistic		325 – 200 BC
Late Hellenistic / late Republican		200 – 30 BC

Table 4.1. Simplified chronological scheme for South Italy.

[1] The current GIA excavations at Timpone della Motta are directed by Prof. Attema and Dr. J. Kindberg Jacobsen.

4.2 ENVIRONMENT AND HISTORIC LAND USE

The study area discussed in this chapter is in the northern part of the present-day province of Calabria, near the modern village of Francavilla Marittima. It comprises the central part of the plain of Sybaris and the surrounding foothills as well as the Raganello valley that runs inland towards the Pollino Mountains (fig. 4.1). It includes parts of the three major physical geographical units of the Sibaritide: the coastal plain, the foothills, and the mountainous hinterland. Each of these in turn has been subdivided into several land systems (fig. 4.2).[2]

The wide coastal and alluvial plain of Sybaris borders to the east on the Gulf of Taranto and is surrounded by the foothills of the Pollino/Dolcedorme massif in the north-west and the foothills of the Sila and Mula mountains in the south-west. Various streams drain the hinterland, of which we mention here the Crati river and the *torrente* (seasonal river) Raganello. These meander through vast beds composed of gravels, stones and boulders that dissect the plain and carve it up into roughly parallel strips of land. The sediments of the plain consist of thick layers of clay and clayey silts, with occasionally intermediary layers of peat or peaty clay.

The foothills that surround the coastal plain reach elevations up to 700 m above sea level. Several ranges have formed that are separated by river valleys. The ranges themselves are dissected by smaller streams and gullies. Over time the major rivers have created broad alluvial fans that extend far into the plain. These are visible in the landscape as gently sloping land surfaces. The foothills have always been favoured as suitable settlement locations as is evident from the even spacing of historical villages such as Dòria, Cassano allo Ionio, Francavilla Marittima, Cerchiara di Calabria and Trebisacce, all located in the northern part of the Sibaritide. The Sibaritide population's preference for the foothills was probably prompted by the marshy and therefore malarial conditions that dominated the plain before the land improvements of the 20th century, as well as by the stifling heat that makes life in the plain during summer quite unpleasant.

The third physical geographical unit consists of the mountainous hinterland along the valley of the Raganello, and the valley itself. Rising in the Pollino massif at a height of 900 m, the Raganello first works its way through a narrow canyon into an upland valley at San Lorenzo Bellizi. It then enters another canyon ending near the village of Città, whence it proceeds through the foothills to enter the plain near the archaeological site of Timpone della Motta. This, with the sites of Broglio di Trebisacce and Torre Mordillo, is one of the main protohistorical settlements in the Sibaritide.

As was the case for the Pontine region discussed earlier in this volume (chapter 3), environmental change in the later Holocene can be described in two sections. The first involves long-term climatic change, especially fluctuations in precipitation, and long-term changes caused by human exploitation of the landscape, such as clearance of woodland for agricultural purposes and grazing, both of which will have intensified erosion and sedimentation. To this end we will discuss a pollen diagram from the mountainous hinterland, and sedimentation studies that we carried out in the plain. The second section deals with the modern mechanized landscape in the plain of the Sibaritide, which led to the virtual elimination of its marshlands, as was the case in the Pontine region in the 20th century.[3] First, however, we present a short overview of climate and human impact as factors in landscape change.

---

[2] Van Joolen (2003, 12-13 and 92-99) classified only a small part of the study area. Van Leusen and Feiken (2007) recently produced a complete landscape classification based on geomorphological criteria.

[3] In both regions, some areas were converted to paddies for *risotto* rice (TCI/CNR 1954-1960).

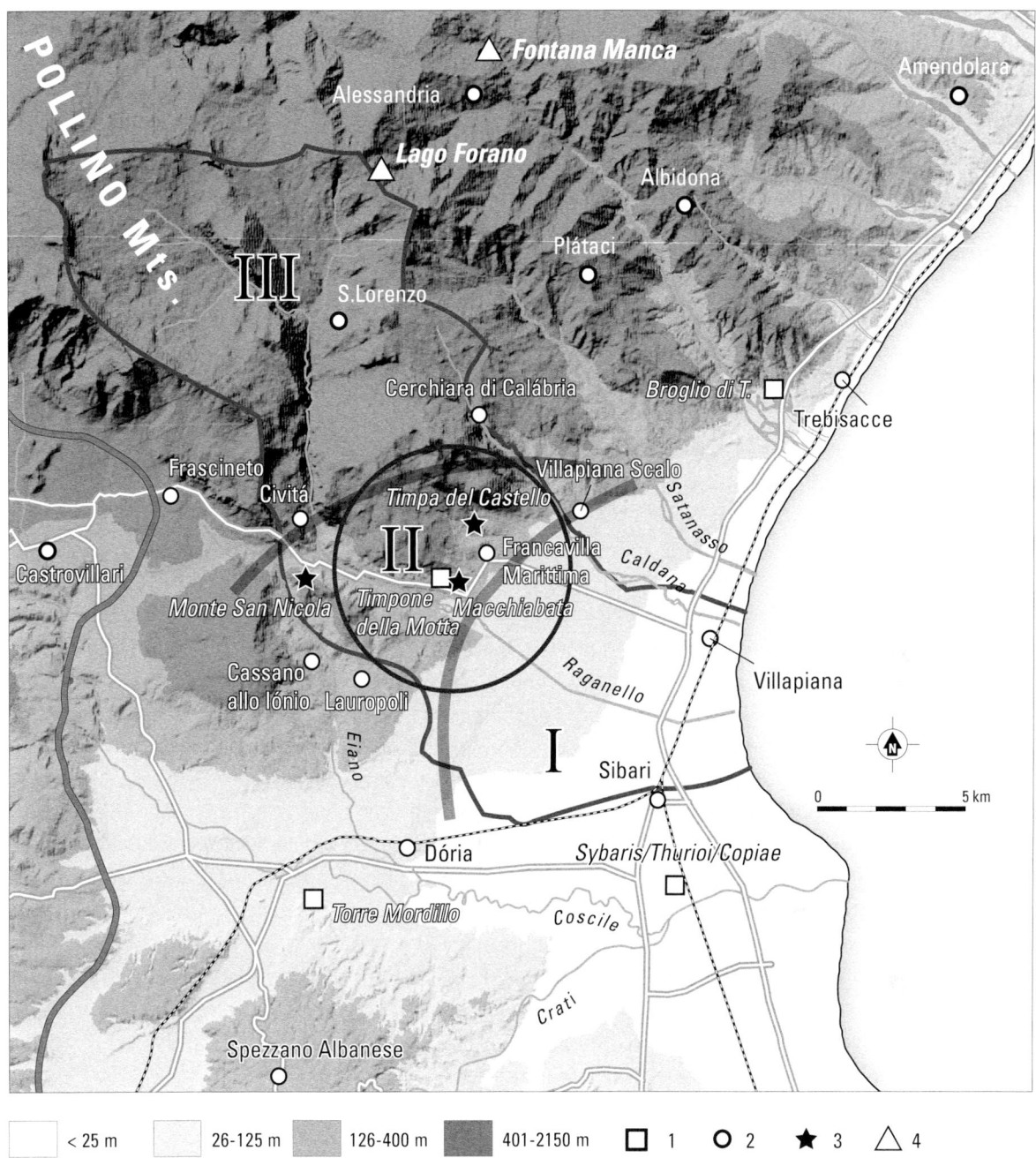

Fig. 4.1. Main features of the Raganello Archaeological Project study area. Main landscape zones: I coastal plain, II foothills, III mountains. 1 main protohistorical sites, with 5km radius catchment of the Timpone della Motta; 2 modern towns; 3 other archaeological sites mentioned in the text; 4 locations of pollen cores. For a colour version of this figure, see page 218.

4.2.1 NATURAL AND HUMAN IMPACT FACTORS IN LANDSCAPE CHANGE

Suitable locations for pollen cores are hard to find in the Sibaritide and its hinterland, and at present pollen-derived information on climate change and human impact on the natural vegetation is based solely on the cores taken at Lago Forano and Fontana Manca.[4] The Lago Forano core was taken in a small depression at 1350 m altitude within the Pollino national park, north of the Monte Sparviere

[4] Kleine et al. 2003 and 2004; Woldring et al. 2006.

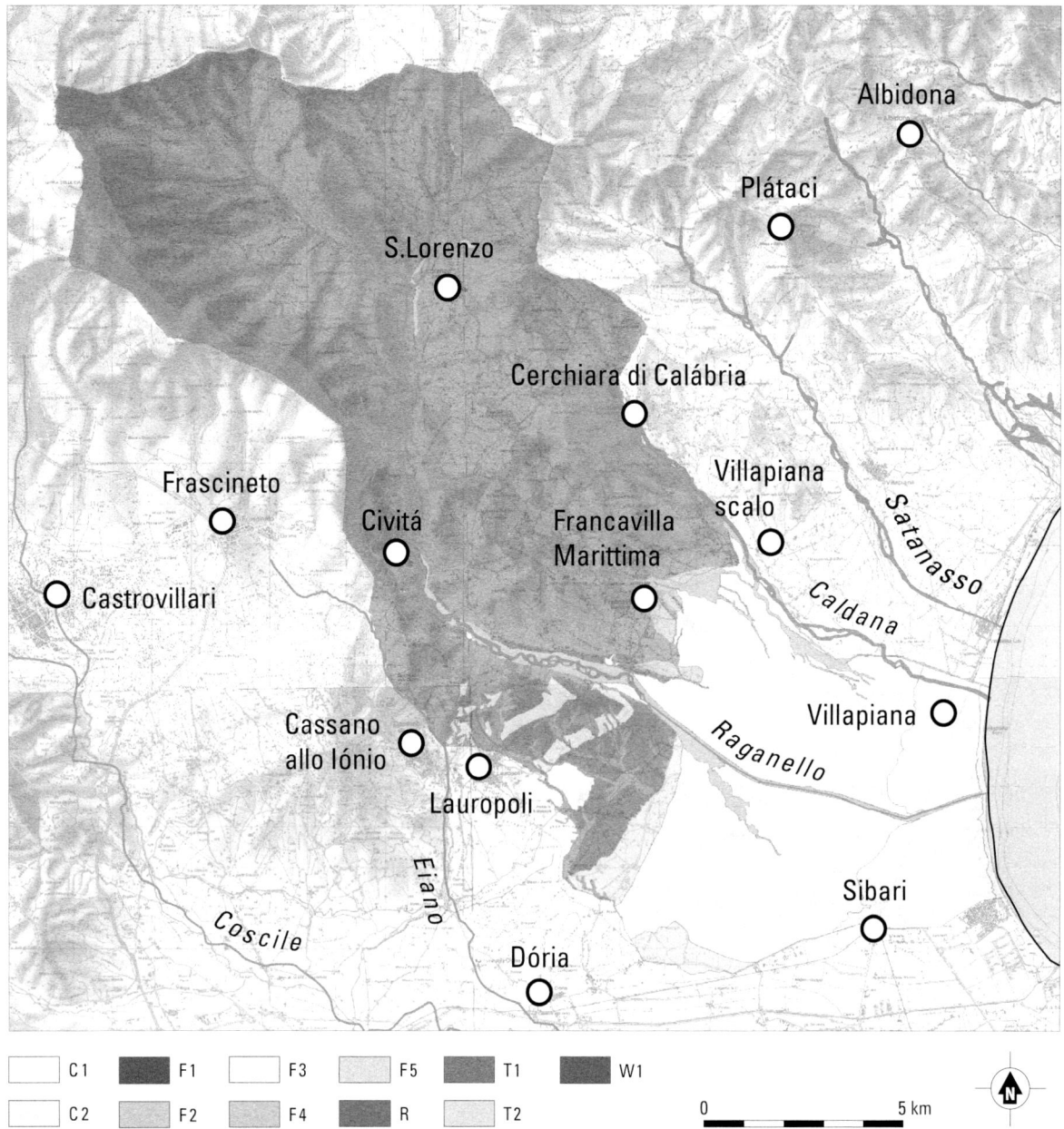

Fig. 4.2. Landscape classification map of the RAP study area. C recent coastal land units with (C2) and without relief (C1); F fluvial land units, ranging from incised gullies (F1) and broader valleys with braided (F2) or meandering (F5) streams to old (F3) and more recent (F4) alluvial fans; T ancient marine cliffs (T2) and terraces (T1); R hard rocks (limestones), forming steep slopes with little soil or vegetation; W1 weak rocks (marls, schists and shales), forming an irregular but gentle topography. For a colour version of this figure, see page 219.

(1713 m) (fig. 4.1). It covers a period from the Late Glacial well into the Bronze Age and contains information on local changes in the vegetation during the Neolithic and Bronze Age. The Fontana Manca core was collected from another small depression, located about 5 km to the north-east of Lago Forano at 960 m altitude; it covers the Final Neolithic and most of the Bronze Age. The pollen diagrams from these two cores add to the overall pollen record of the central and southern Mediterranean.[5] Both contain evidence for human impact on the landscape during the late prehistoric period

[5] cf. Watts et al. 1996; Sadori / Narcisi 2001.

Box 4.1 Pollen evidence for Bronze Age pastoralism

Two pollen cores document the vegetation history of the up- and highland parts of the Raganello watershed area.[A] One was taken at the Lago Forano, on the south-eastern slope of the Pollino massif, in a small depression at 1350 m elevation just to the north-west of the Monte Sparviere (1713 m). The depression consists of an almost horizontal, elongated area of about 100 by 60 m, which is mostly vegetated. At its lowest point, on its eastern edge, there is a small lake in wet periods of the year, turning into a bare patch of soil in dry periods. The flat is surrounded by smooth, not very steep slopes of rounded hills that reach 18 to 60 m above the depression floor. On the 1:10,000 scale topographic map, contour lines show that this assemblage forms part of a zone of subdued topography that is about 1300 m long and 300 m wide and constitutes the divide between two drainage basins. Outside this zone, the landscape is much more dissected and slopes are much steeper. Over the ages the basin has become filled in with sediments that vary from loamy clay in the upper layers to organic clay and clayey peat in the deeper layers. The second pollen core was collected at Fontana Manca, another now desiccated pond located at Alessandria del Carretto, about 5 km to the north-east of Lago Forano. It too has over time become filled with sediments preserving organic materials and peat. The filled-up depression is about 100 m long and 40 m wide. It is the main part of a small plateau at 960 m altitude on a slope that runs down from a ridge at 1080 m to a valley bottom at about 700 m (see fig. 4.3). In recent times the depression at Fontana Manca was covered by a thick layer of soil from elsewhere in order to fill up the lowest parts and improve the quality of the topsoil. In both depressions cores were taken and analysed at the laboratory of the Groningen Institute of Archaeology.[B] Such depressions are very scarce in an erosion landscape such as the Pollino.

The Lago Forano diagram in combination with seven radiocarbon dates at various levels resulted in a general outline of the Holocene vegetation history of the south-eastern part of the Pollino mountains and imparted information on climate change and human exploitation. For the lower levels of this core there are severe problems of interpretation due to the fact that radiocarbon dates of organic material from the Lago Forano pollen core are too old when compared to Fontana Manca dates, while showing the same pollen curves.[C] The Lago Forano diagram indicates that the climate became more humid around 8740 ± 100 BP relative to the preceding steppe climate that dominated southern Italy in the aftermath of the Late Glacial period. Modest human agricultural activity in the Lago Forano area appears to have started around 8700 BP, and more severe impact in the form of forest clearance started around 7500 BP (estimated date) when the diagram shows a decrease in tree pollen. Around ca. 4700 BP however, a clear and undisputed anthropogenic phase can be observed in the diagram as the number of culture indicators increases. The pollen evidence points to grazing rather than to arable farming, suggesting that the area around Lago Forano was used by herdsmen tending their animals. This evidence for the onset of pastoralism in the Middle Bronze Age in the up- and highlands of the Sibaritide is corroborated by the Fontana Manca diagram, which also produced evidence for the onset of grazing during this period. Moreover the Fontana Manca core contained dung-related spores, indicating that these small upland lakes were used as watering places for animals.

[A] Thanks are due to Jan Delvigne (University of Groningen) who wrote parts of this text.

[B] Collected in 2001 by a team from the Groningen Institute of Archaeology, the Lago Forano core was analysed in the period 2002-2003 by E. Kleine (Kleine et al. 2003, 2004). The Fontana Manca core was collected in 2005 and analysed in 2006 by Y. Boekema (Woldring et al. 2006). Both analyses were carried out under the supervision of H. Woldring at GIA's pollen division.

[C] This problem is discussed in Woldring et al. 2006 and raised serious doubts on the reality of an early anthropogenic phase about the transition of the Mesolithic to Neolithic. However, the problematic early date for the lower levels of the Lago Forano core was confirmed by three new AMS radiocarbon dates in March 2007.

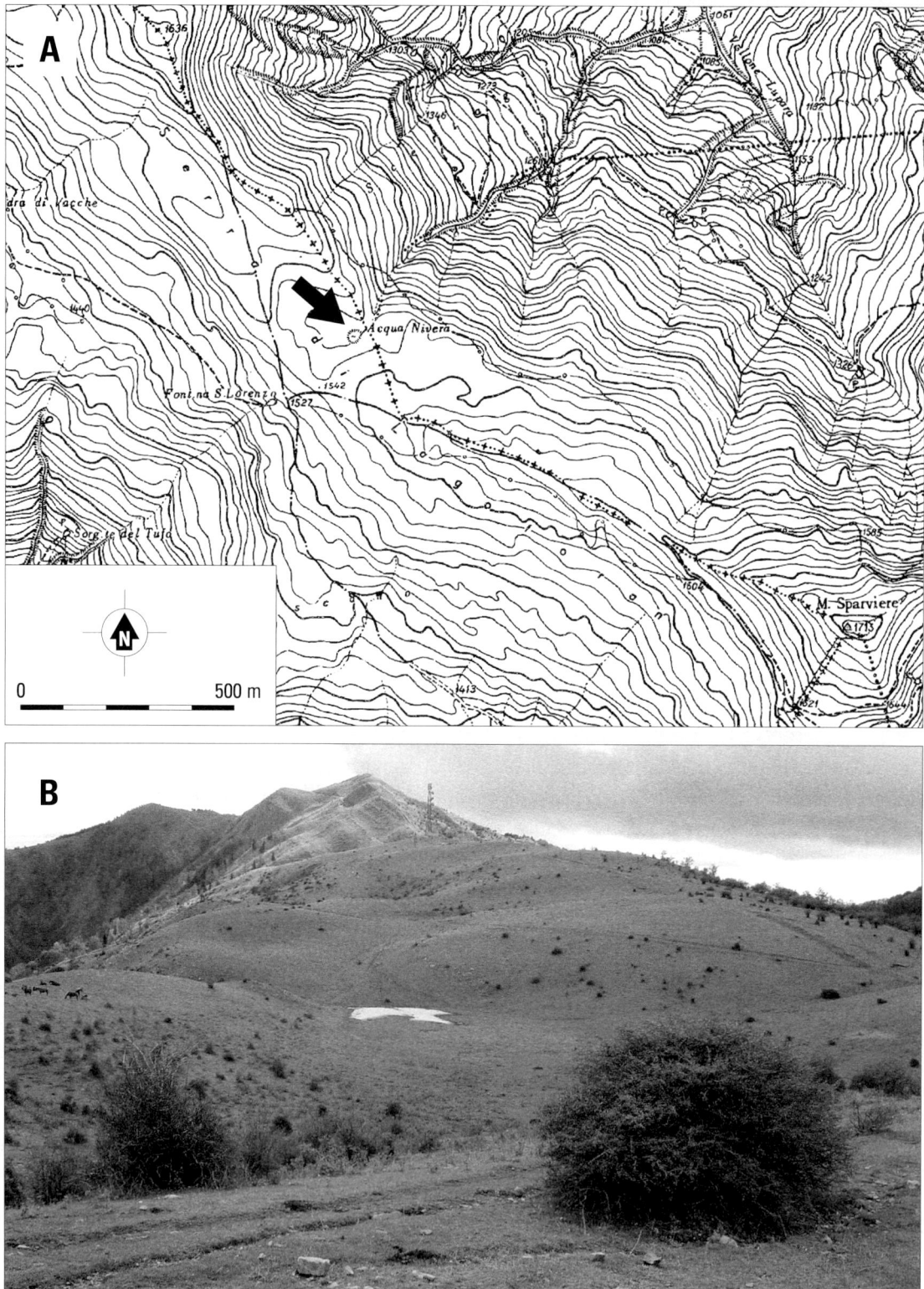

Fig. 4.3. A) orography of the surroundings of the Serra di Lagoforano with the small depression from which the Lago Forano pollen core was collected (Aqua Nivera). Dash-dotted lines: long-distance mule paths (extract from the *Carta Tecnica Regionale*, circa 1955); B) view across the Lago Forano depression, looking south towards the Monte Sparviere (photo Attema, GIA).

> The presence of flocks of sheep or goats in the mountains is often related to short ('vertical') transhumance, which is thought to have been one of the major components of the Bronze Age economy. Before summer herdsmen would go up into the mountains with their livestock to suitable summer meadows, only to return to their winter pastures in the plain before winter set in.[D]
>
> [D] Veenman 2002, 14.

and the Bronze Age, probably in the form of pastoralism. In the Lago Forano diagram this begins around 4700 BP, a period coinciding with the Early Bronze Age, and in the Fontana Manca diagram it occurs slightly later. The pollen evidence indicates grazing rather than arable farming and suggests that the uplands around Lago Forano and Fontana Manca were used by herdsmen tending their flocks. The cores are discussed in more detail in Box 4.1.

A second notable form of human impact on the landscape involves erosion and sedimentation during the later Holocene. From our surveys it appears that protohistorical scatters in the foothills often only surface after serious disturbances of the topsoil, indicating that considerable colluviation has taken place locally. This is a likely indicator of a general vegetational denudation of parts of the foothills from the Neolithic onwards. The same possibly applies to the inland areas along the Raganello. However, our geo-archaeological work in the foothills and uplands has been very limited at the time of writing, and has focused on the plain of Sybaris in order to assess the chronology and rate of recent sedimentation.[6] To this end hand augering up to a maximum depth of 8.5 m was carried out. The sediment type of these cores was studied and peat layers suitable for radiocarbon dating were identified (for details see Box 1.3). There were no radiocarbon dates older than 2150 BP, even at depths over 7 m. From the accumulation of sediments in the plain of Sybaris it is clear that erosion in the hinterland must have been an important factor in landscape change during the Holocene, covering the protohistoric and classical land surfaces under thick sediment and placing them well out of reach of even modern deep-ploughing.

4.2.2 MODERN INFRASTRUCTURAL CHANGE AND THE LANDSCAPE OF ANTIQUITY

In recent times the whole Sibaritide plain has been reclaimed for agriculture. In the 20th century wet areas were eliminated as part of the land improvement schemes, promoted by the Italian state, that have affected most other Italian coastal landscapes as well (cf. the Pontine Region). The main goals were to stimulate arable farming in the fertile parts of the plain and to eradicate malaria. It is unclear whether malaria already reigned in the plain during protohistory and classical antiquity, although a recent thorough study by Sallares based on historiographic research and medical history has made this likely.[7] This means that in antiquity the foothills and inland valleys would have been much healthier places to settle. Historical maps show what the natural environment of the Sibaritide plain may have looked like (fig. 4.4). It was characterized by an alternation of marshy and dry land and dissected by braiding seasonal streams in broad riverbeds full of boulders and stones. It is likely that such marshy conditions also existed in antiquity, on the basis of the peaty layers that characterize the alluvial build-up in the plain but also because the water diverted nowadays for irrigation purposes would still have been available in antiquity. Routes between the coast and the interior probably followed the valley floors, and communication

[6] Hofman 2002; Attema et al. 2004; Van Leusen 2005.   [7] Sallares 2002.

Fig. 4.4. A romantic view of the plain of Sybaris as seen from the foothills (reproduced from P.J. Charrin 1829, *Voyage pittoresque à Naples et en Sicilie*).

between the villages in the foothills was possible by means of a *pedemontana*, a road running along the foothills. Historically known transhumance routes, some of which are still recognizable in the landscape, mark the possible routes that were used to reach the settlements in the interior and the uplands of the Pollino. Some of these routes, which are strongly determined by river valleys and mountain passes, were mapped in the course of the Raganello Archaeological Project (RAP), but it is not yet possible to relate the protohistorical settlement pattern directly to them.[8] The mountainous hinterland of the Pollino today retains much of the original natural landscape and vegetation and is now part of the Pollino national park.

We have briefly illustrated above how natural and anthropogenic changes in the vegetation, geomorphology, hydrology and infrastructure have profoundly affected the landscape of the Sibaritide and its hinterland, and brought about its present state. Obviously it is this latter state that forms the context for our investigation of the archaeological remains, and therefore any reconstruction of the settlement patterns should be evaluated in the light of a paleogeographical landscape reconstruction. Work on this aspect is currently being undertaken in the RAP. Landscape change has also unevenly affected archaeological visibility; the role of visibility and bias in the recording of the archaeological landscape of the Sibaritide from the Neolithic to the Roman period is discussed in Box 1.2.

[8] A full analysis of all protohistorical sites is to take place in 2009-2010.

4.3 SETTLEMENT AND LAND USE IN THE COASTAL PLAIN

4.3.1 PRE- AND PROTOHISTORY

Knowledge of pre- and protohistorical patterns of settlement and land use in the Sibaritide plain is almost non-existent, due to the thick alluvial cover that hides possible remains of those periods (cf. chapter 1 and Box 1.3). Whether or not forms of coastal occupation and exploitation – well attested in other coastal landscapes (e.g., the Pontine Region and Apulia) - existed in the Bronze Age cannot be answered either. The only prehistoric site known in the plain is the Neolithic settlement of Favella, situated on one of the river dunes along the Crati, and this is a strong indication that settlement did take place on favourable locations along the meandering riverbeds.[9] No salt production sites are known in the central Sibaritide, due to the prograding coast in the plain that may have completely covered the type of salt production sites known from the Etruscan and Latial coasts (cf. chapter 2). Apart from its use for human consumption, salt would have been a necessary commodity for cattle in the well-developed pastoral economy of Bronze Age Sibaritide. The nearest protohistorical coastal site that we know of is the Middle Bronze Age site at Tarianne, but this is well outside the actual plain to the north. Agricultural technology in protohistory was probably not developed to such a degree that the heavy alluvial clays could be easily ploughed with wooden ploughshares, and marshy conditions in some places would have precluded arable farming without extensive drainage, but it would be unwise to exclude the plain *a priori* from a reconstruction of the protohistorical subsistence economy. Fishing, hunting, food gathering, winter grazing, and the collection of wood and other resources would have rendered the plain certainly valuable for subsistence, while small-scale arable farming cannot be excluded. The assumption, implicit in the existing literature, that the plain was a marginally settled landscape during protohistory can however not be substantiated because of the thick alluvial cover. Due to this particular environmental circumstance the archaeology of the protohistorical and historical occupation in the foothills of the Sibaritide has received most attention. For various reasons it is, however, likely that permanent settlement first occurred on the elevated parts of the Sibaritide and on the crescent-shaped succession of foothills enclosing the plain. These parts of the landscape offered strategic locations that dominated the plain and controlled the inland routes, contained light and fertile soils and were healthier places to live in, due to their altitude. It is in these parts that centralization of settlement originated, resulting in the important Bronze- and Iron Age settlements of Torre Mordillo, Timpone della Motta and Broglio di Trebisacce. Renato Peroni, the principal investigator of Broglio di Trebisacce, argues that in spite of the incomplete picture of Bronze- and Iron Age settlement in the Sibaritide, we must on the present evidence assume it to have had an unusually high population density, even to the point of reaching the threshold of its carrying capacity.[10] Although this may prove to be overstated, the settlement pattern indicates that when the Greeks arrived to found the colony of Sybaris in the plain near the mouth of the Crati river, they encountered a well-developed indigenous population. Before discussing the recent data and theories on Bronze- and Iron Age centralization in the foothills of the Sibaritide and adjacent uplands, we will first take a look at settlement and environment in the plain during Archaic and Roman times.

4.3.2 ARCHAIC TO ROMAN TIMES: THE COLONY OF SYBARIS

If the plain was indeed hardly inhabited during the pre-Greek period, this situation must have changed very quickly after the Greeks about 720 BC singled out a location in the plain near the coast to found their colony Sybaris. The settlement flourished already by the 6th century BC, and we must assume that

[9] Tiné 1994. [10] Peroni 1994, 835.

the colonists by then cultivated its immediate hinterland on a substantial scale, as they did everywhere else in the wide coastal plains of *Magna Graecia*. They created a *chora* to sustain the growing urban population, in spite of the marshy conditions and endemic malaria from which especially newcomers would have suffered. Although Sallares finds the documentary evidence for malarial conditions in the case of Sybaris not convincing, Bullit points to the passage in Strabo which reads: '… but the city is rendered unhealthy by a river that spreads out into marshes in the neighbourhood'.[11] This implies that the inhabitants of the city and especially those working the land would run a high risk to contract malaria. Even if malaria did not exist, a second disadvantage of settlement in the plain would have been the low workability typical of the heavy alluvial clays that were mentioned earlier. However, in the Iron Age iron ploughshares increasingly replaced wooden ploughshares, and this may have increased the workability.[12] These adverse – at least in principle – environmental conditions apparently did not keep the inhabitants of Archaic Sybaris from developing their initially small colony into a flourishing central place. According to a recent estimate based on a passage in Strabo where he mentions the perimeter of the town in relation to the number of inhabitants: 'Its inhabitants on the Crathis alone completely filled up a circuit of fifty stadia',[13] it may have covered 515 ha.[14] The topographical research carried out by Italian archaeologists into the early phases of Sybaris will hopefully be able to clarify the reliability of this passage.[15]

Apparently the coastal location was so favourable that, according to Strabo, after the destruction of Sybaris in 510 BC by the polis of Kroton Athenians and other Greeks came to live there with the survivors. According to the sources the city would have been refounded in the middle of the 5th century BC. The newcomers, 'although they came there to live with [the survivors], conceived such a contempt for them that they not only slew them but removed the city to another place nearby and named it Thurioi, after a spring of that name.'[16] Ongoing excavations on the site of Sybaris have demonstrated that Thurioi was built in essentially the same location. At the location called Stombi, however, the Archaic houses seemed not to have been overbuilt. Although it grew into a substantial town and the central place for the Sibaritide coastal plain, Thurioi remained smaller than it's predecessor. In its turn, Thurioi was succeeded in the same location by the Roman colony of Copiae, built in the 2nd century BC. The remains of Thurioi and especially of Copiae, which lie at a depth at which groundwater can still be held at bay by continuous pumping, have been extensively excavated, but of the lower levels of Archaic Sybaris little is known outside the Stombi excavations. In section 4.4.5 we will elaborate on the Archaic period found in the lower levels of Sybaris.

In conclusion we may state that the urban continuity of Sybaris-Thurioi-Copiae supports the viability of the town's location in the Archaic period and later, despite the marshy conditions, heavy soils, and malaria. Its success will initially have been mainly due to its position near the coast and on the river Crati, at the hub of inland trade infrastructure and facilitating overseas trade, but it may also have profited from the fertility of the plain. Indeed, the low workability of the alluvial clays does not seem to have prevented the Greeks from farming the plain. The plain's fertility was known in antiquity, and once under cultivation it was very productive. Diodorus Siculus (XI.90.4) states for example that the settlers that refounded Sybaris after its destruction by Kroton 'possessed a fertile land' which allowed them to 'quickly advance in wealth'. That the respective *chorai* of Sybaris, Thurioi, and Copiae were indeed settled appears clear from the extensive augering programme by Rainey and Lerici discussed in chapter 1. On the basis of the augering cores that contained shards dating to the Archaic, Classical and Roman periods De Rossi et al. (1969) indicated several rural sites in their inventory of archaeological sites in the Sibaritide. Unfortunately these augering cores do not allow any precise chronology for the rural infill in the plain, nor do

---

[11] Sallares 2002, 102 and 282; Strabo V.4.13, in Rainey / Lerici 1967, 2.
[12] Van Joolen 2003, 122.
[13] Approximately 10 km; Strabo VI.1.13.
[14] Muggia 2000, 220.
[15] Greco / Luppino 1999.

they offer an understanding of the nature of the buried rural sites, while statistical estimates of the density and extent of the rural site pattern around Sybaris would be unreliable. In the foothills the survey by De Rossi et al. (1969) revealed a dense pattern of isolated Hellenistic farmsteads, hamlets and villages, so we get a much better picture there of the rural infill associated with Hellenistic Thurioi.

In the following sections we will review existing ideas on settlement developments and their historical interpretation, starting with the Middle Bronze Age.

4.4 PROTOHISTORICAL CENTRALIZATION IN THE FOOTHILLS

4.4.1 THE MIDDLE BRONZE AGE

If we accept that people in the protohistorical period, because of the specific environmental conditions and micro-climate in the Sibaritide, would have preferred the foothills and inland valleys as their settlement location over the low-lying and unhealthy plain of Sybaris, then we can sketch the outlines of a model of settlement evolution that centres on the foothills. According to Peroni,[17] the Sibaritide had already by the Middle Bronze Age become a distinct cultural unit divided into territories that were each bounded by two major rivers and characterized by nucleated settlements (fig. 4.5A).[18] How this postulated territorial organization and site pattern of the Middle Bronze Age originated is unknown, as the Early Bronze Age in the Sibaritide is still an enigma in the absence of a clear cultural horizon that would allow us to distinguish the two periods. However, the protohistory specialist, A. Vanzetti, recently tentatively attributed some of the protohistorical surface finds from an intensive survey by the RAP in the catchment area of Timpone della Motta at Francavilla Marittima to the Early Bronze Age.[19] As these finds come from very small scatters widely distributed over the landscape, we may hypothesize that the Middle Bronze Age nucleated pattern grew out of a dispersed Early Bronze Age pattern. The Bronze Age pottery from the survey is now undergoing further study to substantiate this. Other recent research in the Raganello valley suggests that cave sites also must have played an important role in the Late Neolithic and Early Bronze Age settlement system (fig. 4.11).[20]

Peroni and Trucco report a total of 14 sites with shards from the Middle Bronze Age in the Sibaritide, at an average interval of 5 km. These sites fall into two size classes: those of less than 3 ha, and those of 10 ha or more. It should be kept in mind that these estimates are based on geomorphological criteria, not on measurements of actual shard distributions.[21] The total area settled in the form of villages in the Sibaritide would thus add up to over 100 ha. Based on the excavations at Broglio di Trebisacce, village territories would have been completely settled. Taking 100 inhabitants per ha as the norm, Peroni has put forward the hypothesis - already referred to in section 4.3.1 - that certain landscape zones in the Sibaritide may have reached the limits of their carrying capacity already at the end of the Middle Bronze Age.[22] Although he admits that these calculations are highly speculative, Peroni emphasizes that the landscape was probably already under considerable economic pressure. According to Peroni's macro-analysis of the relation between settlement and geological units, sites are preferably located on the natural sand- and conglomerate terraces of the central Sibaritide, which are well-adapted to dry farming. At Broglio di Trebisacce a broad spectrum of cereals that are particularly well adapted to cultivation in an arid climate

---

[16] Strabo VI.1.13.
[17] Peroni 1994, 832-879.
[18] Cf. also Maaskant-Kleibrink 1996-1997, 81.
[19] A. Vanzetti, personal communication.
[20] Larocca 2003.
[21] Vanzetti 2004.
[22] Peroni 1994, 835.

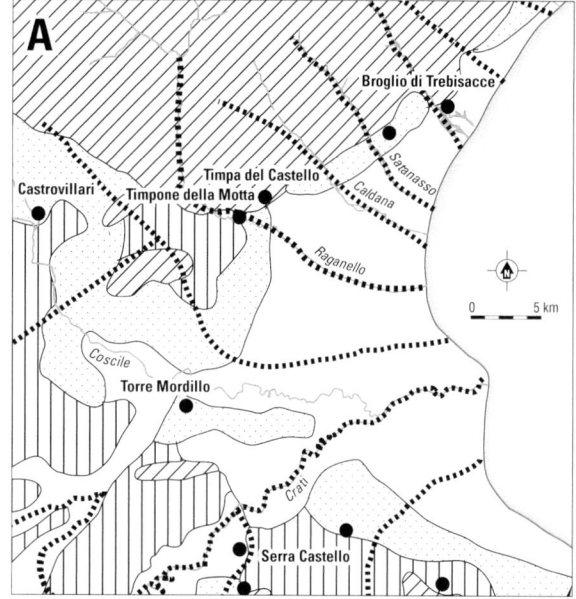
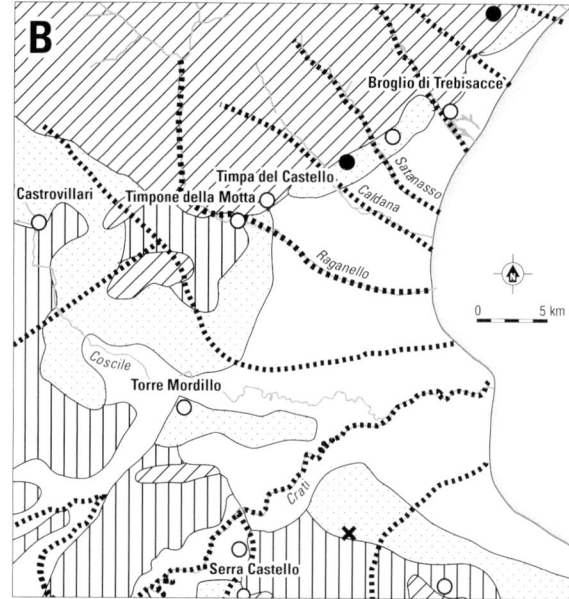
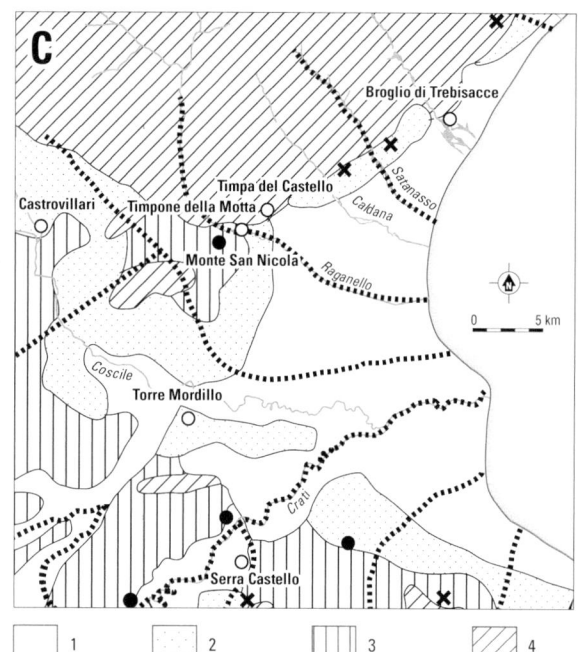

Fig. 4.5. Peroni's Middle (A), Recent (B), and Final Bronze Age (C) settlement models for the Sibaritide (after Peroni / Trucco 1994, figs 227, 229 and 232). Legend: 1 Holocene sediments; 2 terraced sands and conglomerates suitable for seed crops; 3 non-terraced sands and conglomerates; 4 areas suitable for grazing. Closed circle: new site, Open circle: site continuing from previous period, cross: abandoned site. A significant reduction in the number of tribal territories takes place by the end of the Recent Bronze Age.

has been attested from layers dating to the Recent Bronze Age.[23] It seems that the inhabitants chose their settlement locations close to or bordering on, limestone areas which would have provided pasture and woodland. The non-terraced sand- and conglomerate areas of the southern Sibaritide are viewed by Peroni as less suitable for dry-farming. With regard to a possible hierarchy in the settlement system of the Middle Bronze Age, a correlation is noted between the hypothetical size of sites, the quality of their natural defences, and their potential for territorial control.[24] The disparity between the larger, more defensible sites in positions that allow for control over a large territory, and the smaller sites that lack these qualities, suggests that not all sites can be seen as centres of autonomous cells. Peroni does note, however, that at the present state of knowledge 'a true settlement hierarchy was the point of arrival, not of departure, of this

[23] Peroni 1994, 845.

[24] For criteria, see Peroni 1994, 840.

evolution.'²⁵ The non-hierarchical character of the settlement pattern of the Middle Bronze Age is in our opinion supported by the fact that, as far as we know now, a number of potential natural territories did not yet contain a central site.²⁶ Where there was a central site (as at Torre Mordillo, Timpone della Motta at Francavilla Marittima, and Broglio di Trebisacce) the internal settlement hierarchies that led to Bronze Age centralization of settlement in the Sibaritide probably developed gradually. Surveys carried out by the RAP in the territory between the Raganello and Caldanelle rivers now begin to reveal a complex protohistorical pattern of settlement and land use. Analysis of the survey results is expected to reveal the existence of a more complex local hierarchy than has hitherto been supposed.

4.4.2 THE RECENT BRONZE AGE

Society in the Sibaritide had already acquired a certain degree of complexity at the transition to the Recent Bronze Age, and this is expressed in an incipient artisan class and in a control of agricultural production. Such control is especially indicated by olive culture, which requires long-term labour investment needed for this type of agriculture, and is tentatively related by Peroni to a form of elite landownership. Conclusive proof for the production of olive oil is as yet absent for the Recent Bronze Age, but the presence of large storage jars of Aegean type does support it. It is only in the Final Bronze Age that we find such proof at Broglio di Trebisacce through analysis of residues on shards from storage jars (*dolia* in Latin or *pithoi* in Greek) from Final Bronze Age contexts.²⁷ Direct evidence for viticulture has also not yet been found, but given the abundance of drinking cups in Recent Bronze Age layers at this site it seems very likely that there was a local wine production.

Various territories in the foothills and inland were settled in this period, and the correlation between geological units and site location that existed in the Middle Bronze Age becomes less evident (fig. 4.5B). This may indeed point to an increasing pressure on the soils available for dry-farming. An increase in craft specialization is clear, and the finds point to close contacts with the Aegean world. On the basis of this evidence Peroni postulates close contacts between an indigenous artisan class and Aegean craftsmen. These, Peroni believes, were restricted to the larger centres such as Torre Mordillo, Timpone della Motta and Broglio di Trebisacce. The special status of these sites within the settlement system is further emphasized by the investments made in fortification. At the transition between the *Bronze Recente* and *Bronzo Finale* at Torre Mordillo a reinforced earthwork (*terrapieno*) and a wooden palisade were built, whilst palisades with a supposed defensive function have also been found at Broglio di Trebisacce. This is evidence for the creation of defended *acropoleis*, on which structures have been found that must have belonged to the more powerful families within the local communities. Peroni concludes that elite groups became firmly established at the major population centres of the Sibaritide in the Recent Bronze Age.

4.4.3 THE FINAL BRONZE AGE

According to Peroni drastic changes in the settlement pattern occurred in the Final Bronze Age, as 7 out of the 16 sites from the Recent Bronze Age are abandoned at the start of the Final Bronze Age, while 5 new ones are established (fig. 4.5C).²⁸ The latter are reportedly all larger than 10 ha. Peroni notes a tendency for settlements to thin out in the traditionally occupied areas, a process that is partly compensated for by new settlements further inland. There appears to be a difference between the northern and the

---

²⁵ Peroni 1994, 840.

²⁶ Peroni / Trucco 1994, fig. 227.

²⁷ Peroni 1994, 845.

²⁸ Peroni 1994, 855-568.

southern part of the Sibaritide. In the northern part the epicentres are limited to Amendolara, Broglio di Trebisacce and Timpone della Motta/Timpa del Castello, central places that absorbed the territories of the adjacent abandoned centres. We must note, however, that the Final Bronze Age is at present not well-attested on the Timpone della Motta of Francavilla Marittima. No structures from this period have been found on the hilltop, and a 'cabin' on the lower plateau (plateau I) can only hypothetically be placed in the Late Bronze Age. The quantities of material from the Late Bronze Age are, however, convincing enough to allow us to assume continuity of habitation at the site.[29]

In the central and southern part of the Sibaritide the situation is more diverse and discontinuous, with the appearance of new sites and the disappearance of others. The south-eastern part seems quite abandoned, according to Peroni, although this may be due to a lack of research. It has been suggested that the Iron Age settlement at Rossano, at the southern tip of the Sibaritide plain near the coast, was established in this period. The estimated total territory covered by village settlements increased in this period to 150 ha, almost half of which belonged to newly established sites. The abandoned sites were mostly located on or near the sand- and conglomerate terraces, but this does not necessarily imply less emphasis on dry-farming. It is rather very likely that the surviving sites now command larger territories than before, especially in the northern and central Sibaritide where Amendolara, Broglio di Trebisacce, Timpone della Motta/Timpa del Castello at Francavilla Marittima were situated. In the southern Sibaritide there is a tendency to occupy sites located at higher altitudes than before. As Peroni points out, this would have been done for strategic reasons, a trend that was to persist in the Early Iron Age. The new sites are mostly located on the non-terraced sand- and conglomerate units and often near the limestone unit where new territory was being colonized for agriculture. The latter environment is well-adapted to pastoral use.

In Peroni's socio-political analysis the territories controlled by autonomous sites would have been enlarged in tandem with the decrease in site numbers. From north to south, Amendolara now controlled the territory between the rivers Ferro and Avena, Broglio di Trebisacce that between the rivers Avena and Satanasso, and Timpone della Motta and Timpa del Castello together that between the rivers Satanasso and Raganello. Further south, the new site of Monte San Nicola controlled a small territory bordering on the vast one controlled by Torre Mordillo at the confluence of the rivers Crati and Coscile. According to Peroni, Torre Mordillo is the only site with dependent, satellite settlements. On the basis of the geographical analysis as well as its size, it appears that it would have been the dominant site in the Sibaritide. To the south, south-west and west of Torre Mordillo the land was carved up between autonomous sites, similar to the area north of the Raganello.

According to Peroni, the usurpation of new territories and the subjugation of neighbouring sites, as well as the growing preference for strategically located and naturally defended sites, all underscore the belligerent character of Final Bronze Age society. This is also evident from the presence of fortifications and weaponry. Both at Torre Mordillo and Broglio di Trebisacce remains of fortifications from this period have been found. Peroni proposes that the commercial contacts with Mycenaean seafarers in the Recent Bronze Age were part of a redistributive system through which the acquired goods could reach a privileged stratum within the local communities. In the Final Bronze Age this redistributive system appears to have evolved into a regional exchange system, possibly based on objects with an intrinsic value such as the axes and other metal finds that have been found in hoards. The RAP surveys have now revealed a large cluster of small rural sites at Contrada Damale in the vicinity of Timpone della Motta, many of which include *pithos* shards from the Final Bronze Age. This indicates that storage in the Final Bronze Age was no longer restricted to elite families living in the main settlements, but was also practised by families living in the countryside, although these may still have been controlled by elite families.

---

[29] Kleibrink 2006, 177ff.

4.4.4 THE EARLY IRON AGE

There are 18 sites with Early Iron Age material, and as Peroni remarks, that is only four more than the number of sites at the start of the protohistorical cycle in the Middle Bronze Age (fig. 4.5).[30] The area covered by these settlements has, however, doubled to more than 200 ha. If we accept the geomorphological criteria underlying this assumption, and if there were no significant changes in the number of inhabitants per hectare, this would imply that the population at the larger sites doubled during the roughly 700 years of the Middle and Final Bronze Age. No significant changes seem to have occurred at the transition from the Final Bronze Age to the Early Iron Age in the locations of sites in the northern part of the Sibaritide. The situation in the central river valleys and inland was, however, less stable. This may be related to the role of Torre Mordillo, which was now a true central place for the Sibaritide, the socio-political status of which was comparable to that of the large proto-urban centres in the central Tyrrhenian area. In the territory of Torre Mordillo the new satellite site of Pietra Castello di Cassano Ionio was probably founded, which probably had an agricultural function. This is also the case at Cozzo Michelicchio, a site founded on a steep rock at the junction of the rivers Crati and Coscile. There were now three sites at the south-western limit of the territory of Torre Mordillo, while the two sites on the opposite side of the river were abandoned. Inland from Torre Mordillo a new site was founded on the left bank of the river Esaro (Serra Testi) directly opposite the site of Castiglione di Roggiano Gravina. This new site is likewise interpreted by Peroni as part of the defensive system of the territory of Torre Mordillo. In the south-eastern part of the region the Iron Age sites of Rossano and Castiglione di Paludi filled the Final Bronze Age hiatus. The new Iron Age sites were founded on or near good arable land, while the inland sites were abandoned.

In Peroni's view the changes in the settlement pattern in the Early Iron Age were imposed by the elites of the major sites on populations of minor sites in order to expand the population of their territories and strengthen their military and productive potential. The layers with traces of burning at Torre Mordillo that were excavated by the American mission in the 1970s may point to warfare between settlements, although they might just as well result from more innocent causes. The abundance of arms in the graves does indeed suggest that fighting was a regular activity. In the burial grounds of Torre Mordillo and Timpone della Motta lances are frequently present as well as various types of axes. In the Temparella burial ground at Timpone della Motta the lance or spear is part of the standard equipment, and axes also occur frequently.

The growth of the territories of the main settlements may have caused changes in the nature of land ownership. Peroni supposes that there was a development from the earlier 'collective' ownership during the Bronze Age, towards family ownership of the land in the hands of elite families. According to him, the disappearance of the Late Bronze Age *pithoi* suggests that the practice of collective storage was abandoned. It is not yet clear, however, that *pithos* shards from rural sites cannot be dated to the Early Iron Age as well. According to Peroni the appearance of 'satellite sites' on arable soils may be interpreted as an attempt at recolonization of the territory. We think, however, that they may also be interpreted as the spontaneous growth of an inhabited countryside.

4.4.5 THE LATER IRON AGE AND ARCHAIC PERIOD

Evidence concerning the settlement developments in the later Iron Age and Archaic period in the foothills mostly comes from the site of Timpone della Motta. To date, survey in its catchment area has not

---

[30] Peroni 1994, 869-879.

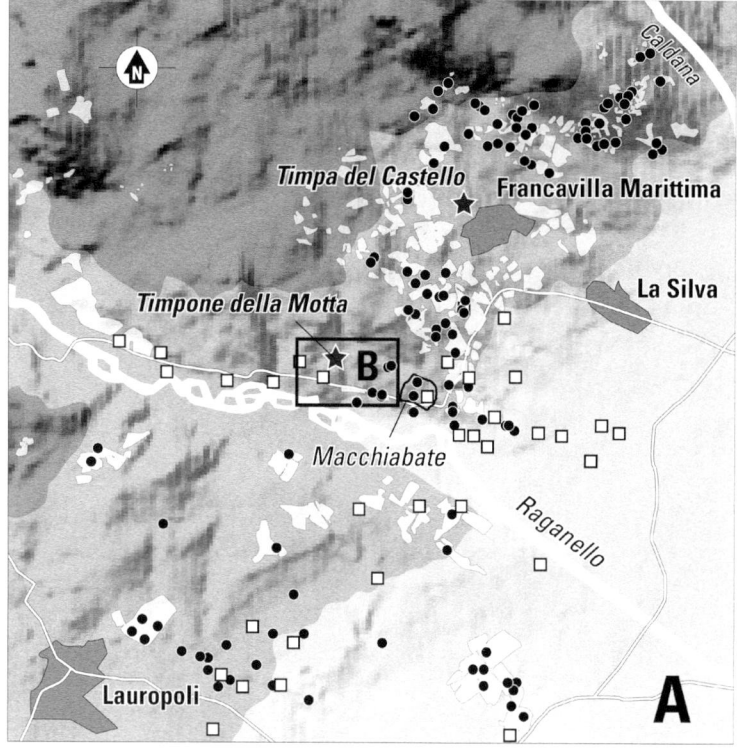

Fig. 4.6. GIA research on and around the Timpone della Motta. A: Areas surveyed intensively in the Timpone della Motta catchment area, with sites recorded in the 1960s (squares) and since 2000 (dots). B: plateaux, trenches and structures on the Timpone della Motta itself. For a colour version of this figure, see page 220.

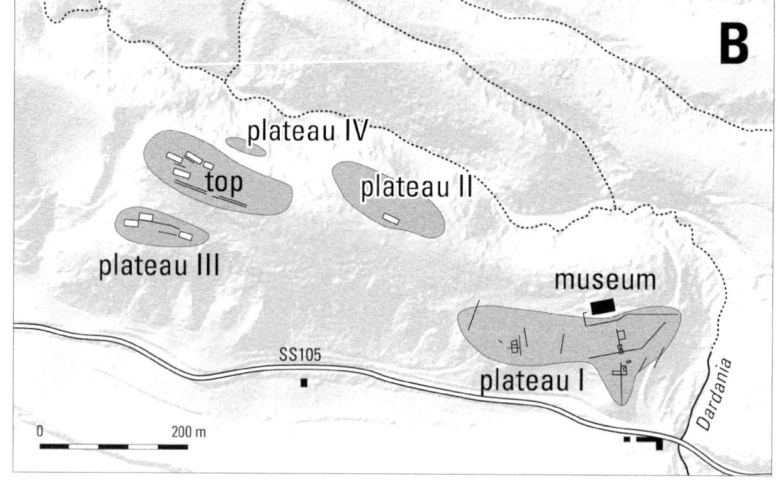

been able to reveal a late Iron Age and/or Archaic rural pattern and we therefore largely depend on the settlement data from the excavations at Timpone della Motta, which we will discuss briefly here.

During the campaigns of 1996-1998 GIA researchers recorded a dense surface distribution of 6th-century BC pottery on the lowest, and most spacious, plateau I of the settlement (fig. 4.6B). Subsequently they located many remains of walls in a number of test trenches. The finds pointed to a phase of intensive use of this plateau in the Archaic period.[31] The excavations that followed the test trenches resulted in the uncovering of one fairly complete house plan (the Casa Aperta) and three less well preserved plans, including that of the Casa al Muro Grande. The latter covered a fine example of an 8th-century BC indigenous hut that probably still stood in the early decades of the 7th century BC, when it was abandoned and subsequently destroyed by fire.[32] However, there remains a gap of at least one century between the

[31] Attema *et al.* 2000; Kleibrink 2006.

[32] The fill probably has a closing date in the last part of the 8th/early part of the 7th century BC, on the basis of pottery attributable to the Thapsos class, and imitations thereof; Kleibrink 2006, 109-110.

'Oenotrian' Iron Age habitation and the Greek 'colonial' house of Muro Grande. In the case of the Casa Aperta in the eastern part of plateau I, no superimposed layers indicating continuous habitation from the Iron Age into the Archaic period were found *in situ* either. However, the fill of a depression that was probably part of a *fossa* defending the lower settlement, to the south of the Casa Aperta, contained settlement debris of both the Bronze Age and Early Iron Age. The excavator believes that this deposit is 'too immense a feature to contain only the debris of one or two earlier huts. […] the Geometric habitation on Plateau I of the Timpone della Motta may have been substantial, but was obliterated prior to the Archaic occupation of the plateau. Considering the richness of the Macchiabate cemetery and the Oenotrian hut underneath the Casa al Muro Grande, this is not surprising.'[33]

Another instance of possible continuity is a house structure on one of the higher plateaus, excavated during the late 1960s and early 1970s, that was known as the Casa dei Pithoi. On excavating the house floors several postholes were observed that had been dug into the conglomerate bedrock. These were interpreted by Kleibrink as postholes indicating the presence of Iron-Age timber buildings that preceded the Archaic building phase. The postholes were reused in the Archaic period as *pithos* pits.[34] It is however not clear whether there were also shards from the 7th and early 6th centuries BC. During the early excavations two more houses were uncovered on plateau II, the Casa della Cucina and the Casa dei Pesi, but these did not show continuity with an earlier phase but were newly founded. In the course of the GIA excavations of the 1990s, more house remains of the 6th century BC were uncovered on the various plateaus of the site, such as the Casa dell'Anfora and the Casa dei Clandestini on plateau III. On plateau II too, another house was found,[35] but none of these houses yielded evidence for previous Iron Age phases. With regard to domestic housing, the period of the 7th and early 6th centuries BC is therefore very poorly represented, and this is in contrast with the monumental ritual buildings found in the sanctuary in this period (see section 4.4.6 and Box 5.1).

On the other hand, we saw above that there is abundant evidence for Archaic housing from the middle of the 6th century BC. The wall foundations of the Archaic houses at Timpone della Motta are in all cases constructed out of river cobbles. This is similar to the construction method of the houses at Stombi and Amendolara San Nicola, while there are also many similarities in the house plans. However, unlike the houses at Stombi and Amendolara San Nicola, the houses at Timpone della Motta are not part of an urban lay-out with paved streets, nor did they have tile-covered roofs. The Archaic settlement at Timpone della Motta is therefore best characterized as a loosely organised rural village with habitations dispersed over the various plateaus.

Simultaneous with the change from huts to houses at Timpone della Motta there was a transition from a tradition with predominantly indigenous handmade impasto pottery in domestic contexts, to contexts in which a locally produced Greek *instrumentum domesticum* became the standard. With a few exceptions, the people living in the Archaic houses at Timpone dell Motta appear to have used the same set of pots as those living in the Archaic habitation quarter of Stombi in the Greek colony of Sybaris.[36] This is a clear cultural break with the preceding period. Fabric research conducted by Mater indicated that almost all fabric groups from Timpone della Motta are represented in the pottery sample from Sybaris/Stombi, which suggests close cultural relationships and participation in the same trading network. Although pottery kilns have only been recorded in the Sibaritide at Sybaris Stombi (and Amendolara San Nicola), Mater thinks that there is enough evidence to suppose that workshops at several different locations distributed their products around the region.[37]

In conclusion, the introduction at Timpone della Motta during the 6th century BC of houses on stone foundations, as well as the widespread use of Greek pottery in the domestic sphere, can be interpreted as

---

[33] Kleibrink 2006, 54.

[34] Maaskant Kleibrink 1970-1971; 1977.

[35] Attema / Weterings 1999.

[36] Mater 2005, chapter 4.

[37] Mater 2005, 123.

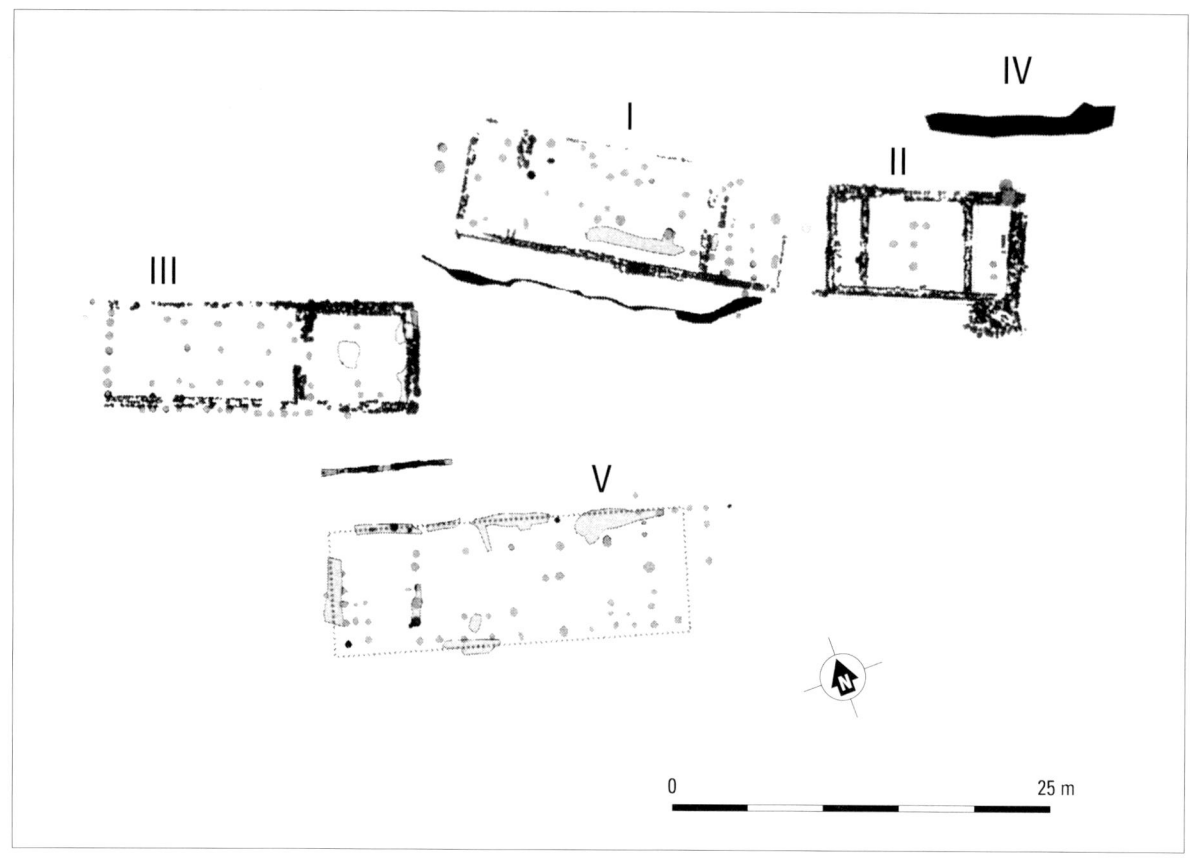

Fig. 4.7. Sacred buildings in the sanctuary on the top of the Timpone della Motta (Francavilla Marittima, Scavi Kleibrink 1991-2005; plan: H. Waterbolk, GIA).

signs of the profound transformation that the local community went through in this period. The archaeological evidence certainly raises the question of continuity or discontinuity between the 'indigenous' Iron Age and the 'colonial' Archaic period on the level of domestic housing. The situation is, however, different in the sanctuary on the summit of the Timpone from that in the contemporary necropolis of Macchiabate, which we will discuss in the next section.

4.4.6 CONTINUITY IN THE SANCTUARY OF TIMPONE DELLA MOTTA AND IN THE NECROPOLIS OF MACCHIABATE

The GIA excavations demonstrated that, whereas the Archaic Athenaion that was discovered and excavated in the 1960s began as an indigenous cult place in the early-8th century BC or before, occupation of the hilltop had already begun by the Middle Bronze Age. The excavations of the 1960s in the sanctuary area resulted in the discovery of three Archaic temples with stone foundations, whilst a fourth building was excavated at a later stage by the Archaeological *Soprintendenza* (fig. 4.7).[38] On the evidence of postholes that were found within these structures, the excavator, Kleibrink, was convinced that there had to be an earlier phase characterized by wooden structures. The postholes were relatively easy to recognize as they were partly dug into the conglomerate bedrock, and it was therefore decided to also clear an area south of building III. Here, beneath a thick layer of loose gravelly soil, the Groningen team found evi-

[38] Kleibrink 2003, with references.

Fig. 4.8. View of the excavations in the Macchiabate cemetery directed in the 1960s by Paola Zancani Montuoro (reproduced from *Scavi a Francavilla Marittima, Estratto dagli Atti e Memorie della Società Magna Grecia* N.S. VI, 1965).

dence for yet another building that was labelled building V. This building was found to have a sequence of construction phases, starting in the Iron Age (8th century BC) with a large wooden house with an apse at its eastern end, a hearth in its western part and a loom in the central space.[39] Around 725/700 BC this was replaced by a wooden temple that was dated on the basis of Thapsos pottery in combination with east-Greek jugs and indigenous 'Oenotrian' matt-painted pottery; and finally around 650 BC by a mud-brick temple. This final building phase was separated from the preceding one by a stratum of yellowish soil that had been used to cover the remains of the wooden temple. The foundation trenches of the mud-brick temple had been cut into the conglomerate rock, and they could be dated on the basis of large quantities of proto-Corinthian shards to the mid-7th century BC. We will not here discuss the details of this excavation or the specific cultic functions of the sacred buildings, for which we refer to Box 5.1. We do, however, wish to emphasize the continuity of cultic occupation on the top of Timpone della Motta and its implications for the interaction between Greeks and Oenotrians, which were both involved in the cult activities. This shows that early Greek colonization was a complex phenomenon of cultural interaction and also that, in the specific ritual context at the Timpone della Motta, it was apparently not necessarily a matter of Greek dominance. The cult place on the Timpone della Motta at Francavilla Marittima presents us therefore with a rare instance of continuity in the settlement history of the Sibaritide, in which indigenous and Greek elements were combined.

A second example of such continuity can be found in the Macchiabate cemetery. The community living in the settlement at Timpone della Motta buried its dead in the nearby cemetery of Macchiabate. Fig. 4.8 is a photograph of the excavations that took place here in the 1960s under Paola Zancani Montuoro. Analyses of the Macchiabate burials by Kleibrink and Vink have indicated that the spatial configuration of the necropolis was based on kinship ties within a ranked community and that it remained stable between the 8th and 7th centuries BC.[40] The chronological analysis of the grave goods further shows that the deposition of sets of indigenous pottery continued despite the increasing presence of Greek pottery, which demonstrates that the indigenous population only gradually adopted Greek material culture in their grave inventories.[41] This suggests continued indigenous use of the cemetery in the 7th century BC, which in turn implies continuous settlement of the area around the cemetery between the Iron Age and

[39] There appears to be no continuity with an earlier hut structure from the Middle Bronze Age in the same location.

[40] Kleibrink 2003.

[41] Vink 1995.

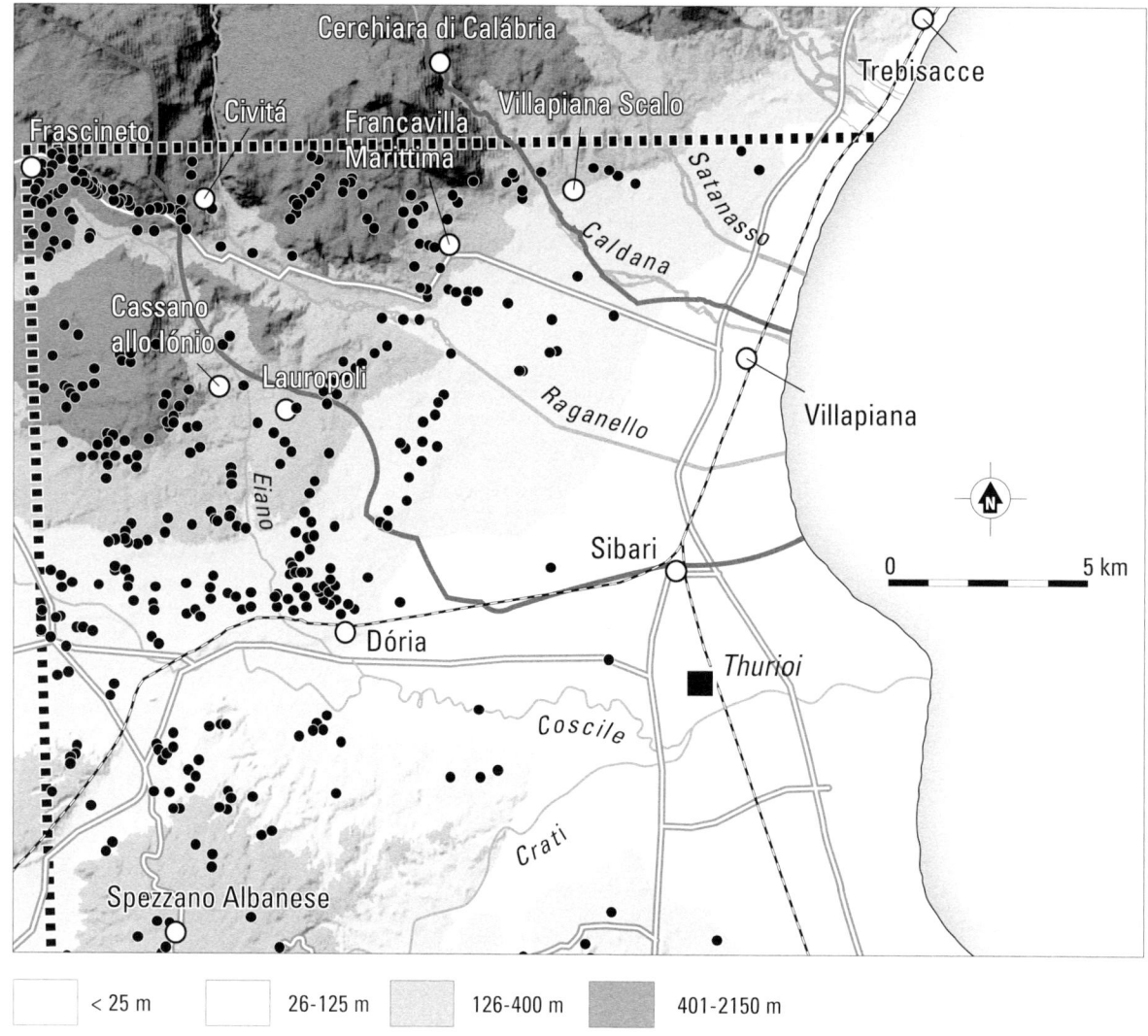

Fig. 4.9. Distribution of rural Hellenistic sites in the central Sibaritide (map compiled from site data published by De Rossi *et al.* 1969; their study area includes the foothill zone but not the mountain area). The outline of the RAP study area is added for orientation. For a colour version of this figure, see page 221.

Archaic periods. So far, however, we have not been able to find signs of 7th-century occupation on the Timpone itself, as was discussed in section 4.4.5, or in the surrounding rural landscape of the foothills. One of the most pressing questions for the RAP is therefore whether any rural infill that can be associated with the period of the indigenous sanctuary at Timpone della Motta and the foundation of Sybaris is present in the wider landscape.

4.5 THE CONTRIBUTION OF FIELD SURVEY: THE RAGANELLO ARCHAEOLOGICAL PROJECT

To conclude this chapter we may briefly review the field survey's contributions to the archaeological evidence for settlement and land use in the Sibaritide. Surface finds of pottery shards and remains of building materials in ploughed fields are our main sources of information for the reconstruction of the

[42] Mater 2005, 101-123.

rural landscape. With regard to the pottery in domestic contexts at Timpone della Motta, the conclusion was that there was a transition in the later Iron Age from a tradition with predominantly indigenous handmade impasto pottery to contexts in which a locally produced Greek *instrumentum domesticum* became the standard. The large-scale adoption of locally-made Greek pottery forms was a 6th-century BC phenomenon, and it has been demonstrated recently that Sybaris played a pivotal role in the distribution of such pottery.[42] Forms and fabrics of pottery found at Timpone della Motta resemble those of pottery manufactured in the kilns found in association with the 6th-century BC houses at Stombi in Sybaris, and this proves the economic and cultural ties between the two sites. With regard to house plans and domestic structures, we concluded that the transition from timber buildings and wattle-and-daub huts to houses with stone foundations must also be dated to the (late) Archaic period. The similarity between the 6th-century BC houses at Stombi in Sybaris and the Archaic houses from Timpone della Motta that we discussed earlier is pertinent. It was already mentioned that the houses at the Timpone do not have tile-covered roofs, and are not part of an urban plan, as do the houses at Stombi in Sybaris. This underscores another relation that arose in the 6th century BC, that of town and countryside. On the one hand there was the expanding urban core of Sybaris – which, as discussed earlier, has been estimated at ca. 500 hectares in this period - and on the other the small rural village at Timpone della Motta. Such a relationship can be seen as an aspect of an urbanizing society. The physical results of this urbanization process become clear when we look at fig. 4.9. The black dots on this map are sites where the Italian survey team in the late 1960s recorded Hellenistic and sporadically also Roman potshards, i.e. materials from the 4th century BC and later. It is an impressive quantity, but this distribution map presents some problems related to archaeological visibility (see also chapter 1). Among other things, the original map (see fig. 1.5) shows the location of the hundreds of mechanical augering samples that were taken by a team of archaeologists from the university of Pennsylvania during the search for Sybaris in the 1960s. It appears from their publication that many of these cores contained archaeological remains. While these cannot be dated precisely and therefore do not constitute proof, it does support the idea that a - locally - densely settled rural landscape developed around Sybaris in the Archaic, Classical and Hellenistic periods, which may have resembled the rural development that we know from the Metapontine plain. Unlike the situation in the Metapontine plain, however, the absence thus far of Archaic and Classical rural sites in the foothills may be attributed to the fact that Sybaris never completed its 5th-century expansion – having been destroyed in 510 BC by its neighbouring polis, Kroton – and that it had an exceptionally large plain in which to expand. Our sedimentation studies have so far shown that the Roman surface in some locations lies buried more than seven meters below the present surface, so that even deep-ploughing could not bring up any buried archaeology. Our knowledge of the rural landscape therefore depends on those areas that have not been covered by alluvium, i.e. the foothills and the uplands. With regard to the rural sites known in the foothills and uplands there is a second problem of archaeological visibility, one concerning the nature of the pottery and the architectural remains. As is well known, the material culture of the Archaic to Hellenistic periods is much more visible than that of earlier periods, since people began to use more durable architectural materials such as stones for the foundations of their farmsteads and houses, and (in the Hellenistic period) heavy terracotta tiles to cover the roofs. The pottery, too, is easier to identify on the surface of ploughed fields because of its often bright-orange or pale-yellowish colours, while its resistance to weathering and mechanical degradation is generally much better as well. To account for this research bias we started a programme of high-intensity surveys in the foothills around Timpone della Motta, using collection units of 50 x 50 meters with a 20% coverage and total sampling.

Fig. 4.6A shows the areas that have been covered since 1995 within the catchment area of Timpone della Motta. This has resulted in a density of protohistorical sites, unprecedented in southern Italy (fig. 4.10). The sites generally appear as small scatters of worn pottery in ploughed fields, and they can only be discovered by means of high-intensity survey techniques or on locations where the soil was recently disturbed by erosion, agriculture or construction work (see Box 4.2). The dissected landscape between

Box 4.2 Research and visibility biases of the Sibaritide hinterland

The Sibaritide foothill zone, between the elevations of about 25 and 400 m above sea level, is where we find the traditional, pre-20th-century villages, a relatively fine-branched infrastructure of roads, paths and tracks, and most of the small-scale arable farming. This is also the zone that is most suitable for modern systematic archaeological surveying, with a high percentage of intensively worked but unenclosed land. It also contains the majority of the known archaeological sites, which is not a coincidence. At higher elevations and further inland, *macchia* and managed oak forest become prominent, and fields tend to be less intensively cultivated because steep outcrops of limestone rocks limit accessibility. It is therefore not surprising that our knowledge is most complete for the foothills and seemingly also least biased. Indeed, our coverage of accessible fields in the foothill zone on either side of the village of Francavilla Marittima is now (2005) almost complete, and some 126 sites have been recorded in an area of just under 6 sq.km.

However, at larger scales new bias factors occur. Our surveys have shown that local slope processes and plough-induced erosion and sedimentation have created agricultural terraces that were later reinforced by the construction of terrace retaining walls. These processes have resulted in a curious phenomenon, viz. that many scatters of archaeological ceramics are discovered at the top of a field – just below one of these terrace walls – and very few at the bottom of a field. The intensity of modern tillage also varies at this scale, with some landowners effecting major changes to the lay-out of their properties (levelling, removal of field boundaries, ploughing unusually deep). The archaeological effects of this vary according to the type of soil disturbance: in one area deep ploughing may turn up several new sites that were previously buried below plough depth, while in another all topsoil may have been bulldozed off to fill a small gully nearby, leaving the field archaeologically sterile. Finally, the geological complexity of the foothill zone means that visibility factors during the survey can vary almost on a field-by-field basis. For example, the underlying geology in some fields consists of strongly to weakly cemented river cobbles and gravel which, when ploughed to the surface, make it very difficult to distinguish archaeological materials such as protohistoric impasto ceramics. In other fields, ploughed-up pieces of schist almost perfectly mimic certain types of ceramics, both in colour and thickness, and even in curvature. If we want to interpret the fine pattern that emerges from this well-investigated zone, we must therefore take land use and land cover, visibility during the field work, and geological and anthropogenic processes into account.

There is as yet no definite boundary between the foothill zone and the hinterland. As one travels inland, the character of the landscape changes gradually with elevation, and at 500-600 m visual contact with the coastal plain and the sea is lost. Here we might posit the beginning of an 'upland' zone, which goes on to rise to some 1400 m in the upper reaches of the Raganello watershed basin (some 15-20 km inland). The upland is characterised by an alternation of hard (limestone) outcrops and softer (schist-based) geology. As already mentioned, land use tends to be much less intensive here, with large areas given over to *macchia* and oak forest. Where agriculture does take place, it is small-scale and less mechanised, so the opportunities for traditional field surveying are correspondingly fewer. The rugged topography also contributes to the difficulty of conducting a systematic archaeological study of this zone. All geological processes (erosion, alluviation/colluviation) are more energetic in such an environment so that archaeological sites in certain locations, such as steep limestone scarps, are quickly eroded away whilst others are equally quickly buried under sediments ranging from fine-grained colluvium to catastrophic rock falls. In terms of biases, the net effect is a strong negative research and visibility bias: the upland is a 'hiatus' in our regional distribution maps. In the absence of information, new discoveries are initially difficult to assess. For example, although over 30 archaeological sites were discovered in the uplands and mountains by the speleological club 'Sparviere' in recent years, their locations (caves, scarps, the foot of limestone rock faces) can hardly be said to be representative of the archaeological record as a whole.

> Besides these physical differences between the landscape zones, variations in the manner in which archaeological research has been conducted can also lead to strong biases in the archaeological record. Thus, the extensive site-oriented methods employed for the archaeological mapping of the Sibaritide in the late 1960s were well adapted to the registration of scatters of highly-visible Hellenistic or Roman tile, building material and pottery, but much less so to that of pre-classical hand-made wares. Given the time constraints under which they probably had to operate, a reliance on reports by farm and construction workers, in combination with motorized site visits, naturally resulted in the clustering of sites near access roads (see Box 1.2). Conversely, the very intensive and systematic surveys conducted by us in recent years resulted in the discovery of a large number of small and unobtrusive, mainly protohistoric, sites. However, since our surveys can only cover small areas they are biased against the discovery of rare, hence significant, site types.

the Raganello and Caldanelle rivers seems to have been preferred over the wide and open marine terraces to the south of the Raganello. The survey also produced evidence for additional Hellenistic sites not reported in the Italian surveys of the late 1960s.[43] Hellenistic period sites recovered by the RAP now include small isolated farmsteads, hamlets and a *fattoria*. This was a larger farm that possibly specialized in olive oil production, judging from the many amphorae that were found in the survey.[44] A restudy of all rural pottery scatters from our own surveys has however not resulted in any site that could be securely dated to the Late Iron Age or the Archaic period. The material recorded in the 1960s, under much better circumstances, has unfortunately not been kept.

Fig. 4.10 is an overview of the locations where archaeological sites have been recorded so far. During the RAP a substantial number were identified in the hinterland of the Sibaritide along the valley of the Raganello. The inland surveys so far revealed many protohistorical sites that form a highly interesting long-term sequence of settlement and land use from the Neolithic to the Final Bronze Age, and which include cave sites and open-air sites up to an altitude of 1600 meters. Evidence for the infiltration of Greek material culture into the upper valley of the Raganello is however slight, although this area is only a day's walk from the coastal plain. The archaeological evidence is restricted to the odd isolated Hellenistic farmstead along transhumance routes leading up into the mountains. This raises another interesting issue: to what extent did the up- and highlands participate in the cultural exchanges that took place in the Mediterranean coastal plains and foothills, and in the subsequent urbanization of these areas that resulted from these encounters? What was the role of these areas? This subject is part of our present studies.

4.6 CONCLUSION

In this chapter we saw how Renato Peroni attributes some influence to the Aegean cultural contacts. These promoted the socio-economic and political developments related to indigenous elite formation and the articulation of power through material culture. Nonetheless, Peroni considers the process of centralization of settlement and the development of territoriality in protohistorical Sibaritide as one that was essentially internally driven. The level of socio-economic and cultural development reached by the indigenous Oenotrian communities of the Iron Age would have been comparable to that of Iron Age communities in mainland Greece. The Greek seafarers from the eastern Peloponnesus, who arrived on the coast of the Sibaritide in the late 8th century BC with the intention of settling, encountered a well-

---

[43] De Rossi *et al.* 1969.

[44] Oome / Attema 2008.

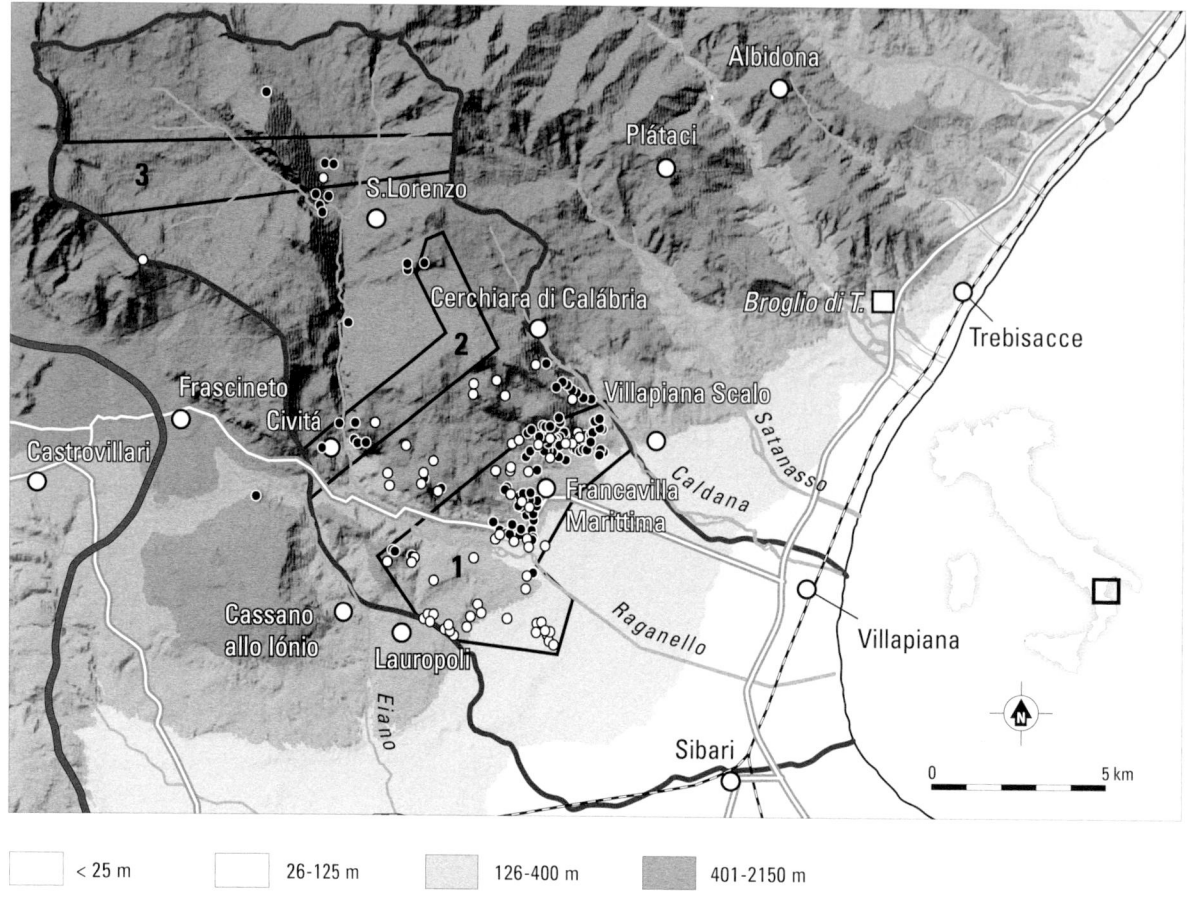

Fig. 4.10. Distribution of archaeological sites recorded by the GIA as part of the Raganello Archaeological Project (situation 2008). Black dots: protohistoric sites, white dots: Hellenistic to late antique sites. Intensive and systematic investigations have mainly taken place in the research transects 1-3. For a colour version of this figure, see page 222.

organized society. That society possessed a strong territorial awareness, marked elite leadership, the means and the knowledge to defend themselves and an advanced level of technology in the field of metallurgy, pottery production, agriculture and husbandry. Such a complex society could not easily be overthrown by what were surely modest numbers of incoming settlers. As Kleibrink noted, the theory of destruction of the indigenous Iron Age villages by the Greek newcomers and their general abandonment is nonetheless still widely adhered to by scholars, even though evidence is accumulating that Greek interventions in the indigenous landscape started out as small-scale enterprises.[45] Moreover, it is hard to deduce from the often poorly preserved archaeological remains of indigenous Iron Age hut compounds whether these were destroyed violently or accidentally, or rather demolished in the course of a necessary replacement of old structures by new ones.[46] The replacement of huts by houses was clearly part of a general process of urbanization in the Sibaritide that entailed the growth of a rural colonial landscape. This process did not necessarily involve a radical cultural break, as the analysis by Vink of the burial sequence in the Macchiabate necropolis of Timpone della Motta has shown.[47] On the basis of her analysis it appears that the indigenous population only gradually adopted Greek material culture in their grave inventories. As

[45] Kleibrink 2003, 22 and cf. chapter 6; Yntema 2000.
[46] Attema 2003, 14.
[47] Vink 1995.

Fig. 4.11. View from the Monte Sellaro toward the south across the Sibaritide coastal plain. The bed of the Raganello river can be seen in the middle distance (photo Nick Ryan, GIA 2000). For a colour version of this figure, see page 223.

such the Macchiabate cemetery would be a convincing example of continuity between the Early Iron Age and the Greek colonial period. The continuity of cult activities at the Timpone della Motta, which involved both Oenotrians and Greeks, can be read as another sign that early Greek colonization was a complex phenomenon involving cultural and socio-economic interaction, not outright subjugation of the indigenous population by the incoming Greeks (cf. Box 5.1). Recent intensive field surveys by the GIA indicated that the development of the sanctuary and settlement at the Timpone della Motta took place within a wider rural landscape that apparently contained dispersed protohistoric habitations. The surveys indicated that there is a dense pattern of small and very small protohistoric rural sites in the foothill zone between the Raganello and Caldanelle rivers, only a minority of which can probably be precisely dated. These sites can be placed in a site-hierarchical context by reference to Peroni's hypothesis of a micro-regional territory based around the twin settlements of Timpone della Motta and Timpa del Castello di Francavilla.[48] Iron Age to Classical rural sites appear to be absent from the foothill zone, which implies that the foothills were 're-colonized' in the early Hellenistic period, unless habitation during this period was concentrated into relatively few villages that are by chance all outside our survey zone. The numerous sites of different sizes from the early Hellenistic period testify to a well-developed rural economy that can be related to the town of Thurioi, successor to Sybaris. Finally it is noteworthy that Roman villa sites are extremely scarce in the region, confirming the pattern that emerged from the topographic inventory made by De Rossi *et al.* in 1969. This is an aspect that requires further study.

---

[48] Peroni / Trucco 1994, 850.

5 Centralization and proto-urbanization in the Bronze and Iron Ages

5.1 INTRODUCTION

In this chapter we will discuss centralization and proto-urbanization in the three RPC study regions for the period of the Bronze Age and Iron Age. Our perspective will be comparative, with occasional references to the broader geographical framework of Central and South-Italy. A first attempt at comparing the three RPC regions was made in a paper presented by one of us during a conference held at the British Academy in November 2002 on Mediterranean Urbanization between 800 and 600 BC.[1] The trends and problems noted in that paper regarding the settlement developments of the three regions have been incorporated in this chapter, although we have extended the comparison to the formative periods of the Bronze Age and Iron Age in which Archaic urbanization is rooted. Moreover, we will place less emphasis on the Late Iron Age and Archaic periods, which are discussed separately in chapters 6 and 7.

In Italian protohistorical archaeology, the terms *centralization* and *proto-urbanization* are used to refer to the physical processes of settlement nucleation, the establishment of central places and the consequent growth of a settlement hierarchy. This process included rural infill of the landscape in the form of smaller 'satellite' sites, 'farmsteads', and other activity areas in the landscape that are related to centralized settlements. Tracing and studying this gradual filling-up of the countryside has been an important goal of the field surveys of the RPC project, and it therefore features prominently in the comparisons drawn in the project. From this perspective, the study of the physical nature and spatial configuration of the archaeological sites encountered during the field surveys, including the smallest, adds significantly to our understanding of centralization and proto-urbanization. Any increase in the complexity of the settlement hierarchy likely indicates an increase in the socio-economic and political complexity of a given society. Various indicators of socio-economical and political complexity may contribute to our analysis, such as the physical nature of the archaeological sites, the configuration of the regional settlement pattern, and factors such as demography and subsistence, that have been pivotal in much of the research by the RPC project. Other indicators include craft specialization, exchange, accumulation of goods, social relations within and between communities, as well as cultural identity.[2] Such factors can be tabulated, and an overview of the crucial elements on which the analysis of socio-economic and political complexity in a protohistorical context may be based is presented in table 5.1. Box 5.1 presents a relevant case study on Broglio di Trebisacce.

---

[1] Attema 2005a. [2] Peroni 2004.

I Integrity of the regional settlement pattern and individual settlement criteria	II Organizational criteria	III Qualitative criteria	IV Intensity of overseas contacts and integration with Aegean people
• presence of 'major centres' • fortification • a high population density • territoriality • intercommunal relationships	• a ranked society and/or a certain degree of social order • a supra-local territorial organization and a supra-communal economic organization	• advanced technological level (craftsmanship) • a relatively uniform material culture • standardization	• long-distance exchange • continuous vs. discontinuous integration of groups of people and cultural traits of Aegean origin

Table 5.1. Indicators of socio-economical and political complexity in protohistorical Italy (after Bietti Sestieri 2005).

5.2 DIFFERING REGIONAL PATHWAYS TO COMPLEXITY IN PROTOHISTORY

Renato Peroni has systematically described the developments in protohistorical settlement in Italy in his recent *L'Italia alle soglie della Storia*, placing its start in the Early Bronze Age (2300 – 1700 BC) with what he calls 'stabilization of settlement' - the process that led to sites that were continuously inhabited for long periods of time.[3] The increasing preference for advantageous locations in the landscape would ultimately lead to the formation of substantial nucleated settlements. In the Early Bronze Age occupation of an open-air site (as opposed to cave sites) for more than two consecutive archaeological phases would still have been a rare phenomenon, according to Peroni, Sicily and the central-eastern area north of the Po river being among the few exceptions. In the Sibaritide and the Pontine region nucleated settlements appear only at later stages of the Bronze Age. In the Sibaritide archaeological indicators of socio-economic complexity are present only from the advanced phase of the Middle Bronze Age onwards. In the Pontine region signs of an incipient settlement hierarchy do not predate the Recent Bronze Age, although there is evidence for centralized settlement in the Middle Bronze Age. On the other hand, a stable site pattern appears along the Adriatic and Ionian shores of the Salento peninsula already in the first half of the 2nd millennium BC, increasing significantly in numbers towards the start of the Middle Bronze Age and becoming particularly dense in the later Bronze Age phases (fig. 5.1).[4]

5.2.1 MIDDLE TO RECENT BRONZE AGE (1700 – 1350 BC)

On the basis of our discussion of excavation and survey data in chapter 4 we concluded that socio-economic and political complexity in the Sibaritide was steadily growing throughout the Middle Bronze Age. This conclusion was based on the observed emergence of substantial, naturally defended settlements and of the carving up of the landscape into communal territories. The possibility of an incipient settlement hierarchy was deduced from the observation that these settlements exist in two size classes, one of up to 3 ha and the other from 10 to over 20 ha. Peroni is inclined to regard the larger sites as autonomous

[3] Peroni 2004, 96-97. [4] Cazzella 1991, 51; Recchia / Ruggini 2009.

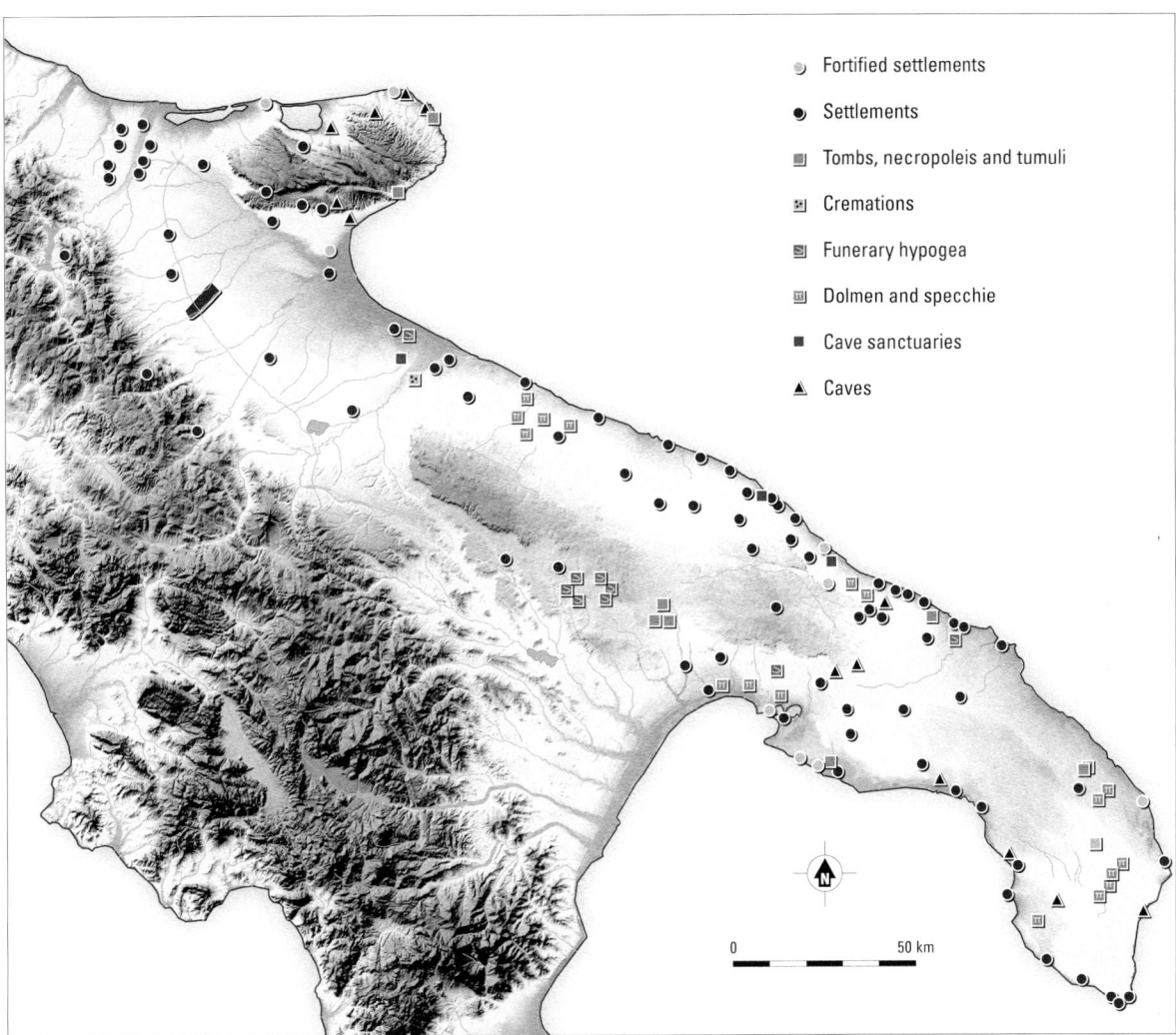

Fig. 5.1. Bronze Age sites in Apulia (after Recchia / Ruggini 2009, fig. 1). For a colour version of this figure, see page 224.

within their respective natural territories, but not as of equal socio-economic status.[5] This he bases on the differences in size and natural defensive potential of individual settlements, as well as on the presence of fine impasto, grey ware, and painted Italo-Mycenaean wares in late Middle Bronze Age layers at Broglio di Trebisacce and Torre Mordillo. Peroni relates such finds to a specialist production controlled by a newly formed elite (cf. the qualitative criteria under III in table 5.1) that would also have been responsible for the observed agricultural intensification in the foothill zone and for the introduction of arboriculture.

The degree of centralization in the Salento isthmus and south-eastern Italy as a whole during the Middle Bronze Age has come under debate in recent decades. Against the prevailing opinion that centralized and fortified settlement began only in the Recent Bronze Age, new excavations and the re-interpretation of chronological sequences now suggest that coastal sites such as Roca Vecchia, Porto Perone and Coppa Nevigata were already surrounded by fortification walls at some point in the first half of the 2nd millennium, and were soon emulated by many inland sites.[6] Typically these fortified sites are only 1-2 ha in size, although some, like those in the Sibaritide, are as large as 10 ha. It remains debatable if particularly the larger sites can be viewed as central places commanding satellite sites and a territory, as has

[5] For Peroni's definition of 'Siedlungskammer': Peroni 2004, 396.

[6] Cazzella 1991, 49. For Roca Vecchia: Pagliara 2005.

been proposed for the contemporary Sibaritide. Alberto Cazzella, another leading Italian protohistorian, argues that the use of differences in site size as evidence of a hierarchy is incorrect for this period and area.[7] He argues that the largest fortified sites would have been relatively empty in comparison to the smaller ones, and points to evidence that a certain degree of functional differentiation existed between the larger settlements: whereas coastal sites are likely to have been involved in supra-regional exchange, the economy of inland sites would largely have been based on subsistence. There is increasing evidence for the existence, in between the larger, stable ones, of sites that were only briefly occupied, such as those found by the RPC surveys on the Murge tableland. We have interpreted these as short-lived sites in a system of shifting cultivation (chapter 3). Cazzella maintains that there is no evidence for the phases under discussion to suggest that a formal, politically hierarchical relationship between the various site types existed.[8] Although funerary data indicate an increasing degree of social hierarchisation of kinship groups within single settlements, Cazzella argues that coastal and inland sites, fortified and open sites, essentially remained peer polities throughout the Bronze Age. They may occasionally have competed with each other, even have been at war, but they maintained a basic political equilibrium. In his view, the fortifications were therefore not expressions of formal hierarchisation; rather they were intended to defend specific landscape features crucial to the protection of overseas exchange or to the control over a territory.

Although these views suggest that the Sibaritide and Salento regions followed different 'pathways to complexity' during the Middle to Recent Bronze Age (with the Sibaritide demonstrating a much higher degree of centralization), the site patterns in both regions do not appear to differ very greatly, especially in comparison with those in the Pontine region. Both are characterized by growing socio-economic complexity in these phases, and even Cazzella in his balanced discussions of Salento and south-east Italy proposes to identify '[...] *un precoce processo di sviluppo verso l'urbanizzazione a partire da una fase antica dell'età del Bronzo* [...]'.[9]

In the contemporary Pontine region, few well-documented Middle Bronze Age sites are known. Even the recent inventory by L. Alessandri hardly allows us to reconstruct the type of 'territorial' landscape Peroni found in the Sibaritide (fig. 4.5).[10] Socio-economic indicators for an early elite formation are absent in Middle Bronze Age settlements in the Pontine region as well. Although for example the pottery finds from the Middle Bronze Age cave burials at Vittorio Vecchi in the Monti Lepini demonstrate a highly developed craftsmanship, there are no indications for the existence of a specialized artisan class such as would have been controlled by an elite. The undifferentiated settlement pattern that characterizes the Pontine region in the Middle Bronze Age fits in the wider picture sketched by Marco Pacciarelli of the settlement dynamics in Latium Vetus. In his overview of Bronze Age to Early Iron Age developments he describes the 'integral' and 'capillary' infill of the landscape by means of constellations of small settlements usually less than 1 ha in size.[11] Many of these small Middle Bronze Age sites did not, however, continue to be occupied into the subsequent Recent Bronze Age, and a change in location preference resulted in the occupation of inland plateaus and heights, as well as areas bordering lakes and lagoons.[12] Socio-economic and political complexity in the Pontine region therefore presumably developed more slowly than in the Sibaritide and the Salento.

[7] Cazzella 1991; Cazzella / Moscoloni 2001.
[8] Cazzella 1991.
[9] Cazzella / Moscoloni 2001, 332.
[10] Alessandri 2005 / 2009; Peroni and Trucco 1994, 834-843.
[11] Pacciarelli 2000, 87.
[12] Pacciarelli 2000, 89.

5.2.2 RECENT TO FINAL BRONZE AGE (1350 – 1200)

Elite groups in the Sibaritide became firmly established in this period at the socio-economically advanced sites of Torre Mordillo and Broglio di Trebisacce. These maintained regular and substantial contact with Aegean seafarers, as shown by the presence of Mycenaean pottery. Peroni suggested that Aegean seafarers may even have become integrated in local communities such as those at Broglio di Trebisacce. On the Salento peninsula, excavations and surveys also indicate that the settlement pattern that developed in the first half of the 2nd millennium BC continued throughout the later Bronze Age (cf. chapter 3). Social stratification in the Salento can be inferred from differences in hut floor sizes, the distribution of Mycenaean wares, and the presence of storage facilities. In this respect Roca Vecchia is in particular noteworthy, one of a chain of fortified settlements on the southern Apulian Adriatic coast.[13] Here, the frequency of imported pottery attests to the importance of contacts with the Mycenaean world. The excavations have further uncovered the remains of substantial storage facilities. These contained large jars probably for storing olive oil, which are believed to have been part of a redistributive system similar in nature (if not in scale) to that of the Mycenaean palaces.

In the later Bronze Age phases, too, the Sibaritide and Salento were probably socio-economically more advanced than the Pontine region, even if we were to include the whole of the Alban Hills in the latter. For an explanation we may again point to the importance of overseas contacts, which were in this period surely more intensive in South-Italy than in Central-Italy. In the Pontine region the Recent Bronze Age is best attested slightly inland along the Astura river at the site of Casale Nuovo, and at several sites bordering the coastal lagoons and the coast itself. As we have seen in chapter 2, there are indications for a growing socio-economic complexity: signs of specialization in pottery production, metallurgy, and saltmaking. Such artisan production may be related to the formation of an elite in the Pontine region (see table 5.1). The presence of Italo-Mycenaean and grey-ware potsherds at Casale Nuovo, and one Italo-Mycenaean shard at the salt production site of P13, suggests that the Pontine region at least was in indirect contact with the material culture of the Aegean world.[14] Moreover, di Gennaro emphasises that the Recent Bronze Age sites recorded in the coastal and sub-coastal zone of the Pontine region were part of a broader central-Italian pattern, which consisted of a string of sub-coastal settlements on sometimes large and well-defended inland plateaus some 5 km from the south-Latial coast.[15] Although little is yet known of the occupation density and duration of these plateaus, the pattern ties in well with the importance ascribed to maritime traffic as a factor triggering a growth in socio-economic complexity in this period (see item IV in table 5.1). Whilst it is possible that the developments in socio-economic complexity in the coastal part of the Pontine region were confined to the vicinity of the valley of the Astura river, which forms a natural corridor between the Pontine coast and the relatively densely settled Alban Hills (cf. chapter 2), Alessandri's recent and forthcoming studies of all known settlement data for central South-Lazio have furnished evidence for a wider geographical scope.[16]

A major factor explaining the relatively high degree of socio-economic complexity in the Bronze Age Sibaritide and coastal Salento is their participation in Mediterranean exchange networks. Located on the Ionian and Adriatic coastlines, these regions were not as peripheral to these networks as the Pontine region would have been, and settlements such as Broglio di Trebisacce and Roca Vecchia were undoubtedly in contact with the Mycenaean world. If we follow Peroni's model for the Sibaritide, these contacts may have spurred local societies within the region into socio-economic and even political complexity (in the sense of territoriality) precisely because of its relatively small scale, well-protected and uniform

---

[13] Excavated scrupulously by Pagliara and Guglielmino: Pagliara 2005; Guglielmino 2005.

[14] Di Giardino 2006.

[15] di Gennaro 2004, 204; for a detailed analysis see Alessandri 2005.

[16] Alessandri 2005 and 2009.

character. This may have stimulated a rapid and even infill of the landscape and promoted a process of cultural homogeneity. Bietti-Sestieri, however, argues that participation in overseas networks was highly 'fragmented' and did not add significantly to the overall socio-economic and political complexity of the settlement system.[17] Cazzella's alternative model for south-eastern Italy states that endemic internal competition between peer polity communities was the major factor inducing growth in complexity, and he denies the emergence of a strongly hierarchical society such as Peroni reconstructed for the Sibaritide.[18]

5.2.3 FINAL BRONZE AGE (1200 – 1000 BC)

In chapter 4 we noted that sites that continue into the Final Bronze Age in the Sibaritide command larger territories and developed defences, whereas there was a growing preference for strategic and naturally defended places in the landscape in the case of newly established sites. We also noted how, in the case of the site of Timpone della Motta, the surrounding landscape filled in with small sites, some of which contained fragments of large storage jars manufactured in Aegean technique (see Box 5.1 for the wider significance of this finds group). It is unlikely that this phenomenon will have been restricted to the catchment area of Timpone della Motta. Most notable is the importance that can be ascribed in this period to the site of Torre Mordillo, thought to have attained already by the end of the Final Bronze Age a central place status for at least the central part of the Sibaritide.[19] We tentatively compared the socio-political status of Torre Mordillo to that of the proto-urban centres in the central Tyrrhenian area in chapter 4, arguing that the Etruscan model of early proto-urbanization can, in fact, be applied some centuries earlier to the Sibaritide.[20] But in the Sibaritide, unlike Etruria, the phenomenon remained geographically very limited.

In Salento, the degree of continuity of Recent Bronze Age sites into the Final Bronze Age is a matter for debate; some sites seem to show continuity, others were abandoned. A case in point is the settlement relocation that took place near Ostuni, where the fortified site of Rissieddi was abandoned after having dominated the coastal plain for centuries (see above, section 3.3.2). It is tempting to relate this to the results of the 1999 'Ostuni' survey of the RPC project, which indicate that dispersed Final Bronze Age occupation occurred in the *lame*, the deeply-incised stream channels in the coastal plain. We may therefore speculate that the nucleated settlement pattern represented by the Rissieddi site gave way to one of dispersion in the course of the 11th/10th century BC. It is not yet clear, however, how this phenomenon relates to the emergence, during the early Iron Age, of a new large site on the hilltops that host the present-day town of Ostuni. Whether this site, which in due time developed into a fortified town, inherited the dominant role from the Rissieddi site, depends on the answer to the as yet unresolved question of how much time elapsed between the abandonment of the first and the emergence of the second. It is, however, likely that the emergence of the site of Ostuni in the Early Iron Age was part of a much wider process of settlement expansion, territorial reorganization, demographic growth, and increasing infilling of the landscape; a process that seems to have become particularly manifest in the 8th century BC and to which we will return in chapter 6.

For South-Lazio in the Final Bronze Age, the general picture is one of an increase in the number of settlements, with the emphasis on sites in a defensible position. In the Alban Hills the settlements are spaced only 2 to 3 kilometres apart, and this pattern of small sites was to continue into the Early Iron Age (Latial period IIA2).[21] In contrast to the developments in the Salento, however, Iron Age proto-

---

[17] Bietti Sestieri 2005, 16-17.
[18] Cazzella 1991, 55-56.
[19] Pacciarelli 2000, 116.
[20] Peroni (2004, 502) notes that we find the Final Bronze Age Torre Mordillo model of 'site and satellite sites' represented some centuries later in South-Etruria.
[21] Pacciarelli 2000, 93.

urbanization in the Pontine plain and along the South-Latial coast generally was foreshadowed, according to Alessandri, by the shift of settlement locations from near water bodies (the peri-lagoonal model) to inland hill plateaus.[22] This would have been accompanied by a shift from a mixed economy, in which hunting and gathering were still important, to an economy in which agriculture formed the basis of subsistence. Hill plateaus occupied in the Final Bronze Age often have settlement continuity into the Iron Age, and some of these, through a process of selection and concentration, were to expand into the proto-urban centres that later form the core of Latial society. This is in line with the accepted Roman school model of how the proto-urban centres of Latium Vetus came into being.

5.2.4 EARLY IRON AGE TO CA. 750 BC

The Early Iron Age up to about 750 BC is regarded as the period of the formation of proto-urban centres in central and southern Italy, and any discussion must start with an observation on the differences in scale of the sites and territories involved in this process. When we put Lazio and Etruria side by side - two regions where the phenomenon has been studied well - it becomes immediately clear that the Etruscan proto-urban centres were of quite a different size class from those in ancient Lazio. The difference was brought out well in the topographical map of Etruria and Lazio published by Pacciarelli (reproduced here as fig. 5.5),[23] in which the known proto-urban centres are plotted according to their estimated sizes. Whilst high-ranking Etruscan proto-urban centres have estimated surface areas in the size classes 100 to 200 ha and 50 to 100 ha, those in Lazio are - with three exceptions in the Tiber and Liri valley - in size classes of 20 to 50 ha and 1 to 15 ha. The size difference between the sites in the vast plains and hills of Etruria and those in south Lazio, in combination with the higher density of proto-urban cores recorded in the latter area, implies that the notional site territories in south Lazio and the Pontine region were far smaller than those in Etruria even though population densities might have been similar. Archaic Etruscan city states at the apex of their power would have controlled areas estimated between 1,000 and 2,000 sq.km with an increasingly hierarchical structure of minor centres, villages, hamlets, and isolated farmsteads. Those in Latium could not have controlled territories much larger than 150 sq.km.[24] In drawing parallels between the sizes of the Latial proto-urban settlements and the southern Italian ones of Torre Mordillo (Sibaritide) and Torre Galli (Tropea), Pacciarelli implies that the same scale difference applies to Calabria.[25] When it comes to chronology, the initial phase of the proto-urban cores, according to current thinking, is dated in Lazio only slightly later than in Etruria. Vanzetti suggested that the time-lag is only half a century - in traditional chronology between the start of the 9th century BC in Etruria and the second half of the 9th century BC in Lazio.[26] In the Sibaritide as well, the Early Iron Age is seen as the period in which the formation of proto-urban centres took place. For the Early Iron Age, Vanzetti notes an expansion directed at the central alluvial plain itself, the result of a 'capillary' occupation by the more important centres that carve out their own territory in a competitive process for expansion and local supremacy. This process unfolded in parallel with the pre-colonial phase, and was finally interrupted by the arrival of the Greeks in the late 8th century BC.[27]

In Salento there is evidence for a nucleated settlement pattern and demographic growth in the Iron Age, but the formation of proto-urban centres is thought to have begun later, in the Archaic period.[28] Here, settlement development is not indicative of so strong and continuous a process of 'capillary' proto-urbanization (with a related strongly politicized landscape) as is claimed in the cases of Lazio and the Sibaritide.

[22] Alessandri 2005.
[23] Pacciarelli 2000, fig.70; cf. Peroni 2004, fig. 116.
[24] Pacciarelli 2000, 124.
[25] Pacciarelli 2000, 119.
[26] Vanzetti 2002, 40.
[27] Vanzetti 2002, 43. Compare also our chapter 6.
[28] D'Andria 1999.

Box 5.1 Indicators of socio-economic complexity in the Sibaritide[A]

Craft specialization at Broglio di Trebisacce in the Recent Bronze Age is evident from four categories of artefacts: drinking cups of fine impasto with a rich form repertoire; the local production of Aegean-type grey ware; painted Italo-Mycenaean ware; and *dolia 'a cordoni e fasce'*. Of these four categories the last three indicate close contacts with the Aegean world. Grey ware is made of depurated clay, is wheel-turned and fired at a high temperature. It is manufactured using *Aegean technology* and reproduces both Aegean and indigenous forms. Besides an abundance of plain grey ware (which, however, demonstrates a large variety of fabrics, colours, surface finish and forms), there is a small quantity of grey ware decorated with dark grey or black paint that imitates motives typical for the Mycenaean repertoire, but applies these in a technique unknown in the Mycenaean world. Painted Mycenaean shards of local production are usually referred to as Italo-Mycenaean ware and are specifically related to elite consumption. Although Italo-Mycenaean pottery normally reproduces true Mycenaean forms, indigenous forms are also sometimes used (fig. 5.2).

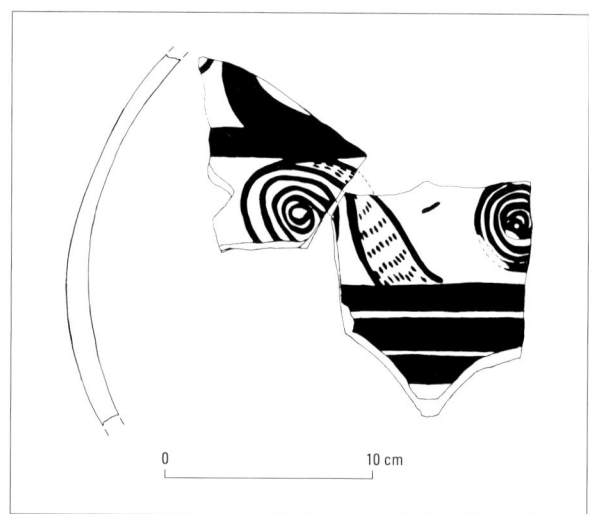

Fig. 5.2. An example of painted Italo-Mycenaean ware from Broglio di Trebisacce (from Peroni / Trucco 1994, tav. 75 no. 5).

The extremely large *dolia* of the *a cordoni e fasce* class are manufactured from depurated clay following Aegean examples, finished on the potter's wheel and fired in high-temperature kilns. The use of these huge containers whose capacity exceeds the needs of a single family unit would point to centralized storage. Evidence for the existence of a *local elite*, however, rests especially on the presence, on the acropolis of Broglio di Trebisacce, of two store-rooms with such dolia. One of the dolia had a capacity of over 500 litres (fig. 5.3).[B] Although residue analysis has provided evidence that some dolia were used for the storage of olive oil, this cannot be generalized since different types of dolia are present that may have served different functions (also for storing wine?). On the basis of the distribution of dolium shards not related to domestic housing features, the Broglio excavation team thinks that there may have been more store-rooms present on the acropolis. These archaeological facts imply an increasing emphasis on arboriculture and forms of territorial control by a well-established local elite. Interestingly the GIA survey team has now identified more than a dozen sites with shards of the *dolii cordonati* class in the foothills of the Sibaritide between the Sciarapottolo and Caldano rivers. These are attested in the catchment area of the centralized settlement of Timpone della Motta (fig. 5.4 and see section 4.4.3). If we accept that this phenomenon was not restricted to Timpone della Motta, but was probably also present in the catchments of Broglio di Trebisacce and Torre Mordillo in the Final Bronze Age/Early Iron Age, then that would imply an early form of *rural infill* that would stand in close

---

[A] After Peroni 1994, 846-847.

[B] Peroni 1994, 856.

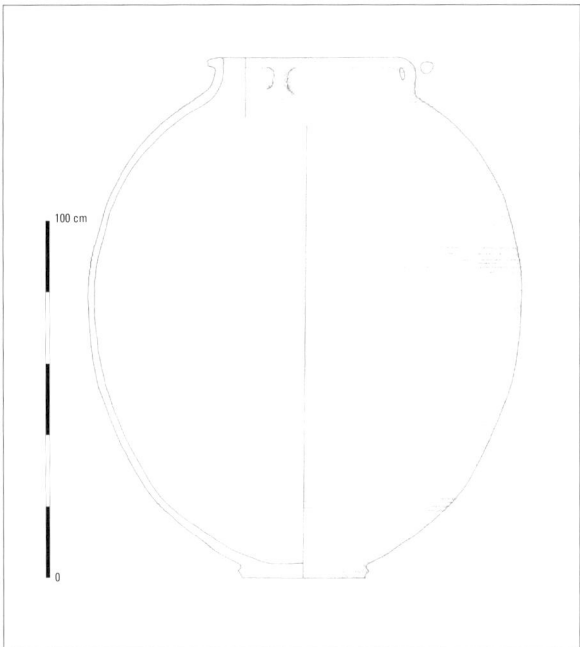

relationship with centralised settlements and craftsmanship there. This could be interpreted as a first stage of proto-urbanization. In the Sibaritide the Aegean contacts in the Recent Bronze Age were certainly conducive to the observed growing complexity in the Final Bronze Age.

Fig. 5.3. *Dolio cordonato* with a capacity of over 500 litres from the acropolis of Broglio di Trebisacce (reproduced from Peroni / Trucco 1994, Tav. 66).

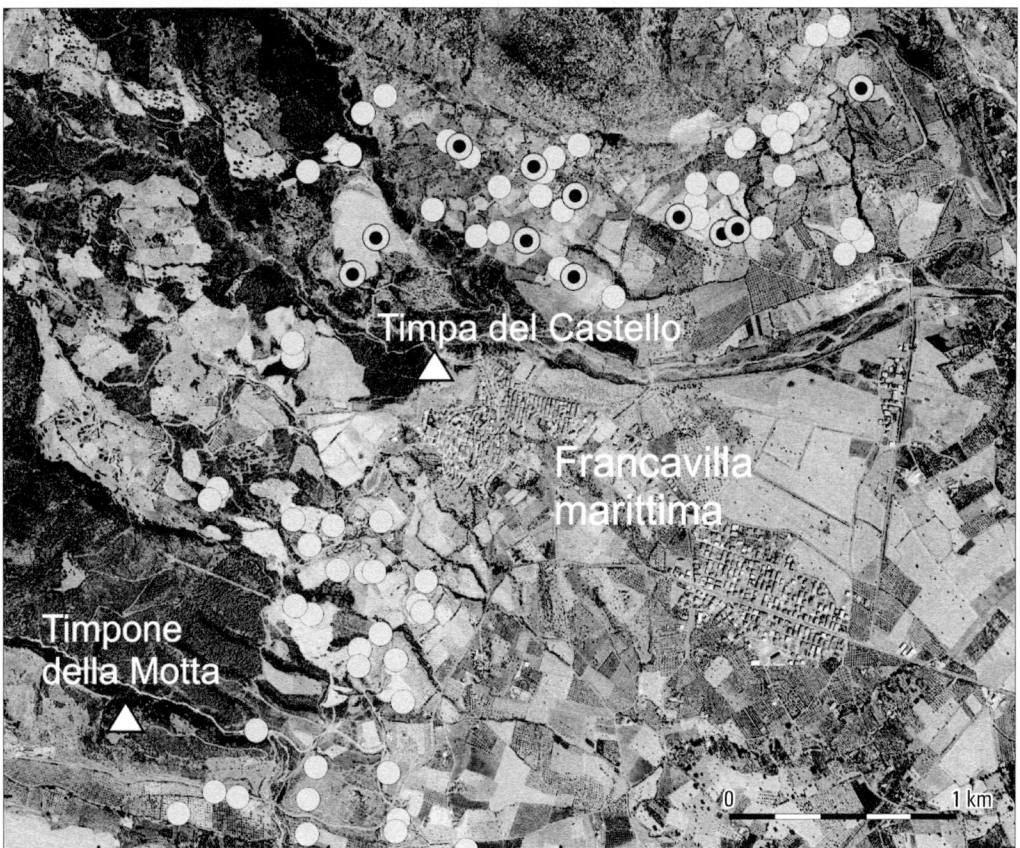

Fig. 5.4. Many of the protohistoric find spots (light dots) recorded by the Raganello Archaeological Project in the foothills between the Raganello and Caldana rivers have yielded sherds of Final Bronze Age *dolii a cordoni e fasce* in recent years (dark dots). The wide distribution appears to contradict Peroni's model of central management of olive oil consumption. For a colour version of this figure, see page 225.

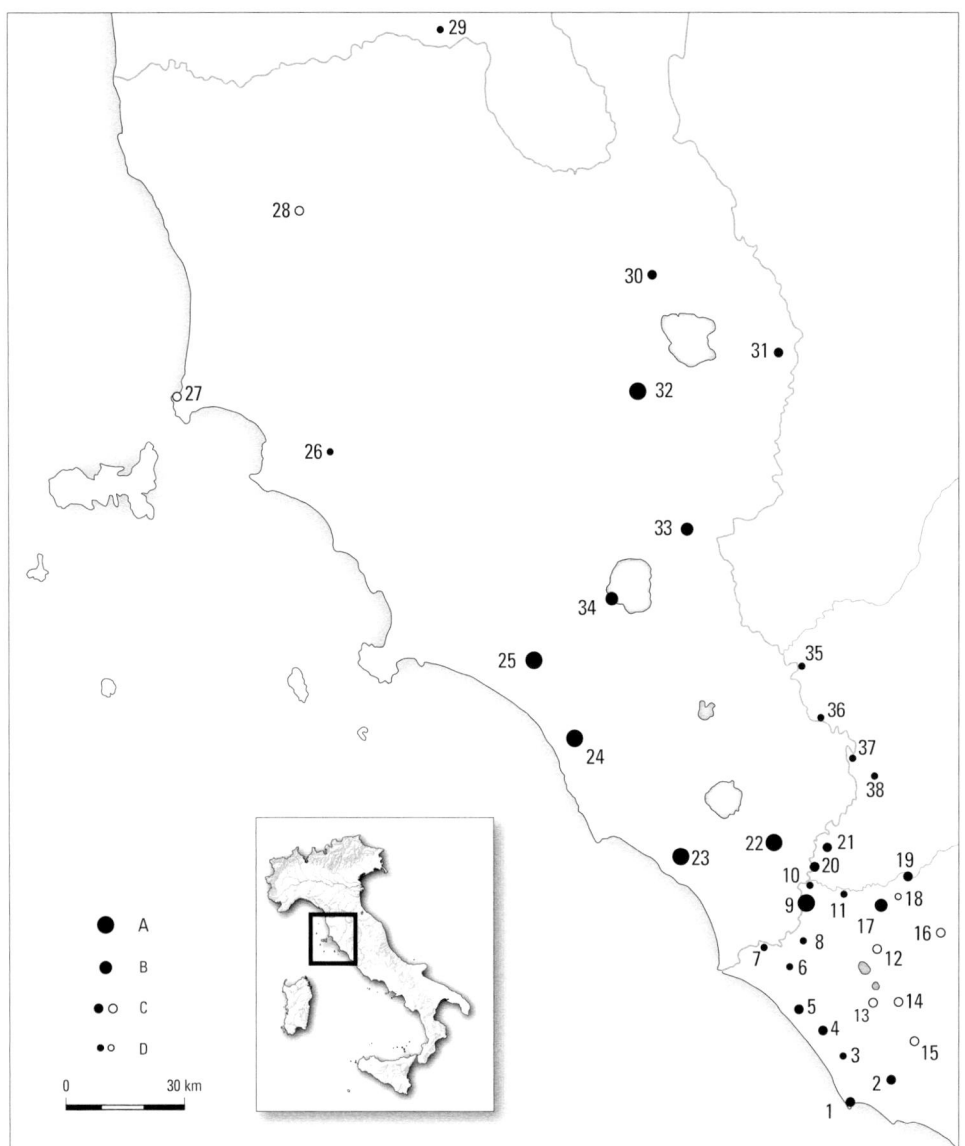

Fig. 5.5. Locations and sizes of proto-urban centres in Etruria and Lazio. A 100-200 ha, B 50 – 100 ha, C 20-50 ha, D 1-15 ha (after Pacciarelli 2000, fig. 70).

Returning to our comparison with Etruria as the main example of proto-urbanization, we must conclude that it is not just in chronology and settlement size that it differs from the RPC regions; there is also thought to be a difference in terms of continuity between the Final Bronze Age and the Early Iron Age (Primo Ferro). Leading Italian protohistorians such as Pacciarelli, Peroni and di Gennaro of the Roman School of protohistory describe the transition from Final Bronze Age to Early Iron Age in Etruria as one of enormous changes and of strong discontinuity, whereas the current model for the Sibaritide and Lazio is rather one of continuity and incremental change. In Etruria, it is thought that the numerous Final Bronze Age settlements on the many tuff plateaus each with a maximum extent of a few hectares only and smallish territories of between 20 and 50 sq.km are abandoned. This was in favour of just five large agglomerations, from which the Etruscan cities of Veio, Cerveteri, Tarquinia, Vulci and Orvieto would arise.[29] For ancient Lazio, Vanzetti notes that one does not find 'such a clear process of

[29] di Gennaro 2000, fig. 6; Peroni 2004, 470; Vanzetti 2002, 37-38.

selection and concentration in particular sites', and that 'the main sites tended to be occupied for long periods, and to grow in stages'.[30] This 'incremental' model also applies to the situation in the Sibaritide, where it is the increase of the total settled surface of existing settlements that indicates the formation of proto-centres, rather than any definite change in the settlement pattern.[31] On the whole, however, it must be remembered that proto-urban formation in the Sibaritide was a limited process, involving only a few settlements of which, as we saw, Torre Mordillo was the dominant one. Despite the differences in scale, timing and degree of continuity, we must conclude that the first signs of urbanization should be placed well before Greek colonization, and even, as Vanzetti emphasizes, before the period of pre-colonization. The contrast with the traditional Etruscological view that identifies Greek colonization as the main force for change in the Iron Age could not be starker.[32]

5.3 CONCLUSION

In this chapter we have discussed the main socio-economic indicators for growing complexity during protohistory (Bronze and Iron Ages) in the three RPC regions. On the subject of settlement development, we saw that stabilization and fortification had an early start in Salento at the turn of the Early to Middle Bronze Age, and the Sibaritide followed suit in an advanced stage of the Middle Bronze Age. In the Pontine region this development occurred much later again, in the Recent Bronze Age. Whereas for the Sibaritide these developments are interpreted according to Peroni's model as indicating the formation of a formal settlement hierarchy and a process of centralisation, no such strong differentiation is recognized in Cazzella's model for Salento and south-eastern Italy in general, where a political equilibrium (even between sites of different extents) is thought to have prevailed throughout the Bronze Age. It may therefore be that the supposed differences in centralization rates and onsets are due more to the dominance of different archaeological models in different areas, then to any actual differences in the archaeological record.

Overseas contacts with the Aegean world played an important role both in the Sibaritide and the Salento peninsula, but evidence for such contacts is poor in the Pontine region, and more generally in South-Lazio. In the Final Bronze Age the first signs of a 'proto-urban' landscape can be observed in the Sibaritide, where intensive surveys now attest to the rural infill of the foothill and upland zones. On the whole, socio-economic and political complexity in the Pontine region in the Bronze Age may be said to have developed at a slower pace than in the Sibaritide and Salento, but in the Final Bronze Age and Early Iron Age all three regions would gradually develop proto-urban forms of settlement. In the Pontine region and in the Salento these evolved into indigenous Archaic proto-urban settlements, whereas in the Sibaritide and in some parts of Salento this process was derailed by Greek urbanism. The interaction between the Greek colonial and the indigenous world will be the subject of the next chapter.

[30] Vanzetti 2002, 40, referring to Peroni 1989; Bietti Sestieri 1992; di Gennaro / Guidi 2000.
[31] This volume, chapter 4; Peroni 2004, 471.
[32] Vanzetti 2002, 37.

6 Rethinking early Greek - indigenous encounters in southern Italy

6.1 INTRODUCTION

Until recently, the study of the protohistorical societies discussed in chapter 5 was strongly overshadowed by that of the Greek colonial world. Indigenous peoples throughout the eastern and western reaches of the Greek colonial ventures have commonly been perceived as socio-politically and culturally subordinate to the Greek colonists who settled among them. In southern Italy, or *Megale Hellas*, most pre-Roman archaeological research concentrated on colonial Greek city-states, from Poseidonia on the Tyrrhenian coast to Sybaris and Taras along the Ionic Sea. Traditionally, these excavations focused – as many continue to do – on Greek colonization and Greek art, architecture and town planning.[1] The merits of this research tradition are indisputable. Unfortunately, however, research of the contemporary indigenous regions was in no way comparable.[2] If these regions were studied at all, it was primarily when indigenous burial grounds were found to contain vast numbers of Greek vases and other artefacts, the style and iconography of which appealed to researchers. At the same time, such finds were seen as a confirmation of the widespread power of Hellenization, the concept denoting the diffusion of Greek culture among indigenous peoples. This, in turn, was felt to support the general belief in Greek cultural, political and technological superiority.[3]

The limitations of this 'Hellenophile' mindset have been made explicit in many publications in recent decades (see section 1.1.3). One aspect of this critical attitude is particularly relevant to the present study: new perspectives have been developed that expand the scope of Classical Archaeology to include regions that the Greeks considered marginal. Recent problem-oriented fieldwork in some of these regions has revealed that many non-Greek groups were far less 'behind' with respect to the Greek city states than previously presumed.[4] It was the explicit aim of the RPC research team to investigate these issues. In this chapter we seek to contribute towards that goal, especially with regard to early Greek colonization in southern Italy, which took place roughly in the eighth and seventh centuries BC.[5] Two of the RPC study regions, the Sybaris region and the Salento isthmus, offer ample scope for a reassessment of long-standing perceptions of Greek impact on local societies. We will trace the active role these societies played in the historical process, and will argue that the Greek migrant settlers of the 8th and 7th-century BC on the shores of southern Italy integrated in a world already characterized by developing settlement hierarchies, land reclamation and territorial expansion.

Since it is our intention to question the presumed dominance of the role of the Greeks from the very start of the colonization process, we cannot limit our analysis to the coastal areas where the Greeks

---

[1] Major volumes, such as those edited by Pugliese Caratelli (1985-1990, 1996) provide comprehensive overviews of the principal issues at stake.

[2] Cf. Morel 1984; Gualtieri 1987; Whitehouse / Wilkins 1989; D'Andria 1991; 2002; Burgers 1998.

[3] See in particular Dunbabin 1948; Boardman 1964.

[4] With regard to Italy see in particular Bottini and Guzzo 1986; Whitehouse / Wilkins 1989; Herring 1991; D'Andria 1991 and 2002; Yntema 1993a; Burgers 1998.

[5] This chapter is based on an article by one of us (Burgers 2004).

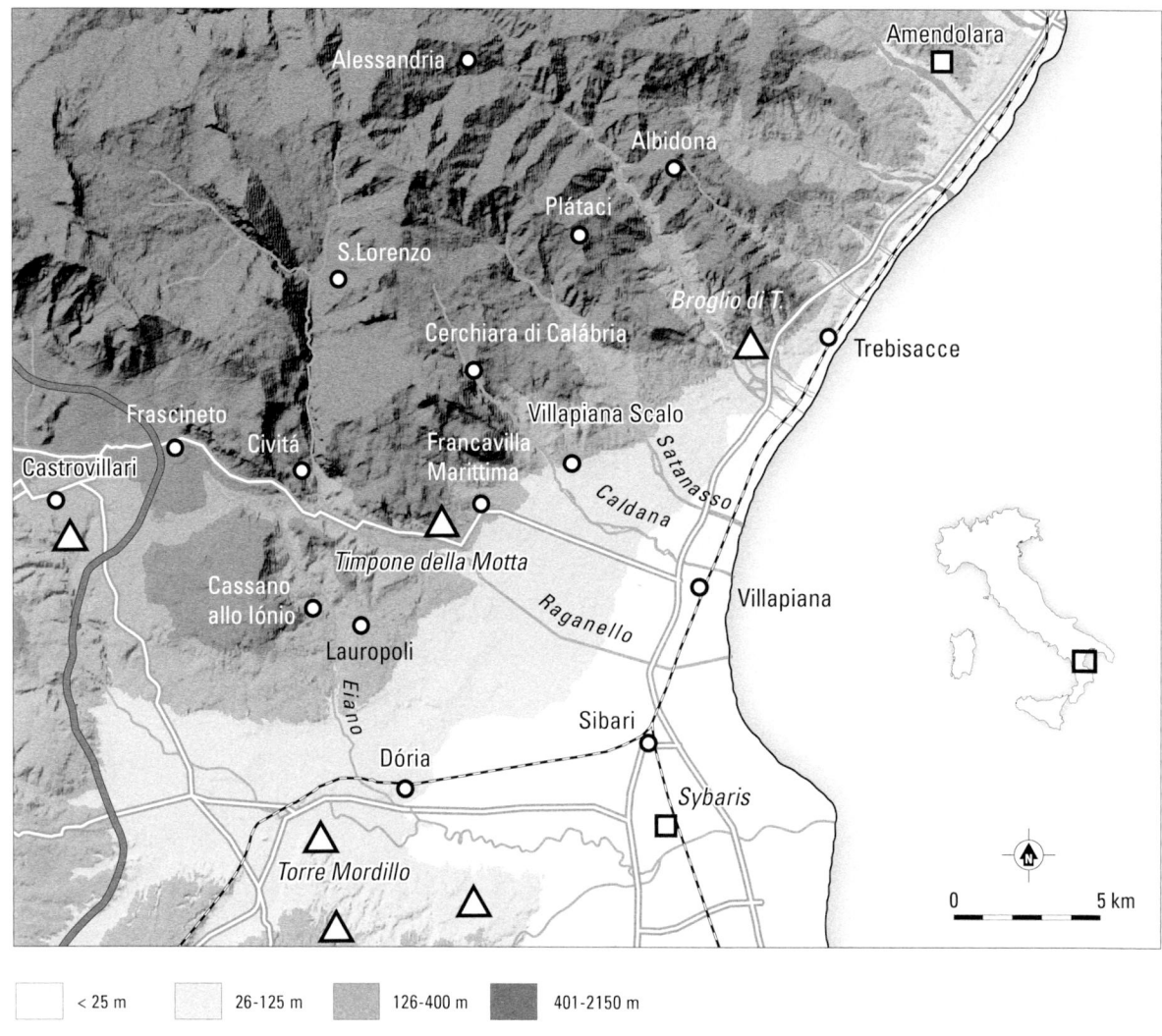

Fig. 6.1. Major Archaic sites of the Sibaritide (triangles; after Vanzetti 2002, fig. 7). For a colour version of this figure, see page 226.

came ashore, but must extend it to the much larger inland indigenous territories. This, unfortunately, is more difficult in the case of the Sibaritide than it is in that of Salento. The Sibaritide was part of a much larger region including the vast inland valleys and uplands of northern Calabria, but these latter areas fall outside the zone for which we have adequate archaeological data. In contrast, the indigenous hinterland of the Salento peninsula, of which the colony of Taras occupied only a small part, has been studied in the context of the RPC-project. Our argument starts with the Sibaritide (sections 6.2 and 6.3) and then widens its scope to include the Salento peninsula (section 6.4).

6.2 THE HEGEMONY OF SYBARIS

The Sybaris plain on the Ionian coast of south Italy is among the regions where the issues discussed above dominate the archaeological agenda (fig. 6.1; see also section 4.3.2). The Iron Age and Archaic settlement configurations there have long been interpreted primarily in the light of early Greek colonialism and territorial expansion. The colony that played a pivotal role in these developments was Achaean Sybaris, which was reportedly founded in the late 8th century BC, exerting a regional hegemonic influence from its very foundation until its destruction in 510 BC by the neighbouring polis of Kroton.[6] One major indication of this dominance can be found in literary sources, notably in an account by Strabo, which states that the town ruled over three tribes (*ethnai*) and 25 towns (*poleis hypekooi*; Strabo, Geogr. VI 1 13).

It was not until fairly recently that archaeologists made a positive identification of Sybaris,[7] buried as it was under the ruins of its successor towns, Thurioi and Copiae. What is more, alluvial deposits that reached 6 m in depth in places covered the town. Located near the confluence of the rivers Crati and Coscile, Sybaris now lies 2.5 km from the coastline, (which is thought to have bordered the town in antiquity). Despite intensive excavations that span decades, few traces of ancient Sybaris have actually been unearthed.[8] The remains of two temples that were found as roman spolia in public buildings of Roman Copiae have received most attention. In addition, a series of private houses dating to the 6th century BC were excavated at Stombi, which lies roughly 1.5 km to the north. The discovery of this systematically organised nucleus of houses at a fairly large distance from what is presumably the town's centre is believed to indicate Sybaris' formidable size.

Similar houses dating to the 6th century BC have been excavated at Amendolara San Nicola and Timpone della Motta near Francavilla Marittima (fig. 6.1).[9] The former site is located some 30 km north of Sybaris, at the extreme end of the plain. The latter lies 18 km from Sybaris, on one of the hills forming the plain's western border, on the eastern bank of the river Raganello. The houses at these sites featured the same construction techniques as the Sybaris houses. They also yielded very similar artefact repertoires.[10] Moreover, the houses at Amendolara were laid out in roman insulae, within a well-defined street pattern: a layout *per strigas* in miniature.[11] These findings are believed to confirm the literary account of contemporary Sibaritide hegemony over the larger part of the region.[12] In the case of Timpone della Motta, this conclusion is reached primarily on the basis of the presence of a Greek-style sanctuary on top of the hill.

Sybaris' dominance during the 6th century BC is generally accepted, at least with regard to the surrounding coastal and alluvial plains. The formative phases of its hegemony, however, are the subject of much debate. Pier Giovanni Guzzo, one of the leading Italian archaeologists involved in the research into Sybaris, contends that its dominance can be traced back to the recorded foundation of the colony in the late 8th century BC. At that time, the few indigenous sites present in the region, including Amendolara, Timpone della Motta and Torre Mordillo, were rapidly falling under colonial control.[13] He adduces archaeological evidence for this theory from the presence, among other things, of Greek ceramics dating to the 1st half of the 7th century BC in an indigenous necropolis at Amendolara. Guzzo interprets the temple structures at Timpone della Motta and those at other sites, such as Torre Mordillo, where similar Greek artefacts were found, along the lines established by De Polignac: he places them in the context of the formation of a 'crown' of frontier sanctuaries that define and defend the early colonial territory.[14]

Although Guzzo draws heavily on datasets from the wider Sibaritide, the region's indigenous communities figure only cursorily in his otherwise rich account. He takes the same approach to the 8th-century

---

[6] This volume, section 4.2.2; see also, e.g., Guzzo 1987 and 1993.

[7] Guzzo 1970, 15-23.

[8] Kleibrink 2001, with extensive bibliography, discusses at length the meagre evidence for early Greek and indigenous groups at Sybaris and in its chora.

[9] For Amendolara see especially De la Genière / Nickels 1975, 483-498; for the site of Francavilla Marittima Kleibrink 2001, 42; cf. Osanna 1992, 159-164; Greco 1993, 469-472.

[10] See chapter 4.3.5 of the present volume, and Mater 2005, chapter 4.

[11] Greco 2001, 177.

[12] Greco 2001, 178; Osanna 1992 and 2001, 210-212; Kleibrink 2001.

[13] Guzzo 1982, 1987. Cf. Greco 2001, 177-178; Osanna 2001, 210-212.

[14] Guzzo 1987, 373-379; cf. De Polignac 1984; Osanna 1992, 122-132 and 157-166; Greco 1993, 467.

BC pre-colonial period, where he focuses primarily on indications of Greek trading activities preceding actual colonization. This exchange is assumed to have taken place based on the occurrence of Greek (and Phoenician) artefacts in the Early Iron Age necropoleis of the native population. Also in this case Greek involvement is considered to have been a decisive factor in the fortunes of the Sybaris region. In fact, Guzzo suggested that the prestigious allure of Greek consumer goods prompted the native population to settle on hilltop sites near the shores.[15] Accordingly, Greek influence is not only thought to have triggered urbanization in the colonial period, but also settlement transformations in the preceding phase.

6.3 IRON AGE INDIGENOUS SETTLEMENT EXPANSION AND EARLY INDIGENOUS – GREEK ENCOUNTERS

Guzzo's views have not gone uncontested. For one thing, they do not appear to tally with the findings of the Roman School of Protohistory's long-standing archaeological research project in the Sibaritide.[16] This project's excavations and extensive surveys indicate that as early as the Middle Bronze Age a stable, centralized settlement system emerged in the Sibaritide (see chapters 4 and 5). Major sub-coastal hilltop sites were built at fairly even distances (3-5 km) apart, each controlling a corresponding territory. After a process of concentration and selection during the Final Bronze Age that favoured the best-defended sites, such as Broglio di Trebisacce and Torre Mordillo, the Roman project team found evidence of settlement expansion in the Early Iron Age (fig. 6.1). This time, the expansion appears to have been concentrated at the centre of the alluvial plain, where minor new – and probably satellite – sites appeared in the territories of major sites (e.g. Terranova and La Prunetta in the territory of Torre Mordillo – see chapter 4).[17] Vanzetti interpreted the emergence of these sites as the infill process by which major centres populated their already established territories,[18] and in line with the Roman School he believes that political and territorial competition between the major centres was the driving force behind this infill. This recon°Greek factor but rather on indigenous processes, especially on the active social strategies of local groups.

Pre-colonial contact with Greeks overseas does not figure prominently in the Roman School's approach. It acknowledges, however, that the Greek role in the indigenous socio-political dynamics of the pre-colonial period was probably not an aggressive one.[19] Even so, the reported colonization of Sybaris in the late 8th century BC is argued to have caused serious indigenous-Greek conflicts and a rather abrupt truncation of indigenous urbanising trends, as it coincided with the abandonment of a number of Iron Age settlements in the region. Recently, Vanzetti has studied these transformations using a rank-size analysis based on Peroni's territorial analysis (see also Box 1.3 on rank-size analysis).[20] The results of the analysis demonstrate that the relations between the major settlements during the Final Bronze Age were non-hierarchical. In contrast, during the transition to the Iron Age, the rank-size structure tends towards log-normality – sign of a mature hierarchy. Vanzetti argues that the latter corresponds to rather sudden (late 8th century BC) and aggressive Greek colonial expansion, which caused the collapse of the traditional settlement system and the formation of Sybaris as a primate central place.[21]

---

[15] Guzzo 1982, 146-151.

[16] Peroni 1994; Vanzetti 2000 and 2002.

[17] The GIA surveys have found no evidence that this type of expansion also took place in the foothills and uplands of the territory of Timpone della Motta.

[18] Peroni 1988; Vanzetti 2002, 43.

[19] Vanzetti 2002, 45.

[20] Vanzetti 2000, 169-183; Peroni 1994.

[21] Vanzetti (2002, 45) notes that the Sibaritide transformation is morphologically analogous to that demonstrated for South-Etruria in the proto-urbanization period during the Early Iron Age.

Recently, Marianne Kleibrink has contested Guzzo's views in a detailed review of academic discourse and historical and archaeological evidence of indigenous-Greek relations in the Sibaritide.[22] Drawing on the Roman School project and other research, Kleibrink argues that the presence of strong indigenous groups in the Sibaritide during the 9th and 8th centuries BC precluded the development of early Greek colonization. By way of a parallel to the Roman School's research, she draws attention to the GIA excavations at Timpone della Motta, which have unearthed, among other things, the remains of an Iron Age indigenous settlement and those of a local cult preceding the construction in the mid-7th century BC of a Greek-style temple complex. A large, apsidal 8th-century BC wooden house with a hearth/altar, which was excavated on a hilltop there, is thought to be one of a group of three large and prominently located aristocratic houses. These houses are accompanied by huts built along the crest of the hill. The presence of finely decorated loom weights (labyrinthine patterns) and votive offerings (bronze jewellery and food items) in the excavated house on the hilltop have been taken as evidence of cult activities focused on a local weaving deity.

Further evidence of a flourishing indigenous community at the site comes from the nearby Macchiabate necropolis. Situated at the foot of the Timpone della Motta hill, this necropolis was excavated as early as the 1960s. Its oldest tumuli burials are contemporary with the wooden elite houses mentioned earlier. The contention is that they belonged to an extended family, one branch of which is thought to have climbed to aristocratic rank in the mid-8th century BC because of its increasingly conspicuous display of wealth and status.[23]

These data are highly significant as they suggest internal social competition in the contemporary indigenous community at Timpone della Motta. Such an interpretation is reminiscent of the arguments proposed by the Roman School in explaining regional settlement expansion in the Early Iron Age (see above). According to Kleibrink, there is nothing to suggest Greek involvement in these processes. Until about 700 BC, hardly any Greek and only few other (e.g. Phoenician) imports occur in the Macchiabate necropolis. It was only in the first half of the 7th century BC that the use of Greek pottery in funerary rites grew in popularity, as Greek artefacts began to be buried alongside traditional indigenous artefacts. Kleibrink takes this evidence to indicate that the native population associated with Greek migrant groups from then on.[24] She approaches the Amendolara necropolis mentioned above along similar lines, contesting Guzzo's interpretation of it as showing evidence of early Greek colonial pressure.

In the same vein, Kleibrink maintains that the historical foundation date of Sybaris does not correspond to a planned, large-scale wave of Greek settlement colonization.[25] She points out that the 7th-century finds at Sybaris come mainly from archaeological contexts in which a mixture of indigenous, imported and locally produced wares were found together with charcoal and bones. Reviewing the very scant evidence of late 8th to mid-7th century BC occupation, Kleibrink argues that the early settlement probably consisted of dispersed nuclei of huts containing dug-out storage facilities.[26] She rejects Guzzo's reading of the fragments of indigenous pottery in the layers related to this settlement as indicative of indigenous labour in the service of the Greeks. Rather, she suggests that indigenous groups, and especially their elites, played an important part in this early settlement. In the model she proposes, Greek colonization at Sybaris did not result in a thorough transformation of the settlement until the latter half of the 7th century BC, when Sybarite power extended across the larger part of the plain. To what degree and how the native population and the Greek immigrant society subsequently integrated to form a new socio-political landscape controlled by Sybaris is still poorly understood.[27]

---

[22] Kleibrink 2001.

[23] Kleibrink 2001, 54-55; see also section 4.3.6 of this volume.

[24] Ibidem.

[25] Cf. in particular Osborne 1998.

[26] Kleibrink 2001, 38-42 and 45.

[27] Attema *et al.* 1998b, 342.

In her belief that settlement expansion and proto-urbanization took place in the phase preceding recorded Greek colonization, Kleibrink follows the Roman School's reconstruction of events. At the same time, however, her contention that the Greeks gained dominion gradually in a relatively late phase diverges significantly from the School's ideas, which is much more in line with Guzzo's interpretation. Neither Vanzetti nor Guzzo devote much attention to the continuity of the local element or to the issue of integration, which Kleibrink stresses in her account of gradual transformations at sites such as Sybaris and Timpone della Motta. In this respect, Kleibrink's approach offers a promising new angle for further research.

Responding to Kleibrink's ideas, Guzzo credits her for questioning and testing traditional interpretive approaches to Greek colonization,[28] but he also makes a number of critical observations. He counters her contention, for instance, that Greek migrants were initially too few in number to be considered a dominant party. He points to the Greeks' indisputable technological superiority (e.g. in seafaring and warfare), which would have counterbalanced any numerical disadvantage, and notes that the Normans too were outnumbered during their conquest of southern Italy in the Middle Ages, and yet dominated over the region for many years to come. Guzzo likewise criticizes Kleibrink for paying little attention to written sources that mention the servile status of the native population, but at the same time acknowledges that these sources are problematic: they are difficult to date, could be viewed as Hellenocentric, and could even be used to support Kleibrink's thesis. Similarly, with regard to his main point, namely that there are still insufficient archaeological data to support Kleibrink's far-reaching conclusions, Guzzo also admits that those data are not sufficient to contradict her convincingly either.

Kleibrink's line of research can be taken further by zooming out and approaching the Sibaritide as just one element in a much wider, regional landscape. For instance, if we were to take the whole of southern Italy as our point of departure, we would see that recent archaeological investigations offer ample new evidence of the continuity of local dynamics and of parallel Iron Age and Archaic processes of growing social complexity in areas that experienced direct colonial interference as well as in areas that did not. Let us turn now to a second RPC study region in exploring these issues further.

6.4 A COLONIAL ENCLAVE AND ITS WIDER CONTEXT: TARAS AND THE SALENTO PENINSULA

The Taranto plain in the north-west of the Salento peninsula is the only place in Apulia where evidence has been found of a lasting Greek colonization venture (fig. 6.2). It was there that the *polis* of Taras developed, which, like Sybaris, is generally considered to have been one of the most powerful of *Megale Hellas*.

The ancient town of Taras is located beneath present-day Taranto, on the Ionian Gulf at the western extreme of the Salento isthmus. The ancient town occupies a strategic promontory, which closes off an internal bay (called *Mar Piccolo*) from an outer one (*Mar Grande*), the latter opening into the Tarentine Gulf. Recent palaeo-geographical investigations indicate that the earliest colonial settlement developed in an insular context, surrounded by lagoonal and marshy zones.[29] Based on the literary sources, Taras is believed to have been founded slightly later than Sybaris, towards the end of the 8th century BC, by Laconian – not Achaean – colonists.[30] Literary tradition has it that in the early days of their existence the two colonies were embroiled in a fierce dispute as to who controlled the land between them (especially Antiochos; in Strabo, Geogr. VI 1 15). This power struggle culminated in the Achaean foundation of the

---

[28] Guzzo 2003.
[29] Piccarreta 2001, 381.
[30] For recent reviews of the literary tradition and of modern studies about it, see in particular De Juliis 2000, Moggi 2002 and Lombardo 2002.

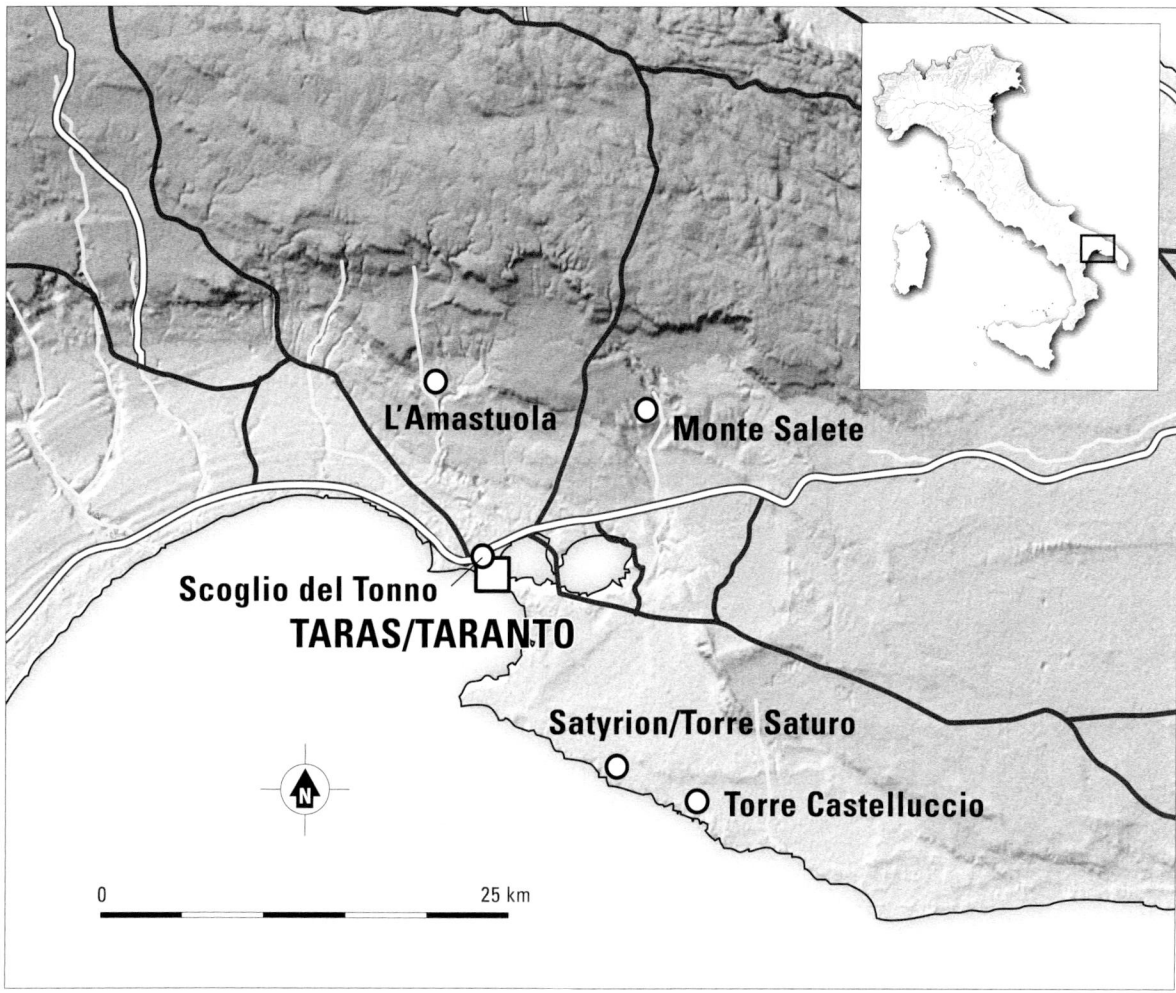

Fig. 6.2. Topography of the Taranto area, with major sites mentioned in the text. For a colour version of this figure, see page 227.

polis of Metapontion between the Bradano and Basento rivers. After that, Taras' expansion proceeded primarily in the direction of its Salentine neighbours, and it ultimately carved out a territory in the Taranto plain.

As is the case at Sybaris, archaeological searches for ancient Taranto, though intensive, have met with limited results as the town lies buried beneath the modern city.[31] Moreover, the territory has not yielded the kind of abundant evidence found for instance in the Metaponto *chora*.[32] However, it is commonly argued that the datasets available indicate the formation of an agrarian system characterised by stable rural settlements in the Taranto *chora*. As in the Sibaritide and other Greek colonies, the establishment of such a stable territory at Taras is viewed as the logical outcome of an expansionist policy, implemented from the time the colony was reportedly founded during the late 8th century BC. As mentioned above, this assumption was long based primarily on written sources (dating to a much later time). A passage in Strabo, which recounts a Delphic oracle advising the founder Phalantos to take

---

[31] See in particular De Juliis 2000, Lippolis 2002 and Dell'Aglio 2001.

[32] Most information can be found in detailed inventories of the *Soprintendenza*'s archival registrations of incidental finds and small-scale excavations; Cocchiaro 1981; Alessio / Guzzo 1989-1990; Lo Porto 1990; Osanna 1992. See also section 3.3.3 for recent topographical research.

possession of the lands of Taras and to become a bane to the local Iapygians, forms the main support for this view.[33] And indeed, the archaeology of both the town and countryside has been interpreted in the light of this. Not surprisingly, it fits well into the conventional model that identifies Tarentine – and more generally Greek - colonization as the primary trigger of urbanization, landscape infill and related transformations in land use patterns in southern Italy.

Our discussion in the introduction to this chapter makes a critical assessment of this view from a theoretical perspective. In it, we have also underscored the fact that this model takes hardly any account of the agency of local peoples living in lands directly contested by the Greeks, or of those living further away. The recent research in the Sybaris plain by both the Roman School of Protohistory and the Groningen Institute of Archaeology has demonstrated that the local perspective adds significant nuances to traditional text-based accounts. This becomes even more evident whenever it proves possible to investigate areas outside the presumptive colonial *chorai*, as in the case of the Salento peninsula. The excavations carried out so far on this relatively flat peninsula point to a single conclusion: the Iron-Age Salento settlements were dispersed, consisting of spatially separated, stable groups of huts of relatively large dimensions.[34] As demonstrated by intensive field surveys, the total settlement space occupied by such groups of huts spanned areas as wide as 90 ha.[35] These were probably open settlements; Iron Age fortifications have as yet rarely been attested. The absence of contemporary funerary evidence is equally conspicuous, and complicates considerably the study of social phenomena in Salento communities.

With regard to funerary practices, it is generally accepted that Salento is exceptional among the South Italian Iron Age regions in that its dead were honoured and disposed of in archaeologically untraceable rituals. Formal burials are unknown until the late 7th/6th century BC, and then they occur in such small numbers that we can only conclude that large segments of the local population continued to be buried with traditional rites for a long time. The well-known series of *stelae* found at indigenous Salento sites, which date as far back as the Early Iron Age, lift a tip of the veil on the nature of these traditional rites since they are thought to be funerary markers (fig. 6.3).[36] They were probably associated with the elite, as has been claimed regarding a stele found at Cavallino featuring a depiction of a chariot.[37] Thus, they may parallel the contemporary elite manifestations in the burial grounds of neighbouring South Italian indigenous regions, which Bottini and Guzzo have tentatively interpreted in terms of social differentiation and increased competition.[38]

We should recall in this context that similar competitive tendencies have been identified in the pre-colonial Sibaritide, where they were related to a process of settlement expansion in the territories of the major sites (as discussed in section 6.3). Although Iron Age Salento has been relatively poorly investigated in this regard, certain broader, regional patterns can be also observed there. These too indicate indigenous landscape infill and territorial expansion, especially during the 8th century BC. The excavations cited above, notably those at Otranto, have been essential in clarifying the stratigraphical sequences of Iron-

---

[33] Antiochos of Syracuse, fr. 13 Jac, in Strabo Geogr. VI 3 2. Cf. Diodoros Siculus, *Bibliotheca Historica*, 8, fr. 21. See in particular Lombardo 1992, 10-11 and 59; 2002 with extensive further bibliography.

[34] Iron Age dwellings have been unearthed at such sites as Otranto, Cavallino, Vaste, Valesio, Oria, S. Vito dei Normanni and I Fani. For a comprehensive overview see especially D'Andria 1991 and Russo Tagliente 1992.

[35] Yntema 1993a, 157.

[36] Lombardo 1994. Unfortunately, most of these *stelae* were found in secondary contexts, which hampers verification of their conventional interpretation as being related to cult activities. Lombardo's interpretation of them as funerary markers is based on a shrewd examination of relevant written sources and archaeological data. Archaeologically, the most convincing argument is that in the few cases where such *stelae* have been found in situ they are related to later, formal graveyards, which suggests continuity in the use of formal space.

[37] Pancrazzi 1979, 233-235; D'Andria 1991, 409-413.

[38] Bottini / Guzzo 1986.

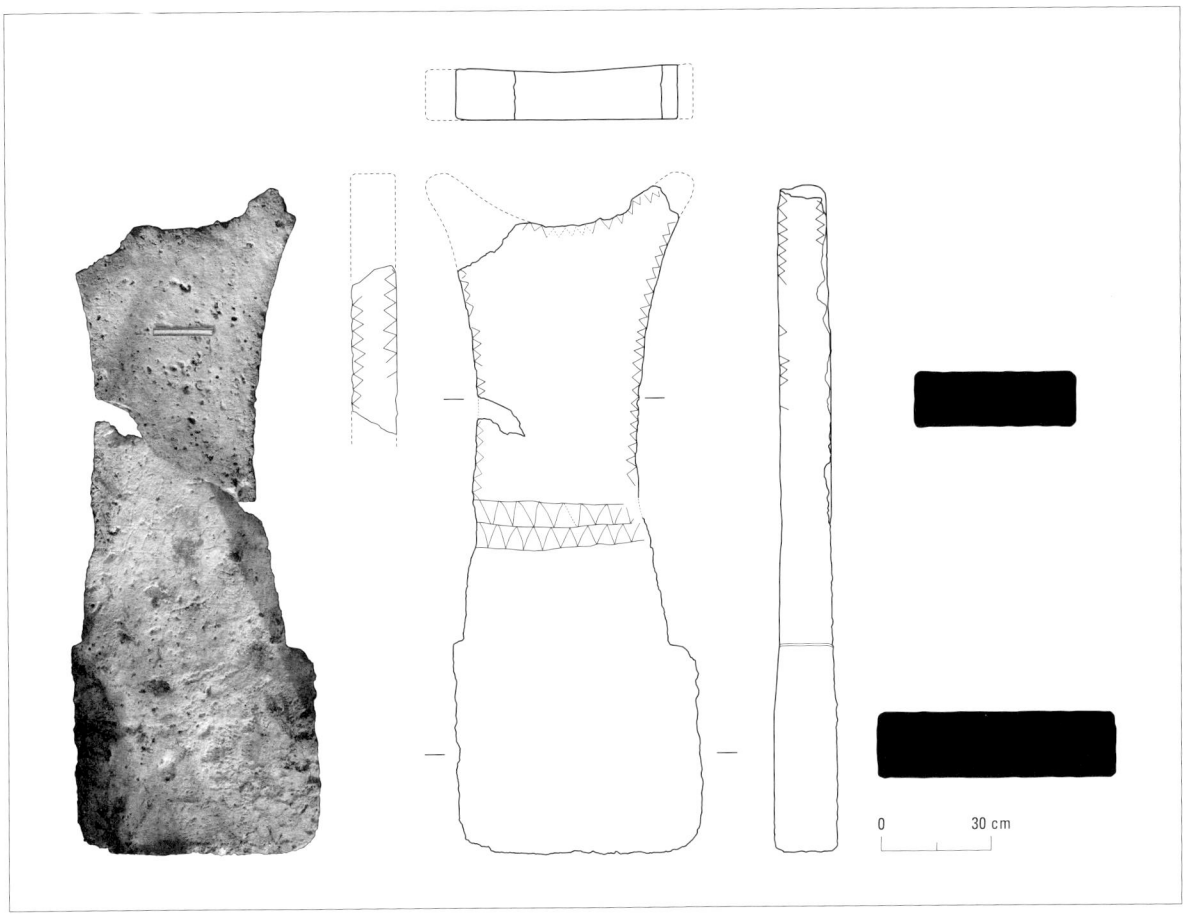

Fig. 6.3. Photo and line drawing of stele from the Archaic necropolis of L'Amastuola (Crispiano, TA). For a colour version of this figure, see page 228.

Age settlement contexts and chrono-typological series of related pottery repertoires. The latter make it possible to track changes in the distribution and density of the many incidental discoveries of Iron Age pottery at sites that have yet to be studied systematically. The major guide-type for this is the regional matt-painted pottery with geometric decoration, the individual type series of which can be dated to within 25-50 years.[39] According to analysis of the incidental Iron-Age finds in Salento, the number of locations with chronologically diagnostic matt-painted pottery types rises sharply during the later 8th century BC.[40] Indeed, these finds suggest that site numbers increased notably during that century, and that both the inland and coastal landscapes in between the pre-existing Iron Age sites were gradually filled in.

In a previous publication, one of us assessed and discounted the possibility that the exponential growth in the number of sites with matt-painted pottery was caused by the slackening of social restrictions on the distribution of matt-painted vessels.[41] The site increase must therefore reflect an actual settlement expansion across the larger part of the Salento peninsula. This thesis was methodically tested during the systematic site surveys launched by the ACVU in the Brindisi plain in north-eastern Salento.[42] From the sandy plains of the central Brindisino to the southern clayey soils of San Pancrazio and the coastal

[39] Yntema 1990.
[40] D'Andria 1991, 405; Burgers 1998, 186-189.
[41] Burgers 1998, 173-191
[42] Yntema 1993b; Burgers 1998.

Fig. 6.4. Oria in the Iron Age: find scatters (dark grey) and single finds (dots) (after Yntema 1993a, fig. 59). The thick line indicates the current extent of the urbanized area of Oria.

Adriatic area near Valesio, the surveyed areas all yielded incidental finds of Iron Age pottery. Remarkably, however, the results of the surveys also pointed to the 8th century BC as the period to which the earliest diagnostic pottery could be dated.[43] The distribution of the surface scatters within the survey areas in all cases conforms to the dispersed habitation patterns established for other Iron Age Salento sites on the basis of excavations. It contrasts strikingly with nucleated patterns such as those of the Roman surface concentrations recorded at the same sites.

A further comparison of the Iron Age settlement areas surveyed in this manner reveals rapid expansion at all of them. Although the sites presumably originated as fairly ephemeral rural settlements at various times throughout the 8th century, they all appear to have grown into substantial (dispersed) villages by the later 8th or early 7th century BC. Moreover, judging by the ACVU's additional rural surveys, isolated rural occupation seems to have been a limited phenomenon in Iron Age Salento. These surveys detected only a handful of such sites, which do not seem to have been occupied for more than one generation.[44] This indicates that the newly emerging habitation pattern was of a village type; the conclusion might be that villages constituted the rural landscape infill that characterised Salento in the (late) 8th century BC.

The aggregate extent covered by the individual new villages does not differ greatly, varying between

[43] Burgers 1998, 174-179.

[44] Yntema 1993a: Oria sites 7-1 and 13-7; Burgers 1998, 61: Muro Tenente site 7-4A.

[45] Burgers 1998, 174-179. These figures include open spaces between the nuclei; the surface effectively covered with scatters varies between 4 and 10 ha.

Box 6.1   Greeks and natives at L'Amastuola

In 1988, the late Grazia Angela Maruggi of the *Soprintendenza ai Beni Archeologici della Puglia* reported the find of an extensive necropolis just south of a hill called L'Amastuola, some 15 km north-west of the modern city of Taranto.[A] Most of the necropolis turned out to be robbed, but Maruggi was able to excavate some thirty tombs that had been overlooked. These tombs are all cut into the bedrock and were once covered by one or more stone slabs. The burials resemble closely the Greek ones common at Taranto, not only with regard to tomb architecture but also to the type of deposition (inhumation in a supine position), grave goods and related burial rites. It is particularly significant that the earliest burials were dated ca. 675 BC, i.e. shortly after the recorded foundation of Taras in the late 8th century. Right from the start of its discovery the necropolis aroused much scientific interest. It is commonly argued to be proof of the presence of a stable Greek community in the area and accordingly to attest to the northward territorial expansion that quickly followed the Spartan colonization of Taras.[B]

In 1991 Maruggi found and excavated the associated settlement some 800 m to the north of the necropolis, on a flat-topped ridge that reaches an altitude of c. 200 m above sea level.[C] Her trenches were located on the south-facing terrace, right behind the 18th-century *masseria* (centre of a landed estate) of L'Amastuola which crowns the highest point of the ridge. In 2003 these excavations were resumed by the ACVU in close collaboration with Maruggi, and they were accompanied by systematic field surveys and geophysical research.[D] The results of these investigations indicate that the settlement in fact started already in the second half of the 8th century BC, with hut-structures of a type common in the contemporary indigenous world. That the site was indeed inhabited by indigenous groups at this time can be inferred also from the ceramic repertoire used, which largely consists of characteristic indigenous coarse impasto and fine matt-painted wares.

In the light of the culturally very different cemetery discussed above, attention then shifted to the vicissitudes of the site in the 7th century BC. The initial excavations had suggested that the huts had been abandoned between 680 and 660 BC, and had been overbuilt rather abruptly with small rectangular dwellings using a different construction technique (mud brick or stone superstructures and tile roofs as compared to the wattle and daub of the previous huts). Since these new rural houses were similar to those current in contemporary contexts on the Greek mainland, the observed settlement transformation at L'Amastuola seemed to correspond with the start of the Greek-type necropolis nearby and was quickly taken to support the theory of a rather sudden Greek take-over at the cost of the original local community.[E]

However, ongoing fieldwork showed the situation to have been more complex. From the third quarter of the 7th century BC onwards, both settlement and necropolis seem to have been characterized not by a homogenous Greek material culture but by a heterogeneous one, with 'typical Greek' features such as burial customs and house plans, mixed with 'typical indigenous' features such as the defensive system, hut plans, ceramic repertoires, and a stele found in the middle of the necropolis (fig. 6.3). Such a context is hardly proof of the presence of an ethnically Greek community controlling part of an extensive Greek territory, as has been proposed before. Instead, Burgers and Crielaard emphasize the complexity of the colonial encounter and argue that Greek and indigenous groups lived together at l'Amastuola.[F]

[A] Maruggi 1996.
[B] De Juliis 1996; Greco 2001.
[C] Maruggi 1996.
[D] Burgers / Crielaard 2007 and 2008.
[E] Greco 2001.
[F] Burgers / Crielaard 2007 and 2008.

Fig. 6.5. Bird's-eye view of the archaeological site and masseria of L'Amastuola, with ACVU trenches visible to the left of centre (photo by permission of Mr. Giuseppe Montanaro). For a colour version of this figure, see page 229.

15 and 28 ha.[45] However, a definite hierarchy emerges when we consider the site of Oria, whose total settlement area Yntema estimates at nearly 90 ha (fig. 6.4).[46] Significantly, Oria is also the only Iron Age site in this part of the Brindisi district that is known to have been continuously occupied from the Bronze Age onwards.[47] In fact, it expanded into a major fortified settlement in the Late Bronze Age, and is thus arguably one of the few sites that survived the process of selection in the Final Bronze Age. Apparently, it expanded again during the 8th century BC, when it became the largest population centre in the Brindisi region. In this phase there also emerged small sites in its territory, including that of Muro Tenente. In other cases, like Valesio, the new village was probably laid out *ex novo* on previously untilled land. Significantly, the locations of most of the new settlements seem to have been selected with a view to exploiting a range of resource zones.[48] Once again, Valesio is an example: its catchment area offers both fertile soils for cereal cultivation and a coastal lagoon environment suitable for animal husbandry.[49]

A similar argument can be advanced regarding the western part of the Salento isthmus. Like Oria, various sites there, including Taranto/Scoglio del Tonno, Torre Castelluccia, Torre Saturo and Monte Salete, have Bronze Age origins and were undoubtedly also inhabited by native communities during the 8th century BC.[50] Analysis of the surface scatters detected during Fornaro's extensive topographical

[46] An estimate based on all available information from archives, excavations and surveys; Yntema 1993a, 157.
[47] Maruggi 2001.
[48] Burgers 1998, 190.
[49] Bijlsma / Verhagen 1989.
[50] It was not until recently that a systematic survey project was launched there (the 'Murge Upland Survey'), and it is therefore more difficult to arrive at any reconstructions of regional settlement configurations. On Scoglio del Tonno and Torre Castelluccio, see in particular Taylour 1958; on Torre Saturo: Lo Porto 1964; on Monte Salete: D'Andria 1991, 414 note 20.

research into the limestone Murge landscape around Grottaglie suggests that this upland area was also characterised by Iron-Age settlement expansion and infill.[51] In most cases, the origins of the new sites recorded by Fornaro proved impossible to date more precisely than that, but the only systematically excavated site yielded stratigraphical proof that it was founded during the 8th century BC.[52] A similar conclusion can be drawn with regard to the site at L'Amastuola, which is strategically located on a hilltop at approximately 8 km from the Ionian gulf and overlooks the larger part of the Taranto coastal plain (fig. 6.5; see also Box 6.1). The recent excavations and field surveys by the *Soprintendenza ai Beni Archeologici della Puglia* and the ACVU at this site suggest that it, too, was founded sometime during the second half of the 8th century BC. If the results of these systematic excavations and surveys are indeed representative of the many incidentally discovered Iron Age sites in Salento, we must conclude that during the 8th century BC the region's native communities engaged in settlement expansion, rural infill and reclamation of previously non-exploited or only marginally exploited landscapes. These processes seem to have involved virtually all major Salento landscape units, including the Taranto plain, and would have conditioned the circumstances in which early Greek colonisation took place.

In recent years various hypotheses have been proposed to explain the developments outlined above. Population growth, socio-economic differentiation and related elite proliferation as well as the quest for control over agricultural and pastoral resources were certainly among the most prominent factors.[53] One almost inevitable conclusion is that the transformations in the arrangement of settlements indicate a redefinition of territorial boundaries within the local communities, as well as territorial expansion and corresponding conflicts between indigenous groups.

6.5 QUESTIONING EARLY GREEK COLONIAL IMPACT

In view of the above we must seriously question the importance of Greek trade or Greek migrants in triggering changes to contemporary indigenous settlement and social configurations in general, and especially in Salento. In the introduction to this chapter, we argued that this role has long been over-emphasized in the light of a Hellenist tradition that leans heavily on a literal reading of the ancient written sources. This explains the classical-archaeological focus on Greek contexts in the colonial enclaves and on the presence of colonial Greek artefacts in indigenous contexts. In turn, the very discovery of these contexts encouraged theories of Greek colonial expansion, power and impact.

Besides the theoretical objections discussed in the introduction, this Hellenist focus is subject to other criticisms as well. First, it should be noted that early colonial Greek objects do not abound in indigenous contexts. Most Greek artefacts in Salento, including those dating to the early colonial and pre-colonial periods, arrived there by means of trans-Adriatic contacts,[54] now interpreted in terms of indigenous-Greek exchange networks. There is no evidence to suggest that the Greeks dominated this exchange, or that the Greek objects had an intrinsically prestigious allure. In a review of relevant datasets, one of us had therefore already set aside the one-sided Greek perspective and argued that the constant internal pressures of social reproduction and the accompanying tendency towards emulation were what prompted indigenous elites to grasp opportunities for exchange.[55] These elites began using Greek objects and may have associated themselves with Greek ideas and customs, redefining and appropriating them as well as integrating them into existing aspects of the local value systems. Ultimately, the appeal of Greek objects

---

[51] Fornaro 1976-1977; Fornaro / Alessio 2000.

[52] The site of masseria Vicentino; see especially Fornaro / Alessio 2000.

[53] E.g., D'Andria 1991, 405; Yntema 1993a, 161; Burgers 1998, 190-191.

[54] D'Andria 1984.

[55] Burgers 1998, 179-194.

and of associating with Greeks in general may well have depended on autonomous indigenous strategies.

And there is yet another reason to think that exchange with overseas Greeks played a subordinate role in local social dynamics. The Iron-Age settlement pattern that developed in the Salento peninsula displays remarkable similarities in its geomorphological location and spacing of settlements to that in the Sibaritide. Here, too, sites are spaced some 10-12 km apart, often in defensible positions. This pattern continues into the interior, and may in fact be more strictly related to the mobilization of and control over high-quality agricultural and pastoral resources.[56]

Our second objection to the focus on colonial Greek contexts is closely related to the first. Compared to the indigenous southern-Italian archaeological records, Italiote-Greek contexts are highly visible. Hence, the visibility of the formation of a colonial *chora* is disproportionately high as compared to that of indigenous territories. Viewed the other way around, indigenous expansion and territorial disputes are disproportionately invisible because of the relative uniformity in local material culture. In our discussion above, we have considered a range of new evidence to overcome this bias. We have every reason to posit a regional process involving internal colonization, expansion and territorial redefinition by indigenous groups. Correspondingly, the Greek migrant groups in the Sybaris and Taranto plains are arguably just one more participant in this process.

There is yet more to support this argument. Yntema approached the subject from a different angle in his review of the historical and archaeological data available on the early Greek presence in south-east Italy.[57] Drawing on modern studies on social identity, one of Yntema's major arguments is that the oracles and colonial foundation accounts recorded by the written sources should be viewed as origin myths created or transformed during the Archaic and Classical periods to conform to specific contemporary socio-political circumstances and agendas. Contextualising the myths primarily in these later phases, Yntema argues that they were redefined or invented to provide the rapidly developing urban communities of the time with a heroic colonial, and ethnically Greek, past. Accordingly, the colonial charters cannot be considered reliable accounts of the early, 8th and 7th-century BC contact phases. Nor should they be taken literally in their portrayal of the colonial ventures as mass migrations inherently marked by aggression and expansion.

In the first part of this chapter we have already discussed at length the case of the Sybaris region, concluding with Kleibrink's contention that the latter witnessed gradual, and relatively late, Greek settlement colonialism.[58] In the case of Salento a similar argument must be proposed on the basis of sites such as those at Otranto and Tor Pisana/Brindisi, which merit special attention as they are generally considered to have harboured small Greek communities among, or on the fringes of, established indigenous settlements. This conclusion is based on the presence of specific closed assemblages of Greek artefacts amongst local indigenous contexts.[59] The traces of these communities can be compared with those of a small dispersed hut settlement from the mid-7th century BC excavated at Metapontion/Andrisani-Lazzazzera. Due to the patently Greek ceramics in this settlement it is thought to have been inhabited by Greek migrants only.[60] In southeast Italy, parallels for both of these contexts can be found at L'Amastuola

---

[56] Van Leusen 2002, chapter 11, 22; cf. Burgers 1998, 190.
[57] Yntema 2000; cf. Osborne 1998.
[58] Yntema 2000; Kleibrink 2001.
[59] Yntema 2000, 23-25; cf. D'Andria 1988, 655-656 and 1991, 403; Lombardo 1995. The Otranto and Brindisi contexts are dated to the late 8th/mid-7th and the middle of the 7th century BC, respectively. At Otranto, the presence of Greeks has been inferred from warehouses containing unusually large numbers of Greek and notably Corinthian imports. At Brindisi/Tor Pisana a small graveyard has been discovered with cremation and inhumation burials containing only Greek ceramics.
[60] De Siena 1996.

(see above, Box 6.1), L'Incoronata, Siris-Polieion in Basilicata, and possibly at Taras and Torre Saturo in Salento.[61] In comparing these data to the evidence of indigenous settlements discussed in more detail above, we can deduce that migrant Greeks were indeed present in south-eastern Italy from at least the later 8th century BC, albeit mainly in relatively small groups living in indigenous settlements or at the margins of indigenous territories.[62] If we substitute the conventional Graeco-centred perspective for an 'indigenous' one, as proposed in the introduction, we could argue that these small early Greek groups were involved in the contemporary indigenous socio-political arena. Association with foreigners may not only have enhanced prestige among one's own and other indigenous communities; the newcomers may also have played a role in internal political/territorial struggles as well as in intertribal warfare.[63]

Admittedly, these reconstructions of early indigenous-Greek encounters are largely hypothetical. However, the same is true for theories emphasizing early Greek colonial interventions and territorial expansion. The merit of the reconstructions presented here is that they place those written sources in a sociologically embedded context related to their own time. Finally, it should be noted that the text-based tradition takes hardly any account of the increasing amount of data on indigenous settlement transformations, hierarchies, territorial expansion and reclamation. In reviewing these data, we have every reason to question the dominant role of relatively small groups of Greek migrants and to propose a different theory of cooperation and co-habitation, or even of indigenous domination.

---

[61] Yntema (2000) briefly discusses the archaeology and the bibliography of these sites. No early Greek settlement traces have been recorded at Taranto. Only a very small number of Greek burials can be dated to the first half of the 7th century BC (Dell'Aglio 2001). The number does not rise significantly until the 2nd half of the 7th century. For Torre Saturo, Yntema contests the rigid separation of 8th-century BC indigenous strata from the successive, entirely 'Greek' layers recorded by Lo Porto (1964). He notes that the most recent indigenous wares can be dated roughly to 680/660 BC, i.e. later than some of the wares in the Greek strata (Yntema 2000, 21-23). Yntema suggests that the site harboured a small, mixed indigenous-Greek community in the first half of the 7th century BC, which erected a Greek-like sanctuary and began to bury their dead in Greek-style cemeteries in the 2nd half of that century.

[62] Yntema 2000; cf. Burgers 1998, 180-194; Kleibrink 2001. The archaeological data suggest that it was only towards the later 7th century BC that a few of these sites (Siris, Metapontion and Taras) began to grow rapidly, subsequently developing into flourishing population centres characterized by an urban material culture.

[63] Burgers 1998, 183-194; Yntema 2000.

7 Indigenous Urbanization in the Archaic Period

7.1 INTRODUCTION

Recent archaeological research has demonstrated that 7th and 6th-century BC urbanization in central and southern Italy was a process that involved non-Greek and non-Roman regions to a much greater extent than was previously believed. Whilst urban characteristics had been recognized in these regions before, they barely received archaeological attention, and when they did, it was mainly as cursory asides in studies focusing on Greek or Roman colonization and urbanism. In southern Italy, for instance, the 'Greek' aspect of indigenous Archaic fortifications was seen as an indication of the diffusive strength of the urban culture of the coastal poleis, along the lines of the Hellenization paradigm discussed in chapter 6. Nowadays the same Archaic fortifications are seen as symbols of the central role of the settlements they defended, each of which came to dominate an extensive territory in what can be defined as a basically autonomous process. Similarly, in central Italy the study of indigenous territories has traditionally been guided by a focus on Roman colonization and domination. This is especially true for the Pontine region and for Latium in general, which in ancient accounts of the history of Rome figures as a laboratory of early Roman colonization. Here again, more recent approaches have abandoned such perspectives in favour of a focus on endogenous developments. In this chapter the new insights this has brought will be illustrated by a discussion of two of the RPC regions, both of which provide evidence of essentially indigenous urbanization in Archaic Italy.

7.2 ARCHAIC URBANIZATION IN THE SALENTO PENINSULA

7.2.1 URBANIZATION AND SETTLEMENT SPACE

The site of Castello in the foothills of the Murge plateau near San Vito dei Normanni, in the north of the Salento peninsula, is an example of the recent rapid progress of archaeological research and the corresponding need to revise traditional views (fig. 7.1). Until 1985 it was not even formally registered, and it has only attracted substantial scientific attention since 1994.[1] Subsequent excavations by the *Soprintendenza ai Beni Archeologici della Puglia* and by Lecce University have demonstrated that the site was first inhabited in the 8th century BC. The excavations demonstrated especially the significance of its Archaic occupation phase, when the previous Iron-Age hut settlement was thoroughly transformed. The best evidence for this transformation is the presence of stone foundations of a monumental rectangular building located at the highest point of the site.[2] This building differs in many respects from the more common domestic structures in Archaic Salento. For example, the associated layers contain large numbers of imported ceramics and amphoras mainly imported from Corinth and Corcyra. These are related to the acquisition and consumption of wine and olive oil, and indicate wide-ranging international contacts. The dimensions of the building, its architectural features and its prominent location have caused the excava-

---

[1] Cocchiaro 1998; Semeraro 1998a. [2] Semeraro 1998a.

tors to interpret it as a palatial structure intended for elite residence. It dominated a settlement area of approximately 3 ha that was itself surrounded by a monumental stone rampart.

The urban characteristics of the site of Castello di San Vito dei Normanni are paralleled at a grander scale by those at Cavallino in the very heart of the Salento peninsula (fig. 7.1).[3] Currently the most extensively excavated Archaic site in the region, the Lecce University excavations at Cavallino have demonstrated that it began as a dispersed hut village during the general 8th-century settlement expansion (see section 6.4). Around the mid-6th century BC it underwent major changes and acquired an urban appearance. Hut compounds were replaced by houses with a rectangular plan, stone foundations carrying stone or mudbrick walls, and roofs covered with tiles. As at Castello, variations in house size and in the complexity of the ground plan as well as the occasional presence of architectural roof decorations suggest that social differentiation was expressed in the residential sphere. The presence of imported architectural decorations has even led the excavators to argue that specialised foreign craftsmen were involved in the building projects. That these projects required a considerable degree of planning can be deduced from the fact that most of the houses are arranged in large habitation quarters, with blocks of adjoining houses flanking paved roads. Moreover, in a recently excavated section of the site a large water reservoir was found that was fed through an ingenious system of numerous channels cut into the limestone bedrock and covered by massive stones.[4] Finally, three monumental stone wall-circuits were uncovered, the outer one of which enclosed a total settlement area of 69 ha.

These two sites are merely the first examples of the scale of urbanization of the Archaic settlement system in the Salento. Similar urban features are gradually being uncovered at other sites as well, from Masseria I Fani in the southern tip of the peninsula to Oria on the Salento isthmus.[5] All of them appear to have developed a greater degree of internal articulation in the Archaic; they are also rather regularly distributed over most of the region at approximate intervals of 10-12 km, which suggests that the larger part of the peninsula was involved in this urbanization process. Moreover, as will be discussed in the next section, there is evidence for the emergence of a settlement hierarchy, with smaller centres functioning as satellites in the territories of the major ones.

7.2.2 SETTLEMENT HIERARCHIES IN THE BRINDISI REGION

It is unfortunate that the extent of most Archaic sites is as yet unknown, for this severely restricts the possibilities for evaluation of the degree to which settlement hierarchies had developed (cf. Box 8.1). Here lies a major task for survey archaeology, which is particularly suited to confront this issue. More generally, the details of the spatial and social dynamics of the urbanization process are yet to be established. In the case of one of the core research areas of the RPC project, the Brindisi region in northern Salento, this central theme is being studied through a combination of surveys, excavations and other datasets.

ACVU surveys in the Brindisino indicate that most landscape units were already reclaimed in the Iron Age, and that the transition from the Iron Age to the Archaic period was not marked by the founding of new sites, villages or farms. In addition to demonstrating a basic continuity in site pattern, the surveys suggest that the settlement hierarchy that had developed in the course of the 8th-7th centuries BC stabilized in the Archaic period (fig. 7.1 and table 7.1). Whilst sites such as Li Castelli di San Pancrazio, Muro Maurizio and Muro Tenente are each estimated to have covered some 20-25 ha in the Archaic phase, contemporary Oria still exceeded them by far at 40-50 ha. The site of Valesio arguably occupied

---

[3] On the Cavallino excavations see especially Pancrazzi 1979, Nenci 1987, and D'Andria 1988 and 1990, all with extensive bibliographies.

[4] Mastronuzzi 1999, 56.

[5] On Masseria I Fani see Descoeudres / Robinson 1993; on Oria see sections 7.2.2 and 7.2.3.

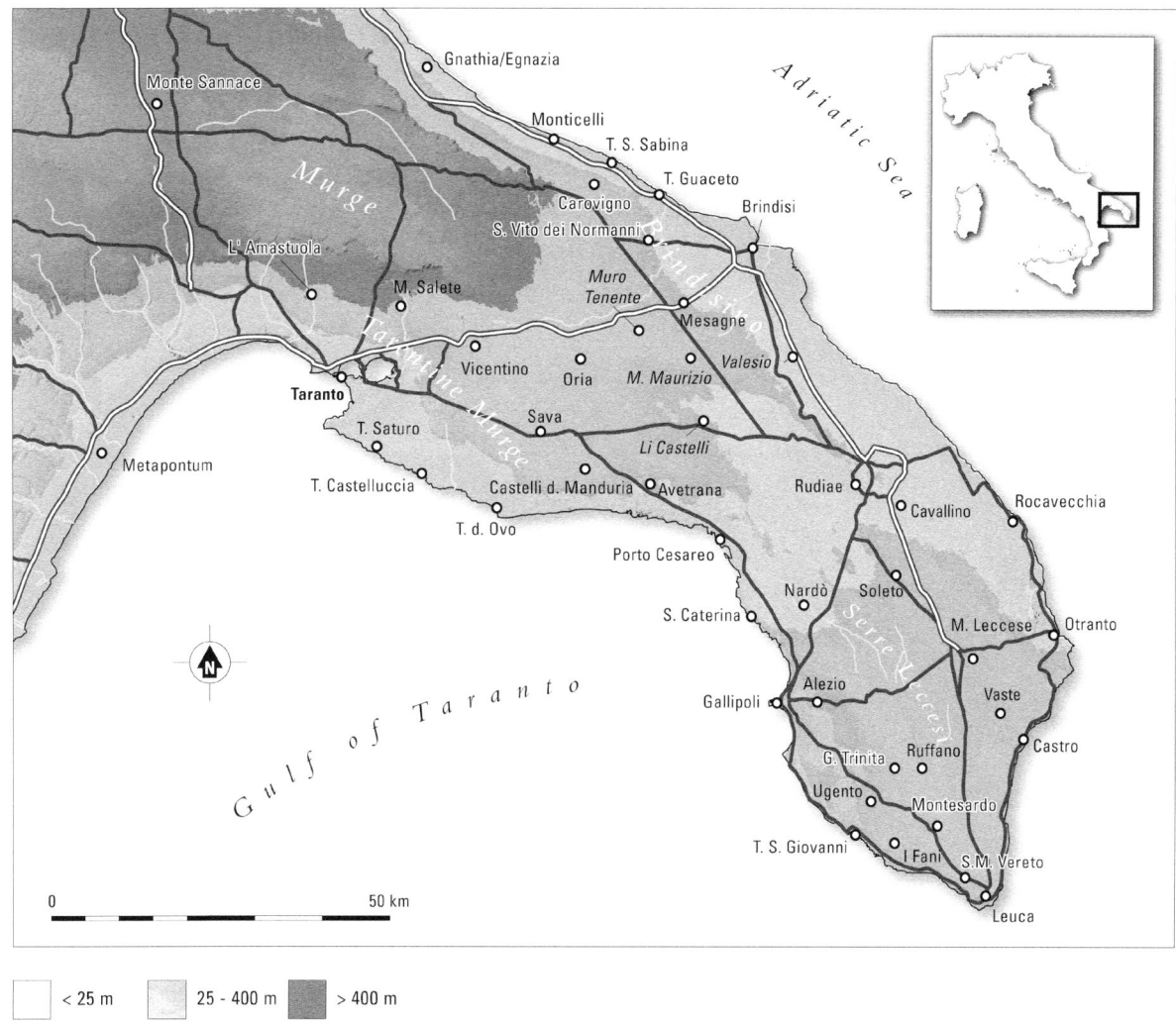

Fig. 7.1. Archaic sites of the Salento (after Semeraro 1998, 6). For a colour version of this figure, see page 230.

an intermediate level, with some 30 ha covered by dispersed surface scatters. Neither the local geomorphology nor any differences in occupation density are likely to have caused this variation in site sizes.

There is some evidence to suggest that Oria was not the only site of outstanding size. A comparison of estimated Archaic site dimensions with those for the better documented Hellenistic period (table 7.1) shows that these towns more or less doubled in size in the Hellenistic period. Oria (118 ha) continued to exceed by far sites of secondary significance like San Pancrazio (57 ha), Muro Tenente (52 ha) and Muro Maurizio (34 ha). At 83 ha Valesio continued to occupy an intermediate level in the Hellenistic hierarchy. Indeed, all sites for which estimates can be made seem to have grown proportionally in the early Hellenistic period. The Hellenistic dimensions of Ceglie Messapico (118 ha) and Brindisi (104 ha) may therefore indicate that these sites already ranked equally with Oria (and Valesio?) in the Archaic period. If it is accepted that the Hellenistic size ranking may be projected back in time in this manner, an Archaic settlement configuration may be proposed for the Brindisi region that was dominated by a handful of 'primary' sites of equal status that were located at intervals of some 20-30 km from each other and incorporated a range of satellite sites within their territories.

137

Site	Estimated extent (ha.)	
	Archaic	early Hellenistic
Oria	40-50	118
Ceglie Messapico	?	118
Brindisi	?	104
Valesio	30	83
Li Castelli di San Pancrazio Salentino	25	57
Muro Tenente	20-25	52
Muro Maurizio	20-25	34
Loc. Castello di San Vito	3	--
Cavallino (Lecce province)	69	--

Table 7.1. Aggregate and effective extent of the largest Archaic and early Hellenistic sites in the Brindisino.

Of course, our hypothesis about the emergence of such a settlement configuration should also be tested against qualitative data. Most of the larger sites have yielded very few data bearing directly on their status in the regional settlement hierarchy, but it seems highly significant that both Brindisi and Valesio have produced written symbols of socio-political self-identification or self-definition as early as the Archaic/Classical period. On the basis of epigraphic and numismatic evidence both sites therefore appear to have constituted autonomous socio-political polities, where concepts of communal organization and central management of public affairs were institutionalized.

7.2.3 ORIA: ARCHAIC URBANIZATION IN THE CENTRAL BRINDISI PLAIN

At the moment, the central Brindisi plain, with the site of Oria at its centre, offers the best data for interpreting site size hierarchy in social terms. At Oria a number of small trenches dug by the *Soprintendenza* provide the evidence for an Archaic urban rearrangement along the lines of Cavallino as discussed above, in the form of traces of late 6th-century dwellings and roads. Moreover, previous excavations brought to light the remains of a late-Archaic monumental stone fortification that probably surrounded the summit of the central Oritan hill.[6] The site itself physically changed in the Archaic, and so did its socio-economic and religious relationship with its territory

The evidence for this comes from various contexts. First, Oria probably began to supply its territory with pottery: Maruggi's intensive explorations at Oria have uncovered part of an Archaic potter's quarter producing wheel-thrown banded cups of Greek type.[7] Similar banded wares have been found at neighbouring secondary sites such as Muro Tenente,[8] and whereas the more abundant handmade impasto wares there were very probably locally made, it is doubtful if this applied to the finer wheel-thrown products as well. Certainly no kilns of the Oria type have been discovered yet at Muro Tenente, despite extensive excavations by both the *Soprintendenza* and the ACVU. Detailed characterization studies are still needed to support the impression based on macroscopic analysis, that the wheel-thrown banded wares found at Muro Tenente and other Brindisino sites were actually produced at Oria, and that the latter therefore was the regional central place for the production and distribution of these types of ceramics. It must also be pointed out in this context that the local production of banded wheel-thrown pottery was a novelty in 6th-century BC Salento. This required new skills and a higher degree of labour organization, as was also the case for the new building programmes.[9] Indeed, this craft specialization must be considered another trait typical of Archaic urban development in Salento; it most likely manifested itself first in urbanising contexts such as Oria.

[6] Andreassi 1981; Maruggi 2001.
[7] Maruggi 1995; 2001, 18-19 and 59.
[8] Burgers 1998, 53-59.
[9] Yntema 2001, 109; Mater 2005, 48-50.

There are other lines of argument to support a role for Archaic Oria as a central place. As discussed in the previous chapter, burial rites have not yet been recognized for Iron Age Salento. It is only from the late 7th/6th century BC that archaeologically recognisable funerary depositions were introduced, in the form of inhumation burials in pit- or cist graves containing mainly ceramic grave goods. Since the number of such formal burials was initially very small and increased only gradually, large sections of the community probably continued to dispose of their dead in traditional, archaeologically invisible ways (see also the discussion in section 6.4). This has led one of us to argue that the introduction of the new burial types and the associated funerary rites was linked to social differentiation and elite manifestation.[10] Significantly, the new burial rites seem to have made their first appearance at Oria, and were afterwards only gradually emulated by neighbouring groups on the Salento isthmus. It seems therefore justified to emphasize the role of the Oritan elites in introducing a new ritual grammar in communications with the ancestors.

This line of reasoning can be expanded to include Archaic transformations in other types of ritual contexts as well. Along with urbanization, another marked phenomenon associated with the transition from the Early Iron Age to the Archaic period is the formalization of religious space through the introduction of sanctuaries as major landscape features. These are commonly found outside the immediate settlement areas, making use of prominent landscape features like hilltops or cliffs, both inland and on the coast. In the Brindisino this is particularly apparent in the hilly landscape around Oria. Here, excavations carried out by the University of Lecce have demonstrated that a sanctuary was founded in the course of the 6th century BC on a small natural terrace on the western slope of the Monte Papalucio hill, some 300 m east of Oria's acropolis. At the back of the terrace is a cave dug into the hill, and it is the cave which is thought to have been the focus of the sanctuary. Archaic structures are present only in the form of terrace walls delimiting the cult area. The great abundance and diversity of votives offered, ranging from objects of gilded silver-plate to a wide variety of pottery types, suggest that the sanctuary was used by many strata of society. Whitehouse and Wilkins have proposed to interpret the site on Monte Papalucio, and other similar sanctuaries in south-east Italy, as the spatial setting for native trade and contact with Greeks.[11] In support of this 'port of trade'-theory they point out that a great variety of Greek pottery is generally found at these sites, as is indeed the case at Oria. Attractive as this idea may sound, it has been objected by others that the imported pottery may represent votives offered by the local people rather than any direct involvement of Greeks.[12] We are more inclined to interpret the relatively sudden emergence of the sanctuaries as spatial settings for religious worship, and interpret their relatively sudden emergence in the 6th century BC in the light of the introduction of new, more formal rituals for communicating with the supernatural. The contemporaneity of this phenomenon with the introduction of a new ritual/symbolic burial grammar discussed above reinforces our view that elite strategies underlie both developments.

There is evidence to suggest that these strategies served to integrate larger sections of the local communities. This can be deduced from the great variety of sanctuary votives, which suggests that the cult was not at all restricted to elite circles. It can further be observed that the nearest potentially analogous sites are found near Ceglie Messapico and Valesio, two of the sites that we have already argued to have been equal in status to Oria (see above, table 7.1). The sanctuary near Ceglie Messapico, the Grotta Abate Nicola, is also a cave site and is interpreted as a cult place on the basis of occasional finds of votives such as terracotta figurines and miniature pottery. The same materials have also been discovered in what appears to be an open-air context at Campisani, some 400 m north of the Valesio settlement.[13] The ACVU Valesio Survey demonstrated that this site covered the same time span as the Monte Papalucio sanctuary, likewise starting in the 6th century BC. Both these sanctuary sites must await further investigation to establish the precise extent of their similarity to Oria-Monte Papalucio, but it is safe to observe, for now, that they

---

[10] Burgers 1998, 195-224; Burgers / Yntema 2000.

[11] Whitehouse / Wilkins 1989.

[12] Burgers 1998, 216-217.

[13] On the Valesio sanctuary: Marzano 1964; Burgers 1998, 202-207.

seem to be the only ones in the Brindisi region that come close. No similar sites were discovered by the ACVU surveys in the countryside around other nearby, but smaller Archaic population centres. It appears that the formalization of cult places did not affect the entire region equally; the distribution of the sanctuaries rather suggests a political-geographical differentiation structured around the presumed major central places.

Summarizing the line of argument presented above, one may conclude that Salento in the Archaic period was characterized by a process of urbanization which involved the larger part of the peninsula. This process is best documented at Oria and Cavallino, but the recent intensification of archaeological research elsewhere indicates that a wide range of sites shared in it, from Masseria I Fani in the far south to Castello di San Vito dei Normanni in the foothills of the northern Murge. Although it affected a large area within a relatively short period, it also introduced archaeologically visible differences in site status. In the Brindisi region a few sites stand out; apart from Oria these are Ceglie Messapico, Brindisi and possibly Valesio. To evaluate the wider implications of the transformations of these primary sites, we have elaborated on the role of Oria in the central Brindisi plain. Oria not only acquired an urban appearance in the Archaic period, but at the same time began to function as a central place for the other settlements in its immediate hinterland in more ways than one. If Oria is typical for the other presumed primary settlements of the Brindisino, the Archaic urbanization process must have been accompanied by the formation of a series of independent socio-political entities, each centred on an urban nucleus and incorporating a number of secondary settlements in its territory.

7.3 URBANIZATION AND EARLY ROMAN COLONIZATION IN THE PONTINE REGION

7.3.1 LATIAL URBANIZATION AND ROMAN COLONIZATION IN THE PONTINE REGION

As was argued in chapter 2, Satricum is a key site for the study of urbanization in south Latium, since excavations have shown that the initial late-9th century BC hut settlement gradually expanded in the course of the Iron Age, and was thoroughly rearranged during the 6th century BC.[14] In this later phase the Iron Age structures were levelled to provide space for a new urban area consisting of rectangular and tile-roofed structures (referred to with the Greek term *oikoi*) grouped around a temple with three adjacent courtyard buildings. Towards the end of the 6th century this temple was replaced by a larger one with long *stoai* arranged in an orthogonal plan. Other public works were carried out simultaneously, such as the construction of an impressive defensive work in the form of an *agger*, an earth rampart which delineated the western part of the settlement area (cf. our discussion in section 2.3.1).

As in Salento, increased territorial organization in Archaic Latium is above all apparent in the regular distribution of similarly-sized Archaic towns (fig. 7.2), with Rome being merely the best known of them. Throughout the region the Iron Age proto-urban settlements increased in size and assumed a formal layout (streets, aligned buildings, defences), within which the buildings became differentiated architecturally into cultic and domestic variants.[15] An interpretation of the Late Iron Age/Archaic settlement configuration in Latium as an interacting system in the sense of Renfrews' peer polities model therefore seems warranted (Box 1.3).[16] The evident signs of socio-economic differentiation in Latial burial grounds of the 7th century BC can also be interpreted in this light. Clearly the competitive strategies employed in this peer-polity

---

[14] See especially Maaskant-Kleibrink 1987 and 1992 with bibliographies; Gnade 1992; Attema 1993; and most recently Gnade 2008.

[15] Van 't Lindenhout forthcoming.

[16] cf. Bouma / Van 't Lindenhout 1996-1997.

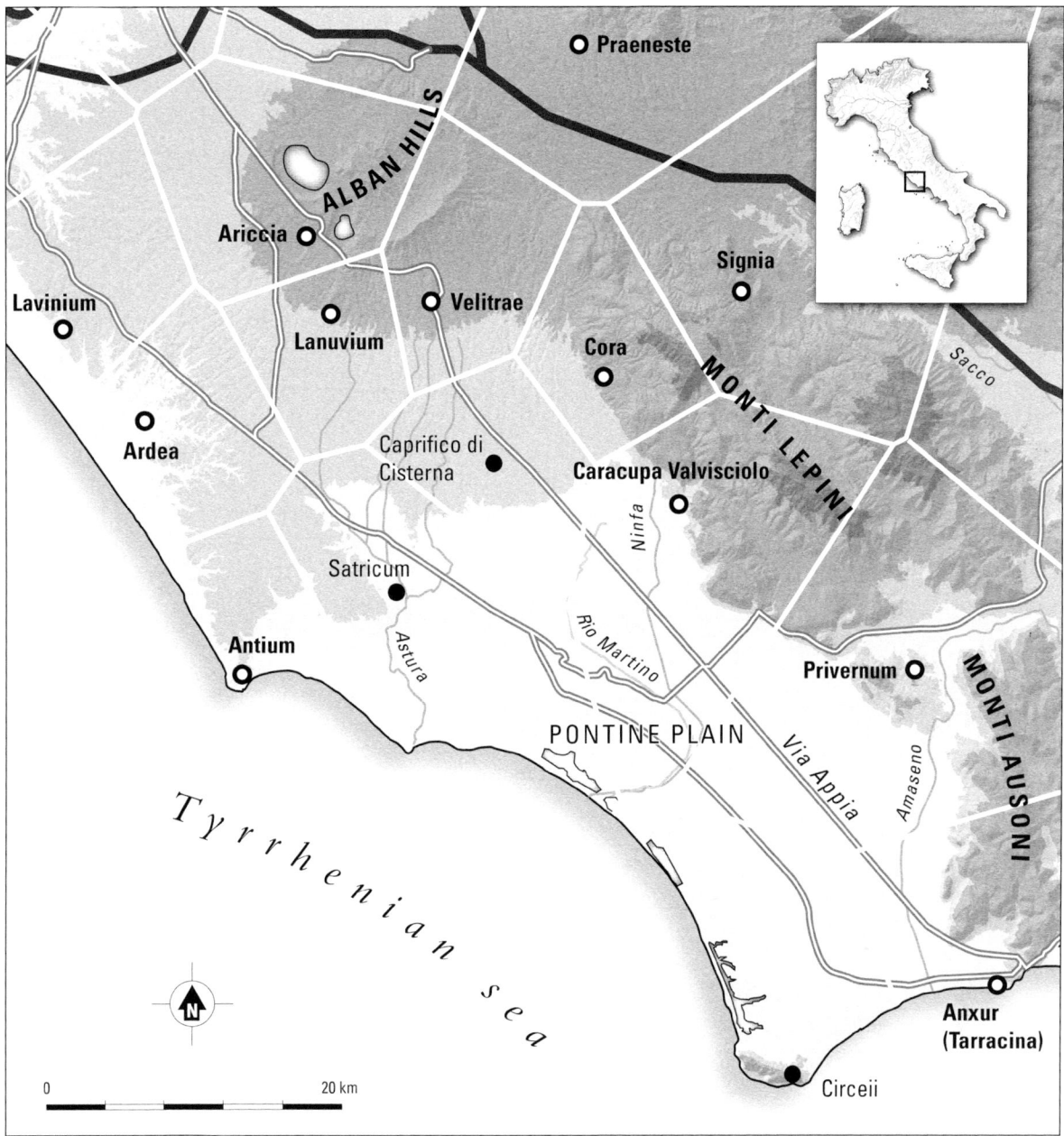

Fig. 7.2. Archaic proto-urban sites in south Lazio, with hypothetical territorial boundaries based on Thiessen polygons (T. de Haas, GIA). For a colour version of this figure, see page 231.

interaction included wide-ranging external contacts. Such contacts demonstrably still existed in the Archaic period, even though the almost complete absence of graves indicates that the practice of elite burial had already been discontinued. Imported goods were by then used mainly in religious contexts. In view of the fact that Archaic towns at the same time developed a rich cultic life, which is archaeologically visible in the form of decorated temples and votive deposits, it may be postulated that Latial urbanization at this time was accompanied by a transfer of wealth display from person-centred to commune-centred contexts.

With increasing urbanization in Latium, the political equilibrium implicit in the peer-polity system gradually broke down in favour of a more prominent and finally dominant role of Rome. Whilst the earliest Roman expansion was directed mainly at its immediate neighbours, it is the slightly more remote Pontine plain that – according to literary tradition – was the first region to be actually colonised. This colonization is sometimes argued to have started under the monarchy, in the course of the 6th century BC, although generally the early-Republican foundation dates of the so-called *priscae coloniae latinae* recorded by Livy are thought to be more plausible. Thus, according to Livy (II, 34.6) in 492 BC a colony was sent to Norba '*quae arx in Pomptino esset*', perched on the Lepine scarp and overlooking the Pontine plain. Other recorded early colonies include Setia, Signia and Cora, all of them located in dominant positions on the outer rim of the Lepine mountain range. Unfortunately Livy does not provide any clear information on the nature of Roman occupation at these sites, nor is it possible to tell from his accounts if they were already inhabited by a local population. This has led modern scholars to assume that these early colonies were settled in a sort of no-man's land. Indeed, the Lepine mountains and the Pontine plain are often considered to have been of merely marginal significance in the general swing of Latial developments, before Roman colonization finally triggered far-reaching transformations. This issue was central to the GIA surveys of the Pontine Region Project that were carried out in the mid-1990s in the framework of the research programme 'Roman colonization south of Rome, a comparative archaeological survey of three early Romanized landscapes'.[17] Just as recent fieldwork in southern Italy has allowed us to re-assess the history of native regions and the impact of Greek colonization, the results of the surveys carried out under this programme, in combination with the later RPC surveys in the same region, call for a critical re-evaluation of conventional views on the Pontine region and especially of the impact of Roman colonization.

7.3.2 NEW INSIGHTS IN ARCHAIC URBANIZATION IN THE PONTINE REGION

The Pontine region surveys discussed in chapter 2 include, as was explained earlier, surveys of urban areas that had not been built over in later periods. One of these is the fortified site of Caracupa-Valvisciolo (cf. the discussion in 2.3.1). Whilst its defences can plausibly be dated to the Archaic period, the surveys indicate a contemporary urban territorial expansion similar to that demonstrated for Satricum.[18] Other surveys attest to the emergence of hilltop sites in the Monti Lepini as early as the 7th century BC,[19] and later urban settlements on the Lepine mountains (including Segni, the later Roman colony of Signia, and Cori, the Latin settlement of Cora) have also produced protohistoric finds. Whilst it is difficult to assess the significance of these two sites in earlier phases because of later overbuilding - both were allegedly colonised by Rome in the 5th century BC - similarities with other contemporary sites suggest that they may also be interpreted as hillforts or *oppida*.[20]

On the basis of the combined Pontine research as described in section 2.3, it may be concluded that at least the Astura river basin, the uplands and slopes of the Lepine mountains, and the contact zone between coastal and volcanic landscapes were all regular components of the Latial protohistoric settlement pattern from the Early Iron Age onwards, and that they were subsequently integral elements of the Archaic urbanising landscape. Only the Pontine plain proper seems to have remained in the periphery of the urbanization development that took place elsewhere. If our failure to find large nucleated sites in the Pontine plain accurately reflects ancient reality, then the relatively small Archaic scatters recorded by our surveys around Fogliano indicate the presence of a dispersed rural population without close relations to any central place. On the basis of the available evidence it seems likely that the economic basis of life in this coastal landscape during the entire protohistoric period was intimately tied up with the (seasonal?) exploitation of the lagoonal environment. Subsistence farming would have taken place in the immediate vicinity of simple hut dwellings.[21] Additional support for this idea comes from the agricultural evaluation carried out in the context of the RPC project, which indicates that, before exploitation of the heavier lagoonal clay soils had become possible by technological advances, only the light and fertile aeolian sandy

---

[17] See especially Attema / Van Leusen 2004.

[18] Attema 1993, 157-180.

[19] Attema 1991.

[20] Attema / Van Leusen 2004, 158-159.

[21] Attema *et al.* 2001a, 158.

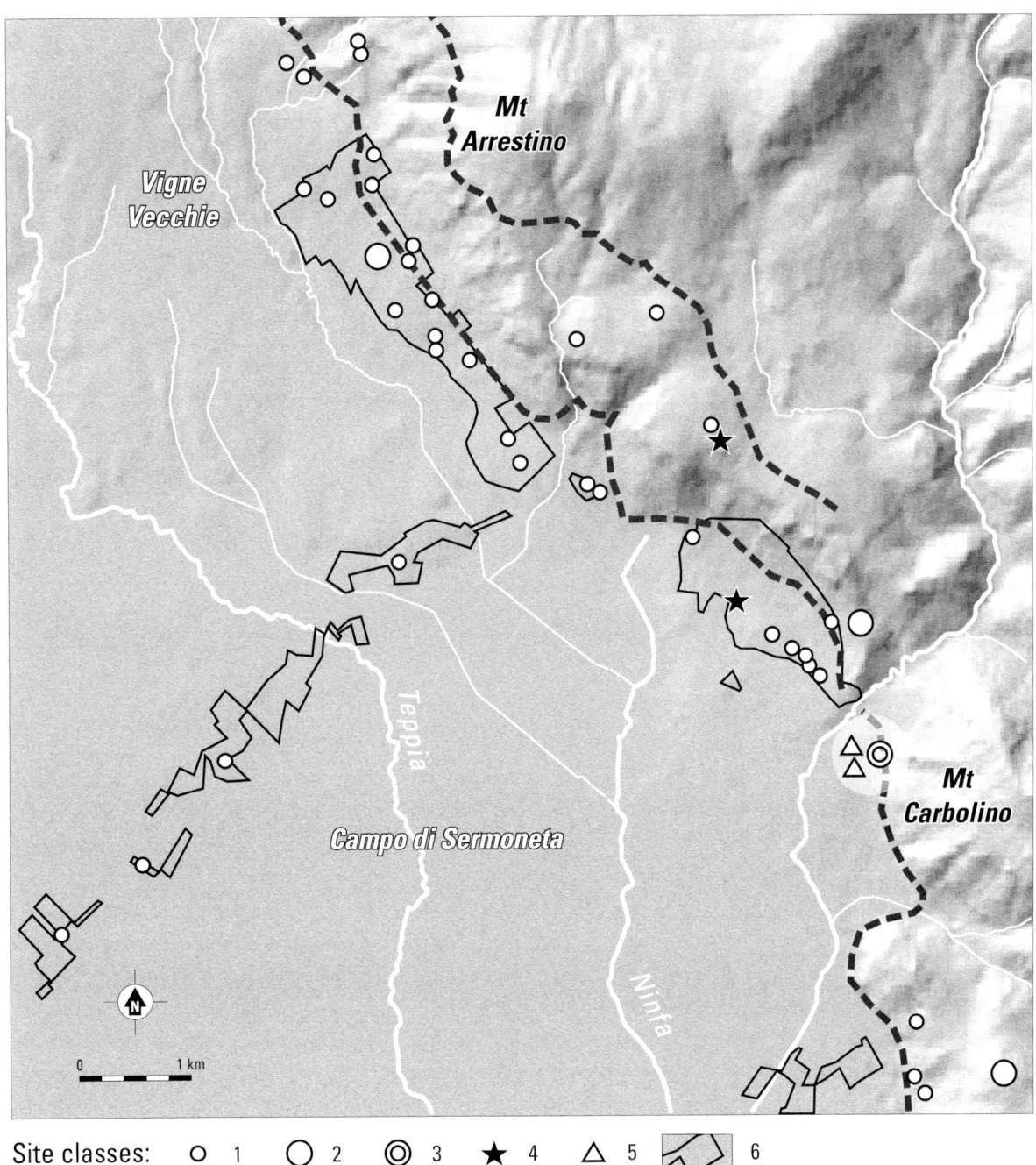

Fig. 7.3. Archaic settlement on the Lepine margins near Norba (compilation of survey results of the Pontine Region Project and sites published in the literature; after Van Leusen et al. 2005, fig. 7). 1. small sites, 2. large sites, 3. proto-urban site, 4. cult site, 5. graves, 6. intensively surveyed areas. Dashed lines: probable routes along the Lepine scarp. For a colour version of this figure, see page 232.

deposits were suitable for arable farming. Most of the remaining land would only be suitable for extensive use, such as rough grazing.

Nevertheless, the sheer number of ceramic scatters identified by the RPC surveys in the Fogliano area indicates that the protohistoric Pontine plain cannot be dismissed as a no-man's land. It appears that the larger part of the plain was regularly exploited since at least the 7th century BC. By the time of the Iron Age/Archaic transition (around 600 BC) exploitation of the coastal landscape had probably intensified, because site numbers double in this phase and a background noise of ceramics (1 to 5 shards per hectare) occurs in almost all fields. The clayey hinterland or *graben*, where protohistoric artefacts are very thinly represented in the present-day plough soil, currently forms an exception to the general picture, but this may well be a consequence of later sedimentation that placed most of the protohistoric landscape below plough depth.

GIA research in the higher parts of the Pontine plain and the adjacent Alban hills thus points to a more intensive rural exploitation there during the Iron Age and Archaic period than in the Pontine plain proper. Surveys in the Alban hills around the protohistorical central place of Lanuvium have demonstrated that incipient rural infill occurred as early as the 8th/7th centuries BC and intensified towards the end of the 7th century BC.[22] Fabric analysis demonstrates that subsequently, in the late 6th century BC, the rural landscape around Lanuvium was characterized by the large-scale diffusion of red-fired Archaic fabrics.[23] This fabric group included roof tiles and coarse ware pots and replaced traditional local Iron-Age fabrics.

The Doganella di Ninfa survey, on the western lower Lepine slopes near the later Roman colony of Norba, likewise showed that rural infill began in the Late Iron Age at the latest, and intensified considerably in the Archaic period. It also led to a reinterpretation of the Iron Age and Archaic scatters that were found during earlier surveys along the western slopes of the Lepine mountains, between Norba and Cori. For the Archaic a three-tier settlement hierarchy was proposed (fig. 7.3).[24] The top level is represented by the fortified proto-urban settlement of Caracupa-Valvisciolo, the bottom level by a range of small and scattered sites, interpreted as single-family farms. A middle level of hilltop sites and 'hamlets' can also be recognised. Similarly, there was a significant protohistorical component in the surveyed parts of the territory of the Roman colony of Signia, on the northern side of the Monti Lepini.[25] Extrapolation from these surveyed zones to the wider landscape leads to the conclusion that landscape infill in all these areas was well under way by the 7th and 6th centuries BC. Moreover, this urbanization and the significant intra-regional differences in settlement and land use of the Pontine landscape both appear to have had their roots in the Iron Age. This differentiation was therefore probably to a large degree conditioned and constrained by a pre-existing physical and social landscape.

7.3.3 TRACING EARLY ROMAN COLONIZATION

One of the major aims of the 1994-1997 GIA research project 'comparative archaeological survey of three early Romanized landscapes' in the Pontine region was to assess continuities and discontinuities in rural settlement and land use patterns during the alleged early phase of Roman colonization, i.e. the late- to post-Archaic period of the 5th and early 4th centuries BC. This is a notoriously difficult period from both an archaeological and an historical point of view. The surface archaeological record is not very diagnostic: wares and forms have a long circulation period which does not allow precise dating. Whilst the historic upheaval in the Archaic proto-urban settlement pattern is archaeologically visible in the abandonment or contraction of some sites, and the relaxation of the rules of spatial lay-out in others, this kind of change is much more difficult to detect and date in rural settlements. Furthermore, the reliability of Livy as our main historical source for the wars between Latins, Romans, and mountain peoples, as well as for Roman attempts at colonization such as at Norba in 492 BC and at Setia in the early 4th century, is doubtful. To address these issues comparative surveys were carried out in the catchment areas of two Roman colonies in the Monti Lepini (Setia and Signia) and in the catchment area of a protohistorical settlement of Latin origin in the Alban Hills (Lanuvium).[26] The major thesis to be tested was if the historically reported influx of colonists could in fact be ascertained around Roman colonies. The fabrics of

---

[22] Attema / Van Oortmerssen 2000, 424; Attema 2005b.

[23] Attema / Van Oortmerssen 2000, 424.

[24] Van Leusen *et al.* 2005

[25] Attema / Van Leusen 2004, 166-173.

[26] Attema / Van Leusen 2004.

the pottery collected during the surveys were analyzed to obtain a more detailed chronological framework for this previously rather undiagnostic phase of the 5th and 4th centuries BC, as explained in Box 1.1.

The comparison of the survey results from all three areas showed that there is a high degree of settlement continuity on most sites in the catchment areas of Lanuvium, Signia and Setia. This directly contradicts the apparent discontinuities in the older, 'topographic' field data that were due to a strong bias in favour of the Roman periods. Around both Lavinium and Signia there was clearly already a rural infrastructure of Archaic farmsteads, on which the Roman rural landscape was later superimposed. It is less clear whether the same is true in the case of Setia, because here natural sedimentation processes in the plain form an obstacle to the interpretation of the archaeological surface record.[27] The natural environment around Lanuvium and Signia, with its fertile volcanic soils and its morphology of plateaus, was certainly very conducive to demographic expansion and rural infill from the protohistoric period onwards, and the two areas show a very similar diachronic development of site densities. The sudden rise in site density recorded for the post-Archaic to Republican period in the Sezze survey, however, followed on a relatively low site density for the Iron Age and Archaic period. Of the three landscapes investigated, only the *ager* of Setia appears to show the expected intensification of rural exploitation contemporary to and following the recorded early Roman colonization. Significantly, neither at Sezze itself nor in its immediate surroundings have there been found indications for the presence of a substantial protohistorical settlement. The development of the *ager* of Setia may therefore be viewed as a more truly 'colonial' enterprise, in the sense that a thinly populated area was claimed by incoming colonists from Rome or its allies. Alternatively, the post-Archaic remains in the *ager* of Setia may be interpreted as the result of a gradual process of indigenous rural infill progressing north-west to south-east along the lower slopes and colluvial deposits of the Monti Lepini, a process that came to include the future *ager* of Setia in the 5th and 4th centuries BC. In this view, the pre-Roman population would have been integrated in the Roman colony that was historically founded on a hilltop overlooking the Pontine plain in the early 4th century BC.

7.4 CONCLUSION

Our main argument in this chapter has been that Archaic urbanization in both Salento and south Latium must be interpreted as a sign of the gradual formation of a number of autonomous local polities, each of which was focused on a single urban centre. In Salento this process became prominent only in the second half of the 6th century BC, and then it involved most of the peninsula. A number of primary sites can be pointed out that, at least in socio-economic and religious terms, came to play the role of central places to other nearby settlements. The accumulated data thus make it clear that processes such as urbanization and socio-economic differentiation were *not* confined to the *polis* of Taras, with minor side effects in its supposed hinterland. Rather, the indigenous Salento communities played a prominent and decisive role in effecting changes in all parts of the peninsula in the Archaic period, just as they did in the Iron Age.

In south Latium too, the local communities can be argued to have been decisive forces in the urbanization process. For Latium Vetus we may postulate the formation of a loosely integrated regional system of independent settlements interpreted as modest 'city states', each boasting temple architecture and elite housing. It is commonly accepted that these polities manifested themselves in the course of the 7th century BC primarily through political unification, enhanced by an aristocracy the emergence of which is so clearly attested in contemporary necropoleis. Italian archaeologists have called this process the *formazione della città*.[28] For the Pontine region, its importance is now being backed up by an increasing amount

---

[27] However, the presence of an Archaic rural temple in the plain below Sezze suggests that some kind of Archaic rural infrastructure would have been present here as well.

[28] Dialoghi di Archeologia 1980.

of field data from both surveys and excavations, which provide insight into the spatial dynamics of the process. The Pontine Region Project is producing increasingly clear information on how both individual settlements and entire territories were rapidly urbanising in the late $7^{th}/6^{th}$ centuries BC. Its surveys have shown that early Roman colonization should not be viewed as a unitary and all-pervasive process. Wherever it may have taken place, the colonists had to come to terms with sometimes densely populated urban and rural landscapes. Even for the recorded late-6th and 5th-century phases of Roman colonization the surveys indicate a large measure of settlement continuity in the rural landscapes of Latium Vetus.

8 Rural Infill, Urbanization and Roman Expansion

8.1 ROMAN CONQUEST AND COLONIZATION

According to tradition the 4th century BC marked the end of a phase of military and territorial turmoil in the Pontine region that was won decisively by the expanding Roman Republic. In the early decades of the century, Rome rapidly ensured its grip on its southern neighbours and their land, founding or reinforcing a series of colonies at strategic points in the Pontine landscape. However, the two southern regions central to our project, the Sibaritide and the Salento peninsula, would still remain outside the tentacles of Roman expansion for more than a century. According to the records of the *Fasti Triumphales Capitolini*, Roman victories over the Salento Messapii were not celebrated until 267/265 BC. At the time, again according to literary tradition, the Messapii were allied with the *polis* of Taras that had become one of Rome's major adversaries.[1] Indeed, the political histories of our southern Italian regions diverge significantly from that of our central Italian one during this phase. Whilst political history in itself is not the theme of our research, we must also discuss the Roman conquest of Italy in the 4th and 3rd centuries BC since this is often assumed to have triggered far-reaching transformations in the settlement and landscape of Italy.

For the early phase of Roman expansion, the disruptive consequences of the wars of conquest and their aftermath are often highlighted.[2] In particular in southern Italy these wars are reported to have caused dramatic losses to the vanquished, of people and material resources as well as of community land, the best of which was usually confiscated by the Romans as *ager publicus*. In addition, Roman colonization intensified considerably in this phase; colonies were established all over the Italian peninsula, including the three regions central to the RPC project. Examples range from the fortress of Norba perched on the inaccessible cliffs of the Lepine mountains in the Pontine region (fig. 8.1; founded 492 BC), via the incipient trading port of Brundisium on the Salento Adriatic coast (ca. 245 BC) to Copiae, built on the ruins of ancient Sybaris/Thurioi (194 BC). These colonies proved powerful instruments not only of Roman military conquest, but also of socio-economic integration of the conquered communities, most of which had by then become allies of Rome. Thus, the urban character of the colonies arguably presented a role model to the allied communities. This is especially the case from the later 2nd century BC onwards, when these communities are thought to have conformed increasingly to the Roman ethics of *urbanitas*, fashioning their hometowns on urban ideal types.[3]

Besides colonization other factors related to the Roman conquest are also considered important in having brought about major changes in the landscape of ancient Italy. Such factors include the alleged ruinous effects of the Punic wars by the end of the 3rd century BC, the Roman military levies and land

---

[1] Lombardo 1992, 146-147 no. 272.

[2] See especially Toynbee 1965, Brunt 1971, and Torelli 1999. An extreme position is taken by La Bua 1992, who argues that a flourishing pre-Roman Messapian society was largely wiped out by the Roman wars of conquest.

[3] The theme of late Republican urbanization figured prominently in the Göttingen conference on 'Hellenismus in Mittelitalien' (Zanker 1976), and the London conference on Urban Society in Roman Italy (Cornell / Lomas 1995). See also Gros / Torelli 1988; Dyson 1992; Morley 1996 and 1997; Lomas 1997; Torelli 1999, 11-12.

Fig. 8.1. Wall circuit and part of the plateau of the Roman colony of Norba, perched on the Lepine cliffs overlooking the Pontine plain (photo Attema, GIA).

confiscations, and the rise of large-scale transhumant pastoralism. These are often argued to have contributed to a disruption of the traditional socio-economic structures of the regional societies, affecting above all the farming populations.[4] One of the consequences was large-scale migration to urbanized areas, notably in central Italy, leaving southern Italy in particular in a state of marginality.

The recent increase in archaeological research into Roman Italy has contributed much to demonstrate that the peninsular landscape as a whole was indeed characterized by profound transformations in the course of the Republican period. Although, thanks to systematic excavations and field surveys, this view has been differentiated for individual regions as well as for Italy as a whole, its basic structure continued to figure prominently as a model for a range of archaeological projects until recently.[5] Of particular interest here is the application of long-term, regional perspectives such as the one used by the RPC project. Instead of mainly emphasizing sudden changes and focusing on political and military events as the principal causes, such a perspective also allows the study of the interaction of these phenomena with societal *conjonctures* and the *longue durée*. In the present chapter this perspective is again central to our comparative analysis of contemporary trends in settlement and landscape organization in the three regions studied. Rural occupation of the middle Republican phase, i.e. the 4th and 3rd centuries BC, is at the focus of this analysis, and our argument will be structured around our observation of an increase in such occupation in the three RPC study regions. We will question the role of Roman expansion in this trend and offer alternative explanations. We start by defining the nature of this rural occupation (section 8.2), linking it to urban development (8.3) and identifying it as a means to expand and intensify agriculture (8.4). We then

[4] De Neeve 1984.

[5] See for instance the various contributions on Italy in the Roman Landscapes conference edited by Barker and Lloyd (1991).

highlight specific regional variations in rural trends and identify local stimuli and strategies that caused them (8.5). Widening our scope, we then evaluate contemporary data from intensive surveys throughout central and southern Italy and conclude that, notwithstanding a certain degree of regional variability, a basic cross-regional trend is apparent and should be explained (8.6 and 8.7). The chapter closes with an epilogue on the late Republican period.

8.2 RURAL SETTLEMENT

In one particular sense the RPC surveys in the three study regions provide similar results, i.e. with regard to the scale of rural settlement attested for the middle/late Republican period. Whereas in the Pontine region rural sites dating to these phases are found in abundance from the scarp and footslopes of the Monti Lepini to the former wetlands of the Pontine marshes, in the Salento isthmus they are abundantly present from the central Brindisi plain to the upland karst plateau of the Murge. In the Sibaritide the topographic research of Lorenzo Quilici and the selective surveys carried out by the RPC team likewise indicate intensive contemporary rural occupation in the hinterland of Thurioi/Copiae. Here, Hellenistic sites have recently even been recorded at altitudes of up to 900 m.[6] Indeed, the overall impression is that a transformation took place in the use of various parts of the landscapes of the three regions, with large-scale rural occupation extending even to marginal lands. This transformations is central to the present chapter. As stated in the introduction to this volume, our study of the Italian landscape focuses explicitly on rural histories of settlement and land use, in an attempt to complement the traditional urban focus. From this perspective the apparent similarity in the three regional rural settlement trends deserves particular attention, since we are interested not only in specific regional *conjonctures*, but also in their interaction with contemporary macro-regional trends.

Our interpretation of the apparent parallelism in rural expansion has to be qualified by an evaluation of possible biases involved in its identification, in particular those that potentially prevent us from recognizing prior rural occupation patterns that are less obtrusive in a survey context than the ones detected (cf. chapter 1). This could be due either to factors relating to the archaeological record itself or to the way research has been conducted in these areas. Such factors have been re-evaluated for the regions central to the RPC project by carrying out additional analyses of post-depositional processes and of artefacts, in combination with highly intensive survey techniques in potentially marginal areas and excavations of extant stratigraphies. These new problem-oriented investigations have been discussed in previous chapters and in particular in chapter 1. They did indeed attest to earlier phases of landscape infill, notably in the Pontine region. Nevertheless it must be emphasized on the basis of all the evidence available at the moment that neither the biases involved, nor the detected variability invalidate the observed trend of a considerable increase in rural occupation.

As several RPC surveys demonstrated before, isolated farmsteads and dispersed hamlets are among the most common forms of rural occupation that were found. The surface debris recorded at many of them – roof tiles and household pottery with a little fine ware – points to a domestic use. The occasional presence of rural burial grounds near quite a few of these farms and hamlets means that it was not unusual for rural dwellers to be buried in the countryside. This suggests that they lived on their farms permanently on a year-round basis, and that they were deeply committed to the land. However, the evidence from surface data certainly does not suggest that rural necropoleis were associated with all farms. Quite a few of them may in fact have been only seasonally inhabited and their inhabitants buried in nearby central places.

---

[6] Attema *et al.* 2001b, 52.

The compositions of site assemblages are not necessarily conclusive either in this respect. The surface debris recorded at many rural sites for this period points to a domestic use: it consists of roof tiles, household- and fine pottery. However, farmers that every year temporarily moved to the countryside for the harvest period may have brought the same sets of artefacts with them as did their neighbours who lived in the countryside on a permanent basis. After all, the number of pots that seems to have been used on most farm sites is generally low and unlikely to have created transportation problems. Moreover, most rural site assemblages consists predominantly of coarse and plain domestic pottery, fine wares being relatively rare. Even for those farmers that resided permanently on their fields, life on the farm seems to have involved no particular degree of luxury. Yet other rural structures may not have been inhabited at all, as is suggested by the discovery of sites that completely lack domestic pottery. These may be interpreted as sheds for the storage of agricultural implements or as mere seasonal shelters for pastoral use or during harvest time. The latter would not justify the relatively high investments needed to build structures with tiled roofs.

8.3 URBAN DEVELOPMENT

The apparent inter-regional similarity of the dispersed, rural settlement patterns documented by our field surveys could well be superficial, masking different regional pathways. The rural settlement patterns in each region must therefore be studied separately with regard to their relation to the rest of the settlement system and in particular to the larger nucleated settlements and towns. We need to ask if these larger settlements and towns were abandoned in favour of a dispersed settlement pattern, or if instead they continued or even expanded.

With regard to the Pontine region, we have already alluded to the apparent relation of the mid-Republican rural settlement trends to the presence of the early Roman colonial towns. Substantial rural occupation is attested notably along the slopes of the Monti Lepini and the adjacent plain near the colonies of Cora, Norba and Setia. From the mid-4th century BC these colonies were characterized by urban development. Cora and Setia are comparable in their topography and urban structure, and are both situated on hilltops that, although steep, are connected with the plain by relatively gently sloping alluvial fan deposits.[7] In both cases the urban plan is adapted to the geomorphology, resulting in concentric plans with a central *arx* from which streets radiate downhill. Norba, on the other hand, was built on a steep cliff, several hundred meters above the plain and accessible only by means of an arduous climb. The architects projected an orthogonal plan characterized by a strict functional zoning onto the plateau on top of the cliff.[8] The religious buildings were situated on the two small hilltops within the town walls (the minor and major acropoleis), whereas the level area in the south-west part of the site was reserved for civic quarters and public spaces.

We have argued that Cora, Setia and Norba played a crucial role in the mid-Republican reordering of the Pontine region.[9] These towns became the central places of an expanding, complex and hierarchical settlement system that no longer centred on the volcanic areas alone but came to include the Lepine side of the Pontine plain and the Sacco valley. Likewise, the slopes of Monte Circeo and the Monti Ausoni became part of the Roman settled landscape under the influence of the towns of Circeii and Tarracina, and rural occupation around the colony of Antium intensified.[10]

On the Salento isthmus rural infill is apparent in most of the land systems investigated by means of intensive surveys (chapter 3). Here, the results of the field surveys clearly indicate that contemporary villages expanded considerably, whereas at the same time they were gradually arranged in a more nucleated

[7] Attema 1993, 82-89; Attema / Van Leusen 2004.
[8] Quilici / Quilici Gigli 1988.
[9] Attema 1993, 230-232.
[10] Attema *et al.* 2009.

Fig. 8.2. Artist's reconstruction of the early Hellenistic fortified site of Muro Tenente (Mesagne, BR), based on excavations and field surveys (drawing by mr. V. Camassa). For a colour version of this figure, see page 233.

way. Moreover, many of these larger sites were defended with monumental fortifications; the individual settlement areas enclosed in this way vary from a few to more than a hundred hectares (fig. 8.2). The excavations also indicate that specific intra-mural areas were rearranged to accommodate public-ceremonial buildings and other cult places, craft workshops, storage sheds and cemeteries. Indeed, physically these settlements were increasingly acquiring urban features. Thus far, the evidence comes from a small set of sites which have been well investigated. However, when the results of surveys and excavations are both related to other available datasets, the impression one gets is that similar transformations were occurring throughout the larger part of the Salento isthmus, from the northern Murge plateau to the southern extents of the Brindisi plain. None of the major land systems seem to have been excluded.

The contemporaneity of this phenomenon with the large-scale dispersion of more isolated residences has led us to interpret it as the formation of central places with urban functions: furnishing settled hinterlands with craft products, offering them facilities for the processing, storage and exchange of agricultural products, and supplying religious/ceremonial/administrative and political services. Admittedly the evidence in some cases is still insufficient. Whereas the production of the tiles, pottery and probably also other artefacts that characterize the many rural sites was probably located at or near the urban settlements, and can be attested archaeologically, evidence for political/territorial dependency is much harder to produce. Here the territorial divisions and hierarchies obtained using Thiessen polygons and XTENT modelling (see Box 1.3) may be taken only as indicative, not as evidence. Moreover, the bond between centre and hinterland may have varied in strength and character between polities and through time. Despite these reservations, we can conclude that rural infill made the relationship between the central places and their hinterlands much closer, as it did in the Pontine region.

In the Sibaritide the rural infill is likewise to be interpreted in a hierarchical framework. Here, a central role must be attributed to the polis of Thurioi. Although so far excavations have managed to uncover only very few traces of the town, its urban character is undisputed. From as early as its foundation in 445 BC as a pan-Hellenic colonial venture promoted by Athens, the polis is frequently praised in ancient written sources for its urban achievements. Its lay-out, in particular, was regarded as exemplary for Magna Graecia: according to literary tradition, the town plan was designed by the legendary architect Hippodamos of Miletus, the alleged father of the orthogonal lay-out. As discussed in chapter 4, extensive alluvial flooding has completely hidden the ruins of Thurioi and the contemporary surrounding land surface from view. We have, however, earlier presented the probability that this landscape in the late 4th/3rd century BC was characterized by dispersed rural occupation similar to that established for the territories of other poleis on the Ionian coast. Although this still awaits direct proof, the topographical research conducted by Lorenzo Quilici and his team in the 1960s and the intensive surveys of the RPC team since 2000 have already provided ample evidence for the presence of early Hellenistic farmsteads in the foothill zone. At the same time this research has demonstrated the absence of contemporary larger settlements in the foothill zone; such sites seem to have developed only in the mountainous inland areas, as at Cassano allo Ionio. For the Sibaritide, then, one may conclude that the landscapes of the coastal plain and of the surrounding terraces and foothills were oriented towards urban Thurioi.[11]

We must therefore conclude that in all three research areas the evolving rural settlement patterns gravitated around a range of urban sites of various statures. We are tempted to quote Sir Moses Finley, who in his work on the Graeco-Roman city stated boldly that '... even the agrarian populations, always a majority, most often lived in communities of some kind, hamlets, villages, towns, not in isolated farm homesteads'.[12] Although there is abundant evidence in our regions for isolated farmsteads, yet on the basis of the evidence presented above we broadly agree with Finley's statement, at least for our research area in the periods discussed here. Even in regions with a traditionally fairly dispersed settlement pattern, such as Salento, a range of large nucleated settlements emerged or was consolidated in tandem with the expansion of isolated rural occupation. Like Thurioi and the Pontine colonies, these settlements functioned in various ways as urban central places within an increasingly complex network of rural settlement.

8.4 RURAL INFILL AND THE EXPANSION OF AGRICULTURE

In view of the high degree of urban development it is remarkable that dispersed rural occupation occurs so frequently. It is commonly thought that isolated rural occupation severely hampers contact with larger communities living in regional centres, and therefore carries with it strong anti-social implications.[13] Similarly, farmers actually living on the land are more vulnerable to annual variations in crop productivity than those dwelling in towns, since after a poor harvest it is more difficult in the countryside to exchange surpluses or to find additional subsistence means. For rural dwellers dispersed land holdings were not a feasible option to overcome these problems. Growing crops on holdings dispersed over a variety of landscape units can be a strategy to reduce the risks of crop failure at one particular holding. However, such a strategy is only possible if the farmer's dwelling is located at a central location from which the scattered holdings can be reached with relative ease; correspondingly, commuting farmers normally indicate nucleated settlement rather than isolated rural residence.

Significantly, traditional settlement systems as delineated for early-modern central and southern Italy by historical geographers and anthropologists are of a highly nucleated kind, with farmers by and large concentrated in 'agro-towns'.[14] Much less common is dispersed rural residence on a significant scale. The Salento Murge is, however, an exception. Here, nucleated settlements like Locorotondo and Ostuni were until well within the 20th century accompanied by highly dispersed rural settlement in so-called *trulli* (i.e.

---

[11] Oome / Attema 2008.

[12] Finley 1981, 3.

[13] Osborne 1987, 59; Alcock 1993, 61.

[14] Blok 1969.

Fig. 8.3. Dispersed settlement pattern in the Murge countryside (photo G.-J. Burgers, ACVU). For a colour version of this figure, see page 234.

the traditional name of the characteristic isolated rural dwellings of the region; fig. 8.3). This pattern can be traced back at least to the 18th century, and its emergence was studied in detail by the anthropologist Galt (1991), who unravelled the social strategies of both the elites and the rural dwellers involved. Galts' central thesis in this regard is that 'the settlement patterns [...] of the *Murgia dei Trulli* are the result of a local land owning class strategy to realize income from a landscape which was agriculturally marginal, and which could only be made productive through massive amounts of intensive labor'.[15] In a more general article, Anthony Blok builds on a range of studies on the subject of dispersed rural occupation as well as on his own anthropological fieldwork in concluding likewise that the dispersed pattern in modern southern Italy accompanied intensive agriculture.[16] As has also been argued for antiquity, expansion of rural occupation accompanying urban development is commonly associated with a process of expansion and intensification of agricultural production.[17]

Strategies to increase agricultural production relate either to land already under cultivation (ranging from the suppressing of fallow and crop diversification to a closer symbiosis of arable cultivation with animal husbandry) or to previously untilled land (e.g. the application of drainage systems and/or new ploughing techniques in compact, water logged clayey soils).[18] Clearly, not all of these strategies will be

[15] Galt 1991, 9.
[16] Blok 1969, 132.
[17] Halstead 1987, 83; Alcock 1993; Bintliff 1997; Barker / Rasmussen 1988.
[18] Cf. chapter 1 on land evaluation analysis, and Van Joolen 2003.

readily traceable in the archaeological record; archaeological research that focuses on the reconstruction of agricultural production modes in Italy is in many ways still underdeveloped, not in the least where archaeobotany is concerned. An important exception is the evidence from pollen studies in the Pontine region, which indicates that olive cultivation was introduced in the 4th and 3rd century BC on the lower slopes of the Monti Lepini on a substantial scale. As is discussed in chapter 2, this evidence can be related to Roman Republican farm sites along the Lepine margins that we believe were involved in the production of olive oil.

Evidence from intensive surface surveys may to some extent compensate for the relative lack of botanical data. It is by now generally acknowledged that manuring practices are a major contributor to the formation of the off-site scatters that are regularly encountered in the Mediterranean landscape (see above, chapter 1). An exponential increase in the amount and dispersion of such off-site material is therefore often taken as an indication of (more) intensive manuring or of the reclamation of previously untilled land.[19] Other explanations must be considered with regard to scatters in areas where manuring is not likely to have occurred, as in the Pollino mountains, where Hellenistic artefact scatters have been found at high altitudes. Possibly these represent farms specialising in cattle breeding or horse raising, but other explanations may be found in the intensification of seasonal activities related to pastoralism or forestry.

Not only off-site material but also rural residential sites may be instructive in this regard. Some of the strategies discussed above require higher investments of time and energy in the land, which in turn requires residence on the land itself. Halstead discussed experiments relating to this point that were carried out in Greece and focused on the benefits of manure-based agriculture and cereal/pulse rotation over growing cereals in a bare fallow system.[20] These experiments showed that the former are much more productive per unit area than the latter. That the bare fallow system has nonetheless been so pervasive in Greece's recent past is closely related to the traditional Greek settlement pattern, in which farmers live almost exclusively in nucleated settlements, far from the (generally scattered) fields. In such a context cereal/pulse rotation is likely to have been an option beyond the reach of most town dwellers because of its relatively high labour demand. Moreover, living away from the fields is a severe obstacle to the grazing (and thus the manuring) by the households' small herds of their own land. If farmers on the other hand reside on their land both these options can be used. Although unattractive from a social viewpoint, the intensification of production that then becomes feasible potentially allows higher yields from the same holding. Other advantages of rural residence include the possibility to apply more effective sowing techniques and the reduced need for work animals and the associated high feeding costs. Evaluating all variables involved, Halstead concludes that 'extensive and intensive farming are characterized by different cultivation technologies, by different harvesting and crop processing techniques and so by different labour inputs and production outputs at almost every stage in the agricultural cycle'.[21] Intensive farming is most efficient in combination with dispersed rural settlement. Indeed, the remarkable increase in rural occupation attested by our field surveys may be interpreted in this perspective. We therefore conclude that the observed dispersion of surface scatters in most of the land systems of our research areas, representing both sites and off-site material, probably relates to strategies that focused either on the intensification of production of land already under cultivation or on the reclamation of previously unexploited land.

We will try to explain this phenomenon by focussing in section 8.5 on differences between, as well as within, the various regions. In section 8.6 we will argue that in spite of some regional variation a basic cross-regional trend is still apparent.

---

[19] Halstead 1987, 83ff.
[20] Halstead 1987, 82.
[21] Halstead 1987, 84.

8.5 LOCAL VARIABILITY IN RURAL TRENDS

Finding explanations for the increase in rural occupation for each region separately is imperative, since the phenomenon is certainly not as uniform as it might seem: upon close scrutiny chronological and spatial differentiation both between and within the three RPC study areas become apparent.

In the Salento isthmus region fluctuations in the sizes, composition, density and distribution of rural sites are found throughout the period under study. Late Republican sites are for instance generally larger than those of the preceding phase but are also far less numerous. An initial wave of new rural sites seems to have occurred in the late 4th/early 3rd century BC, when many sites of similar composition and extent, interpreted as isolated farmsteads, spread out over the countryside and only occasionally clustered into hamlets. In the course of the 3rd century BC the number of isolated sites rose further, at least in the Valesio coastal area; moreover, they appear to be located at such regular intervals (of approximately 500 m) that some degree of central management appears likely, possibly in connection with the establishment of a centuriation system in the territory of the newly founded Latin colony of Brundisium. Such a distribution pattern is absent from the survey areas outside the territory of the colony, where early Hellenistic sites seem often to be aligned along roads radiating from the nearest central town. With regard to spatial differentiation, it must also be observed that some landscape units seem to have been less favoured for rural settlement, or even not at all, such as the limestone plateau south of Oria or the lagoonal system and narrow strip of loamy soils along the Adriatic coast immediately north of Brindisi.

Although much less information on spatial differentiation is available for the Sibaritide due to the relative scarcity of intensive surveys, chronologically the general impression for the investigated areas is also one of decreasing site numbers in the late Republican period. As in the Salento isthmus region, rural infill is particularly apparent for the late 4th/3rd century BC. Still, the impact of environmental diversity was considerable in the Sibaritide as well, where the coastal plain, the surrounding terraces and the enclosing mountains each generate different conditions for human exploitation. It is very probable that rural infill affected these landscape units in varying degrees. Early Hellenistic surface scatters are extremely rare in the mountains and internal valleys, but abound at the interface of the coastal and alluvial plains with adjacent landscape units not covered by more recent alluvium. It is likely that the thick alluvial deposits laid down in the coastal plain in more recent times (see Box 2.2) cover a system of early Hellenistic rural sites, similar to those recorded in the territories of other Greek towns on the Tarantine Gulf, like Metapontion and Taras. We must conclude that a very large territory around Thurioi was settled within a relatively short period.

In the Pontine region the general trend in the late Republican period is one of increasing site densities. Rural occupation is not limited to the areas traditionally favoured for settlement such as the Alban hills or the lower slopes of the Lepine mountains and adjacent plain, but it is attested even in the wetlands and beach ridges of the Pontine plain. For the preceding middle Republican period, on the other hand, these areas seem to have been largely unaffected. This doesn't mean that no transformations can be observed in the Pontine region in the 4th century BC. On the contrary, the Lepine side of the Pontine plain is characterized in the middle Republican period by investments in infrastructure and agricultural construction. The phenomenon has been related to the contemporary foundation of colonies at Cora, Norba and Setia, which suggests that colonists settled not only in the towns themselves but also on the land they had been allotted. These land assignments are echoed by the actual discovery on air-photographs of two centuriation systems, one on the colluvial slopes north-west of Terracina and the other in the plain south of Setia. One may conclude that much energy was invested particularly in the colonization of the low-lying part of the Pontine region. Further indications for this are the canals, dikes and roads that were discovered in connection with the centuriation systems. Of particular interest is the construction of the Via Appia through this area, historically dated to the late 4th century BC, which

[22] Halstead 1987, 85.

considerably improved not only the infrastructure of the region in general, but also communications with and transportation to and from the city of Rome.

We may conclude that despite an apparent parallelism in rural trends, regional differentiation cannot be ignored. As is clear from the evidence discussed above, environmental variability is certainly one of the most prominent factors accounting for differentiation in strategies between regions as well as between landscape units within a single region. However, we do not wish to suggest that the physical environment was the only determinant: social factors must have been equally important. Variation in social strategies of individual households is often overlooked.[22] These strategies are to a significant extent determined by variability in the households' life-cycle, e.g. in the availability of labour force, in the number of mouths to feed, or in ceremonial obligations (e.g. dowry, funerary rites). Considering also fluctuations in external factors like climate, external demand and access to a market, Halstead lucidly remarks that the peasant farmer 'is aiming at a moving target with a weapon of gradually shifting calibre... So each year the farmer may be aiming for a different production target, from a different area of land, with a different labour force and with the cushion of a greater or lesser amount of produce in store'.[23] Of course, such individual, highly flexible strategies are hard to cope with in archaeology, especially since field surveys, our main source of information, provide less specific data. This makes it often highly complicated even to identify the 'type' or function of individual sites; their range of possible functions would have been much greater than may seem obvious to the present-day urban outsider. As has recently been suggested by Alcock as well with regard to rural occupation in late Classical/early Hellenistic Greece, 'many of these sites probably shifted in their precise function through time, as a family's size, needs and aspirations varied'.[24]

Because this type of micro-variability evens out at coarse spatial and temporal resolutions, we may confine ourselves to a more generalised evaluation of social factors in a context of concrete datasets. It must be emphasized here again that the observed archaeological phenomena are not restricted to a few fields and a few years only, which might reflect occasional individual farmers' strategies. Instead, the observed patterns clearly demand a much wider spatial and chronological framework of analysis, to the extent that we may speak of regional *conjunctures*. We must accordingly discuss the impact of more general socio-political transformations, of demography and of landholding patterns. Of the three RPC study areas, the Pontine and Salento regions provide datasets that allow such an evaluation, albeit only up to a point.

8.5.1 THE PONTINE REGION

One of the most significant factors determining differentiation in regional settlement trends in the period under discussion has already been emphasized: the impact of Roman political, military and demographic expansion. This factor clearly sets apart the Pontine region from the other two research areas. In the Pontine region external forces, notably Roman colonization, were a significant trigger to urban development and rural infill. The Roman colonial towns came to dominate the Pontine region. Besides being political-military strongholds, the new towns must have fulfilled a central role in Pontine society as signposts of Roman authority. They certainly did so with regard to the gradually developing regional economy, performing urban functions to the dispersed colonial settlers and absorbing the increased surpluses that had been made possible by the intensification of agricultural production. Infrastructural improvements such as the construction of the Via Appia and the imposition of centuriation systems likewise stimulated the economy and at the same time symbolized the increasing Roman grip on the Pontine landscape. Indeed, not only the Pontine colonies benefited from the increase in agricultural production in their hinterland; the Pontine region became in this phase of early expansion an agricultural resource zone of Rome.

[23] Ibidem.
[24] Alcock 1993, 60.

[25] Following Rathbone 1981, 16-18; cf. Morley 1996, 131 with regard to the recolonization of Cosa.

Although Roman influence in the Pontine Region was undeniably strong in the mid-Republican phase, two objections may be raised to the idea that this was due to a significant influx of colonists. Firstly, one can seriously question the net demographic effect of colonization as attested in the ancient texts. Population trends for the earlier phase have hardly been studied, nor do we have sound archaeological information about the subsequent effects of Roman intervention on such trends. Secondly, the repeated sending of contingents of colonists as mentioned in the written sources doesn't necessarily imply a parallel increase in the Pontine colonist population. On the contrary, it may well reflect the inability of the colonist population to stabilize, with colonists repeatedly failing to set up a viable colony and opting to transfer to their home towns or elsewhere.[25]

The Groningen surveys made clear that no uniform system of settlement and land use can be projected onto the Pontine region, neither in the pre-Roman phase nor in the Roman period. In fact, new surveys by the RPC project indicate that various landscape units, notably in the coastal plain, remained largely unaffected by settlement transformations in the mid-Republican period, whether these involved urban development or rural infill.[26] Here, traditional settlement and land use seems to have prevailed. What remains to be established is the extent to which this situation applies to the colonial core areas, where indigenous groups are likely to have integrated more fully into the Roman sphere of influence. Unfortunately the (mis-) fortunes and strategies of the indigenous populations are not easily identifiable. Although the pace of colonization is likely to have depended in part on the claims and resilience of these local populations, it is not clear as yet to what extent these were integrated in the new territorial-administrative order and had their properties respected. In this context it must be noted that there is no archaeological evidence either for or against the notion that local farmers were dispossessed in favour of Roman colonists. One may hypothesize that the process was rather differentiated, as exemplified by the superimposition of the new *agri* of Cora and Norba on an already settled countryside, whereas the colonial territory of Setia seems to have been created *ex novo* around a new town, and consisted at least partly of reclaimed wetlands.

8.5.2 THE SALENTO ISTHMUS

On the Salento isthmus and in the Sibaritide Roman intervention cannot have caused the wave of rural infill that marked large parts of these regions in the late 4th/early 3rd century BC.[27] The local communities are generally considered to have remained politically autonomous and outside the sphere of influence of the Urbs, right up to the Roman conquest some decades later. Correspondingly, settlement trends for this phase have primarily been analysed in a local or regional context, and they can be mainly explained by internal factors. In order to explore in more detail the social mechanisms at work we focus in particular on the Salento isthmus region, where these have been amply studied.[28] Here, the rural infill was arguably induced by local social strategies.

The division of the land is a major variable in this argument, as one of the factors that 'dictate the appearance of the countryside, set the level and nature of its utilization, and underlie demographic change'.[29] Of course, landholding patterns are notoriously difficult to investigate archaeologically, especially without having access to written sources. In Salento, it is only through circumstantial reasoning that we may be able to comment on landed property. The land that became filled with early Hellenistic

---

[26] Attema *et al.* 2001; Van Leusen 2002, ch. 10.
[27] Cf. Terrenato 2001, 2-3.
[28] D'Andria 1991 and 2002; Yntema 1993a and 1995; Burgers 1998.
[29] Alcock 1993, 55.

farms was possibly common land that was rented out to individual farmers, or made available to them in some other way. Another possibility is that the land, or part of it, was privately owned. If private ownership already existed in the preceding Archaic/Classical period with its nucleated settlement system, then scattered holdings are likely to have been the norm, as these reduce the risks associated with crop failure (see above, section 8.4). In such cases the subsequent exploitation of the holdings would be most efficient if others than the proprietors themselves were to reside on them. In that case the residents of the early Hellenistic farms may have been tenants or people otherwise bound to the land, and the ownership probably lay in the hands of urban elites. This strategy would have allowed the elites to intensify production and thus to procure a larger income from that same land. This idea has been supported by Yntema, who advances the increasing archaeological visibility of specific contemporary elite groups as evidence. This visibility is enhanced by residential as well as funerary architecture, among other things. Notable examples of residential buildings have been excavated at the *oppida* of Monte Sannace and Vaste.[30] The clustering of residential complexes in the centre of these settlements, as well as their size, their architecture and the artefacts associated with them, all clearly point to their special status. They are tentatively interpreted as elite residences with a public-ceremonial function, perhaps similar to early examples of Roman Republican civic buildings, the architecture of which also refers to the domestic sphere.[31] The emergence of these buildings is generally linked to the contemporary incipient custom of opulent burials. The so-called *hypogeum* of the Caryatides at Vaste is a much-cited example of such burials.[32] A modest number of similar monumental *hypogea* is known to have existed in other major Salento sites of the early Hellenistic period. They resemble the chamber tombs found in southern Italian Greek cities, notably Taras and Metapontion, and are plausibly argued to have been local elite burials.

The conspicuousness with which specific Salento elite families manifested themselves during this phase suggests that they had access to more than average means, and these may well have derived from their exclusive ownership of the land. It is likewise being argued that letting tenants settle on their land allowed these families to procure higher yields from it. It may be recalled that a parallel argument was proposed by Galt with regard to the 19th-century dispersed rural settlement pattern of the *trulli* on the Murge table land (see above, section 8.4). However, Galt explicitly takes into account the agency of non-elite groups as well, which do not yet figure in the socio-economic models for the ancient Salento. There is every reason to investigate the role of such groups, since elite groups were not the only ones that became archaeologically more visible. Much stronger than the correlation between a few elite residences and opulent burials, is that between the exponential growth of the number of rural settlements and burial grounds in general.

Although statistical information is lacking, there is no doubt that the early Hellenistic phase in Salento was marked by an increase in the number of graveyards as well as in the density of burials within them. The general impression is that large, more nucleated necropoleis were formed during this phase that have a greater homogeneity in architecture, grave structure and content than before. For instance, the observed

---

[30] Of those at Monte Sannace, two have a central colonnaded court (Russo Tagliente 1992, 126-136) surrounded by rooms of various dimensions and character - from kitchens and small storage rooms to representation chambers comparable to the Greek *andron* and *exedra*, which were meeting rooms. Other distinguishing features include decorative elements such as plastered walls, antefixes and sculptured stone slabs, which embellished the courtyards. Another example comes from Vaste (D'Andria 1991, 465-476), where recent excavations by the University of Lecce at Fondo San Antonio have uncovered the remains of a complex covering more than 600 sq.m (1100 sq.m including the paved open court in front). The L-shaped structure, which is adorned with a portico and other architectonic refinements, is divided into a series of rectangular spaces, one of which contains rooms for representation and storage.

[31] D'Andria 1991, 47; Gualtieri 1993, 332.

[32] Lamboley 1981; Lippolis 1991; D'Andria 1991, 472-475.

[33] D'Andria 1991, 475.

[34] Cf. Osborne 1996, 83-84.

uniformity in the various early Hellenistic necropoleis at Vaste led D'Andria to interpret them as reflecting a homogeneous stratum in the social hierarchy of the resident community.[33] From the early Hellenistic period onwards the greater part of the local population seems to have been buried in cemeteries that were larger and more nucleated than before. Moreover, the homogeneity of these new cemeteries suggests that local groups had begun to share a common funerary grammar, one in which differences in wealth and status were not displayed. In addition, these cemeteries were located in areas which were apparently specifically reserved for burial purposes. This implies that a formal distinction between domestic and burial areas must have been recognized, enforced and maintained.[34] Abundant burial grounds accompany the rural infill in the countryside in the early Hellenistic period. These rural graveyards seem to have been much smaller than the urban ones, related as they probably were to single hamlets or farms. Although by no means elaborate, the common grave in the countryside was not a poor one either.

In his classic study of a comparable increase in burials in late Geometric Greece, Ian Morris convincingly argued that any interpretation of this phenomenon in terms of demographic growth is prone to be criticized because of its unwarranted assumption that all groups in local society throughout the period under study would have been buried in ways that leave archaeologically visible traces.[35] Morris' argument also applies to Salento in the early Hellenistic phase. Here, there is every reason to suggest that existing burials from pre-Hellenistic periods only represent specific social groups and that large segments of the local communities disposed of their dead in ways that left no traces. Adult funerary practices first become archaeologically visible from the late 7th or early 6th century BC onwards, mostly taking the form of single inhumation burials in cist or pit graves. The number of burials subsequently rises gradually, and only increases exponentially in the later 4th century BC.[36] Drawing on Ian Morris' approach, one of us suggested elsewhere that this increase is related to the fact that larger segments of the population started to bury their dead in a formal fashion, abandoning previous funerary practices that were archaeologically invisible.[37] Possibly old rules that had restricted formal burial to elites were now relaxed or abandoned. If this line of reasoning is applied to early Hellenistic Salento, population growth may have been less significant here than was previously thought. The phenomenon would instead suggest an emancipation and a change in the fortunes of a significant part of the local communities. Not only did they obtain the right to formal burial, but they must also have acquired the necessary resources to do so. Agriculture is the key here: permanent or seasonal residence on the land was one of the strategies that were used to intensify production and/or reclaim marginal land. It is therefore likely that the rural infill discussed in the present chapter not only favoured elite proprietors, but also farming communities, either as tenants or as owners. Even a redistribution of land, public or private, must be considered as a possibility, with land being assigned to the landless. Unfortunately, any discussion on this point or on the legal status of farmers must remain hypothetical. We must acknowledge that, at the present state of research and in the absence of written documents, we cannot reach any firm conclusions other than that none of the options mentioned here can be excluded. Future research of this major issue should also take into account that these options need not be mutually exclusive - farming communities' social strategies most likely interacted with those of the elite.

[35] Morris 1987, *contra* Snodgrass 1980; but see Snodgrass 1991.

[36] Lombardo 1994; Burgers 1998, 241.

[37] Burgers 1998, 244-246.

8.5.3 CONCLUSION ON LOCAL VARIABILITY AND RURAL TRENDS

The central issue in the current chapter is the 4th/3rd-century BC expansion of rural occupation that has been documented by the various RPC field surveys. In the present section 8.5 the focus has been on variation within and between regions, in particular with regard to the Pontine region and the Salento isthmus. The aim has been to detect region-specific stimuli and strategies that brought about the observed rural patterns.

As discussed in the introductory sections of this chapter, Roman expansion and in particular colonization are often seen as having caused profound changes in the physical and social landscape of the Italian peninsula. Roman influence is even considered to have been the principal trigger of these transformations. We have argued that early colonization was indeed a significant factor in shaping the mid-Republican Pontine region. Close political and economic ties with Rome developed in tandem with colonization. Significant infrastructural improvements were undertaken, and are likely to have benefited the rural economy. However, similar processes of urbanization and rural infill that were demonstrably for the most part determined by internal factors occurred at the same time in other parts of Italy, and this is a warning against relying exclusively on a top-down colonial approach even in the Pontine region.

First, it must be stressed that no uniform system of settlement and land use can be projected on all three regional landscapes, as was also the case for the pre-Roman phases. The primary differentiating factors are the constraints and possibilities inherent in the local environment. This is for instance the case in the Sibaritide, where the undulating sloping land, the marine terraces and the uplands each produced different rural settlement patterns in the period under study. It is certainly also true in the Pontine region, and may serve as an argument to de-emphasize the alleged universal impact of Roman expansion in this region. It now seems likely that the landholding systems and land use patterns here evolved in response not only to Roman intervention, but also to traditional socio-economic patterns. Moreover, it remains to be established to what extent this was also the case in the colonial territories, where indigenous groups were probably integrated more fully into the Roman way of life. We argued earlier that even in these areas significant differences can be assumed between the *agri* of Cora and Norba, with their ample evidence of pre-Roman rural occupation on the fertile Lepine footslopes, and that of Setia in the Pontine plain, which seems to have been largely colonized *ex novo*.

The contemporary settlement trends on the Salento isthmus were arguably determined by internal factors to a much greater degree than in the Pontine region. Although demographic increase is also likely to have had an effect, it is important not to over-interpret particularly the apparent increase in burial evidence, which may instead be attributed to a growing socio-economic prominence of parts of the local farming population. The same is the case for the rural infill, which probably enabled farmers to increase agricultural production and to reclaim new land. Unfortunately, it is as yet impossible to establish reliably to what extent this rural infill was also caused by changes in landholding patterns that may have favoured small independent landholdings over common or elite-owned land. Such changes may have been complex, for there is ample evidence to suggest that local elites also benefited from higher agricultural yields, possibly employing resident tenants on their land.

8.6 COMPARING RURAL SETTLEMENT PATTERNS IN CENTRAL AND SOUTH ITALY

Earlier we emphasized geohistorical conditions, socio-economic cycles and short-term events as the major variables determining interregional differentiation in rural and urban settlement patterns. Nonetheless there is also a significant degree of structural similarity in regional trends. In all three RPC study regions much of the rural landscape was restructured during the 4th/3rd centuries BC to accommodate a more intensive agricultural exploitation, and previously marginal land was reclaimed. The scale of this phenomenon becomes even more apparent once datasets from field surveys throughout Italy are taken into consideration. Rural occupation is then no longer confined to the classic 'growth' areas along the Ionian and central Tyrrhenian shores, but is attested as well in the lowlands, uplands, and intermontane basins and valleys. Here we will review the general trends that emerge from relevant field surveys, starting with the earliest, the South Etruria Survey, and working our way down to the far South.

8.6.1 CENTRAL ITALY

The most important of the Central Italian surveys is clearly Ward-Perkins' South Etruria Survey, the first large-scale intensive field survey project ever conducted in Italy. This project, carried out by the British School at Rome between the 1950s and the 1970s, comprised a range of field surveys in adjoining territories on the south side of the Tiber, immediately north of Rome, between the *Ager Veientanus* and the *ager* of Falerii. In the 1980s surveys were also carried out on the other side of the Tiber, notably around Farfa. The first major synthesis of the South Etruria Survey results was published in Tim Potters' *The Changing Landscape of South Etruria* (1979), a book with an admirably wide scope that has been very influential in Mediterranean landscape archaeology. Potter's interpretation of the survey results, however, has not been shared by all, especially where the Roman Republican period is concerned. His conclusion that this period was marked by a strong continuity in site numbers has recently been challenged in the context of a systematic restudy of the South Etruria Survey data, again under the aegis of the British School at Rome, by the Tiber Valley Project.[38] As the results of this project, which started in 1997, are gradually becoming available it is increasingly clear that site numbers were not as stable as Potter thought. Especially the late 4th and 3rd centuries BC (mid-Republican) site densities turn out to be higher than was thought before.[39] We will see this again below for south Italy, and for the results of other surveys in Etruria, such as the one at Cerveteri.[40]

The settlement trends on the border between Latium and Campania, in the Liri valley, are less clear. Here a systematic survey project was carried out between 1978 and 1983 under the direction of the late Edith Wightman.[41] The valley is part of a large intermontane basin between the pre-Apennine Monti Aurunci to the west and the central Apennine mountain chain to the east. Some 30 km towards the south-east the Matese mountains, which lie on the western border of the Biferno valley survey, can just be seen. Although the Liri Valley survey was multi-period and the final publication discusses the valley's history from prehistory to the 17th century AD, the survey's main focus was on the Roman rural landscape. Contrary to what we have seen in South Etruria, mid-Republican sites in the Liri Valley appear to have been relatively scarce in comparison to the large number of late Republican sites recorded. However, Hayes and Martini also state that many of the latter contain 'flimsy' traces of late 4th/3rd-century BC occupation. They acknowledge that the various bias factors discussed in chapter 1, and especially the rather low diagnostic value of the ceramic assemblages, may have seriously affected the identification of mid-Republican occupation phases.[42]

The same problem may also affect the data available for northern Campania, where in the 1980s Paul Arthur investigated some 100 sq.km of the Garigliano basin and the Massico mountain.[43] As Arthur freely admits, his field walking did not meet the standards of modern surveys. It was mostly carried out by one person only (over a period of three years) and focused on the identification of the more obtrusive

[38] Patterson 2004; Patterson / Di Giuseppe / Witcher 2004.
[39] Patterson / Di Giuseppe / Witcher 2004; cf. Liverani 1984.
[40] E.g. Enei 1995.
[41] Hayes / Martini 1994.
[42] Hayes / Martini 1994, 36.
[43] Arthur 1991.

Roman period sites. It therefore seems probable that this survey, too, suffered from a severe bias against the identification of small, low-density artefact scatters that predate the formation of the large, obtrusive late Republican villas that were so successfully documented by Arthur.

More in line with the results of our own surveys are the intensive surveys in the Biferno valley (Molise) carried out between 1974 and 1978 and directed by Graeme Barker.[44] This is one of the few fully published survey projects in Italy. Inspired notably by the French School of Annales history, the project aimed to reveal the long-term settlement history of the valley, and the survey area was chosen to encompass a range of topography from coast to inland mountains. The project combined intensive and intermediate levels of survey as well as reconnaissance surveys, covering just over 400 sq.km, or 18% of the study area. For the Republican period a peak in site numbers in all parts of the valley was dated to the period 350-80 BC. In the upper valley a remarkable intensification of settlement probably started in the late $4^{th}/3^{rd}$ centuries BC and continued in the 2nd century BC, resulting in a highly structured landscape of major and minor fortified hillforts, villages, rural sanctuaries, farmsteads, huts and shacks. The lower valley too is characterized by urbanisation, settlement expansion and a developing settlement hierarchy in the later $4^{th}/3^{rd}$ centuries BC. Here the major town of Larinum developed along with a range of smaller towns and villages. The number of contemporary sites in the lower valley is much higher than that in the upper valley, and most of them probably represent farms or buildings related to agricultural or pastoral exploitation.

Other central Italian upland areas that have been intensively investigated, such as the Rieti intermontane basin ca. 80 km north-east of Rome,[45] the Cicolano mountains ca. 20 km south-east of Rieti,[46] and the Sangro Valley in the Abruzzo region,[47] also seem to have been marked by an increase in rural settlements in the late $4^{th}/3^{rd}$ centuries BC, although the surveyors explicitly state that the relatively undiagnostic character of the surface debris only allows for general impressions.

8.6.2 SOUTHERN ITALY

Similar patterns are obtained for southern Italy, where the work carried out in the territory of Metapontion is among the most widely published large-scale studies. As early as the 1960s topographical research revealed major trends in the organisation of the colonial landscape around Metapontion, including substantial rural occupation from the Archaic period onwards and the regular subdivision of the *chora* by at least the early 5th century BC.[48] From the early 1980s onwards these data were supplemented by intensive surveys carried out by the University of Texas.[49] Initially these were limited to a single transect crosscutting the undulating landscape of hills, valleys and marine terraces so typical of the Metapontino, between 6 and 10 km west of the town of Metaponto. Subsequently they were extended to cover an estimated quarter (35 sq.km) of its total territory, and together they mainly highlighted rural trends for the Greek and Roman period.[50] If we focus on the phases relevant to the present argument, we observe that the number of sites, which diminished in the later 5th to mid-4th century BC in comparison to the Archaic phase, rose again sharply in the later 4th to early 3rd century BC. This increase is accompanied by a parallel increase in site dimensions.[51] The new sites are distributed throughout the area investigated, including the upland marine terraces.

---

[44] Barker 1995.
[45] Coccia / Mattingly 1992, 1996.
[46] Barker / Grant 1991.
[47] Lloyd / Christie / Lock 1997; Faustoferri and Lloyd 1998.
[48] Recently established with certainty: Carter 2001, 779-781.
[49] Carter 1981, 1987, 1998, 2001, and 2006; De Siena 2001; Thomson 2002.
[50] Carter 2001, 772.
[51] Carter 2001, p786; Thompson 2002.

The results of the Metapontine research are echoed by small-scale but still intensive surveys by the University of Texas in the *chora* of Kroton and by the most recent surveys in the territory of Taras. Here, field walking by the University of Lecce and the ACVU has confirmed the conclusions of the Apulian *Soprintendenza* (see above, section 3.3) that the maximum rural expansion occurred during the early Hellenistic phase.[52]

Until fairly recently, the inland regions of southern Italy were much less well known than the Italiote Greek territories. The earliest systematic surveys here were those of Vinson in the rugged highland of eastern Basilicata and western Apulia, carried out in the context of the British School excavations at the fortified hill of Botromagno. Most of the work was done between 1968 and 1979 when wide tracts were investigated along the ancient road system that connected the Roman colony of Venusia to the west with Potenza in the heartland of the Lucanian Apennines, and also to the south with the town of Gravina di Puglia on the fringes of the Murge plateau. Other surveys in the context of this project were undertaken by Joan Taylor, Alfred Ammerman and others between Gravina and nearby Matera. Constituting the largest body of survey data in Italy since the pioneering South Etruria Survey, the potential contribution of this research project to the settlement history of southern Italy is undoubtedly great, but primary data and interpretations have unfortunately remained largely unpublished. On the basis of some preliminary information provided by Vinson and Small, we can surmise that some 518 sites were recorded in a surveyed area of 615 sq.km.[53] An overall rise in the number and extent of sites appears to have been recorded for the 4th-3rd centuries BC, but specific quantitative and qualitative information is largely lacking and concerns about the methodology mean that the results must be used with caution. Small explicitly states that the survey focussed on the detection of communication routes and related obtrusive sites of the Roman period, so that pre-Roman sites, which were presumably much less obtrusive, are very likely to have escaped detection. In this particular case, therefore, source criticism throws doubt on the supposed mid-Republican increase in site numbers. On the other hand, later, more intensive and reliable surveys in neighbouring landscapes seem to demonstrate the same patterns. One of these centred on an 80-sq.km area in the heart of the Lucanian uplands in the southern Apennines, just north-west of Potenza, and was carried out between 1979 and 1983 to accompany the excavations of the University of Alberta at the Roman villa site of San Giovanni Ruoti.[54] Aiming to establish the highland settlement pattern of which the site at Ruoti was part, this survey covered the area within a 6 km radius around the excavations and found an unusually high site density there of one site for each 1.2 sq.km surveyed. A total of 18 sites could be dated to the period between 500 and 300 BC, whereas 38 sites were dated to the subsequent Roman Republican period, most of which could be subdated to the phase 300-200 BC. Again, the early Hellenistic phase seems to have been marked by a rise in site numbers.

Since the 1980s other teams from the University of Alberta have conducted surveys throughout southern Italy, around Tempa Cortaglia in south-eastern Basilicata, along the Basentello valley on the Basilicata/Apulia border and in the mountainous region of Cilento, in Campania.[55] Densely-settled early Hellenistic rural landscapes were recorded in all of these surveys, but especially in Cilento. Here, the survey focused on the landscape surrounding the fortified Lucanian site of Roccagloriosa, which was being excavated at the same time. Roccagloriosa is located at ca. 500 m above sea level on a limestone ridge that forms the watershed between the valleys of the Mingardo and Bussento rivers. Towards the south these valleys converge on the Tyrrhenian sea, while mountain ranges reaching heights of between 1200 and 1900 m enclose the area to the north, east and west and constitute a major barrier to communica-

---

[52] For the Kroton surveys see Carter / D'Annibale 1985; for topographical research in the Tarantino see, section 3.3.

[53] Vinson 1972; Small 1991.

[54] Roberto / Plambeck / Small 1985; Small 1991; Roberto and Small 1994.

[55] Tempa Cortaglia: Fracchia 1985. Basentello-valley: Small *et al.* 1998. Cilento: De Polignac / Fracchia / Gualtieri 1990; Gualtieri / De Polignac 1991; Fracchia / Ortolani 1993.

tions with other parts of western Lucania. Within this naturally enclosed region the area most suitable for agricultural exploitation consists of a series of gently sloping terraces on either side of Roccagloriosa. Both this area and part of the uplands were included in the surveys. Between 1983 and 1985 two sample zones (30 sq.km in total) were investigated in the Roccagloriosa catchment area, and from 1987 onwards most of the Mingardo river valley was included as well. The average density of sites recorded in these surveys is 3 sites per sq.km. Although the survey was multi-period and regional in scope, the principal aim was to investigate the relationship between the fortified site and its surrounding landscape in the period 350-250 BC. During this phase the area was found to be marked by a sharp increase in the number of rural sites both in the catchment area of Roccagloriosa and up to 20 km away in the upper Mingardo valley. Most of these sites were interpreted as permanently occupied small farmsteads, but there are also hamlets, tombs, votive deposits and watch towers. In general, the Roccagloriosa area seems to fit a model of isolated farms, clustered settlements and fortified nucleated centres that can be distinguished into major and minor categories on the basis of size, position, political and religious function.

In 1996 another large-scale survey project was launched in the middle and upper Sinni valley jointly by the *Università degli Studi di Bologna* and the *Seconda Università degli Studi di Napoli*.[56] Although it adheres to the topographical tradition of the *Forma Italiae* series, the Sinni project adopted modern, intensive line walking techniques for a total coverage and documentation of all pre-modern archaeological sites in the study area. In this way some 1240 archaeological sites, dating from prehistory to medieval times, were recorded within the ca. 1130 sq.km of the project area. Hundreds of these find spots, which measure between 400 and 900 sq.m and are mostly interpreted as small farm sites, date to the second half of the 4th and the 3rd centuries BC. This represents a clear increase relative to the preceding phase. Whilst most of these sites are located on terraces, slopes and hilltops, some occurred up to 800 m above sea level in marginal upland areas where standing structures such as wall foundations and polygonal terrace walls are often preserved. Moreover, remains of tile- and coarse-ware kilns were frequently recorded in the vicinity of these sites. Besides small farms there are necropoleis, rural cult places, hamlets, villages, towns and hillforts.

The Sinni Valley surveys are exceptional in their documentation of standing rural structures, probably thanks to the use of the site-oriented judgemental topographic techniques so characteristic of the *Forma Italiae* tradition. Being relatively rare, such ruins will always be poorly represented in survey projects that use intensive probabilistic sampling procedures.

8.7 EXPLORING A MACRO-REGIONAL EXPLANATION

On the basis of the central- and south-Italian surveys outlined above we can safely conclude that the expansion of rural occupation in the late $4^{th}/3^{rd}$ century BC in the three regions studied by the RPC team was not an isolated phenomenon. As we have already discussed, this transformation was connected to the introduction of a variety of innovative agricultural strategies that enabled a more intensive exploitation of existing landholdings (e.g. manure-based agriculture) or the reclamation of previously untilled, formerly marginal areas (e.g. the construction of drainage systems). Remarkably, these trends were not longer confined to the Ionian and central Tyrrhenian coastal plains, where rural territories had been filled in as early as the Archaic period. In the late $4^{th}/3^{rd}$ centuries BC rural infill became manifest even in mountainous inland areas such as Samnium and Lucania. When the traditionally dominant role of animal husbandry in the economies and societies of such inland regions is considered, the variation in local conditioning factors becomes even greater. However, even in these regions the density and nature of the archaeological surface finds that were detected during surveys confirm that similar processes occurred. The fact that even here innovative agricultural strategies were adopted is an additional argument to

---

[56] Quilici / Quilici Gigli 2001.

Fig. 8.4. Hellenistic fortifications of the Apulian coastal town of Egnazia (Fasano, BR; photo: ACVU-archive). For a colour version of this figure, see page 235.

investigate the impact of supra-regional factors. Once again Roman expansion can only partially explain the apparent cross-regional affinities, especially because in large parts of southern Italy it postdates the observed transformations.

As it has become clear that macro-regional explanations cannot be based exclusively on Roman colonization as the 'moving force', we must look at alternatives that stress the role of interregional exchange networks. It is by participating in such networks that local communities throughout Italy were able to adopt the concepts necessary for rural infill to be effected. Archaeological contexts clearly indicate an unprecedented growth in exchange systems in the early Hellenistic period. This can for example be deduced from the wide circulation of manufactured and luxury items such as Red-figure ceramics. However, not only goods but also technological concepts clearly had a wide circulation. Good examples are the monumental fortification walls that are abundantly attested in central and southern Italy from the late 4th century BC onwards, even in mountainous inland regions (fig. 8.4). Here, as in many other Italian regions, few such defensive circuits existed in pre-Hellenistic times. On the basis of (admittedly still meagre) stratigraphical evidence and typological affinities it is generally believed that the fortifications only became widespread in the course of the later 4th century BC. We must conclude that building techniques such as these could be quickly adopted, even by communities far from the urban core areas, through the mechanisms of interregional contact, and that innovative agricultural strategies are likely to have been adopted the same way.

Although few regions have produced hard evidence for innovations in agricultural strategies or technology, the infill of the landscape in many of them during this period is a strong argument in favour of various forms of intensification of the exploitation of landholdings and of reclamation of formerly marginal areas. New agricultural techniques, that made it possible to cope with the local environmental conditions in a different way than before, were probably introduced to achieve this. The adoption of these innovations, and also of those observed in ceramic technology, architecture and many other areas, clearly coincided with the attested integration of the regions' elites in interregional social and economic networks. One may therefore conclude that socio-economic integration on a macro-regional scale was the trigger for the flow of technological innovations and the subsequent rural infill of the Italian landscape during the late 4th and 3rd century BC.

8.8 EPILOGUE: LATE REPUBLICAN AGRICULTURE AND THE CITY OF ROME

In this chapter we have discussed at length the process of landscape reorganization that characterized the Italian peninsula during the mid-Republican phase. We have questioned, however, the impact of Roman expansion and colonization on this process. An important aim of this volume is to assess critically the traditional emphasis on the allegedly decisive role of Greek and Roman colonization in the formation of the protohistoric and early historic Italian landscape. The later Roman Republican period is less controversial in this respect. With the socio-political unification and integration of Italy under the hegemony of Rome, metropolitan influence on this process and on the organization of the Italian landscape in general became more manifest, especially through direct interference in the form of municipal legislation, centuriation, and the siphoning off of manpower by the Roman military levies. Placing these processes into a long-term perspective, we conclude this chapter with a summary evaluation of major rural occupation trends in the three RPC regions in the late Republican period, when urban development in Italy reached new levels.

8.8.1 TRANSFORMATIONS IN THE AGRARIAN ECONOMY

Late Republican urbanization is generally argued to have been accompanied by a rearrangement of the agrarian economy and a subsequent drastic reshaping of the Italian landscape as a whole. Central to this argument, which was long based mainly on references in ancient texts, is the formation of market-oriented rural enterprises throughout central and southern Italy.[57] On the basis of these texts it was concluded that such enterprises in central (Tyrrhenian) Italy specialised in growing olives and especially in viticulture. Southern Italy was seen as largely dominated by extensive estates that focused on cereal cultivation and grazing, producing likewise for urban markets. The growing demand by urban markets was, however, not the only factor behind this transformation. The Roman wars of expansion in the Mediterranean basin also provided new markets, capital (war booty) and work force (slaves), enabling wealthy landowners and especially metropolitan elites to undertake such enterprises. It is also deduced from historical sources that land was abundantly available especially in southern Italy, thanks to the large-scale additions to Roman *ager publicus* after the Second Punic War, additions that followed confiscations of land from Italian communities that had been disloyal to Rome. It is this combination of factors which is generally supposed to have severely disrupted autonomous regional socio-economic structures.[58] Farming populations already weakened by continuous war probably suffered most from the economic competition by the new estates. The resulting migration was directed primarily to the urbanized areas of central Italy, depopulating southern Italy in particular.

---

[57] This is one of the most discussed themes in Ancient History (connected as it is to contemporary political strife) and it has also aroused much attention in Italian survey archaeology in recent decades. Consequently, the literature on the subject is extensive. For overviews see especially Rathbone 1981, De Neeve 1984, and Morley 1996.

[58] De Neeve 1984.

We reiterate that this model has long been based mainly on ancient written sources, and the details of the causes of the decline of small subsistence farming are disputed, with different scholars emphasizing one or more of the factors discussed above. As the geographical scope of the written sources is limited and the model therefore depends heavily on support from epigraphy and archaeology, the relative lack of archaeological data from the south was until recently seen as evidence of its economic and demographic marginality. A more critical look suggests that the poor datasets rather reflect a long-standing lack of interest by archaeologists in systematic archaeological research, and therefore result from, rather than support, the assumptions underlying this model (see also chapter 1 on research biases). In the last decades this situation has changed considerably, thanks to the introduction of landscape studies and survey archaeology. A wealth of data is gradually becoming available which allows us to re-assess the model and to study late Republican settlement trends for individual regions. In the following sections we will briefly do so, focusing first on the three RPC regions and then presenting an overview of broad trends in survey patterns in late Republican central and southern Italy.

8.8.2 DIVERGING TRENDS: COMPARATIVE SETTLEMENT ARCHAEOLOGY

As discussed in section 8.3, the results of the analysis of the RPC survey data reveal elements of both continuity and change in the process of rural infill that is apparent in the three study regions from the later 4th century BC onwards. In the Pontine area, the late Republican settlement pattern in the Alban hills and down to the coast is characterised by a contraction into fewer but larger rural sites. We have tentatively dated this development to the 2nd century BC (mostly on the basis of building techniques). In contrast, our surveys in the territory of Antium in the coastal zone indicate an increase in site density in this period, reaching a peak in the late Republican and early Imperial period. A similar but slightly later and less intensive trend could be observed further south along the coast, in the Fogliano surveys of 1998-1999. As new GIA surveys are being carried out in the coastal landscape to the northwest of Fogliano, and as older surveys are being analysed more thoroughly, such spatial variation becomes gradually more apparent.[59] In all landscape units a general decrease in the number of sites occurs only after the early Imperial period, a phenomenon consistent with the idea that the intensive rural exploitation of the Hellenistic/Republican period was replaced by a more extensive mode of exploitation. So far, there is, however, little archaeological evidence for the existence of so-called *latifundiae* in the Pontine plain.

Both in the Sibaritide and in the Brindisino the general trend in rural settlement patterns resembles that of the Alban hills and the Lepine side of the Pontine plain, where site numbers decrease notably. In the Sibaritide the Roman colony of Copiae was founded on the site of Thurioi in the early 2nd century BC, but only a handful of rural *villae* from this period are attested in the foothill zone (the absence of evidence for such villas in the plain is probably caused by continuing alluviation). Less than a quarter of the Hellenistic sites that are reported in the Quilici survey continued into the Roman period, and the limited evidence provided by our own survey suggests that the presence of a few larger and richer villa sites must be linked to this reduction. The decline in the number of rural sites is less pronounced in the Brindisi region, which has been more thoroughly investigated. However, local differentiation can be observed in relation to site sizes. In the northern periphery of Brindisi and in the fertile plateau around Oria, the Siena and AIVU surveys respectively suggested an increase in site sizes, while in the southern coastal transect near Valesio no such increase was observed. In the Murge area evidence for late Republican occupation is limited to a few shards from sites whose major component was debris of the Imperial period. This demonstrates how varied such developments can be, even within a single land system.

---

[59] Attema *et al.* 2008; Attema *et al.* 2009.

Of course, it is often extremely difficult to explain such local variations in socio-economic terms. In this particular case, however, we can point to the development of an amphora production industry in the periphery of Brindisi, investigated mainly by the Siena project. As we have seen earlier (chapter 3), industrial amphora production is generally related to the emergence of market-oriented olive oil production, practised on larger and more centralised farms of the kind detected by the Siena surveys and the ACVU survey around Oria. Production was geared towards the urban market at Brindisi, which in this phase developed into a major harbour for the overseas export of regional agricultural products, notably olive oil. In contrast, in the areas further away from Brindisi and the Via Appia - which was extended to Brindisi in this phase and thus provided good transportation facilities - small subsistence farms seem to have prevailed; the Valesio and Ostuni survey transects are a case in point. Elsewhere we have argued that these data agree with a model that predicts that these areas did not participate in the increased trade and export, while their pre-Roman *oppida* lost their previous functions as local central places and dwindled into hamlets.[60] Conversely, the rapidly expanding town of Brindisi emerged as the undisputed central place.

The late Republican settlement trends visible in the RPC study regions cannot be neatly fitted into the generalised model of contemporary Italian agriculture. This is especially the case in the Brindisino which clearly does not conform to the conventional picture of southern Italy after the Punic Wars, supposedly a landscape of extensive cereal cultivation and grazing. In reality the flourishing of intensive arboriculture in specific Brindisi areas remained a very significant factor. Moreover, intra-regional variation is again obviously present, with local landscape units responding in remarkably different ways. Such examples warn against any cross-regional generalizations for Italy as a whole.

Surveys in the wider peninsula confirm this view. In central Italy the picture is rather varied, with some regions being characterised by expansion or consolidation in site numbers, others by contraction. In southern Italy rural site decline seems to be rather common in most of the surveyed areas. However, as in the Brindisino the case of Daunia also argues against any bleak scenario of a uniformly deserted south Italy. Daunia has long been considered to be emblematic of such a scenario, but this view was already modified to some degree by Volpe's systematic inventory of all excavations and other find reports of rural sites of the Roman period in Daunia.[61] Volpe concludes that these data conform only to a limited degree to the traditional literary picture of the economic geography of the region. Large parts of late Republican Daunia seem actually to have been characterised by dense rural settlement and intensive cultivation, and only an estimated 25-30% of the region was used for cereal cultivation and grazing.[62] Like the earlier case of the Brindisino, which demonstrates that the combination of a reduction in rural sites and a decline of *oppida* should not be uncritically interpreted as evidence for a crisis in agriculture, the Daunian example warns against over-reliance on literary tradition. We may conclude that the model of a uniformly depressed southern Italy after the Punic Wars is incorrect, and that even within each region there are marked differences in prosperity and demographic trends. Clearly, a more refined model is needed.

8.8.3 ECONOMIC ZONATION IN THE LATE REPUBLIC

Recently, Neville Morley discussed a number of Italian surveys in his important work on the late Republican transformation of Italian settlement and land use, and he offered a more differentiated model than the conventional one.[63] Morley's major concern is the effect of Rome's economic demands on the Italian peninsula. Morley argues that some economic growth was possible also within the limits of a pre-indus-

---

[60] Burgers 1998, 265-281.
[61] Volpe 1990.
[62] Volpe 1990, 78.
[63] Morley 1996.

trial economy, and that the demographic growth of Rome created an urban market of an unprecedented size, which would have significantly enhanced economic growth in late Republican Italy. He proposes a model of agricultural change that borrows heavily from geographical theory. His main point is that the growth of the Roman market led to the formation of an Italian landscape which was differentiated in zones of varying economic profitability. In this model distance-to-market and related transportation costs are among the more important variables that dictate the different types of farming systems in each zone.

Morley applies the model to the available historical and archaeological data, and argues that an intensive farming system came to dominate in the *suburbium*, the immediate hinterland of Rome (up to 30 km away). The economy of this zone focused on the provisioning of Rome with perishable food such as fruit and vegetables, and luxury goods such as fish. Major factors contributing to the emergence of this system were high urban market prices and relatively low transportation costs. The increased rural prosperity which resulted was accompanied by a decline of traditional urban nuclei, which where increasingly by-passed by the flow of goods and money between Rome and its hinterland particularly in this zone. A second economic zone, limited to the central Tyrrhenian coastal areas, was characterised mainly by the emergence of intensive slave-run villas that focused on olive oil production and above all viticulture, and which produced for the Roman market as well as for markets outside the Italian peninsula. The third and final zone in Morley's model comprises those parts of Italy that are even further removed from Rome and were correspondingly less influenced by its demands. Here it was the production of surpluses of specific regional specialities (notably the products of pastoralism) which was demonstrably intended to satisfy the demands of the market of the Urbs. The introduction of long-distance transhumance, favoured by the expansion of *ager publicus*, the establishment of political control and the relative peace resulting from it, fits well into this model. It can indeed be argued that these developments would have promoted the conversion of good arable land into pasture and consequently the desolation of the countryside. However, studies in Daunia and Samnium suggest that long-distance transhumance was still a relatively restricted phenomenon and other, more traditional (short-distance, sedentary) forms of pastoralism that were combined with arable cultivation should not be ignored. This is also the case for agricultural land use in general. The Brindisi region, for example, demonstrates that estates practising intensive arboriculture flourished in the hinterland of towns in southern Italy, where they served local markets as well as a wider Mediterranean network.

Morley's geographically oriented model offers a powerful instrument for understanding the transformations in Italy as a whole as well as in its individual regions. Particularly instructive in the present context is Morley's insistence not to view the zonation as absolute and to allow for regional variation. As is predicted in the original economic-geographical models, a range of factors is likely to distort the ideal zonation.[64] Although the growth of Rome definitely had a major impact on the socio-economic development of Italy, it did not have the same influence throughout the various zones. Other factors, like variations in climate and soil fertility, regional socio-economic power relations, unequal access to the primary market, and the presence of alternative urban markets within and outside Italy, have to be taken into account as well.

The Italian settlement trends reviewed above were influenced not only by the hegemonic rule and the market demands of Rome, but also by the interaction of a range of other factors that probably operated at various geographical scales. At the local scale the environment is likely to have been a significant determinant in specific socio-economic trajectories followed by individual communities. At the regional scale, the settlement trends also reflect social patterns and economic structures of centre and periphery. Finally, at the macro-regional scale, the trends reflect the position of Italy within the changing economy of the Mediterranean. The Italian regions that began to supply areas outside Italy, as the Brindisino did, illustrate this.

---

[64] Cf. De Neeve 1984; Burgers 1998, 286-289; 2001.

9 A Supra-regional Comparative Perspective

9.1 INTRODUCTION

The main goal of the RPC project, as set forth in the project design, was to gain insight into processes of centralization and urbanization taking place over a long period from protohistory into Roman times, within three regions studied since the early 1980s by the participating Dutch archaeology departments (GIA and ACVU). The spatial, ecological, technological, socio-economic, and political aspects of these processes were to be analyzed from a long-term and comparative perspective.

This was an ambitious goal, as it involved the study and explanation of observed changes in settlement and land use patterns in geographically diverse areas and over a long period of time. These changes were in our opinion the outcome of a complex interaction of internal and external forces, and eventually they resulted in more complex forms of society in all three study areas – hence the project title 'Regional Pathways to Complexity'. Additional fieldwork was conducted in all three regions to collect urgently needed data on the hitherto neglected 'marginal' areas (coastal margins, former marshes, and uplands). These, though perhaps economically less productive in the past, nonetheless represent a significant percentage of both the ancient and the modern landscape, and no modern regional archaeological study can afford to ignore them.[1] Specialist studies were conducted into the application of palaeo-economic land evaluation, historical and ethnographic aspects of pastoralism, the analysis of site distribution patterns and the production and distribution of pottery.[2] Where relevant, the results of these studies have been integrated in this monograph.

Here we will present the methodological advances and increased understanding that the RPC project has resulted in.

9.2 METHODOLOGICAL ADVANCES

The methodological advances coming out of the RPC project may be grouped under three headings. Firstly, the importance of a proper assessment of research- and visibility biases in archaeological field walking surveys, and of the relationship between potential and actual land uses, will be argued. Secondly, the importance of studying historic and ethnographic aspects of pastoralism will be stressed, since this is a type of land use that was a major factor in past subsistence and economic strategies but is not included in formal land evaluation studies using the FAO method. Thirdly, the potential of technological pottery studies to improve the chronological resolution of survey finds will be assessed, as well as its potential to reconstruct socio-economic aspects of past societies. The section will be concluded by a discussion of some remaining methodological issues.

---

[1] In 2005, the NWO-funded research programme 'Hidden Landscapes' was initiated by the GIA to focus on precisely these landscapes.

[2] Veenman 2002; Van Leusen 2002; Van Joolen 2003; Mater 2005.

9.2.1 RESEARCH AND VISIBILITY BIASES

The RPC project has paid special attention to the important role played by research- and visibility biases in the process of gathering and processing data during field walking surveys. Moreover, it has done so at all spatial scales from the regional down to the local. From a methodological point of view, the landscape-oriented RPC surveys have been amongst the most intensive ever performed in Italy. This has resulted in the creation of a surface record that through its high spatial and chronological resolution makes visible low-intensity uses of the past landscape as well as the effect of bias factors such as geomorphological processes and anthropogenic soil disturbance. The detailed recording of visibility factors for every 50 by 50 m unit enables us to study how the surface record varies with visibility. Likewise, the standard collection of *all* pre-modern material in the field-walkers' transects means that a specialist re-study of the finds can reveal patterns that were overlooked during the survey itself.[3] Once we realized that the vegetation cover was not the only, or even the main, factor affecting ground visibility within our study area, we introduced a recording system that allows for the assessment of the relative importance of a range of locally significant visibility factors. It is now clear that visibility factors should be assessed within the framework of both geomorphological and land use/land cover variation. For example, a large part of the Sibaritide foothill zone consists of marine or fluvial terraces formed on top of conglomerate rock of varying composition, and when these terraces have been ploughed the many curved fragments of stones of different colours make effective surveying, even in otherwise excellent circumstances, extremely difficult.

Likewise, it is now apparent that the degree in which visibility and research biases affect the major finds groups greatly varies. An assessment of existing site records at the time when the project started had already made visible a widespread and severe bias towards 'Hellenistic-Roman' sites, and field experience soon showed that, even in the absence of structural remains, the quantity and type of material remains from these periods is by far the most likely to be noticed by farmers, farm- and construction workers, and archaeologists. Activities which resulted in less densely concentrated or less obtrusive remains simply went unnoticed as field walkers passed over them. Consequently, the most obvious and immediate result of our more intensive and systematic surveys is the discovery of many very small protohistoric (in south Italy) and Archaic (in the Pontine region) sites, sometimes spaced as little as 100 m apart. To achieve this result the surveys have had to be slowed down almost by a factor of ten: whereas typical site-oriented surveys of the early 1990s covered an average of 10 hectares per person per day, ours cover only 1 hectare. Clearly, the loss of speed has to be weighed against the greater quantity and quality of information gained from the landscape – future projects should make a rational decision about this.

In the case of the RPC project, we can conclude that our surveying strategies have paid off, since they uncovered much more spatial variation in settlement- and land use histories than had been attested previously. This spatial differentiation has forced us to abandon some of the generalizing scenarios that had been used to describe the protohistoric and early historic settlement and land use histories in the three study areas. In particular, the surveys have resulted in more detailed knowledge of what was going on *outside* the central settlements, not only in their immediate surroundings but in the more remote parts of the landscape as well. Moreover, we are now able to detect the impact of core processes on these landscapes. Thus, for the protohistorical Pontine region we have identified a range of small rural sites on the ancient beach ridge (well outside the territories of any proto-urban settlement), that indicate the existence of a widespread and long-term exploitation of this marginal land system. In this case there is

---

[3] For example, the presence of depurated storage pottery dating to the Final Bronze Age on some sites surveyed in 2002 became apparent only in 2005; older collections were then restudied and further storage vessels identified. Likewise, a specialist re-examination of our protohistoric sites resulted in the discovery of a few fragments of matt-painted depurated pottery dating to the Iron Age.

no need to assume that this phenomenon was linked to the development of centralized and proto-urban settlements elsewhere. In contrast, early Hellenistic urbanization in the Salento region seems to have had an impact even on such relatively marginal areas as the Murge tableland, parts of which were in this phase reclaimed for permanent rural occupation, albeit to a lesser extent than in the coastal plain.

One as yet unresolved methodological issue is the publication of survey results: should we publish the 'raw data' or the 'corrected' density maps, or both?[4] Debate has so far concentrated on problems surrounding the interpretation of 'corrected' density maps, and indeed correction methods currently rely wholly on the individual project director's judgement. More fundamentally, however, the RPC project experience has shown that there is no such thing as 'raw data': beside the visibility and research biases operating during the survey, many projects still rely on team members' judgement to collect 'important' finds while ignoring or discarding the more than 90% of undiagnostic pottery. Furthermore, density maps are based on each projects' classification of find types and dates, with major problems such as the chronology of local coarse wares still unresolved.

Finally, the importance of geo-archaeological studies has been driven home to us in the course of the RPC project, as it became increasingly clear that natural and anthropogenic processes may either cause, or have a major influence on the discovery of, many of the archaeological patterns recorded in our field surveys (see sections 2.2 and 4.2). These processes operate on all spatial and chronological scales, and a systematic assessment of them is therefore vital to the interpretation of the results.[5]

9.2.2 ACTUAL AND POTENTIAL LAND USE: CLASSIFYING THE LANDSCAPE

The main attempt by the RPC project at systematic landscape classification has used the economic land-evaluation approach, which determines the potential suitability of different landforms for different crops, given a certain technological level. Land evaluation seems best suited for societies that use the simple types of agriculture that the method was originally designed to assist, but both the study area and the archaeological dataset must satisfy a large number of additional conditions. The study area must be large enough to contain considerable environmental and physiographic variation, as well as good opportunities for collecting palaeo-ecological data. The archaeological dataset, too, must be of a sufficient size and quality to capture any spatial or typochronological patterning present in the archaeological record. Land evaluation as a formal method for modelling environmental potential and constraints can be applied to any early-agriculturalist society for which the physical landscape can be reconstructed to a sufficient degree. Models based on land evaluation have the further advantage that they are *generic* (they can be applied to any area with a similar environment without reference to its archaeology) and *falsifiable* (they can be tested both against existing archaeological records and by a straightforward program of fieldwork). These models therefore enable a fundamentally more constructive and objective approach to the study of past landscapes than was previously possible. However, since land evaluation will often require a large investment in palaeo-geographic reconstruction (coring programmes, palynological reconstructions), other means of reconstructing past landscapes also deserve attention. Some early-historic landscapes can, for instance, be partially reconstructed on the basis of additional sources of historical information deriving from place name etymology or historical literary and cartographic sources.[6]

---

[4] Density maps have been published for the following RPC surveys: SIBA2000 (Van Leusen / Attema 2003), Fogliano (Attema *et al*. 2001a), and Ostuni (Burgers *et al*. 1998 [2004]).

[5] In recent years the GIA has focused its efforts on paleo-geographical reconstruction of the Pontine plain and computer simulation of slope processes in the Raganello watershed: see Feiken, forthcoming.

[6] Satijn 2003.

In the RPC project the emphasis has been on a classification of the landscape into so-called land systems.[7] This has provided additional support for some of our 'environmental' explanations of large-scale patterns (e.g. agriculture before the introduction of the iron ploughshare avoiding heavy alluvial soils) but its a-historical character means that it can only help to explain why a particular development did *not* occur in a specific land system, not why it did. For example, according to Van Joolen's land evaluation the plain around Brindisi is one of the most suitable landscapes for ancient agriculture in the entire Salento isthmus. Its soils are considered to be suitable for a range of ancient land use types, from the typical Mediterranean polyculture system to monoculture of cereals, olives or grapes. However, this suitability does not mean that it was actually used intensively, even in the late Republican period when agriculture in this region became commercialized. The archaeological data from field surveys and excavations indicate that agricultural intensification and commercialization in the late Republican period in the Brindisi plain were largely limited to specific areas with good infrastructure, whereas other, previously intensively settled and worked areas in the same land system were largely abandoned. Clearly, predictions based on land evaluation alone should always be tested, and historical conditions should be taken into consideration. Furthermore, the land evaluation approach ignores many other factors (such as accessibility and microclimatic conditions) that affected past choices in settlement and land use. This became evident as more detailed archaeological research found much unexplained variation in types and quantities of archaeological remains within each land system or land-form class. A further spatial refinement on the basis of FAO-type criteria, however, seems useless. We have therefore also introduced alternative and more fine-grained landscape classifications based mainly on geomorphological criteria.[8]

However, an *expected* form of land use for any particular (agricultural) socialeconomic model of past societies can still be derived from economic land evaluation. The main use of land evaluation in archaeology therefore is that it allows us to assess the viability of these socio-economic models. Comparison of the expected form of land use with the archaeologically observed form could in theory provide a basis for modifying these models, but the requisite ecofacts and artefacts can only be derived from targeted palaeo-environmental studies and excavation projects. In the Pontine region pollen analysis of various cores taken in different land systems proved a useful tool to test the kinds of land use predicted in Van Joolen's land evaluation models. Pollen analysis in the highlands of the Pollino mountains in the Sibaritide proved useful to detect and date the impact of grazing, a type of land use that receives less attention in landscape archaeological studies.

9.2.3 PASTORALIST STRATEGIES

The specialist study on pastoralism carried out by Veenman was deemed necessary as the FAO land evaluation method does not consider this form of land use. Pastoralism has always been important in the longue durée of the Italian landscape as an essential component of subsistence farming, although more specialized strategies also existed such as short- and long-distance transhumance. Veenman linked various ethnographically recorded strategies to specific socio-economic situations. Short-distance transhumance has traditionally been considered a fundamental component of Italian society since the Bronze Age, linking the upland with lowland land systems and settlements. Evidence for the grazing of flocks in the uplands of the Sibaritide from an early phase of the Bronze Age onwards was indeed found in two of the pollen cores that we discussed in chapter 4 and Box 4.1, while ethnographic evidence for this type of transhumance is available for the Pontine plain. Here, herdsmen until recent times used to move with their flocks in the autumn from the mountainous hinterland into the Pontine plain to stay there dur-

---

[7] For a definition, see section 1.2.1.

[8] Van Leusen *et al.* 2005; Van Leusen / Feiken 2007.

ing the winter and early spring. Marginal parts of the landscape, such as the uplands of the Murge, the Pollino and the Lepini and parts of the Pontine and Sibaritide plains, may thus in the past have been intensively used for grazing and as such have been areas of considerable economic interest. Long-distance transhumance along so-called *tratture* benefited notably from the Roman political unification of Italy and the growth of markets for dairy products. Archaeological or documentary evidence for long-distance transhumance is, however, absent in the RPC regions for the periods under study. Veenman's studies of recent vegetation degradation caused by grazing may be incorporated into future work once such degradation can be identified in the ancient pollen record.[9] Veenman's comparative study of bone collections from excavated sites pointed to variations in meat consumption and grazing in the three regions over time and by implication in the overall composition of the animal stock that was raised (pig, sheep/goat, cow). She noted a certain conservatism in the type of stock-raising in the sense that, for instance, central Italy was always more dedicated to sheep-farming. Such data would underline the power of the longue durée. The weak statistical basis of the study, however, precludes a systematic incorporation of the results in our land use analyses, and further studies are needed.

9.2.4 POTTERY PRODUCTION AND DISTRIBUTION

Mater's pottery studies have proved important on different levels. On the macro-level, her inventory and typology of pottery production sites by period showed regional trends from household- via workshop- to early industrial production over the long period from the Bronze Age to the Roman Republican period. This gradual transition from household-based pottery production to industrial workshops is fundamental for our understanding of centralization and urbanization in the regions studied.

On an intraregional level, evidence for changes in the scale and type of pottery production may be used to assess the degree of centralization within a region, as in the Bronze Age contexts discussed above or indicate increasing urbanization, as in Archaic Sybaris and its surrounding sites.[10] In her dissertation Mater extended this argument to the Roman world by looking at amphora production as an example of the unprecedented scale of specialized production in this period (see also section 3.3.1).[11] This is particularly evident in the immediate hinterland of Brindisi, where several amphora production centres emerged in the Late Republican period. The rapid urbanisation of the colonial territory of Brindisi was therefore demonstrably accompanied by an industrialization of the amphora production that was necessary to support the commercialization of the regional agriculture and especially the overseas trade of olive oil and wine.

Some of the pottery studies were dedicated to the study of pottery fabrics. In our discussion of the surveys it was noted how in some cases the low dating resolution hampers the assessment of continuity or discontinuity in rural site patterns, as in the Pontine region for the 5th and 4th century, and more in general in the case of scatters of worn impasto pottery found in the intensive surveys in all RPC regions. Although some work on the pottery fabrics has already been published, still further studies are therefore needed.[12]

Full publication of diagnostic survey materials from both sites and off-site contexts is necessary to enable sound comparisons between projects and regions. We have already published detailed site- and find catalogues for most of our surveys in the Pontine region.[13]

[9] Veenman 2002, chapter 4.
[10] Mater 2005, 101-126.
[11] Mater 2005, chapter 5.
[12] Attema *et al.* 2003a; Mater 2005, chapters 3 and 4.
[13] The Fogliano (Attema *et al.* 2005), Monti Lepini (Van Leusen *et al.* 2005), and Astura/Nettuno (Attema *et al.* 2008) surveys.

9.2.5 DISCUSSION: PROBLEMS AND ADDED VALUE OF THE COMPARATIVE INTEGRATED APPROACH

There remain still many methodological problems to be solved. The comparison and combination of the results of two or more field walking surveys, for instance, presents a surprisingly difficult problem to the archaeologist. In the majority of cases, field survey practice and recording methods are simply not sufficiently standardized for the results to be 'normalized' with any degree of confidence. We have found this to be the case to some extent even when comparing two RPC surveys that made use of identical methods in the same landscape type, since other important variables (especially the expertise of individual field team members and the expertise of finds processing staff) can have a great impact on the detection and recording of specific find groups. The current debate on 'comparative survey' must therefore perforce shift towards the comparison of *trends* in individual survey results.[14] Also, we have found that field walking surveys have their limitations. Archaeological remains ploughed to the surface and left to weather help us to identify the rough date and, in a few cases, type of activity at a site, but they leave many other questions unanswered. The more emphasis is placed on off-site surveying, the greater this problem becomes as surface visibility and the quality and density of finds all tend to become less. More intensive forms of research, both on-site (coring, geophysical mapping, trial trenching, environmental sampling) and off-site (geophysical prospection and remote sensing), are needed to answer these questions, and should therefore be integrated in any future research proposals.

In spite of these methodological problems, the integrated approach elaborated in the RPC project shows promise for the comparative study of centralization and urbanization processes in past landscapes. It has been shown that these processes can be profitably studied using data other than those concerning the apex of regional settlement hierarchies. Data on land use, technological improvements, rural settlement hierarchy, off-site archaeology and the organization of production add significantly to our understanding of these processes. We have hopefully also shown that the perspective of the longue durée is helpful in overcoming the artificial divide between protohistory and the classical periods as well as the disciplinary divide between archaeology and history. Both these divides hamper a view on centralization and urbanization as long-term processes.

9.3 INTERPRETATIONS

In our introductory chapter we referred to Braudel's framework for understanding history as being articulated in three different time-scales, corresponding to the long-term 'structural' and physical change of the landscape, the medium-term 'conjunctural' demographic and economic cycles, and short-term human actions or 'events'. The regional studies in this volume show that increased and combined knowledge of settlement- and land use patterns covering a long period will often dissolve apparent 'conjunctural' discontinuities in settlement histories. With hindsight, these discontinuities are seen to have been caused by a fragmented and poorly controlled approach to the use of archaeological evidence, in which landscapes are studied period by period and biases in the archaeological record are not taken into account.

Processes that appear 'revolutionary' in a long-term perspective, such as Bronze Age centralization, the historical Greek and Roman colonizations, and Archaic and Roman urbanization, can now be studied at the 'conjunctural' scale, where they are found to have roots in the indigenous landscapes of the three

---

[14] See, for example, our discussion of Hellenistic settlement trends in section 8.6. The problem is more broadly discussed in Alcock / Cherry 2004.

regions. The Mediterranean landscape itself is no longer the static, unchanging backdrop of Braudel's *Mediterranée*, but a changing and in some cases highly dynamic environment both influencing and influenced by the societies living in the regions we have studied. The introduction of new ways of cultivating the landscape sustained long-term demographic growth in all three landscapes, but now as a result of our work Braudel's medium-term demographic and economic cycles also become visible. Thus, specific urbanization trends, e.g. during the late Iron Age and Archaic periods in Lazio and the Hellenistic period in the Salento isthmus and the Sibaritide, can be shown to have been accompanied by an exponential increase in the number of rural sites, indicative of a flourishing of the countryside. Phases of stagnation and decline are also evident in all three landscapes, as for instance in the Pontine region during the 5th and 4th centuries BC or in the Roman period in the Sibaritide, and in all three regions in the final stages of the late antique period and early medieval period.[15]

Due to the limitations of the methods and data we used for our study of the settlement histories in the RPC regions, we have not been able to incorporate Braudel's short-term scale of human actions and the world of events, and we might therefore be accused of having committed 'structural determinism'. We already mentioned in the introduction to this book how later generations of Annales historians and post-processual archaeologists have criticized Braudel for this same reason. They wished to restore a dialectical relationship between landscape, structures and events and to question the fundamental primacy of landscape and social structures over individual human actions, on the grounds that human actions also create, reproduce and transform these structures. Whilst acknowledging that events and political actions by individuals leading for instance to warfare certainly had their effects on regional settlement developments, we feel that the use of whatever fragmentary and often severely biased epigraphical and especially historical sources are available presents major problems of its own. Such an approach would also lead to particularist explanations at the level of case studies, losing sight of the regional or supraregional trends that we set out to study.

9.3.1 LOCAL TRAJECTORIES TOWARD CENTRALIZATION

One specific trend that was discussed is the development in the Bronze Age of centralized and (proto-)urban forms of settlement organization by local indigenous groups. We concluded that the three regions followed different trajectories. Although there is evidence in Salento for the fortification of settlements as early as the first half of the 2nd millennium BC, the prevailing view among Italian archaeologists working in the region is that the degree of centralization was limited and that no formal settlement hierarchy developed throughout the Bronze Age (see section 5.2). Social differentiation, however, is argued to have increased from the Middle Bronze Age onwards and to have caused a competitive relationship between the various communities, a relationship otherwise marked by a political equilibrium. By contrast, in the Sibaritide the early development of local elites in the Sibaritide was the crucial element that triggered the establishment of central places and the consequent growth of a settlement hierarchy in the Recent Bronze Age, at least according to the Roman School of Protohistory. Such elites would have controlled most agricultural and craft production, as well as (overseas) exchange with the Aegean world. But these differences between the Sibaritide and Salento in the start and the growth rate of socio-economic complexity were small compared to those in the Pontine region. Such comparisons should be central to the debate on interregional variability.

---

[15] Though beyond the scope of this book, subsequent GIA research in the Pontine region has aimed to study these periods, e.g. Attema *et al.* forthcoming.

Early Iron Age and Archaic settlement hierarchies appear to have been much more stable and well-defined in the Pontine Region and the Salento isthmus than in the Sibaritide. In the latter, local indigenous development appears to have been cut short by the historical Greek colonization. Archaic urbanisation in the Pontine Region and the Salento isthmus was probably triggered by the interaction between peer polities, each of which was focused on a single urban centre (chapter 7). For Latium we may postulate the formation of a loosely integrated regional system of independent 'city states', a development which in the Pontine Region can be dated to the late 7th and 6th centuries BC. In Salento a similar process, involving the larger part of the peninsula, took place in the second half of the 6th century BC. A number of primary sites can be pointed out that, at least in socio-economic and religious terms, came to function as central places to the other settlements in their territories. The Sibaritide, due to its relatively small size, offered space for only one such polity; historically Sybaris' peers would have been the neighbouring coastal Greek colonies.

9.3.2 DIFFERENTIAL IMPACT OF GREEK COLONIZATION

Much chronological and geographical detail has been added to our understanding of the impact of the historical Greek and Roman colonization movements on the indigenous societies in our three regions. In chapter 6, for example, we argued that early Greek colonization in the Sibaritide and the Salento isthmus was very probably not the dominant force for socio-political change, nor did it affect all parts of the landscape to the same extent. Large parts of each region initially fell outside the direct control of the Greek colonies. Conversely, it is also quite possible that Greek claims to the landscape and its resources initially did not conflict with those of the indigenous communities, with the colonists using those parts of the coastal plain that were of only marginal significance to the indigenous farmers and pastoralists. The colony of Sybaris was initially a modest settlement that increased in size significantly only in the Archaic period. The impact of this development on the landscape immediately surrounding Sybaris is far from clear because of the thick sediment that covers this alluvial plain, but recent work on the Metapontino demonstrates that Archaic Greek farmsteads do indeed lie buried under such alluvium.[16] Surveys in the foothills show, however, that Greek rural infill emanating from Sybaris had barely reached the foothills by the end of the Classical period. Two possible explanations for this difference between the Sibaritide and the Metapontino come to mind: either Sybaris never completed its 5th-century expansion because it was destroyed by the Krotonese in 510 BC; or the traces of its expansion may simply lie hidden below the alluvium, since Sybaris had an exceptionally large coastal plain to expand into (see section 4.5 and Box 4.2). If the latter were the case, then the differences with the Metapontino are not so great after all. Although 7th-century Greek influence is evident from the cultural transformations taking place in the sanctuary of Timpone della Motta, it wasn't until the 6th century BC that the adjoining settlement transformed into a village that resembled residential areas at Sybaris itself. Rural infill of the foothill zone was primarily a Hellenistic phenomenon.

Our analysis of the Salento isthmus (chapters 3, 6 and 7) showed that trends of growing complexity of settlements and society were not restricted to Taras and its immediate hinterland in the early Iron Age, but occurred also in the indigenous areas. Moreover, we argued that Greek interference was not the only cause of the settlement transformations and landscape infill that can be demonstrated for Salento in the Iron Age. Rather, they seem to reflect a more general phenomenon, one primarily involving the indigenous coastal communities and induced by social differentiation, population growth and increased competition for available resources and territorial expansion. We concluded that the Greek colonists that settled the south Italian shores in this phase constituted not the dominant, but merely one of the elements in the ferment of shifting power structures. We argued that the immigrants were allowed to exchange, settle among and integrate with

---

[16] Carter 2006, 115-117.

the indigenous communities, because association with them or with the items they traded or produced was deemed useful in the context of indigenous competitive social strategies.

9.3.3 DIFFERENTIAL IMPACT OF ROME

Direct Roman influence on settlement patterns was, of course, felt much earlier in the nearby Pontine region than in either of the South Italian regions. From the 4th century BC onwards, a wholesale restructuring of the landscape took place in the Pontine plain, epitomised by the urban development of the Roman colonies of Cora, Norba and Setia. It was accompanied by investments in infrastructure (e.g. the construction of the Via Appia) and agriculture, notably in rural settlement on the Lepine side of the Pontine plain and along the coast around the colonies of Antium and Tarracina. However, in chapter 8 we warned against putting too much emphasis on this Roman colonial impact. We argued that landholding systems and land use patterns evolved in response to traditional, local socio-economic patterns. We called attention to the fact that similar processes of urbanisation and rural intensification occurred in other parts of Italy not yet under Roman influence at this time, and that these processes can be shown to have been largely internally driven (e.g. the Salento region). Our discussion of the major field survey projects south of the Tiber valley demonstrated that patterns of rural settlement similar to those attested in the Pontine, Salento and Sibaritide regions have been documented in lowlands, uplands, intermontane basins and valleys alike from the late 4th–3rd centuries BC onwards. We can only explain such a widespread trend by using a macro-regional approach that emphasizes demographic growth and the role of interregional exchange networks. It was through integration in such networks that local communities throughout Italy came to share similar socio-economic structures and material cultures.

In the late Republican period integration on a macro-regional scale further increased under the influence of the socio-political unification of all of Italy under Rome. Following Neville Morley, we emphasized the growth of the Roman urban market during this phase, which led to the formation of an Italian landscape that was differentiated into zones of varying economic profitability.

9.4 FINAL REMARKS

In this book we have highlighted similarities and differences between local trajectories of change in three regions in Italy: the Pontine region in central Italy and the Salento isthmus and Sibaritide regions in south Italy. We have observed how society in these regions between the Bronze Age and the Roman Empire became more complex in terms of its social, cultural, economic and administrative organisation. The rise of the large-scale, powerful and hierarchical Roman Empire as perceived in the tradition of neo-evolutionary thinking (see chapter 1) was, however, not our main focus. Our aim was rather an understanding of how and why local indigenous societies developed towards more complex forms of socio-economic and political organization, and why they did not all follow the same route. We focused on what we termed the 'core processes' of settlement centralization and proto-urbanization in the Bronze Age and Iron Ages respectively, as well as on indigenous urbanization and local responses to Greek and Roman colonization in the Archaic period, and the growth of Roman towns and countryside. Although these processes were broadly comparable in the three landscapes in the sense that, in all three, settlement hierarchies developed and comparable cultural transformations took place, the timing, the spatial scale and the nature of socio-political organization in each were significantly different. By first in chapters 2-4 outlining the long-term trajectories of change in the three individual regions and then in chapters 5-8 comparing them thematically, we were able to highlight the main differences and similarities that constitute each region's 'pathway to complexity'.

BIBLIOGRAPHIC REFERENCES

Abbott, J.T., 1997: *Late Quaternary Alluviation and Soil Erosion in Southern Italy* (PhD thesis, the University of Texas at Austin), Ann Arbor.

Abbott, J.T., in press: Geomorphology and Geoarchaeology of the Metapontino, in J.C. Carter (ed.), *The Chora of Metaponto. Archaeological Field Survey I, Bradano to Basento*.

Adams, W.Y. / E.W. Adams, 1991: *Archaeological typology and practical reality*, Cambridge.

Alcock, S.E., 1993: *Graecia Capta. The Landscapes of Ancient Greece*, Cambridge.

Alcock, S.E. / J.F. Cherry (eds), 2004: *Side by Side Survey: Comparative Regional Studies in the Mediterranean World*, Oxford.

Alessandri, L., 2000-2001: *L'occupazione costiera protostorica del Lazio centromeridionale*, unpublished graduate thesis, Università degli Studi di Roma La Sapienza.

Alessandri, L., 2005: L'occupazione costiera nell'età del bronzo media, recente e finale del Lazio centromeridionale, in P. Attema / A. Nijboer / A. Zifferero (eds), *Papers in Italian Archaeology VI* (BAR International Series 1452), 637 – 645.

Alessandri, L., forthcoming: *Il Lazio centro-meridionale nelle età del Bronzo e del Ferro*, PhD thesis, University of Groningen.

Alessio, A., 2001: L'area a S.E. di Taranto, in *Taranto e il Mediterraneo. Atti del XLI Convegno di Studi sulla Magna Grecia. Nuovi documenti dai territori tarantini (dalla tavolo rotonda di Taranto, 7 giugno 2001)*, Taranto, 87–116.

Alessio, A. / P.G. Guzzo, 1989-1990: *Santuari e fattorie ad est di Taranto. Elementi archeologici per un modello di interpretazione* (Scienze dell'Antichità 3-4), 363-396.

Ammerman, A., 1981: Surveys and archaeological research, *Annual Review of Anthropology* 10, 63-88.

Ammerman, A., 1985: Plow-Zone Experiments in Calabria, Italy, *Journal of Field Archaeology* 12, 33-40.

Anastasia, C., 2002-2003: *La protostoria nelle valli dell'Amaseno e dell'Ufente*, unpublished graduate thesis, Università degli Studi di Roma La Sapienza.

Andersen, H.D. / H.W. Horsnaes / S. Houby-Nielsen, 1997: Urbanization in the Mediterranean in the 9th to 6th centuries BC – An Introduction, in H.D. Andersen / H.W. Horsnaes / S. Houby-Nielsen (eds), Urbanization in the Mediterranean in the 9th to 6th centuries BC, *Acta Hyperborea* 7, 9-16.

Andreassi, G., 1981: Oria – Brindisi, *Studi Etruschi* 49, 466-468.

Angle, M., 2003: Il popolamento del sistema montuoso dell'Artemisio durante la pre- e protostoria, in *Lazio e Sabina. Atti del convegno primo incontro di studi su Lazio e la Sabina, Roma 28-30 gennaio 2002*, 139-150.

Angle, A. / A. Zarattini, 1987: L'insediamento protostorico di Casale Nuovo, *Archeologia Laziale* VIII / *Quaderni del Centro di studio per l'archeologia etrusco-italica* 14, 250-252.

Angle, M. / A. Gianni, 1985: La morte ineguale: dinamiche sociali riflesse nel rituale funerario. Il caso della necropolis dell'età del ferro di Caracupa, *Opus* IV, 179-216.

Angle, M. / C. Caneva / A.M. Conti / R. Dottarelli / A. Gianni / C. Giardino / C. Persiani, 1987: Casale Nuovo (LT) e la tarda età del Bronzo nel Lazio meridionale, *Atti del 3° Convegno di studi "Un millennio di relazioni fra la Sardegna e I paesi del Mediterraneo"*, Selargius – Cagliari, 265-303.

Angle, M. / F. Lugli / A. Zarattini, 2002: Lago Albano: il villaggio delle macine, in S. Rizzo (ed.), *Roma: città del Lazio. Catalogo della mostra, Roma, 12.10-24.11.2002*, 52-56.

Aprosio, M. / F. Cambi, 1997: La ricognizione archeologica nell'agro brindisino, in *Metodolologie di catalogizzazione dei beni archeologici*, Martano (Beni Archeologici - Conoscenza e Tecnologie, Quaderno 1.2), 177-180.

Aprosio, M., 2008: *Archeologia dei paesaggi a Brindisi dalla romanizzazione al Medioevo*, Bari.

Arthur, P., 1991: *Romans in Northern Campania: Settlement and Land-use around the Massico and the Garigliano Basin* (Archaeological Monographs of the British School at Rome 1), London.

Attema, P.A.J. 1991: The Contrada Casali, an intensive survey of a new Archaic hilltop settlement in the Monti Lepini, South Lazio, *Antiquity* 50, 7-62.

Attema, P.A.J., 1993: *An Archaeological Survey in the Pontine Region*, PhD thesis, University of Groningen.

Attema, P.A.J., 1996: Inside and outside the landscape. Perceptions of the Pontine Region in Central Italy, *Archaeological Dialogues* 3(2), 176-194.

Attema, P.A.J., 1998: Romeinse kolonisatie ten zuiden van Rome (4), veldverkenningen in het hoogland van de Romeinse kolonie Setia (centraal Italië), *Paleo-aktueel* 9, 46-50.

Attema, P.A.J., 2000: Landscape archaeology and Livy: warfare, colonial expansion and town and country in Central Italy of the 7th to 4th c. BC, *BABESCH* 75, 115-126.

Attema, P.A.J., 2003: From Ethnic to Urban Identities? Greek Colonists and Indigenous Society in the Sibaritide, South Italy. A Landscape Archaeological Approach, in H. Hokwerda (ed.), *Constructions of Greek Past, Identity and Historical Consciousness from Antiquity to the Present*, Groningen, 11-24.

Attema, P.A.J., 2005a: *Early Urbanization between 800 and 600 BC in the Pontine Region (South Lazio), the Salento Isthmus (Apulia), and the Sibaritide (Northern Calabria)* (Proceedings of the British Academy 126), 113-142.

Attema, P.A.J., 2005b: L'occupazione della campagna nel periodo protostorico, nell'ager di Lanuvio, in M. Angle / A. Germano / F. Zevi (eds), *Museo e Territorio, Atti della IV convegno, Velletri, 7-8 maggio 2004*. Roma, 143-152.

Attema, P.A.J. / J.W. Bouma / A.J. Nijboer / R.A. Olde Dubbelink, 1992: Il sito di Borgo Le Ferriere <Satricum> nei secoli V e IV A.C, *Archeologia Laziale* XI(1) / *Quaderni del Centro di studio per l'archeologia etrusco-italica* 20, 75-86.

Attema, P.A.J. / A.J. Nijboer / G.J.M. van Oortmerssen, 1997: Romeinse kolonisatie ten zuiden van Rome (3): het aardewerkonderzoek, *Paleo-aktueel* 8, 84-88.

Attema, P.A.J. / G.-J. Burgers / M. Kleibrink / D. Yntema, 1998a: Centralization, early urbanization and colonization in a regional context, Dutch excavations and landscape archaeology in central and southern Italy, *Saguntum* 31, 125-132.

Attema, P.A.J. / G.-J. Burgers / M. Kleibrink / D. Yntema, 1998b: Case studies in indigenous developments in early Italian centralization and urbanization, a Dutch perspective, *Journal of European Archaeology* 1(3), 326-381.

Attema, P.A.J. / J.J. Delvigne / B.J. Haagsma, 1999: Case studies from the Pontine Region in central Italy on settlement and environmental change in the first millennium BC, in P. Leveau / F. Trément / K. Walsh / G. Barker (eds), *Environmental Reconstruction in Mediterranean Landscape Archaeology*, Oxford, 105-121.

Attema, P.A.J. / J.J. Delvigne / E. Drost / M. Kleibrink, 2000: Habitation on plateau I of the hill Timpone della Motta (Francavilla Marittima, Italy). A preliminary report based on surveys, test pits and test trenches, *Palaeohistoria* 39/40 (1997/1998), 375-411.

Attema, P.A.J. / E. van Joolen / P.M. van Leusen, 2001a: A Marginal Landscape: Fieldwork on the beach ridge complex near Fogliano (South Lazio), *Palaeohistoria* 41/42 (1999/2000), 149-162.

Attema, P.A.J. / T. de Haas / J. Huis in 't Veld / P.M. van Leusen / M. Rooke, 2001b: SIBA2000, voorbereidend landschapsonderzoek in de Sibaritide, *Paleo-aktueel* 12, 47-53.

Attema, P. / G.-J. Burgers / E. van Joolen / M. van Leusen / B. Mater (eds), 2002: *New Developments in Italian Landscape Archaeology*, Oxford (BAR International Series 1091).

Attema, P.A.J. / A.J. Beijer / M. Kleibrink / A.J. Nijboer / G.J.M. van Oortmerssen, 2003a: Pottery classifications: ceramics from Satricum and Lazio, Italy, 900-300 BC, *Palaeohistoria* 43/44 (2001-2002), 312-396.

Attema, P.A.J. / T. de Haas / A.J. Nijboer, 2003b: The Astura project, interim report of the 2001 and 2002 campaigns of the Groningen Institute of Archaeology along the coast between Nettuno and Torre Astura (Lazio, Italy), *BABESCH* 78, 107-140.

Attema, P.A.J. / J.J. Delvigne / P.M. van Leusen, 2004: Recenti ricerche nei pressi di Timpone della Motta, vicino Francavilla Marittima (Calabria), in *Atti della XXXVII Riunione Scientifica, Preistoria e protostoria della Calabria, Scalea, Papasidero, Praia al Mare, Tortora, 29 settembre – 4 ottobre 2002*, Volume II, Firenze, 825-833.

Attema P.A.J. / T. de Haas / M. La Rosa, 2005: Sites of the Fogliano survey (Pontine Region, Central Italy), site classification and a comment on the diagnostic artifacts from prehistory to the Roman period, *Palaeohistoria* 45/46 (2003-2004), 121-196.

Attema, P.A.J. / P.M. van Leusen / P. Roncoroni (eds), sd (2006): *Il progetto archeologico Raganello, rapporto preliminare 2002-2003*, Francavilla Marittima, Associazone per la Scuola Internazionale d'Archeologia "Lagaria" / Groningen Institute of Archaeology.

Attema, P.A.J. / H. Feiken / T.C.A. de Haas / G.W. Tol, 2008: The Astura and Nettuno surveys of the Pontine Region Project (2003-2005), first report, *Palaeohistoria* 49/50 (2007/2008), 415-516.

Attema, P. / T. De Haas / G. Tol (eds), 2009: *Nettuno. Il Territorio dalla Preistoria al Medioevo: La Carta Archeologica*, Nettuno.

Attema, P.A.J. / T. Derks / G.W. Tol, forthcoming: The 'Carta Archeologica' of Nettuno, evidence for late antique and early medieval settlement on the coast of south Lazio near Antium and Torre Astura (Italy), in S. Menchelli / M. Pasquinucci / S. Santoro (eds), *LRCW 3: late Roman coarse wares, cooking wares and amphorae in the Mediterranean: archaeology and archaeometry*, Oxford (BAR International Series).

Attema, P.A.J. / T. de Haas, 2005: *Roman Landscapes of the Pontine Region between ca. 300 BC and 300 AD, continuity and change*, in B. Santillo Frizell / A. Klynne (eds), *Roman villas around the Urbs. Interaction with landscape and environment. Proceedings of the conference at the Swedish Institute in Rome, September 17-18, 2004*: 97-112.

Attema, P.A.J. / J.J. Delvigne, 2000: Settlement dynamics and alluvial sedimentation in the Pontine Region, central Italy: a complex relationship, in F. Vermeulen / M. de Dapper (eds), *Geoarchaeology of the Landscapes of Classical Antiquity*, Leiden, Stichting BABESCH, 35-47.

Attema, P.A.J. / A.J. Nijboer, 2007: Le Grottace / PIC 13, in C. Belardelli / M. Angle / F. di Gennaro / F. Trucco (eds), *Repertorio dei siti protostorici del Lazio. Province di Roma, Viterbo e Frosinone*, Firenze, 219-221.

Attema, P.A.J. / P.M. van Leusen, 2004: The early Roman colonization of South Lazio; a survey of three landscapes, in P.A.J. Attema (ed.), *Centralization, early urbanization and colonization in first millennium BC Italy, part I, Italy*, Leuven/Paris/Dudley MA, 157-195.

Attema, P. / G. van Oortmerssen, 2000: Ceramics of the first Millennium BC at Lanuvium in the Alban hills, central Italy: method, aims and first results of regional fabric classification, *Palaeohistoria* 39/40 (1997/1998), 413-439.

Attema, P.A.J. / J. Weterings, 1999: Francavilla Marittima, het nederzettingsonderzoek in 1999, *Paleo-aktueel* 11, 32-36.

Banning, E.B., 2002: *Archaeological Survey*, New York (Manuals in Archaeological Method, Theory, and Technique vol. 1).

Barker, G., 1995: Landscape Archaeology in Italy - Goals for the 1990's, in N. Christie (ed.), *Settlement and Economy in Italy 1500 BC - AD 1500. Papers of the Fifth Conference of Italian Archaeology*, Oxford, 1-11.

Barker, G. (ed.), 1995: *The Biferno Valley survey: the archaeological and geomorphological record*, London.

Barker, G. / A. Grant (eds), 1991: Ancient and modern pastoralism in central Italy: an interdisciplinary study in the Cicolano Mountains, *Papers of the British School at Rome* 59, 15-88.

Barker, G.W. / C.O. Hunt, 1995: Quaternary valley floor erosion and alluviation in the Biferno Valley, Molise, Italy: the role of tectonics, climate, sea level change and human activity, in J. Lewin / M.G. Macklin / J.C. Woodward (eds), *Mediterranean Quaternary River Environments*, Rotterdam, 145-157.

Barker, G. / J. Lloyd (eds), 1991: *Roman Landscapes. Archaeological Survey in the Mediterranean Region*, London (Archaeological Monographs of the British School at Rome 2).

Barker, G., / T. Rasmussen, 1988: The Archaeology of an Etruscan Polis: a preliminary report on the Tuscania Project (1986 and 1987 seasons), *Papers of the British School at Rome* 43, 25-42.

Berry, B.J.L., 1961: City Size Distributions and Economic Development. *Economic Development and Cultural Change,* 573–588.

Betelli, M., 1997: *Roma, la città prima della città: i tempi di una nascita*, Roma.

Bietti Sestieri, A.M., 1992: *The Iron Age community of Osteria dell'Osa: a study of socio-political development in Central Tyrrhenian Italy*, Cambridge.

Bietti Sestieri, A.M., 2005: A reconstruction of historical processes in Bronze and early Iron Age Italy based on recent archaeological research, in P. Attema / A. Nijboer / A. Zifferero (eds), *Papers in Italian Archaeology VI, Communities and Settlements from the Neolithic to the Early Medieval Period* (BAR International Series 1452), 9-24.

Bijlsma, J.W / J. Verhagen, 1989: *Geologie, bodems en landschap in de omgeving van Valesio.* Internal report, Vrije Universiteit Amsterdam.

Bintliff, J., 1991: *The Annales School and Archaeology*, Leicester.

Bintliff, J., 1997: Regional Survey, Demography and the Rise of Complex Societies in the Ancient Aegean: Core-Periphery, Neo-Malthusian and Other Interpretive Models, *Journal of Field Archaeology* 24, 1-38.

Blok, A., 1969: South Italian Agro-Towns, *Comparative Studies in Society and History* 11, 121-135.

Boardman, J., 1964: *The Greeks Overseas*, London.

Boersma, J.S., 1990: Oria and Valesio. Dutch Archaeological investigations in the Brindisi region of Southern Italy, *Mededelingen KNAW afd. Letterkunde (new series)* 53, no. 3.

Boersma, J.S., 1995: *Mutatio Valentia. The late Roman baths at Valesio, Salento*, Amsterdam.

Boersma, J.S. / H. van Wijngaarden / D.G. Yntema / L. Zomer, 1990: The Valesio Project. Fifth Interim Report (Excavations and Survey of 1989), *BABESCH* 65, 81-96.

Boersma, J.S. / G.-J. Burgers / D. Yntema, 1991: The Valesio Project: final interim report, *BABESCH* 66, 115-131.

Boersma, J.S. / D.G. Yntema, 1987: *Valesio. History of an Apulian settlement from the Iron Age to the Late Roman Period*, Fassano di Puglia.

Bottini, A. / P.G. Guzzo, 1986: Greci e indigeni nel Sud della penisola dall'VIII secolo a.C. alla conquista romana, in *Popoli e civiltà dell'Italia antica vol. VIII* (Rome), 9-39.

Bouma, J.W. / P.A.J. Attema / A.J. Beijer / A.J. Nijboer / R.A. Olde Dubbelink, 1995: The economy of an early Latin settlement, Borgo Le Ferriere Satricum, 800 -200 BC, in N. Christie (ed.), *Settlement and Economy in Italy, 1500 BC to AD 1500. Papers of the 5th Conference of Italian Archaeology*, Oxford (Oxbow Monographs 41), 183-195.

Bouma, J.W. / E. van 't Lindenhout, 1996-1997: Light in Dark Age Latium. Evidence from settlements and cult places, in M. Maaskant Kleibrink (ed.), *Caeculus III, Debating Dark Ages, Papers on Mediterranean Archaeology*, Archaeological Institute, Groningen University, 91-102.

Brandizzi Vittucci, P., 1968: *Cora* (Forma Italiae regio I, Vol 5), Roma.

Brandizzi Vittucci, P., 2000: *Antium. Anzio e Nettuno in epoca romana*, Roma.

Brandt, R.W. / J. Slofstra (eds), 1983: *Roman and Native in the Low Countries. Spheres of Interaction*, Oxford (BAR International Series 184).

Brinkman, R. / A.J. Smyth, 1973: *Land evaluation for rural purposes*, Wageningen (Publications of the International Institute for Land Reclamation and Improvement 17).

Brückner, H., 1983: Holozäne Bodenbildungen in den Alluvionen süditalienischer Flüsse, *Zeitschrift für Geomorphologie* N.F. 84, 99-116.

Brunt, P.A., 1971: *Italian Manpower 225 BC - AD 14*, Oxford.

Burgers, G.-J., 1998: *Constructing Messapian Landscapes: Settlement Dynamics, Social Organization and Culture Contact in the Margins of Graeco-Roman Italy*, Amsterdam.

Burgers, G.-J., 1999: Antieke koloniale situaties in Zuid-Italië. Een regionaal perspectief, *Tijdschrift voor Mediterrane Archeologie* 21, 19-26.

Burgers, G.-J., 2001: L'archeologia e l'Italia meridionale post-annibalica: una prospettiva regionale e diacronica, in E. Lo Cascio / A. Storchi Marino (eds), *Modalità insediative e strutture agrarie nell'Italia meridionale in età romana*, Bari, 249-266.

Burgers, G.-J., 2004: Western Greeks in their regional setting. Rethinking early Greek - indigenous encounters in Southern Italy, *Ancient West and East* 3(2), 252-282.

Burgers, G.-J. / P.A.J. Attema / M. van Leusen, 1998 (published 2004): Walking the Murge: Interim report of the Ostuni field survey (Apulia, Southern Italy), *Studi di Antichità* 11, 257-282.

Burgers, G.-J. / J.P. Crielaard, 2007: Greek colonists and indigenous populations at l'Amastuola, southern Italy, *BABESCH* 82, 77-114.

Burgers, G.-J. / J.P. Crielaard, 2008: Paesaggi del contatto. Indigeni e greci nelle Murge Tarantine, in M. Bettelli / C. De Faveri / M. Osanna (eds), *Prima delle colonie: organizzazione territoriale e produzioni ceramiche specializzate in Basilicata e in Calabria settentrionale ionica nella prima età del ferro*, Venosa, 337-353.

Burgers, G.-J. / D.G. Yntema, 1999: The Settlement of Muro Tenente. Third Interim report, *BABESCH* 74, 111-132.

Burgers, G.-J. / D.G. Yntema, 2000: Town and countryside in pre-Roman Southern Italy: A regional perspective, in F. Krinzinger (ed.), *Die Ägäis and das westliche Mittelmeer. Beziehungen und Wechselwirkungen 8. Bis 5. Jh. V. Chr. Akten des Symposions Wien 1999*, 95-104.

Cambi, F., 2000: Pottery and territory: a tormented relationship, in R. Francovich / H. Patterson / G. Barker (eds), *Extracting meaning from ploughsoil assemblages, The Archaeology of Mediterranean Landscapes 5*, Oxford, 174-184.

Cambi, F. / N. Terrenato, 1995: *Introduzione all'archeologia dei paesaggi*. Roma.

Cancellieri, M., 1990: Il territorio pontino e la via Appia, *Archeologia Laziale* 10(1) / *Quaderni del Centro di studio per l'archeologia etrusco-italica* 18, 61-72.

Carafa, P., 1995: *Officine ceramiche di età regia: produzione di ceramica in impasto a Roma dalla fine dell'VIII alla fine del VI secolo a.C*, Roma.

Carter, J.C., 1981: Rural Settlement at Metaponto, in G. Barker / R. Hodges (eds), *Archaeology and Italian Society, Papers in Italian Archaeology II*, Oxford (BAR International Series 102), 167-178.

Carter, J.C., 1987: Agricoltura e pastorizia in Magna Grecia (tra Bradano e Basento), in G. Pugliese Caratelli (ed.), *Magna Grecia. Lo sviluppo politico, sociale ed economico*, Milan, 173-212.

Carter, J.C., 1998: *The Chora of Metaponto: the Necropoleis*, Austin.

Carter, J.C., 2001: La chora di Metaponto. Risultati degli ultimi 25 anni di ricerca archeologica, in *Problemi della chora coloniale dall'Occidente al Mar Nero. Atti del 40° Convegno di Studi sulla Magna Grecia*, Taranto, 771-792.

Carter, J.C., 2006: *Discovering the Greek countryside at Metaponto*, Ann Arbor.

Carter, J.C. / C. D'Annibale, 1985: Metaponto and Croton, in S. Macready / F.H. Thompson (eds), *Archaeological Field Survey in Britain and Abroad* (Society of Antiquaries of London Occasional Paper 6), 146-157.

Cazzella, A., 1991: Insediamenti fortificati e controllo del territorio durante l'età del Bronzo nell'Italia sud-orientale, in E. Herring / R. Whitehouse / J. Wilkins (eds), *Papers of the Fourth Conference of Italian Archaeology 1, The archaeology of power Part 1*, 49-59.

Cazzella, A. / M. Moscoloni, 2001: Non più villaggi, non ancora città: gli insediamenti dell'età del bronzo dell'Italia sud-orientale, in J. R. Brandt / L. Karlsson (eds): *From Huts to Houses. Transformations of Ancient Societies. Proceedings of an International Seminar Organized by the Norwegian and Swedish Institutes in Rome, 21–24 September 1997*, Stockholm, 331-336.

Chapman, R., 2003: *Archaeologies of Complexity*, London and New York.

Cherubini, C. / V. Cotecchia / R. Pagliarulo, 1994: Geological and geotechnical problems connected with the disappearance of the ancient city of Sybaris. *Science and Technology for Cultural Heritage* 3, 95–112.

Chiarucci, G., 1985: Materiali dell'età del Bronzo nelle acque del Lago Albano, *Archeologia Laziale* VII, 34-39.

Chiarucci, P., 1983: *Lanuvium*, Roma (Collana di Studi sull'Italia Antica 2).

Chiarucci, P., 1988: *Le città dei Colli Albani, origine e sviluppo*, Roma.

Cipriano, M.T., 1985: Le anfore. Alcune produzioni documentate a Roma tra Repubblica e Basso Impero, in *Misurare la terra: centuriazione e coloni nel mondo romano. Città, agricoltura, commercio: materiale da Roma e dal suburbio*, Modena, 190-199.

Cipriano, M.T. / M.-B. Carre, 1989: Production et typologie des amphores sur la côte adriatique de l'Italie, in *Amphores romaines et histoire économique, dix ans de recherches*, Rome, 67-104.

Cocchiaro, A., 1981: Contributo per la carta archeologica del territorio a sud-est di Taranto, *Taras* 1, 53-75.

Cocchiaro, A., 1997: Carovigno (Brindisi), *Notiziario delle attivita di tutela* 1997, 59-60.

Cocchiaro, A., 1998: La ricerca archeologica in località Castello a S.Vito dei Normanni (1994-95), in *L'Area archeologica di località Castello a san Vito dei Normanni. La ricerca come risorsa*, Brindisi, 13-26.

Coccia, S. / D. Mattingley (eds), 1992: Settlement History, environment and human exploitation of an intermontane basin in the central Apennines: the Rieti survey, 1988-1991, part I, *Papers of the British School at Rome* 60, 213-290.

Coccia, S. / D. Mattingley (eds), 1995: Settlement History, environment and human exploitation of an intermontane basin in the central Apennines: the Rieti survey, 1988-1991, part II. Land-use patterns and gazetteer, *Papers of the British School at Rome* 63, 105-158.

Coppola, D., 1977: La ricerca paletnologica nel brindisino: storia degli studi e nuove prospettive di indagini, *Brundisii Res* IX(2), 261-306.

Coppola, D., 1983: *Le origini di Ostuni. Testimonianze archeologiche degli avvicendamenti culturali*, Martina Franca.

Cornell, T.J. / K. Lomas (eds), 1995: *Urban Society in Roman Italy*, London.

Cotecchia, V. / R. Pagliarulo, 1996: State of the art in geological, hydrogeological and geotechnical researches carried out on the archaeological site of Sybaris, *Geologia applicata e idrogeologia* 31: 43–54.

D'Andria, F., 1984: Documenti del commercio arcaico tra Ionio e Adriatico, in *Magna Grecia, Epiro e Macedonia, Atti del XXIV Convegno di Studi sulla Magna Grecia*, Taranto, 321-377.

D'Andria, F., 1988: Messapi e Peuceti, in *Italia, omnium terrarum alumna: le civiltà dei Veneti, Reti, Liguri, Celti, Piceni, Umbri, Latini, Campani e Iapigi*, Milano, 653-715.

D'Andria, F. (ed.), 1990: *Archeologia dei messapi*. Exhibition catalogue, Museo Provinciale Lecce, Bari.

D'Andria, F., 1991: Insediamenti e territorio: l'età storica, in *I Messapi, Atti del XXX Convegno Internazionale di Studi sulla Magna Grecia, Taranto 1990*, Napoli, 393-478.

D'Andria, F. (ed.), 1999: *La forma della città e del territorio: Esperienze metodologiche e risultati a confronto. Atti dell'Incontro di studio, S. Maria Capua Vetere 27 – 28 novembre 1998*, Roma.

D'Andria, F., 2002: Greek Colonization and Romanization From a Native Perspective, in P. Attema / G.-J. Burgers / E. van Joolen / M. van Leusen / B. Mater (eds), *New Developments in Italian Landscape Archaeology*, Oxford (BAR International Series 1091), 152-59.

De Haas, T.C.A., 2005: *The Pontine Region Project 1987-1999*. Internal report, Groningen Institute of Archaeology.

De Haas, T.C.A., 2008: Comparing settlement histories in the Pontine Region (southern Lazio, central Italy): surveys in the coastal landscape near Nettuno, *Digressus* 8, 1-32.

De Juliis, E.M., 1996: *Magna Grecia: l'Italia meridionale dalle origini leggendarie alla conquista romana*, Bari.

De Juliis, E.M., 2000: *Taranto*, Bari.

De la Genière, J. / A. Nickels, 1975: Amendolara (Cosenza) – Scavi 1969-1973 a S. Nicola, *Notizie degli Scavi* 29, 483-498.

Delano-Smith, C., 1981: Climate or Man? The Evidence of Sediments and Early Maps for the Agents of Change in the Post-Medieval Period, in C. Delano-Smith / M. Parry (eds), *Consequences of Climate Change*, Nottingham, 88-105.

Delano Smith, C., 1992: The Annales for archaeology? Review article, *Antiquity* 66, 539-441.

Dell'Aglio, A., 2001: La proschoros tarentina, in *Taranto e il Mediterraneo. Atti del XLI Convegno di Studi sulla Magna Grecia. Nuovi documenti dai territori tarantini (dalla tavolo rotonda di Taranto, 7 giugno 2001)*, Taranto, 171-194.

De Michele, V., 1986: *Locorotondo. Rinvenimenti archeologici in contrada Grofoleo. Origini di un centro abitato della Valle d'Itria*, Martina Franca.

De Neeve, P.W., 1984: *Peasants in peril. Location and economy in Italy in the second century B.C.*, Amsterdam.

Dent, D. / A. Young, 1981: *Soil survey and land evaluation*, London.

De Polignac, F., 1984: *La naissance de la cité grecque*, Paris.

De Polignac, F. / H. Fracchia / M. Gualtieri, 1990: Siti nel territorio e vie di comunicazione, in M. Gualtieri / H. Fracchia (eds), *Roccagloriosa I. L'Abitato: scavo e ricognizione topografica (1976-1986)*, Napoli, 171-201.

De Rossi, G.M. / L. Pala / L. Quilici / S. Quilici Gigli, 1969: Carta Archeologica della piana di Sibari, extract from *Atti e Memorie della Societa' Magna Grecia, Nuova Serie IX-X (1968-1969)*, Roma, 91-155.

Descoeudres, J.-P. (ed.), 1990: *Greek colonists and native populations. Proceedings of the first Australian Congress of Classical Archaeology held in honour of emeritus professor A. D. Trendall, Sydney, 9-14 July 1985*, Canberra.

Descoeudres, J.-P. / E. Robinson, 1993: *La "chiusa" alla Masseria del Fano: an early Messapian Site near Salve in the Province of Lecce*, Lecce.

De Siena, A., 1996: Metapontino: strutture abitative e organizzazione territoriale prima della fondazione della colonia achea, in F. D'Andria / K. Mannino (eds), *Ricerche sulla casa in Magna Grecia e in Sicilia. Atti del colloquio*, Lecce, 161-195.

De Siena, A., 2001: Il territorio di Metaponto, in *Problemi della chora coloniale dall'Occidente al Mar Nero. Atti del 40° Convegno di Studi sulla Magna Grecia*, Taranto, 757-770.

De Simone, C., 1956: Un caduceo bronzeo proveniente da Brindisi, *Archeologia Classica* VIII, 15-23.

De Simone, C., 1958: Ancora sul caduceo bronzeo, *Archeologia Classica* X, 102-105.

Désy, Ph., 1989: *Les timbres amphoriques de l'Apulie republicaine: documents pour une historie économique et sociale* (BAR International Series 554).

Désy, Ph., 1993: *Recherches sur l'économie apulienne au IIe e Ie siècle avant notre ère*, Bruxelles.

Dialoghi di Archeologia, 1980: *La Formazione della città nel Lazio* (Dialoghi di Archeologia, nuova serie, anno 2).

Diamond, J., 1998: *Guns, Germs, and Steel: The Fates of Human Societies*.

di Gennaro, F., 2004: Italia Centrale, in D. Cocchi Gennick (ed.), *L'età del bronzo recente in Italia, Atti del Congresso Nazionale di Lido di Camaiore, 26 – 29 ottobre 2000*, Lucca, 201-208.

di Gennaro, F. / A. Guidi, 2000: Il Bronzo finale dell'Italia centrale. Considerazioni e prospettive di indagine, in M. Harari / M. Pearce (eds), *Il protovillanoviano al di qua e al di là dell'Appennino. Atti della Giornata di Studio, Pavia 17-06-1995* (Biblioteca di Athenaeum 38), 99-131.

di Gennaro, F., 2000: "Paesaggi di Potere", l'Etruria meridionale in età protostorica, in G. Camassa / A. De Guio / F. Veronese (eds), *Paesaggi di potere: problemi e prospettive. Atti del Seminario, Udine (16-17-05-1996)*, Roma (Quaderni di Eutopia 2), 95-119.

Di Giardino, C., 2006: Il villaggio dell'età del Bronzo di Casale Nuovo: Lavorazione di rame e piombo in un sito con ceramica di tipo Egeo, in *Astura, Satricum, Pometia, un itinerario alle origini di Latina (Atti del Convegno 27 marzo 2004)*, Associazione Socio-Culturale "Mater Matuta", Assessorato alla qualità Urbana, Comune di Latina.

Drost, E., 1996: Nederzetting en landschap in het stroomgebied van de Astura, zuid-Latium, Italië, *Paleo-aktueel* 8, 79-83.

Dunbabin, T.J., 1948: *The Western Greeks. The History of Sicily and South Italy from the Foundation of the Greek Colonies to 480 B.C.*, Oxford.

Dyson, S.L., 1992: *Community and Society in Roman Italy*, Baltimore.

Eisner, W. R. / H. Kamermans, 2004: Late Quaternary Vegetation History of Latina, Italy: a Final Report on the Mezzaluna Core, in S. Holstrom / A. Voorrips / H. Kamermans (eds), *The Agro Pontino Archaeological Survey*, Leiden (Archaeological Studies Leiden University 11; CD-ROM).

Enei, F., 1995: Ricognizioni Archeologiche nell'Ager Caeretanus: 1990-1992, in N. Christie (ed.), *Settlement and Economy in Italy 1500 BC - AD 1500. Papers of the Fifth Conference of Italian Archaeology*, Oxford, 64-79.

Faustoferri, A. / J. Lloyd, 1998: Monte Pallano: a Samnite fortified centre and its hinterland, *JRA* 11, 5-22.

Feiken, H., forthcoming: *Hidden Landscapes: Geo-archaeological studies into visibility problems,* PhD thesis, University of Groningen.

Foeken, S. / S. Gietema, 2000: *Farming in the good old days: land suitability classification in Salento (Italy) for Bronze Age and Roman agriculture*, unpublished report, Free University of Amsterdam.

Finley, M.I., 1981: The ancient city from Fustel De Coulanges to Max Weber and beyond, in B.D. Shaw / R.P. Saller (eds), *Economy and society in ancient Greece*, London, 3-23.

Fornaro, A., 1976-1977: Ricerche archeologiche nelle gravine di Grottaglie, *Annali della Facoltà di Lettere e Filosofia dell'Università degli Studi di Bari* XIX-XX, 45-47.

Fornaro, A. / A. Alessio, 2000: *L'Insediamento messapico di masseria Vicentino, Grottaglie. Catalogo della mostra documentaria*, Fasano.

Fracchia, H., 1985: The Tempa Cortaglia Survey Project, *Echos du Monde Classique/Classical Views* 29, 243-256.

Fracchia, H. / F. Ortolani, 1993: The Regional Landscape, in M. Gualtieri (ed.), *Fourth Century B.C. Magna Grecia: A Case Study*, Jonsered, 227-254.

Fusco, V., 1964: Ceramica messapica in un castelliere sopra Ceglie Messapico, in *Atti del VIII Riunione dell'IIPP*, 187-190.

Galt, A.H., 1991: *Far from the Church Bells. Settlement and Society in an Apulian town*, Cambridge.

Giangiulio, M., 1987: Aspetti di storia della Magna Grecia arcaica e classica fino alla guerra del Peloponneso, in G. Pugliese Caratelli (ed.), *Magna Grecia, lo sviluppo politico, sociale e economico*, 9-54.

Gierow, P.G., 1964: *The Iron Age Culture of Latium*, vol. 2.1, Gleerup, Lund.

Gnade, M., 1992: *The southwest necropolis of Satricum: excavations 1981 – 1986*, Amsterdam.

Gnade, M., 2002: *Satricum in the post-Archaic period. A case study of the interpretation of archaeological remains as indicators of ethno-cultural identity*, Leuven/Paris/Dudley MA (Satricum VI).

Gnade, M. (ed.), 2008, *Satricum: Trenta Anni Di Scavi Olandesi (catalogo della mostra, Le Ferriere, Latina, 26 ottobre 2007-29 febbraio 2008)*, Leuven.

Graham, A.J., 1983: *Colony and Mother City in Ancient Greece*, Chicago.

Greco, E., 1981: Dal territorio alla città, lo sviluppo urbano di Taranto, *AION. Archeologia e Storia Antica*, III, 139-157.

Greco, E., 1993: L'Impero di Sibari, Bilancio archeologico-topografico, in *Sibari e la Sibaritide, Atti del XXXII Convegno di Studi sulla Magna Grecia, Taranto-Sibari, 7-12 ottobre 1992*, Taranto, 458-485.

Greco, E., 2001: Abitare in campagna, Problemi della chora coloniale dall'Occidente al Mar Nero, *Atti del XL Convegno di Studi sulla Magna Grecia, Taranto, 29 settembre- 3 ottobre 2000*, Taranto, 171-201.

Greco, E., 2003: La colonizzazione greca in Italia meridionale. Profilo storico-archeologico, in *Il fenomeno coloniale dall'antichità ad oggi. Atti dei Convegni Lincei, 189. Roma 19 e 20 marzo 2002,* Roma, 17-35.

Greco, E. / S. Luppino, 1999: Ricerche sulla topografia e sull'urbanistica di Sibari –Thuri – Copiae, *Annali di Archeologia e Storia Antica, Nuova Serie* 6, Napoli, 115-164.

Gros, P. / M. Torelli, 1988: *Storia dell'urbanistica. Il mondo romano*, Bari.

Guaitoli, M., 2002: Il territorio e le sue dinamiche: osservazioni e spunti di ricerca, in *Taranto e il Mediterraneo. Atti del XLI Convegno di Studi sulla Magna Grecia. Taranto 12-16 ottobre 2001*, Taranto, 219-252.

Gualtieri, M., 1987: Fortifications and Settlement Organization: an Example from Pre-Roman Italy, *World Archaeology* 19, 30-46.

Gualtieri, M. (ed.), 1993: *Fourth Century B.C. Magna Graecia: A Case Study*, Jonsered.

Gualtieri, M. / F. de Polignac, 1991: A Rural Landscape in Western Lucania, in G. Barker / J. Lloyd (eds), *Roman Landscapes. Archaeological Survey in the Mediterannean Region*, 194-203.

Guglielmino, R., 2005: Rocavecchia: nuove testimonianze di relazioni con l'Egeo e il Mediterraneo orientale nell'età del Bronzo, in R. Laffineur / E. Greco (eds), *Emporia. Aegeans in the Central and Eastern Mediterranean. Proceedings of the 10th International Aegean Conference*, Athens (Aegeum 25), 637-651.

Guidi, A., 1985: An application of the rank-size rule to protohistoric settlements in the middle Tyrrhenian area, in C. Malone / S. Stoddart (eds), *Papers in Italian Archaeology IV, part iii: Patterns in protohistory* (BAR International Series 245), 217-242.

Guidi, A., 1986: Gli insediamenti perilacustri di riva d'età protostorica nel Lazio centro-meridionale, *Quaderni di Protostoria* I, 239-247.

Guzzo, P.G., 1970: Sulla localizzazione di Sibari, Thurii e Copia, *Notizie degli Scavi*, suppl. III, 15-23.

Guzzo, P.G., 1982: Modificazioni dell'ambiente e della cultura tra VIII e VII secolo sulla costa ionica d'Italia, *Dialoghi di Archeologia* n.s. 2, 146-151.

Guzzo, P.G., 1987: Schema per la categoria interpretativa del 'santuario di frontiera', *Scienze dell'Antichità* 1, 373-379.

Guzzo, P.G., 1993: Sibari. Materiali per un bilancio archeologico, in *Sibari e la Sibaritide. Atti del XXXII Convegno di Studi sulla Magna Grecia, Taranto-Sibari, 7-12 ottobre 1992*, Taranto, 51-82.

Guzzo, P.G., 2003: Sul mito di Sibari, *Bulletin Antieke Beschaving* 78, 221-223.

Halstead, P., 1987: Traditional and ancient rural economy in Mediterranean Europe: plus ça change?, *Journal of Hellenic Studies* CVII, 77-87.

Hayes, J.W. / I.P. Martini (eds), 1994: *Archaeological Survey in the Lower Liri Valley, Central Italy* (BAR International Series 595), Oxford.

Herring, E., 1991: Socio-political change in the south Italian Iron Age and Classical periods: an application of the peer polity interaction model, *Accordia Research Papers* 2, 33-54.

Hofman, B., 2002: *Notes on the Sedimentation History of the Sybaris plain*, internal report, Groningen Institute of Archaeology.

Hodder, I., 1979: Simulating the Growth of Hierarchies, in C. Renfrew / K.L. Cooke (eds), *Transformations: Mathematical Approaches to Culture Change*, New York, 117-144.

Hunt, C.O. / W.R. Eisner, 1991: Palynology in the Mezzaluna core, in A. Voorrips / S.H. Loving / H. Kamermans (eds), *The Agro Pontino Survey Project. Methods and preliminary results*, Amsterdam (Studies in Prae- en Protohistorie 6), 49-59.

Iacovou, M., 2005: The Early Iron Age Urban Forms of Cyprus, in R. Osborne / B. Cunliffe (eds), *Mediterranean Urbanization 800-600 BC*, London, 17-43.

Johnson, G.A., 1985: Monitoring complex system integration and boundary phenomena with settlement size data, in S.E. van der Leeuw (ed.), *Archaeological approaches to the study of complexity*, Amsterdam, 144-179.

Kamermans, H. / S.H. Loving / A. Voorrips, 1985: Changing pattern of prehistoric landuse in the Agro Pontino, in C. Malone / S. Stodddart (eds), *Papers in Italian Archaeology IV.1: The human landscape* (BAR International Series 243), 53-68.

Kamermans, H., 1993: *Archeologie en landevaluatie in de Agro Pontino (Lazio, Italië)*, PhD thesis, University of Amsterdam.

Kleibrink, M., 2001: The Search for Sybaris, an Evaluation of Historical and Archaeological Evidence. *BABESCH* 76, 33-70.

Kleibrink, M., 2002: A short history of Dutch research in the Mediterranean, in Attema *et al.* (eds), *New Developments in Italian Landscape Archaeology (BAR Int. Series 1091)*, 13-17.

Kleibrink, M., 2003: *Van wol tot water, cultus en identiteit in het Athenaion van Lagaria, Francavilla Marittima (Calabrië, Italië)*, Rossano.

Kleibrink, M., 2006: *Oenotrians at Lagaria near Sybaris, a native proto-urban centralized settlement. A preliminary report on the excavation of two timber dwellings on the Timpone della Motta near Francavilla Marittima, southern Italy*, London (Accordia Specialist Studies on Italy, vol. II).

Kleibrink, M. / M. Sangineto, 1998: L'insediamento enotrio su Timpone della Motta I. La ceramica geometrica dal edificio V, Francavilla Marittima, *BABESCH* 72, 1-61.

Kleine, E. / H. Woldring / R.T.J. Cappers / P.A.J. Attema, 2004: Holocene vegetatiegeschiedenis van de Sibaritide (Calabrië, Italië), analyse van het pollenmateriaal uit Lago Forano, *Paleo-aktueel* 14/15, 68-73.

Kleine, E. / H. Woldring / R.T.J. Cappers / P.A.J. Attema / J.J. Delvigne, 2003: Il carotaggio del Lago Forano presso Alessandria del Carretto (Calabria, Italia). Nuovi dati sulla vegetazione olocenica e sulla storia dell'uso del suolo nella Sibaritide interna, in *Preistoria e protostoria della Calabria, scavi e ricerche* (Atti delle giornate di studio, Pellaro-Reggio Calabria, 25-26 Ottobre 2003).

Knapp, A.B., 1992: *Archaeology, Annales, and Ethnohistory*, Cambridge.

La Bua, V., 1992: Il Salento e i messapi di fronte al conflitto tra Annibale e Roma, in G. Uggeri (ed.), *L'Età annibalica e la Puglia, Atti del II Convegno di studi sulla Puglia romana*, 43-69.

Lamboley, J.L., 1981: Note sur l'hypogée de Vaste, *Studi Antichi* 2, 196-206.

Larocca, F., 2003 (ed.): *Calabria Profonda. Guida alla conoscenza del patrimonio sotterraneo regionale*, Bari.

Lepore, E., 1989: *Colonie greche dell'Occidente antico*, Rome.

Lippolis, E., 1991: Vaste, ipogeo delle Cariatidi: sculture architettoniche del vestibolo, in *Vecchi scavi, nuovi restauri*, Taranto, 148-161.

Lippolis, E., 2002: Taranto: forma e sviluppo della topografia urbana, in *Taranto e il Mediterraneo. Atti del XLI Convegno di Studi sulla Magna Grecia. Taranto 12-16 ottobre 2001*, Taranto, 119-170.

Liverani, P., 1984: L'ager veientanus in età repubblicana, *Papers of the British School at Rome* 52, 36-48.

Lloyd, J. / N. Christie / G. Lock, 1997: From the mountain to the plain: landscape evolution in the Abbruzzo. An interim report on the Sangro Valley Project (1994-5), *Papers of the British School at Rome* 65, 1-58.

Lomas, K., 1996: Greeks, Romans, and Others: problems of colonialism and ethnicity in southern Italy, in J. Webster / N.J. Cooper (eds), *Roman Imperialism: Post-Colonial Perspectives*, Leicester, 135-144.

Lomas, K., 1997: The Idea of a city: élite ideology and the evolution of urban urban form in Italy, 200 BC-AD 100, in H.M. Parkins (ed.), *Roman Urbanism. Beyond the Consumer City*, London and New York, 21-41.

Lombardo, M., 1984: Oria e il mondo messapico: orizzonti attuali dell'indagine storica, in *Atti del IX Convegno dei Comuni Messapici, Peuceti e Dauni*, Oria, 7-38.

Lombardo, M., 1991: I messapi: aspetti della problematica storica, in *Atti del XXX Convegno di Studi sulla Magna Grecia, Taranto - Lecce 1990*, Napoli, 35-109.

Lombardo, M., 1992: *I messapi e la messapia nelle fonti letterarie greche e latine*, Galatina.

Lombardo, M., 1994: Tombe, necropoli e riti funerari in 'messapia': evidenze e problemi, *Studi di Antichità* 7, 25-45.

Lombardo, M., 1995: La necropoli arcaica di Tor Pisana a Brindisi. Evidenze e problemi interpretativi, in C. Marangio / A. Nitti (eds), *Scritti di antichità in memoria di Benita Sciarra Bardaro*, 171-177.

Lombardo, M., 2002: Πῆμα Ἰαπύγεσσι: rapporti con gli Iapigi e aspetti dell'identità di Taranto, in *Taranto e il Mediterraneo. Atti del XLI Convegno di Studi sulla Magna Grecia. Taranto 12-16 ottobre 2001*, Taranto, 253-290.

Lo Porto, F.G. 1964: Satyrion (Taranto) - scavi e ricerche nel luogo del piú antico insediamento laconico in Puglia, *Notizie degli Scavi* 1964, 177-279.

Lo Porto, F.G., 1990: Testimonianze archeologiche della espansione tarantina in età arcaica, *Taras* X(1), 67-97.

Lowe, J.L. / C.A. Accorsi / M. Bandini Mazzanti / S. Bishop / S. van der Kaars / L. Forlani / A.M. Mercuri / C. Rivalenti / P. Torri / C. Watson, 1996: Pollen stratigraphy of sediment sequences from lakes Albano and Nemi (near Rome) and from the central Adriatic, spanning the interval from oxygen isotope 2 to the present day, in P. Guillizzioni / F. Oldfield (eds), *Palaeoenvironmental analysis of Italian crater lakes and Adriatic sediments* (Memorie dell' Istituto di Idrobiologia 55), 71-98.

Lugli, G., 1926: *Ager Pomptinus 1: Anxur/Tarracina*, Roma (Forma Italiae I,1).

Lugli, G., 1928: *Ager Pomptinus 2: Circeii*, Roma (Forma Italiae I,1).

Maaskant Kleibrink, M., 1972: Abitato sulle pendici della Motta, *Atti e Memorie della Società Magna Grecia*, n.s. 11-12 (1970-1971), 75-80.

Maaskant-Kleibrink, M., 1977: Abitato sull'altopiano meridionale della Motta, *Atti e Memorie della Società Magna Grecia*, n.s. 15-17 (1974-1976), 169-174.

Maaskant-Kleibrink, M., 1987: *Settlement excavations at Borgo Le Ferriere <Satricum>*, Groningen.

Maaskant-Kleibrink, M., 1992: *Settlement excavations at Borgo le Ferriere 'Satricum', vol 2*. Groningen.

Maaskant-Kleibrink, M., 1993: Religious activities on the Timpone della Motta, Francavilla Marittima – and the identification of Lagaria, *BABESCH* 68, 1-47.

Maaskant-Kleibrink, M., 1996-1997: Dark Age or Ferro I? A tentative answer for the Sibaritide and Metapontine plains, in *Caeculus III, "Debating dark Ages", Papers on Mediterranean Archaeology*, Groningen.

Malkin, I., 1987: *Religion and Colonization in Ancient Greece*, Leiden.

Malone, C. / S. Stoddart (eds), 1994: *Territory, Time and State: The Archaeological Development of the Gubbio Basin*, Cambridge.

Manacorda, D., 1988: Per uno studio dei centri produttori delle anfore brindisine, in C. Marangio (ed.), *Puglia in età repubblicana. Atti del I convegno di studi sulla Puglia romana, Mesagne 1986,* Galatina, 91-108.

Manacorda, D., 1990: Le fornaci di Visellio a Brindisi. Primi risultati dello scavo, *Vetera Christianorum* 27, 375-415.

Marangio, C., 1971-73: Rinvenimenti archeologici lungo alcune antiche strade del Brindisino, *Annali della Facoltà di Lettere e Filosofia dell'Università degli Studi di Lecce* 6, 149-174.

Marangio, C., 1974: Brindisi, masseria Marmorelle, anfore romane di età repubblicana ed imperiale, *Ricerche e Studi* 7, 114-124.

Marangio, C., 1975: La romanizzazione dell'Ager Brundisinus, *Ricerche e Studi* 8, 105-133.

Marangio, C., 1980: Problemi storici di Uria calabra in età romana, *Studi italiani di filologia classica* 52, 222-243.

Maruggi, G.A., 1995: Oria (Brindisi). Via dei Cretesi, angolo via Torneo dei Rioni, *Taras* XV(1), 76-78.

Maruggi, G.A., 1996: Crispiano (Taranto), L'Amastuola, in F. D'Andria / K. Mannino (eds), *Ricerche sulla casa in Magna Grecia e in Sicilia. Atti del colloquio, Lecce,* Galatina, 197-218.

Maruggi, G.A., 2001a: 'Il territorio a Nord di Taranto', in *Taranto e il Mediterraneo. Atti del XLI Convegno di Studi sulla Magna Grecia. Nuovi documenti dai territori tarantini (dalla tavolo rotonda di Taranto, 7 giugno 2001),* Taranto, 79–100.

Maruggi, G.A. (ed.), 2001b: *Oria e l'archeologia. Percorsi di una ricerca*, Oria.

Maruggi, G.A. / G.-J. Burgers (eds), 2001: *San Pancrazio Salentino, Li Castelli. Archeologia di una comunità messapica nel Salento centrale*, San Pancrazio Salentino.

Marzano, G., 1964: Di un tesoro di monete greche di un santuario a Valesio, *Ricerche e Studi* 1, 45-51.

Mastronuzzi, G., 1999: L'età del ferro e l'età arcaica, in D'Andria, F. / M. Lombardo (eds), *I Greci in Terra d'Otranto*, Martina Franca, 50-64.

Mastronuzzi, G. / P. Sansò, 2002: Holocene coastal dune development and environmental changes in Apulia (southern Italy), *Sedimentary Geology* 150, 139-152.

Mater, B., 2005: *Patterns in Pottery. A comparative study of pottery production in Salento, Sibaritide and Agro Pontino in the context of urbanization and colonization in the first millennium BC*, PhD thesis, Vrije Universiteit Amsterdam.

Mater, B. / M.B. Annis, 2002: Some reflections on the meanings of pottery within landscape and settlement archaeology, in P. Attema / G.-J. Burgers / E. van Joolen / M. van Leusen / B. Mater (eds), *New Developments in Italian Landscape Archaeology*, Oxford (BAR International Series 1091), 155-168.

Mattingly, D.J. (ed.), 1997: Dialogues in Roman Imperialism. Power, discourse, and discrepant experience in the Roman Empire, *Journal of Roman Archaeology Supplementary Series* 23.

McIntosh, R.J., 1991: Early urban clusters in China and Africa: the arbitration of social ambiguity, *Journal of Field Archaeology* 18, 199-212.

Millett, M., 2000: Discussion, in R. Francovich / H. Patterson (eds), *Extracting Meaning from Ploughsoil Assemblages* (The Archaeology of Mediterranean Landscapes 5), 92-94.

Moggi, M., 2002: Taranto fino al V sec. a.C., in *Taranto e il Mediterraneo. Atti del XLI Convegno di Studi sulla Magna Grecia. Taranto 12-16 ottobre 2001*, Taranto, 45–78.

Morel, J.P., 1984: Greek colonization in Italy and the west. Problems of evidence and interpretation, in T. Hackens / R. Ross Holloway (eds), *Crossroads of the Mediterranean*, Louvain-la-Neuve, 123-162.

Morley, N., 1996: *Metropolis and hinterland. The city of Rome and the Italian economy 200 B.C.-A.D. 200*, Cambridge.

Morley, N., 1997: Cities in context: urban systems in Roman Italy, in H.M. Parkins (ed.), *Roman Urbanism. Beyond the Consumer City*, London and New York, 42-58.

Morris, I., 1987: *Burial and Ancient society. The Rise of the Greek City-state*, Cambridge.

Morris, I., 1992: *Death-ritual and Social Structure in Classical Antiquity*, Cambridge.

Morris, I., 1994: Archeologies of Greece, in I. Morris (ed.), *Classical Greece. Ancient Histories and Modern Archaeologies,* Cambridge, 8-48.

Muggia, A., 2000: La gerarchia degli insediamenti in Magna Grecia, in G. Camassa / A. De Guio / F. Veronese (eds), *Paesaggi di potere, Problemi e prospettive, Atti del Seminario Udine 16-17 maggio 1996*, Roma, 219-237.

Neboit, R., 1983: *L'Homme et l'erosion* (Fac. Lettres et Sciences Humaines vol. 17), Université de Clermont-Ferrand II.

Nenci, G., 1987: Cavallino, in G. Nenci / G. Vallet (eds), *Bibliografia topografica della colonizzazione Greca in Italia e nelle Isole Tirreniche* V, 194-202.

Nijboer, A.J., 1998: *From household production to workshops. Archaeological evidence for economic transformations, pre-monetary exchange and urbanization in central Italy from 800 to 400 BC*, PhD thesis, University of Groningen.

Nijboer, A.J. / P.A.J. Attema / G.J.M. van Oortmerssen, 2006: Ceramics from a Late Bronze Age saltern on the coast near Nettuno (Rome, Italy), *Palaeohistoria* 47/48 (2005-2006), 141-205.

Oome, N. / P.A.J. Attema, 2008: Portieri, a Hellenistic *fattoria* in the foothills of the Sibaritide (Calabria, Italy), site report and shard catalogue, *Palaeohistoria* 49/50 (2007/2008), 617-685.

Osanna, M., 1992: *Chorai coloniali da Taranto a Locri. Documentazione archeologica e ricostruzione storica*, Roma.

Osanna, M., 2001: Fattorie e villaggi in Magna Grecia, Problemi della chora coloniale dall'Occidente al Mar Nero, *Atti del XL Convegno di Studi sulla Magna Grecia, Taranto, 29 settembre-3 ottobre 2000*, Taranto, 203-220.

Osborne, R., 1987: *Classical Landscape with Figures: the Ancient Greek City and its Countryside*, London.

Osborne, R., 1996: *Greece in the Making. 1200-479 BC*, London.

Osborne, R., 1998: Early Greek colonization? The nature of Greek settlement in the West, in N. Fisher / H. van Wees (eds), *Archaic Greece: New Approaches and New Evidence,* London, 251-269.

Osborne, R., 2005: Urban Sprawl: what is urbanization and why does it matter?, in R. Osborne / B. Cunliffe (eds), *Mediterranean Urbanization 800-600 BC*, London, 1-16.

Pacciarelli, M., 2000: *Dal Villaggio alla Città, la svolta protourbana del 1000 a.C. nell'Italia tirrenica*, Firenze (Grandi Contesti e Problemi della Protostoria Italiana 4).

Pagliara, C., 1989: La costa salentina del Canale d'Otranto. Primi risultati, in *Salento Porta d'Italia*, 121-130.

Pagliara, C., 1991: Santuari costieri, in *I Messapi, Atti del XXX Convegno di Studi sulla Magna Grecia, Taranto - Lecce 1990*, Taranto, 503-526.

Pagliara, C., 2005: Rocavecchia (Lecce): il sito, le fortificazioni e l'abitato dell'età del Bronzo, in R. Laffineur / E. Greco (eds), *Emporia. Aegeans in the Central and Eastern Mediterranean* (Proceedings of the 10th International Aegean Conference, *Aegeum* 25), Athens, 629-635.

Palazzo, P., 1988: Aspetti tipologici della produzione di anfore brindisine, in C. Marangio (ed.), *Puglia in età repubblicana. Atti del I convegno di studi sulla Puglia romana, Mesagne 1986*, Galatina, 109-117.

Palazzo, P., 1994: Insediamenti artigianali e produzione agricola. I siti di Apani, Giancola, Marmorelle, La Rosa, in C. Marangio / A. Nitti (eds), *Scritti di antichità in memoria di Benita Sciarra Bardaro*, 53-60.

Pascucci, P., 1996: Grotta Vittorio Vecchi, in C. Belardelli / P. Pascucci (eds), *Repertorio dei siti protostorici del Lazio. Province di Rieti e di Latina*, Roma, 53.

Pancrazzi, O. (ed.), 1979: *Cavallino I. Scavi e ricerche 1964-1967*, Galatina.

Patterson, H. (ed.), 2004: *Bridging the Tiber. Approaches to Regional Archaeology in the Middle Tiber Valley* (Archaeological Monographs of the British School at Rome 13).

Patterson, H. / H. di Giuseppe / R. Witcher, 2004: Three South Etrurian 'crises': first results of the Tiber Valley Project, *Papers of the British School at Rome* 72, 1-36.

Perkins, Ph., 1999: *Etruscan settlement, society and material culture in central coastal Etruria*, Oxford (BAR International Series 788).

Peroni, R., 1988: Comunità e insediamento in Italia fra età del bronzo e prima età del ferro, in A. Momigliano / A. Schiavone (eds), *Storia di Roma, I: Roma in Italia*, Torino, 7-37.

Peroni, R., 1989: *Protostoria dell'Italia continentale*, Roma (Popoli e civiltà dell'Italia antica 9).

Peroni, R., 1994: Le comunità enotrie della Sibaritide ed i loro rapporti con i navigatori egei, in R. Peroni / F. Trucco (eds), *Enotri e Micenei nella Sibaritide* vol. II, Taranto, 831-879.

Peroni, R., 2004 (1996): *L'Italia alle soglie della Storia*, Bari-Roma.

Peroni, R. / F. Trucco (eds), 1994: *Enotri e Micenei nella Sibaritide*, Taranto.

Piccarreta, F., 1977: *Astura*, Firenze (Forma Italiae Regio I, Vol. XIII).

Piccarreta, F., 2001: Aerofotografia e telerilevamento, in *Atti del XL Convegno di Studi sulla Magna Grecia, Taranto, 29 settembre- 3 ottobre 2000*, Taranto, 365-384.

Price, T.D. 1995: Social inequality at the origins of agriculture, in T.D. Price / G.M. Feinmann (eds), *Foundations of Social Complexity*, New York.

Pugliese Caratelli, G. (ed.), 1985-1990: *Magna Grecia*, 4 vols, Milan.

Pugliese Caratelli, G. (ed.), 1996: *The Western Greeks*, Venice.

Quilici, L., 1971: Latina, *Italia nostra* 79, 25-28.

Quilici, L., 2004: Caprifico di Cisterna di Latina. Una città arcaica nella Piana Pontina, *Ocnus* 12, 247-262.

Quilici Gigli, S. / F. Melis, 1972: Proposta per l'ubicazione di Pometia, *Archeologia Classica* XXIV, Fasc. 1, 219-247.

Quilici, L. / S. Quilici Gigli, 1975: *Repertorio dei beni culturali archeologici della provincia di Brindisi*, Fasano.

Quilici, L. / S. Quilici Gigli, 1988: Ricerche su Norba, *Archeologia Laziale* IX / Quaderni del Centro di studio per l'archeologia etrusco-italica 16, 233-256.

Quilici, L. / S. Quilici Gigli, 2001: Ricerche nella valle del Sinni, in *Problemi della chora coloniale dall'Occidente al Mar Nero. Atti del 40° Convegno di Studi sulla Magna Grecia, Taranto*, 793-806.

Quilici, L. / S. Quilici Gigli (eds), 2000-2003: *Carta archeologica della valle del Sinni*, fasc. 1-8, Roma (Atlante tematico di topografia antica, supplemento X).

Quilici, L. / S. Quilici Gigli, 2005: La cosidetta acropoli del Circeo. Per una lettura nel contesto topografico, in L. Quilici / S. Quilici Gigli (eds), *La forma della città e del territorio* 2, Roma (Atlante tematico di topografia antica 14), 91-146.

Rainey, F.G. / C.M. Lerici, 1967: *The Search for Sybaris, 1960-1965*, Roma.

Rasmussen, T., 1991: Tuscania and its Territory, in G. Barker / J. Lloyd (eds), *Roman Landscapes. Archaeological Survey in the Mediterranean Region*, London (Archaeological Monographs of the British School at Rome 2), 106-114.

Rathbone, D., 1981: The Development of Agriculture in the Ager Cosanus during the Roman Republic: Problems of Evidence and Interpretation, *Journal of Roman Studies* 71, 10-23.

Recchia, G. / C. Ruggini, 2009: Sistemi abitativi dell'età del Bronzo nelle Murge brindisine, in G.-J. Burgers / G. Recchia (eds), *Ricognizioni nell'altopiano delle Murge. La carta archeologica di Costernino*, Foggia.

Renfrew, C., 1978: Space, time, and polity, in J. Friedman / M. Rowlands (eds), *The Evolution of Social Systems*, London, 89-112.

Renfrew, C. / E.V. Level, 1979: Predicting Polities from Centers, in C. Renfrew / K. L. Cooke (eds), *Transformations. Mathematical Approaches to Culture Change*, New York, etc, 145-167.

Renfrew, C. / J.F. Cherry (eds), 1986: *Peer Polity Interaction and Sociopolitical Change*, Cambridge.

Roberto, C. / J. Plambeck / A.M. Small, 1985: The chronology of the sites of the Roman period around San Giovanni: Methods of analysis and conclusions, in S. Macready / F.H. Thompson (eds), *Archaeological Field Survey in Britain and Abroad*, London (The Society of Antiquaries of London, Occasional Paper 6), 136-145.

Roberto, C. / A.M. Small, 1994: The Field Survey, in A.M. Small / R.J. Buck (eds), *The Excavations of San Giovanni di Ruoti. Volume I: The Villas and their Environment*, University of Toronto, 19-22.

Rosini, L., 1996: Longara, in C. Belardelli / P. Pascucci (eds), *Repertorio dei siti protostorici del Lazio. Province di Rieti e di Latina,* Roma, 63-64.

Rowlands, M., 1998: The archaeology of colonialism, in K. Kristiansen / M. Rowlands (eds), *Social transformations in archaeology: global and local perspectives*, London/New York, 327-333.

Rowlands, M. / M. Larsen / K. Kristiansen (eds), 1987: *Center and Periphery in the Ancient World*, Cambridge.

Russo Tagliente, A., 1992: *Edilizia domestica in Apulia e Lucania. Ellenizzazione e società nella tipologia abitativa indigena tra VIII e III secolo a.C.*, Galatina.

Sallares, R., 2002: *Malaria and Rome, A history of malaria in ancient Italy*, Oxford.

Sadori, L. / B. Narcisi, 2001: The Postglacial record of environmental history from Lago di Pergusa, Sicily, *The Holocene* 11, 665-670.

Satijn, O.P.N., 2003: Towards Incastellamento: Combining Archaeology and Texts in Modelling the Post-Roman Landscape in Lazio, in *SOMA 2002 Symposium on Mediterranean Archaeology. Proceedings of the Sixth Annual Meeting of Postgraduate Researchers*, Oxford (BAR International Series 1142), 113-120.

Scarfi, B.M., 1961: Gioia del Colle - Scavi nella zona di Monte Sannace, *Monumenti Antichi* 45, 144-331.

Scarfi, B.M., 1962: Gioia del Colle - L'abitato peucetico di Monte Sannace, *Notizie degli Scavi* 1962, 1-283.

Schojer, T., 2001: Il N.W. tarantino, in *Taranto e il Mediterraneo. Atti del XLI Convegno di Studi sulla Magna Grecia. Nuovi documenti dai territori tarantini (dalla tavolo rotonda di Taranto, 7 giugno 2001),* Taranto, 65-86.

Scollar, I., 1992, The Bonn archaeological database, in C.U. Larsen (ed.), *Sites & Monuments, National Archaeological Records*, The National Museum of Denmark, Copenhagen, 97-117.

Semeraro, G., 1998a: Scavi a San Vito dei Normanni, in *L'Area archeologica di Località Castello a San Vito dei Normanni. La Ricerca come risorsa*, 26-32.

Semeraro, G., 1998b: L'Eta del Ferro e L'Eta Arcaica, in *Messapica Ceglie, Catalogo alla mostra*, Ceglie Messapica, 18-25.

Sevink, J. / A. Remmelzwaal / O.C. Spaargaren, 1984: *The soils of southern Lazio and adjacent Campania*, University of Amsterdam (Fysisch geografisch en bodemkundig laboratorium Publication 38).

Shennan, S., 2001: The history of social hierarchies. Book review essay, *European Journal of Archaeology* 6(1), 91-97.

Small, A., 1991: Late Roman Rural Settlement in Basilicata and Western Apulia, in G. Barker / J. Lloyd (eds), *Roman Landscapes. Archaeological Survey in the Mediterannean Region*, 204-222.

Small, A. / C. Small / I. Campbell / M. MacKinnon / T. Prowse / C. Sipe, 1998: Field Survey in the Basentello Valley on the Basilicata-Puglia Border, *Echos du Monde Classique/Classical Views* n.s. 17, 337-371.

Snodgrass, A., 1980: *Archaic Greece. The Age of Experiment*, Berkeley.

Snodgrass, A., 1986: Interaction by design: the Greek city state, in C. Renfrew / J.F. Cherry (eds), *Peer Polity Interaction and Socio-Political Change*, Cambridge, 47-58.

Snodgrass, A., 1991: Archaeology and the study of the Greek city, in J. Rich / A. Wallace-Hadrill (eds), *City and Country in the Ancient World*, London, 1-23.

Taylour, W., 1958: *Mycenaean Pottery in Italy and Adjacent Areas*, Cambridge.

TCI/CNR, 1954-1960: *Carta dell'utilizzazzione del suolo d'Italia, 1:200.000,* Milan, Touring Club Italiano and Consiglio Nazionale delle Ricerche.

Terrenato, N., 2001: Introduction, in S. Keay / N. Terrenato (eds), *Italy and the West. Comparative Issues in Romanization*, Oxford, 1-6.

Thompson, S., 2002: The Metapontino- and Morgantina Archaeological Survey Projects (Basilicata and Sicily), in P. Attema / G.-J. Burgers / E. van Joolen / M. van Leusen / B. Mater (eds), *New Developments in Italian Landscape Archaeology*, Oxford (BAR International Series 1091), 76-82.

Thompson, S., 2004: Side-by-side and back-to-front: exploring intra-regional latitudinal and longitudinal comparability in survey data. Three case studies from Metaponto, southern Italy, in S.E. Alcock / J.F. Cherry (eds), 2004: *Side by Side Survey: Comparative Regional Studies in the Mediterranean World*, Oxford, 65-85.

Tiné, S., 1994: Il villaggio di Favella della Corte e la neolitizzazione della Sibaritide, *Atti del XXXIII Convegno di Studi sulla Magna Grecia, Taranto, 8-13 ottobre 1993,* Taranto, 85-102.

Torelli, M., 1988: Le popolazioni dell'Italia antica: societa e forme del potere, in A. Momigliano / A. Schiavone (eds), *Storia di Roma, vol. I: Roma in Italia*, Roma, 53-74.

Torelli, M., 1999: The Romanization of Italy, in M. Torelli (ed.), *Tota Italia. Essays in the Cultural Formation of Roman Italy*, Oxford, 1-13.

Toynbee, A.J., 1965: *Hannibal's Legacy*, 2 vols., Oxford.

Trigger, B., 1989: *A History of Archaeological Thought*, Cambridge.

Van Alberda, K. / G.-J. Burgers / H. Burgers / D. Karel / D.G. Yntema, 1999: *Muro Tenente. Centro messapico nel territorio di Mesagne*, Manduria.

Van Dommelen, P., 1997: Colonial constructs: colonialism and archaeology in the Mediterranean, *World Archaeology* 28(3), 305-323.

Van Joolen, E., 2003: *Archaeological land evaluation. A reconstruction of the suitability of ancient landscapes for various land uses in Italy focused on the first millennium BC*, PhD thesis, Rijksuniversiteit Groningen (http://dissertations.ub.rug.nl/faculties/arts/2003/e.van.joolen/).

Van Leusen, P.M., 1996: Unbiasing the Archaeological Record, *Archeologia e Calcolatori* 7, 129-136.

Van Leusen, P.M., 2002: *Pattern to Process: methodological investigations into the formation and interpretation of spatial patterns in archaeological landscapes,* PhD Thesis, University of Groningen (http://dissertations.ub.rug.nl/faculties/arts/2002/p.m.van.leusen/).

Van Leusen, P.M., 2005: Verborgen Landschappen. Naar een alternatieve benadering van de Mediterrane landschapsarcheologie, *Tijdschrift voor Mediterrane Archeologie* 33, 4-9.

Van Leusen, P.M. / P.A.J. Attema, 2003: Regional Archaeological Patterns in the Sibaritide, preliminary results of the RPC Field survey campaign 2000, *Palaeohistoria* 42/43 (2001/2002), 397-416.

Van Leusen, M. / H. Feiken, 2007: Geoarcheologie en Landschapsclassificatie in Midden- en Zuid-Italië, *Tijdschrift voor Mediterrane Archeologie* 37, 6-16.

Van Leusen, P.M. / R.H. White, 1997: Aspects of Romanization in the Wroxeter Hinterland, in K. Meadows / C. Lemke / J. Heron (eds), *TRAC 96. Proceedings of the Sixth Annual Theoretical Roman Archaeology Conference, Sheffield 1996*, Oxford, 133-143.

Van Leusen, P.M. / T. de Haas / S. Pomicino / P. Attema, 2005: Protohistoric to Roman settlement on the Lepine margins near Ninfa (south Lazio, Italy), *Palaeohistoria* 45/46 (2003-2004), 301-346.

Van 't Lindenhout, E., forthcoming: *Bouwen in Latium in de Archaïsche periode. Een vergelijkend onderzoek van constructies als informanten van een urbaniserende samenleving (600 – 450 v. Chr.)*, PhD thesis, University of Groningen.

Vanzetti, A., 2000: Costruzione e problemi dei "paesaggi di potere" nella Sibaritide (Calabria) dall'età del bronzo alla prima età del ferro, in G. Camassa / A. De Guio / F. Veronese (eds), *Paesaggi di potere: problemi e prospettive. Atti del seminario, Udine 16-17.05.1996*, Roma (Quaderni di Eutopia 2), 153-187.

Vanzetti, A., 2002: Some current approaches to protohistoric centralization and urbanization in Italy, in P. Attema / G.-J. Burgers / E. van Joolen / M. van Leusen / B. Mater (eds), *New Developments in Italian Landscape Archaeology*, Oxford (BAR International Series 1091), 36-51.

Vanzetti, A., 2004: Risultati e problemi di alcune prospettive di studio della centralizzazione e urbanizzazione di fase protostorica in Italia, in P.A.J. Attema (ed.), *Centralization, early urbanization and colonization in first millennium BC Italy and Greece, Part 1: Italy*, Leuven (BABESCH Supplement 9), 1-28.

Veenman, F., 1997: Landevaluatie in de Pontijnse regio (Zuid-Latium, Italië), dateringsproblemen rond een bronstijd-akkerbouwfase, *Paleo-aktueel* 8, 59-62.

Veenman, F., 2002: *Reconstructing the pasture, a reconstruction of pastoral land use in Italy in the first millennium BC*, PhD thesis, Vrije Universiteit Amsterdam.

Vink, M., 1995: Confrontatie of coexistentie? De verhouding tussen lokale bewoners en Griekse kolonisten in Zuid-Italië, *Tijdschrift voor Mediterrane Archeologie* 14 (1994-1995), 16-24.

Vinson, P., 1972: Ancient roads between Venosa and Gravina, *Papers of the British School at Rome* 40, 58-90.

Vita-Finzi, C., 1969: *The Mediterranean valleys: geological changes in historical times*, **London.**

Volpe, G., 1990: *La Daunia nell'età della Romanizzazione. Paesaggio agrario, produzione, scambi*, Bari.

Voorrips, A. / S.H. Loving / H. Kamermans (eds), 1991: *The Agro Pontino Survey Project. Methods and Preliminary Results*, Amsterdam (Studies in Prae en protohistorie 6).

Wallace-Hadrill, A., 1992: Introduction, in J. Rich / A. Wallace-Hadrill (eds), *City and Country in the Ancient World*, London, ix-xviii.

Watts, W.A. / J.R.M. Allen / S.C. Fritz, 1996: Vegetation History and Climate of the last 15,000 years at Laghi di Monticchio, Southern Italy, *Quaternary Science Reviews* 15, 114-132.

Whitehouse, R.D. / J.B. Wilkins, 1989: Greeks and natives in south-east Italy: approaches to the archaeological evidence, in T.C. Champion (ed.), *Centre and periphery: comparative studies in archaeology*, London, 60-66.

Wikander, Ö., 1993: From Clay Beds to Excavation, in *Acquarossa VI: the Roof-Tiles. Part 2: Typology and Technical Features*, Stockholm, 100-139.

Woldring, H. / Y. Boekema / P.A.J. Attema / J.J. Delvigne, 2006: Vegetatieontwikkeling en landgebruik in de Monte Sparviere (Calabrië, Italië), *Paleo-aktueel* 17, 82-89.

Yntema, D.G., 1990: *The Matt-Painted Pottery of Southern Italy* (2nd enlarged and corrected edition), Galatina.

Yntema, D.G., 1993a: *In Search of an Ancient Countryside. The Free University Field Survey at Oria, Province of Brindisi, South Italy, 1981-1983*, Amsterdam.

Yntema, D.G., 1993b: The Settlement of Valesio, South Italy: Final Report on the Field Survey in the Town Area, *BABESCH* 68, 45-66.

Yntema, D.G., 1995: Romanization in the Brindisino, Southern Italy: A Preliminary Report, *BABESCH* 70, 53-77.

Yntema, D., 2000: Mental landscapes of colonization: the ancient written sources and the archaeology of early colonial-Greek southeastern Italy, *BABESCH* 75, 1-49.

Yntema, D.G., 2001: *Pre-Roman Valesio. Excavations of the Amsterdam Free University at Valesio, Province of Brindisi, southern Italy. Volume 1: The Pottery*, Amsterdam.

Zaccheo, L. / F. Pasquali, 1972: *Sezze dalla preistoria all'età romana*, Sezze.

Zanker, P., 1976: *Hellenismus in Mittelitalien: Kolloquium in Göttingen vom 5. bis 9. Juni 1974*, Göttingen (Abhandlungen der Akademie der Wissenschaften in Göttingen, Philologisch-Historische Klasse; 3. Folge, Nr. 97).

Zarattini, A., 2003: "Il villagio delle macine" nel Lago di Albano. Insediamento ed addatamento ambientale, in *Atti del II convegno nazionale di archeologia subaquea, Castiglioncello, 7-9 settembre 2001*, 11-19.

Zipf, G.K., 1949: *Human behaviour and the principle of least effort: an introduction to human ecology*, Cambridge.

Index

A
Abruzzo region 162
Adriatic tectonic plate 60
ager
   - of Falerii 161
   - of Setia 145
   - of Veii 160
ager publicus 147, 166, 169
Agro Pontino Survey 5, 56,
agro-towns 152
Alban hills 4, 12, 43, 57, 144, 167
   - Alban caldera 12
   - and Monti Lepini 35
Amaseno river 12, 41
   - Amaseno basin, sedimentation in, 41-42
   - Amaseno valley 56
Amendolara San Nicola 93, 96, 115, 121, 123
Ammerman, A. 162
Andrisani-Lazzazzera 132
Annales historians 10-11, 177, 161
   see also Braudel F.
Antium 54-56, 150, 167,
   - and Terracina 179
Apulia 3, 5, 59, 61, 162, 163
Apulian grey-gloss pottery 16, 69
Archaic urbanization 107, 140, 145
   - and pottery studies 28
   - in Salento and south Latium
   see also urbanization
Ardea 39, 46, 47, 49
Ariccia 46
Arthur, P. 161
Astura (settlement) 142
   see also Torre Astura
Astura and Nettuno surveys 5
Astura river 5, 32, 52-53
   - Astura river basin 54-55, 57, 142
   - at the site of Casale Nuovo 111
Ausoni 12, 32, 40, 43, 53

B
Barker, G. 161
Basentello valley (surveys along) 163
Basilicata 61, 73, 162, 163
biases 19, 176
   - systematic 7, 29,
   - depositional 20
   - visibility and research 20, 172-173
   - bias factors 21, 172
   - classification biases 20
   - resarch biases 20, 56
   - of the Sibaritide hinterland 101-102
   - in archaeological field surveys 171
Biferno valley survey 161
Blok, A. 153
Borgo Grappa 53-55
   - Borgo Grappa plain 14
   - Borgo Grappa land system 14
Botromagno 162
Bottini, A. 126
Braudel, F. 10-11, 176-177
Brindisi 132, 137-138, 140, 155,
   - and the Via Appia 167
   - and amphora production 175
   - Brindisino (areas, region) 5, 139, 140, 167-169
   - Brindisi plain 149, 151, 174
   - *Brundisium* 147, 155
   - central brindisi plain 62
   - hinterland of 175
Brindisino project 5, 6, 16
briquetage 54
   see also salt production
British School at Rome 160, 161
British School excavations 162
Broglio di Trebisacce 81, 82, 88, 90, 92-93, 109, 111, 114, 122
Bussento river 163

C
Cambi, F. 69
Campania 161, 163
Campisani 139
Campoverde 36, 39
   - Campoverde pollen core 36, 39, 46
Caprifico di Cisterna di Latina 46-49, 54
Caracupa-Valvisciolo 40, 46, 50-51, 54, 57, 142, 144
Castello 135
Castello di San Vito dei Normanni 75, 136, 140
Castiglione di Paludi 94
Castiglione di Roggiano Gravina 94
Cavallino 136, 138, 140
Ceglie Messapico 76, 137, 139, 140
central Italy 168
   - pollen cores in 12, 35
   - pottery studies 16
   - urbanization in 17
   - Recent Bronze age in 111
   - study of indigenous territories in 135
   - large scale migration to urbanized areas 138, 156
   - dedication to sheepfarming 135
centralization 107, 177, 179
   - Bronze Age centralization in the Alban Hills 31, 34
   - Iron Age (political) centralization in the Salento Isthmus 79
   - Bronze Age centralization in the Sibaritide 88, 92, 103
   - comparative study of 176
   - as long term process 176
central place(s) 107, 140, 145, 149, 151-152, 167, 177-178
   - in the Pontine Region 46, 143-144, 150
   - in the Salento Isthmus and Brindisi plain 76, 79, 109, 138-140
   - in the Sibaritide 89, 93-94, 122
   - and the development of the countryside 46
   - central places and central place theory 26, 27
centre and periphery 169
centuriation 56, 73, 83, 155, 156, 166

Chapman, R. 8
chora
   - of Metapontum 61, 73, 125
   - of Sybaris (Thurioi and Copiae) 89
   - of Taras 77, 125
   - of Kroton 162
Cicolano mountains 162
Cilento 163
Circeii 150
Cisterna di Latina 40, 46
city states (in the Pontine Region) 146, 168
   - colonial city states 1
   - Etruscan city states 113
   - Greek city states 119
climate
   - of the Pontine region 35
   - of the Salento Isthmus 60
coastal area(s) 9, 119,
   - of the Pontine Region 5, 32-33, 39, 44, 45, 54-55, 57
   - of the Metapontino 62
   - south of Brindisi 71, 79
   - north of Brinsisi 73, 79
   - of the Salento Isthmus 72, 75, 78
   - Valesio coastal area 154
coastal land system (Pontine Region) 43, 45, 52-57
coastal land system (Brindisi plain) 70
Colle San Lorenzo (pollen core) 36, 39
Colonization 10
   - Greek and Roman colonization 10, 18, 165, 176, 178-179
   - early Greek colonization 103, 119, 178
   - (early) Roman colonization 12, 31, 56-57, 135, 142, 144-147, 156, 164, 177
comparative regional approach 7-8
complexity (definition of) 8, 107
   - complexity (and rank-size analysis) 26
   - in Bronze Age Sibaritide 92
   - geological complexity in the Sibaritide 101
   - socio-economic and political complexity (in the RPC regions) 108, 110-112, 114-115, 117, 124
Contrada Casali 51
Contrada Trentossa 40
Copia 121, 147, 149
Copiae 22, 89, 121, 167
Cora 142, 150, 155, 157, 160, 179
Cori 142, 144
Coscile river 23, 93-94, 121
   - floodplain 22
Cozzo Michelicchio 94
craft specialization (in the Sibaritide) 114
crater lakes 35, 44, 57
Crati river 22, 88-89, 93-94, 121
   - plain 21, 23

   - basin 24

D
data quality 25
Daunia 168-169
Diodorus Siculus 89
di Gennaro, F. 111, 116
Doganella di Ninfa survey (Pontine Region) 144
domestic housing (at Timpone della Motta and Broglio di Trebisacce) 96-97, 114

E
elite 47, 94, 109-111, 131, 153, 157-159, 177
   - social strategies 7
   - Roman 49, 53, 56
   - landownership 92
   - groups 92
   - families 93, 158
   - indigenous 103, 131
   - leadership 103
   - consumption 114
   - local 114, 160, 177
   - houses 123, 146
   - residence 136, 158
   - burial 141, 158
   - urban 157
   - non elite groups 158
   - elite-owned land 160
   - metropolitan 166
erosion (and sedimentation) 24, 34, 36, 38, 40, 43, 46, 58, 61, 70-71, 79, 85-86, 100-101
exchange 107
   - exchange systems 164
   - exchange and trade systems 8
   - market exchange 9
   - cultural exchange 103
   - regional exchange system 93
   - long-distance exchange 108
   - supra-regional exchange 110
   - overseas exchange 110
   - Mediterranean exchange 111
   - Greek exchange networks 131
   - surplus exchange 142
   - interregional exchange networks 164, 179
   - exchange with the Aegean world 177

F
fabric analysis (of pottery) 11, 16, 144
   - fabrics from Satricum, Sezze, Segni, and Lanuvium 17
FAO 2, 13
   - method 171
   - criteria 174
   - and evaluation 174
farm sites
   - Roman Republican farm sites 153

   - Hellenistic farm sites 73, 90, 103, 152, 157
   - isolated 52, 57, 76, 102, 113, 149, 152, 154
Favella 88
field survey 15, 99, 107
   - by the Pontine Region Project 47, 48, 55
   - throughout the Metaponto landscape 62
   - ACVU field surveys 62, 71, 74, 79
   - of the RPC project 107
   - by the GIA 105
   - throughout Italy 150
Fogliano 39, 142, 144
   - pollen core and diagram 38, 39, 53
Fogliano surveys 5, 54-55, 167
Fontana Manca (pollen core and diagram) 83, 85-86
Fornaro, A. 130-131
fortification(s) 8, 18, 47, 68, 73, 75-76, 92-93, 108-110, 117, 136, 167
   - pre-Roman 47
   - Archaic 135
   - stone 138
   - monumental 151, 164
   - Hellenistic 165

G
Galt, A.H. 153, 158
Garigliano basin 161
geo-archaeological studies 42, 86, 173
Gravina (di Puglia) 162
Groningen Institute of Archaeology 1, 11, 49, 54, 81, 85, 126
Grotta Abbate Nicola 139
Grotta di Santa Maria d'Agnano 75
Guidi, A. 53
Guzzo, P. G. 121-124, 126

H
Halstead, P. 154-155
hamlets 9, 50, 52, 55, 67, 79, 90, 102, 113, 144, 149, 152, 154, 163-164, 167
Hellenization 10, 26, 119, 135
Herring, E. 26
high-intensity surveys 100
see also intensive survey
Hippodamos of Miletus 152
Holocene 35, 86
   - climate 12, 35
   - forest 36
   - erosion and sedimentation 40, 46, 64, 70,
   - dune belts 61, 64
   - lagoons 64
   - vegetation history 85
   - environmental change 86
   - landscape change 86
hypogea 158

I
ideal zonation 169
(intensification of) agricultural production 92, 153, 156, 160
intensive survey 5, 7, 51, 53, 56-59, 65, 73, 90, 117, 149-150, 152, 155, 161-162, 175
Iron Age Salento 126, 128, 139
isolated farmsteads 52, 67, 76, 102, 113, 149, 152, 154

K
karst phenomena 55, 60, 64, 73, 149
Kleibrink, M. 7, 16, 81, 122-124, 132
Kroton 89, 100, 121, 162
   - the Krotonese 178

L
Laghi di Vescovo (pollen core) 39
lagoons (in the Pontine Region) 5, 12, 22, 33, 35, 38, 41, 43-45, 52-53, 56-57, 64, 110-111
   - lagoonal sediments 12
   - lagoonal environment 12, 35-36, 43, 55, 143
   - Fogliano lagoon 38
   - lagoonal deposits 41-42
   - peri-lagoonal model 113
   - lagoonal clay soils 144
lagoons (Salento Isthmus) 62, 64, 77-78
   - lagoonal area 64
   - lagoonal landscape 69
   - lagoon-dune-beach system 70
   - lagoonal and marshy zones (at *Taras*) 124
   - lagoonal environment 130
   - lagoonal system 155
lake
   - lake of Ariccia 44
   - lake Albano 44
   - lake Nemi 44
   - lake of Campoverde 36
   - lake Fogliano 38, 43
   - lake of Vescovo 39
L'Amastuola 78, 129, 132
land evaluation 5, 11, 13-14, 171, 173-174
   - Automated Land Evaluation System (ALES) 2
   - in the Pontine Region 36-37
   - of the Salento Isthmus 63, 66-67, 77, 174
   - FAO land evaluation method 174
landscape classification 82, 84, 173-174
landform characteristics 45
land systems 13-14, 40, 144, 174
   - of the Pontine Region 31-33, 36, 39, 40, 43, 50-52, 56-58
   - of the Salentho Isthmus 59, 62-63, 77, 79, 140-141
   - of the Sibaritide 82
land-use studies 11-15

Lanuvium 46, 48, 145
Larinum 162
latifundiae 50, 52, 167
Latina land system 56
'Latina' plain 56
Latium 178
   - Archaic Latium 140
   - Latium Vetus 48, 110, 146, 113
   - and peer polity 141-142
   - and city state 178
Lavinium 145
Lazio 3, 32, 35, 39, 44, 113, 116, 177
   - northern 35
   - southern 17, 39, 44, 111-112, 117, 141
   - ancient Lazio 116, 133
Lepine mountains 142, 144-155, 175
   - Lepine margins 39, 50-52, 57, 143, 153
   see also Monti Lepini
Li Castelli di San Pancrazio 67, 72, 136
L'Incoronata 132
Liri Valley (survey) 161
Livy 48, 51, 55, 142, 145
Locorotondo 152
longue durée 8, 10, 29, 32, 148, 174, 175-176
Lucania 163-164
   - Lucania Apennines 162
   - Lucanian uplands 163

M
Macchiabate necropolis 96-98, 103, 123
Manacorda, D. 69
manuring practices 153-154, 164
Maruggi, G. A. 129
masseria I Fani 136, 140
masseria Mea 67
Massico mountain 161
Mater, B. 18, 96, 175
Matera 162
Mesagne 65-66, 73
Metapontino 62, 162, 178
Metapontion 124, 132, 158, 162
Metaponto 162
   see also Metapontion
Mezzaluna (pollen core) 35, 39
Mingardo river 163
   - valley 163
Monte Circeo 55, 150
Monte Papaluccio 72, 139
   - sanctuary 139
Monte Salete 130
Monte Sannace 158
Monti Aurunci 161
Monti Ausoni 12, 32, 40, 43, 53, 150
Monticchio (pollen core) 39
Monti Lepini 4, 5, 12, 33, 35-36, 39-41, 43, 45, 49-51, 53, 56-58, 110, 142, 144-145, 149-150, 153, 175
Morley, N. 168-169, 179

Morris, I. 9, 159
Mottola land system 77-79
Murge 149
   - Murge area 167
   - Murge plateau 151, 162
   - Murge table land 73, 158, 173
   - Murge uplands 5
   - Murge land system 78
Muro Maurizio 136, 137
Muro Tenente 6, 67, 130, 136-138

N
Nettuno 52, 54-55
Norba 51, 142, 144-145, 147, 150, 155, 157, 160, 179

O
oikoi 140
olive culture 92
Olmobello 48
oppida 142, 158, 167-168
Oria 5, 128, 130, 136-140, 155, 167
   - Archaic Oria as a central place 139
   - Oria catchment area 16
   - Oria field survey 16, 67
Ostuni 5, 61, 75-76, 112, 152
   - Ostuni survey 75-76, 112, 167
Otranto 126, 132

P
Palaeogeographical reconstructions 12-14, 29, 173
pastoralism 85, 154, 169, 171, 174, 178
   - pastoral and agricultural activities 12, 34
   - pastoral society 14
   - pastoralist strategies 174
   - pastoral economy 88
   - pastoral resources 131-132
   - transhumant pastoralism 148
   - pastoral exploitation 162
peer-polity (interaction) 10, 26, 29, 112, 141-142
Peroni, R. 7, 81, 88, 90-94, 103, 105, 108-110, 112, 114, 116, 117, 122
physical landscape (changes in) 32
Pietra Castello di Cassano Ionio 94
pollen cores 31, 83, 85, 174
   - of Central Italy 35
   - of the Pontine region 36-39
   - of the Sibaritide 85-86
   - pollendiagrams 35, 84
   - pollen evidence 12, 36, 38, 46-47, 85-86
   - pollen studies 36
Pollino mountains 82, 85, 87, 154, 174-175
   - national park 83, 87
Pometia 46-47
Pontine and Sibaritide plains 175
Pontine region 4, 29, 31-32, 35-36, 38, 142, 147, 149-151, 155-156, 160,

167, 172, 174-179
- colonies 152, 156
- graben 12
- plain 4-5, 12, 22, 25-26, 29-30, 41, 44, 57, 142, 144-145, 150, 155, 160, 167, 174, 179
Pontine Marshes 32, 149
Potenza 162, 163
Potter, T. 161
pottery production 16, 18, 47, 54, 103, 111, 175
pottery studies 16, 48, 171, 175
Priverno 12, 50
proto-urbanization 57, 107, 112-113, 115-116, 122-123, 179
- proto-urban settlements 15, 25, 27, 46, 54-57, 117, 140-141, 172-173
- proto-urban society 46
- proto-urban centres 94, 112-113
- Etruscan proto-urban centers 113
- proto-urban landscape 117
- proto-urban settlement pattern 144
Punic Wars 147, 168

Q
Quilici, L. 47, 65, 81, 149, 152, 164
Quilici Gigli, S. 47, 65, 164
Quilici survey 167

R
Raganello river 23, 82, 86, 92-93, 100, 102-103, 105, 121
- alluvium 24
- valley 82
- watershed 85, 101, 173
Raganello Archaeological Project 3, 81, 83, 87, 102
rank-size analysis 26-27, 122
redistributive system 93, 111
regional settlement models (scope and limitations of) 29
Renfrew, C. 26-27, 29
research biases
see biases
Rieti intermontane basin 162
Rissieddi 75-76, 112
ritual 47, 126, 139
- ritual architecture 47
- monumental ritual buildings 96
- ritual context 98, 139
Roccagloriosa 163
Roman colonization
see colonization
Roman conquest 147, 157
Roman expansion 142, 147-148, 159-160, 164-165
Roman Italy 148
Romanization 5, 10, 17, 51, 59
Roman market 168-169
Roman School of Protohistory 122, 126, 177

Rome 47, 49, 51-52, 55, 135, 140, 142, 145, 147, 155-156, 159, 166, 168-169, 179
- growth of Rome 169
- impact of Rome 179
Rossano 93-94
Rowlands, M. 29
RPC surveys 15-16, 110, 142, 144, 149, 172-173, 176
rural infill 151, 155, 159-160, 164-165, 167
- prior to Greek or Roman colonization 1
- in the Sibaritide 22, 151, 178
- in the Pontine Region 45-46, 48, 57, 144-145, 156-157
- Hellenistic rural infill 67
- in the Brindisi plain 67
- on the Salento Isthmus 67, 76, 150, 157-159
- Greek rural infill 178
- in Samnium and Lucania 164
rural settlement patterns 150, 152, 160, 167

S
Sacco valley 150
Salento 128, 131-132, 152, 157-159, 177-179
Salento isthmus 5, 28, 151, 154, 157, 160, 174, 177-178
Salento isthmus landforms 14
Salento Murge 152
Salento peninsula 126-127, 132, 135
salt production 53-54, 88, 111
Samnium 164, 169
sanctuary of Timpone della Motta 97
San Giovanni Ruoti 163
Sangro valley 162
San Lorenzo 39
San Pancrazio 137
San Vito dei Normanni 135
Satricum 5, 16, 19, 46, 48-49, 140, 142
Second Punic War 166
sedimentation 40
see also erosion
Segni 142
see also Signia
Serra Testi 94
Setia 40, 41, 51, 142, 145, 150, 155, 160, 179
settlement distribution 2, 29
- comparison of 25
- in the Pontine Region 46, 108
settlement hierarchy 8, 107, 117
- modelling of 26
- in the Pontine Region 51, 144
- in the Salento Isthmus 58, 62, 68, 72, 136, 138, 177
- in the Brindisi region 136
- in the Sibaritide 91, 108, 177
- in the Biferno valley 161

- rural settlement hierarchy 176
settlement models 29
Sezze 12, 40, 41, 52
- Sezze alluvial fan 41
see also Setia
Sezze survey 145
Sibaritide 6, 21, 132, 151-152, 155, 157, 160, 167, 174, 177-179
- Sibaritide foothill zone 172
- Sibaritide plain 13
Siena and ACVU surveys 167
- Siena project 167
- Siena surveys 167
Signia 142, 144-145
Sinni valley 164
- Sinni Valley surveys 164
Siris-Polieion 132
'site' databases 20
Small, A. 163
Socio-economic complexity (in the Sibaritide) 114
South Etruria Survey 160-161, 163
Stombi (at Sybaris) 89, 121
Strabo 89, 121
suburbium (the) 168
Sybaris 21, 88, 100, 120, 124, 178
- Archaic Sybaris 89, 175

T
Taylor, J. 162
Taranto 78, 124-125
- Taranto chora 125
- Taranto plain 124-125
- Taranto/Scoglio del Tonno 130
Taras 77, 79, 124-126, 132, 145, 147, 158, 162
Tarianne 88
Tarracina 150, 179
Tempa Cortaglia 163
Terracina 32, 35, 56, 155
see also Tarracina
Thiessen polygons 26-28, 151
Thurioi 22, 89, 121, 149, 151-152, 155, 167
Tiber Valley Project 161
Timpone della Motta 7, 81, 94, 96, 99, 121, 123-124, 178
- continuity of cultic occupation at 98
Theory of practice 18
Tor Pisana 132
Torre Astura 56
Torre Castelluccia 130
Torre Mordillo 6, 88, 92-94, 109, 111-113, 115, 117, 121-122
Torre Saturo 130, 132
Torelli, M. 9
transhumance 174
- long-distance transhumance 169, 175
- short-distance transhumance 50, 53, 57, 174

- vertical transhumance 86
tratture 175
Tres Tabernae 49
trulli 153, 158

U
University of Alberta 163
University of Lecce (excavations) 75, 77, 135-136, 139, 162
up- (and high)lands 103, 160, 171, 174, 179
   - uplands of the Monti Lepini 5, 25, 40, 43, 50, 57, 142
   - uplands of the Murge 5, 63, 75-76, 130, 149, 175
   - uplands of the Italian peninsula 35
   - Sezze uplands 50
   - protohistorical upland sites 50
   - Metapontino uplands 62, 162
   - of the Salento Isthmus 79
   - of the Sibaritide 81-82, 86-88, 100-101, 174
   - upland zones in the Pontine Region 117
   - upland zones of northern Calabria 120
   - uplands of the territory of Timpone della Motta 122
   - other central Italian upland areas 152
   - Lucanian uplands 163
   - uplands of the Sinni valley 164
urbanization 8-9, 79, 100, 135, 146
   - Greek urbanism 117, 135
   - indigenous urbanization 122, 135-146
   - and pottery studies 17-18
   - early Hellenistic urbanization 173
Urbs (the) 157, 169

V
Valesio 5-6, 70, 72-73, 130, 136-140, 154, 167
   - Valesio and Ostuni survey transects 167
   - Valesio surveys 71
Van Joolen, E. 12-13, 36, 38-43, 50, 52-53, 56, 62-63, 66, 74, 77-78, 174
Vanzetti, A. 90, 113, 116-117, 122, 124
Vaste 158
Veenman, F. 14, 174-175
vegetation degradation 175
Velletri 46
Venusia 162
Via Appia 49-50, 56-57, 79, 155-156, 167, 179
villae maritimae 53, 56
villaggio delle macine (Alban Hills) 44
Vinson, P. 162-163
visibility and research biases 172-173
  (*see biases*)
Vita-Finzi, C. 61

Volpe, G. 168
Volscian wars 48

W
wars between Latins, Romans, and mountain peoples 145
Whitehouse, R. D. 139
Wightman, E. 161
Wilkins, J. 139

X
XTENT modelling 27-29, 151

Y
Yntema, D.G. 16, 67, 72, 130, 132-133, 157

Colour plates

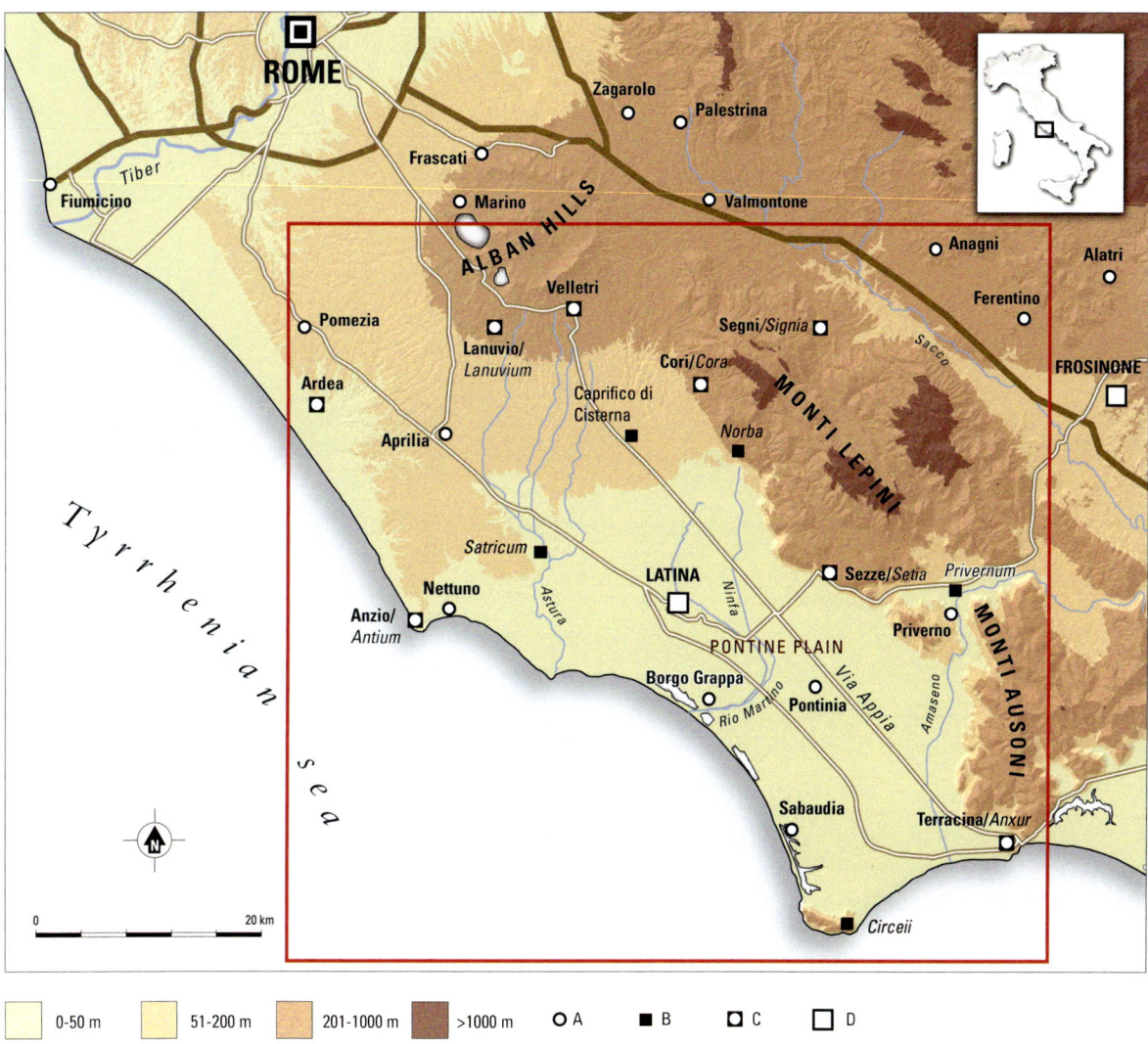

Fig. 1.2. Geography and topography of the Pontine region. A modern town; B ancient town; C ancient and modern town; D modern provincial capital. The RPC study area is indicated by a box.

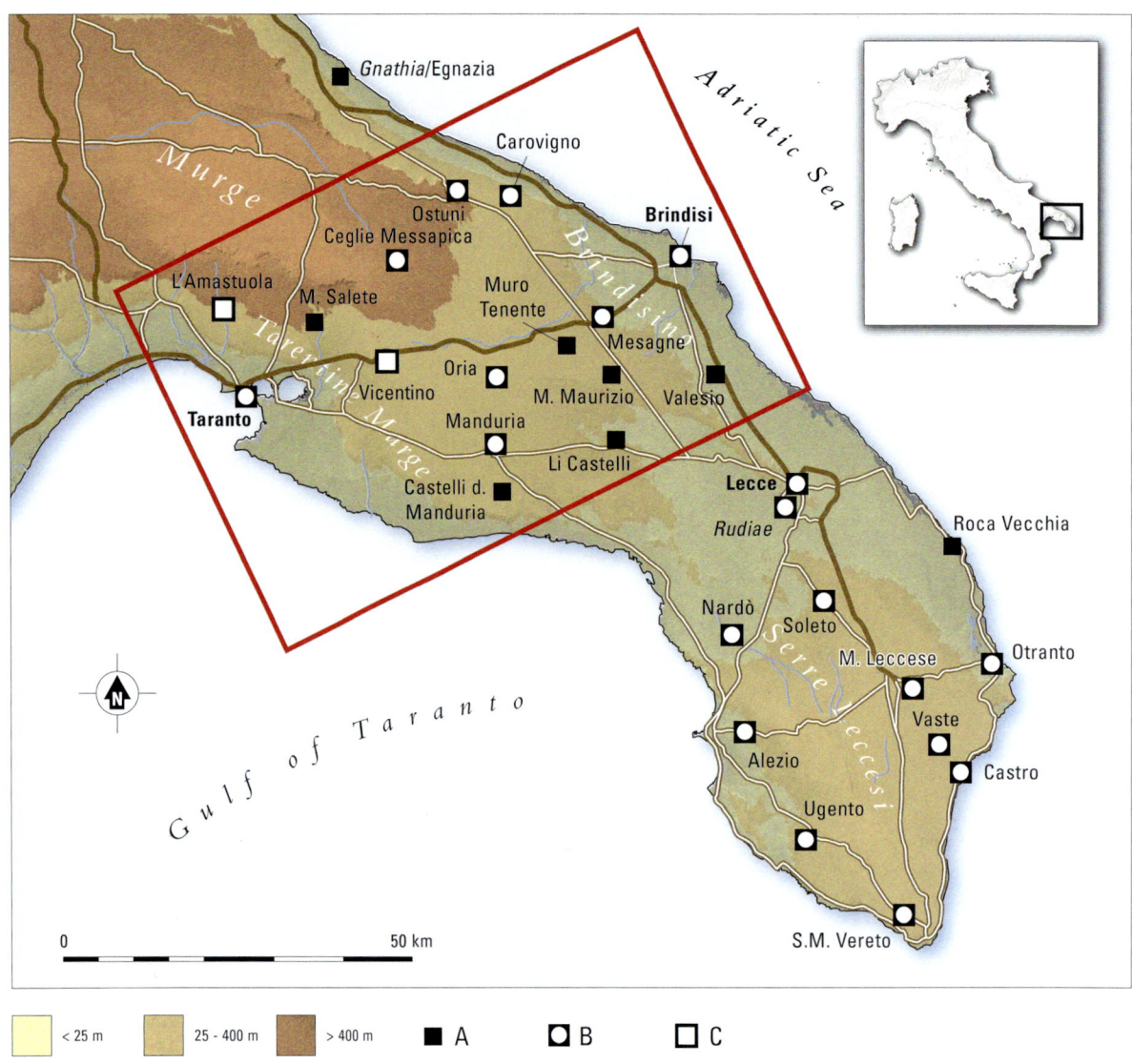

Fig. 1.3. Geography and topography of the Salento peninsula. A ancient town; B ancient and modern town; C named archaeological site. The Salento Isthmus is outlined.

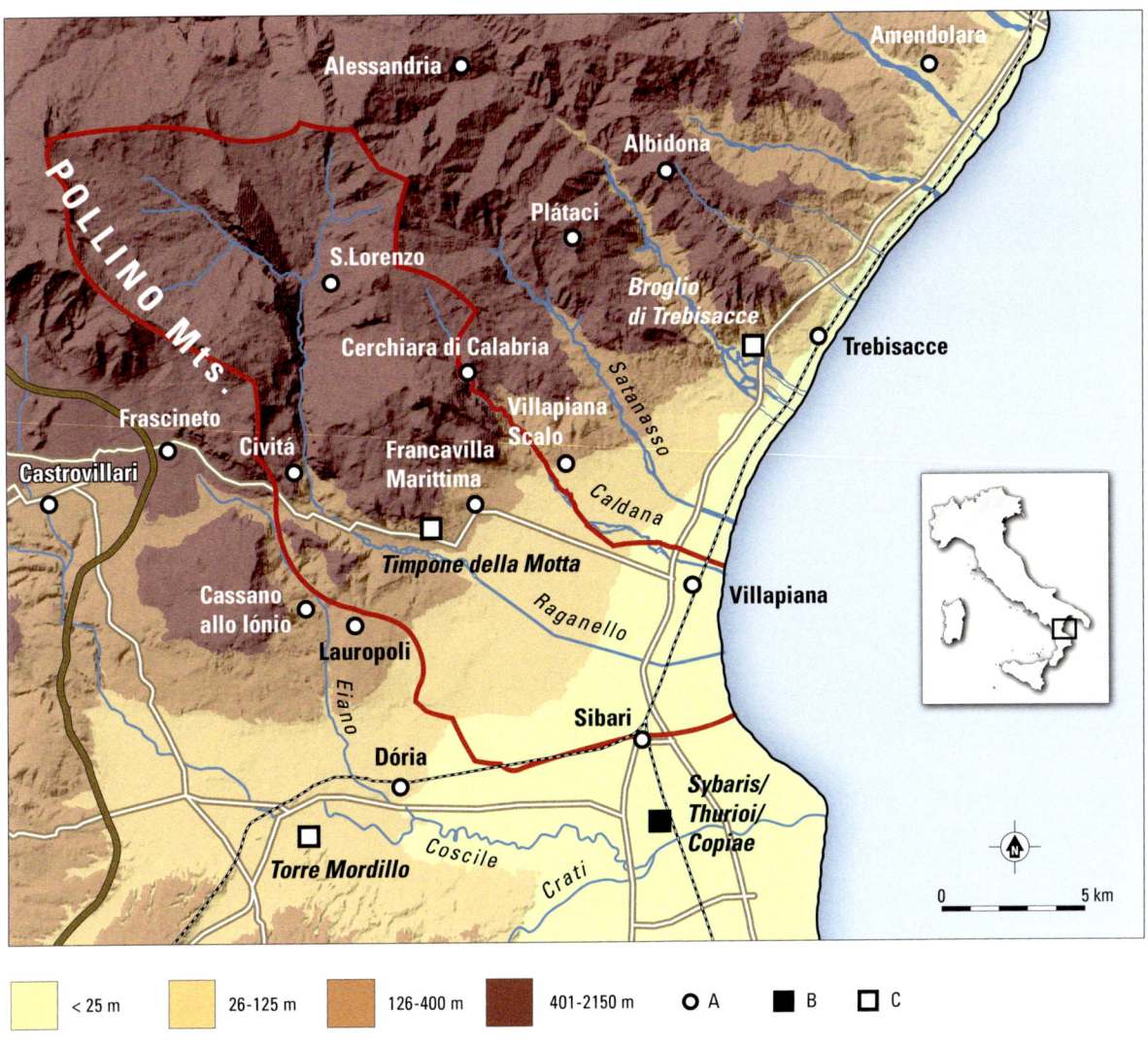

Fig. 1.4. Geography and topography of north-eastern Calabria. A modern town; B ancient town; C major archaeological site. The RPC study area is outlined.

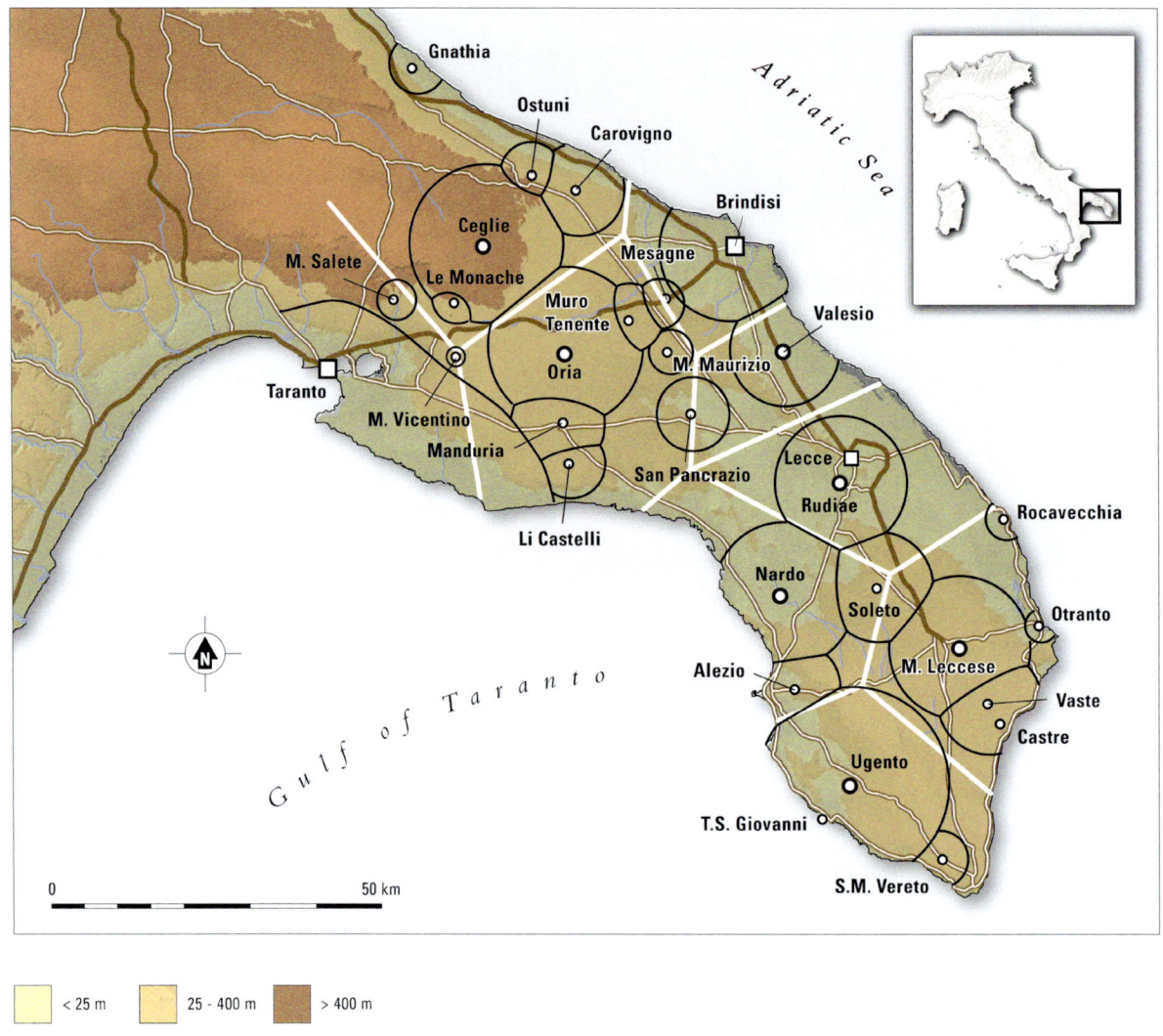

Fig. 1.8. Modelling early Hellenistic territorial organization of the Salento peninsula using Thiessen polygons for the largest sites (white) and XTENT 'bubbles' for all sites (black) (after Burgers 1999, 26-27).

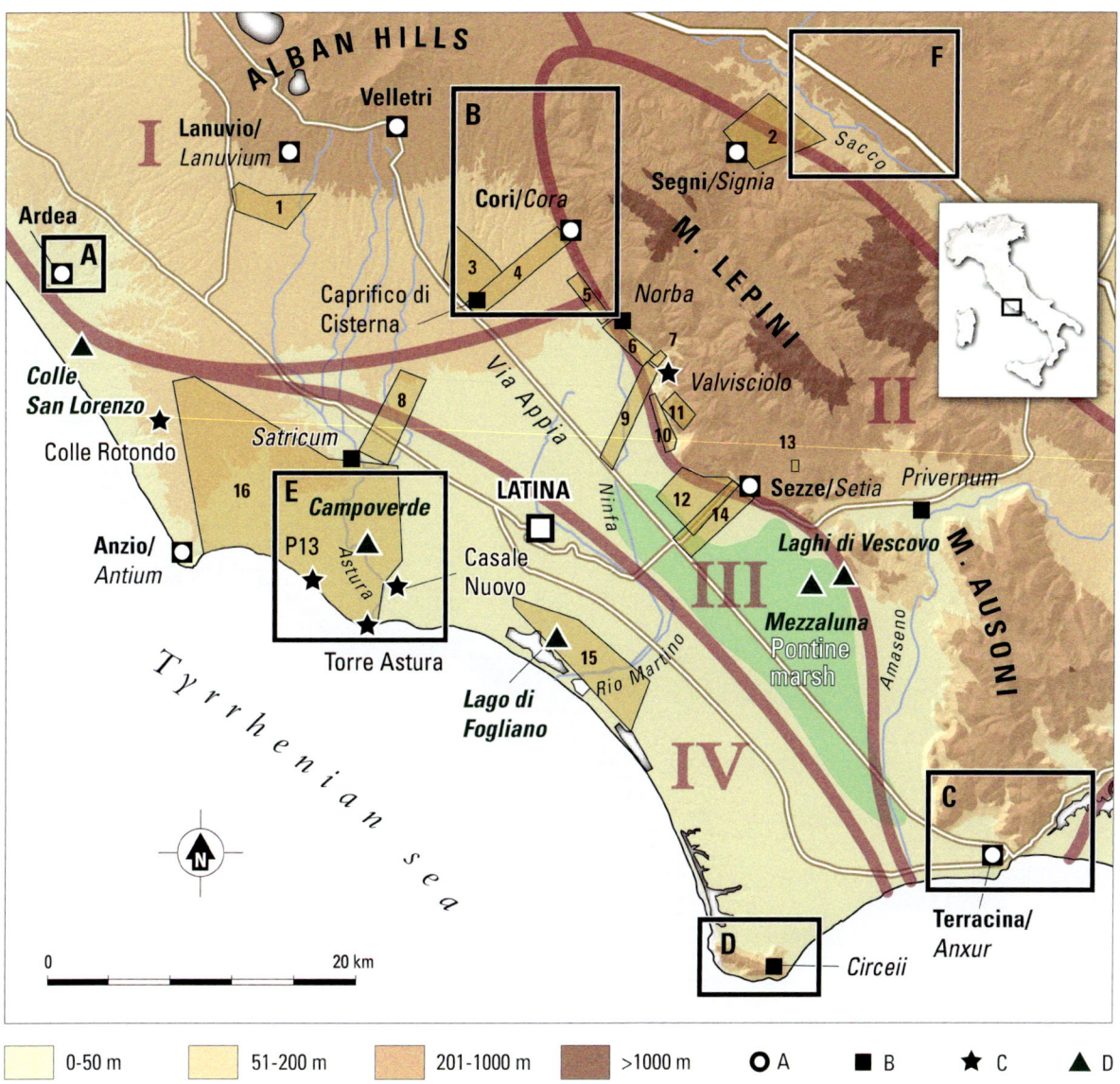

Fig. 2.1. The main land systems of the Pontine region (I - IV), with areas investigated for the *Forma Italiae* series (A - F), areas investigated by the GIA (1 - 16), and pollen locations mentioned in the text. Legend: A modern town, B ancient town; C named archaeological site; D pollen location.

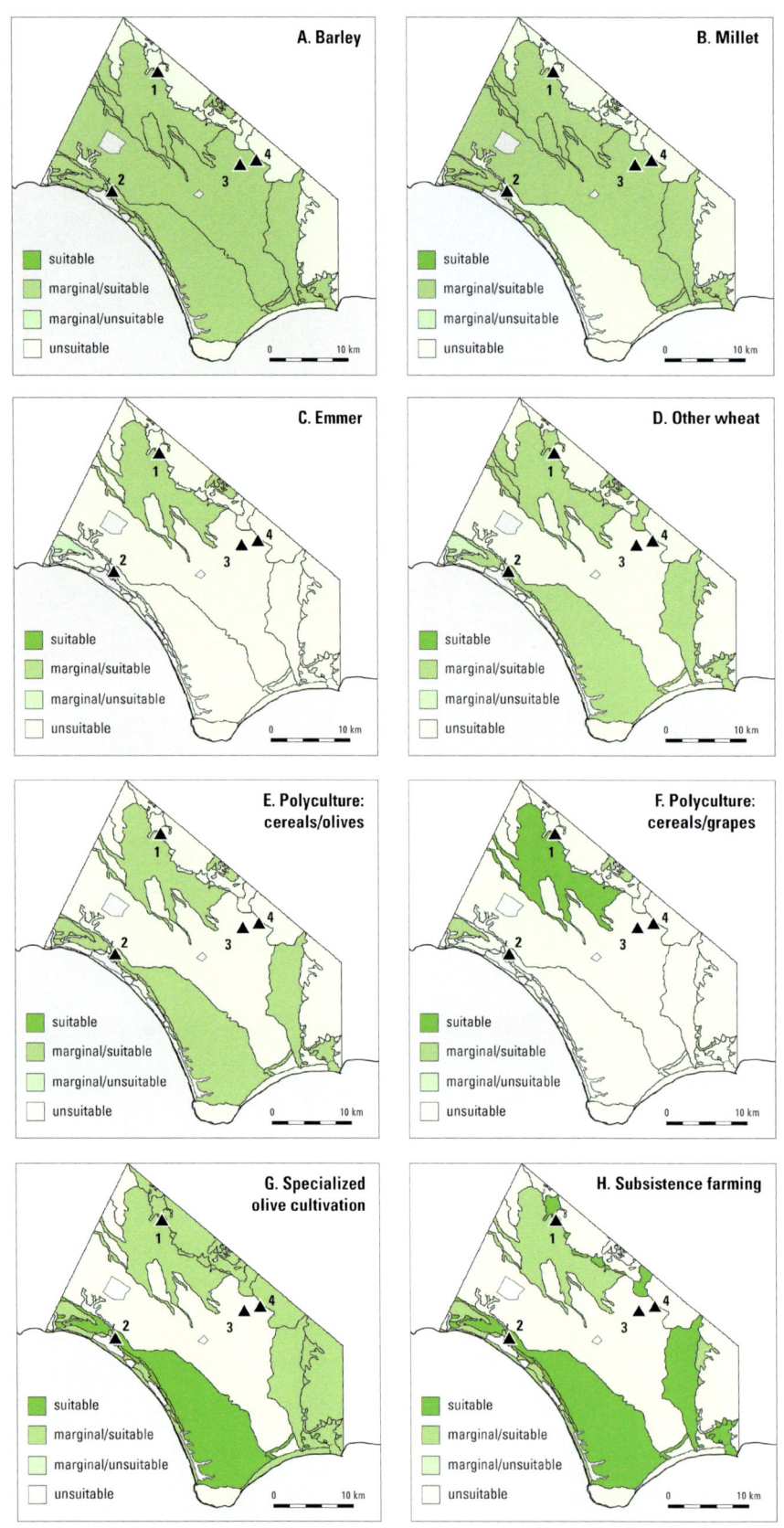

Fig. 2.3. Land evaluation models for four grain types and four cultivation types in the Pontine region (after Van Joolen 2003, figs 5.8 and 6.2). Locations of relevant pollen cores: 1. *Monticchio*, 2. *Lago di Fogliano*, 3. *Mezzaluna*, 4. *Laghi di Vescovo*.

Fig. 2.6. View south from the Monti Lepini across the Pontine plain towards the Tyrrhenian Sea and the Monte Circeo (photo W. de Neef, GIA 2009).

Fig. 3.1. The Salento Isthmus study area, with modern topography, archaeological sites mentioned in the text, and ACVU survey areas.

Fig. 3.3. View of the Brindisi plain, part of the Brindisino land system (photo: G.-J. Burgers, ACVU).

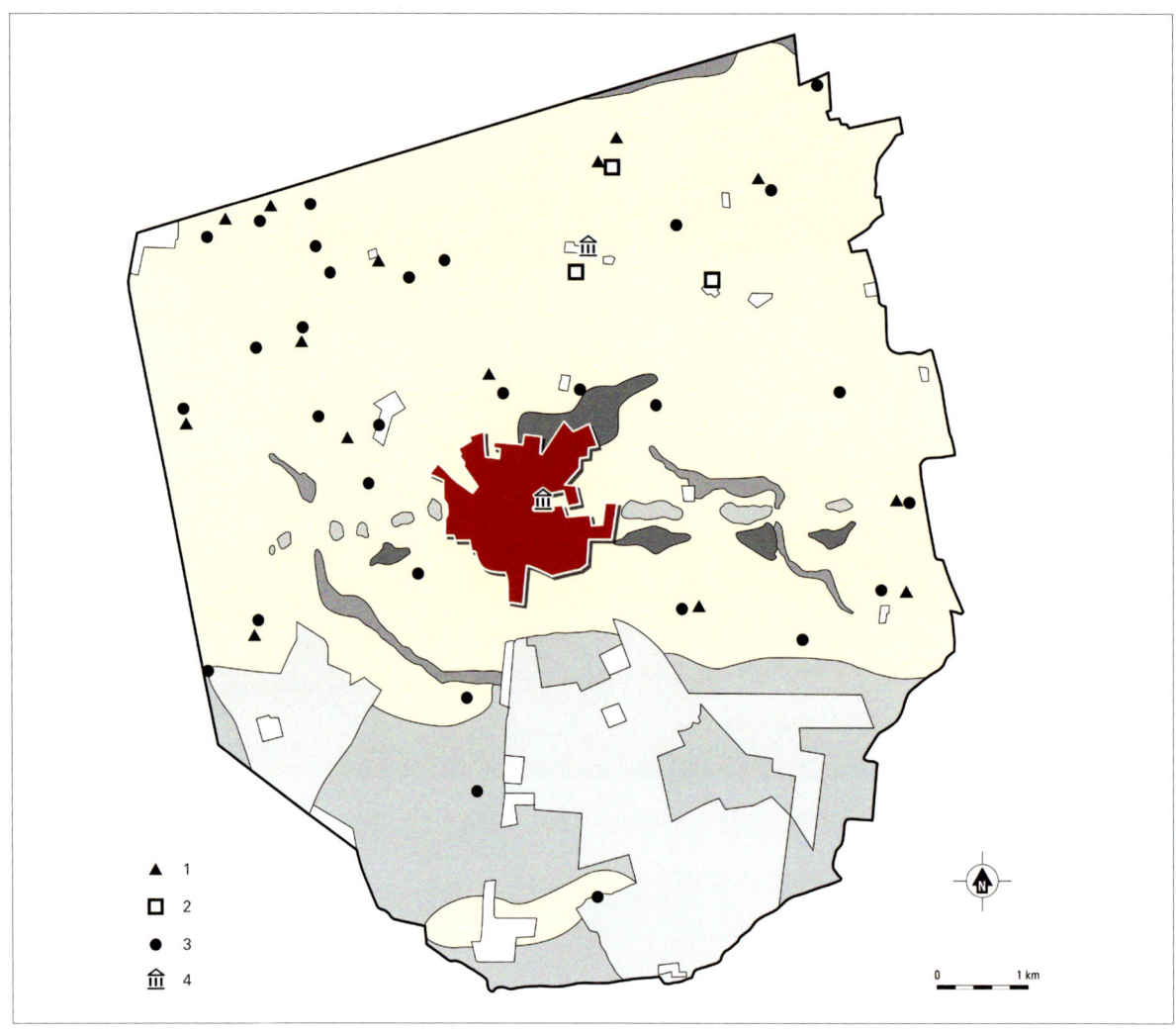

Fig. 3.4. Distribution of early Hellenistic sites in the Oria survey area. 1 necropolis; 2 hamlet; 3 isolated farmstead; 4 sanctuary. Colours represent different geophysical units (after Yntema 1993, fig. 74).

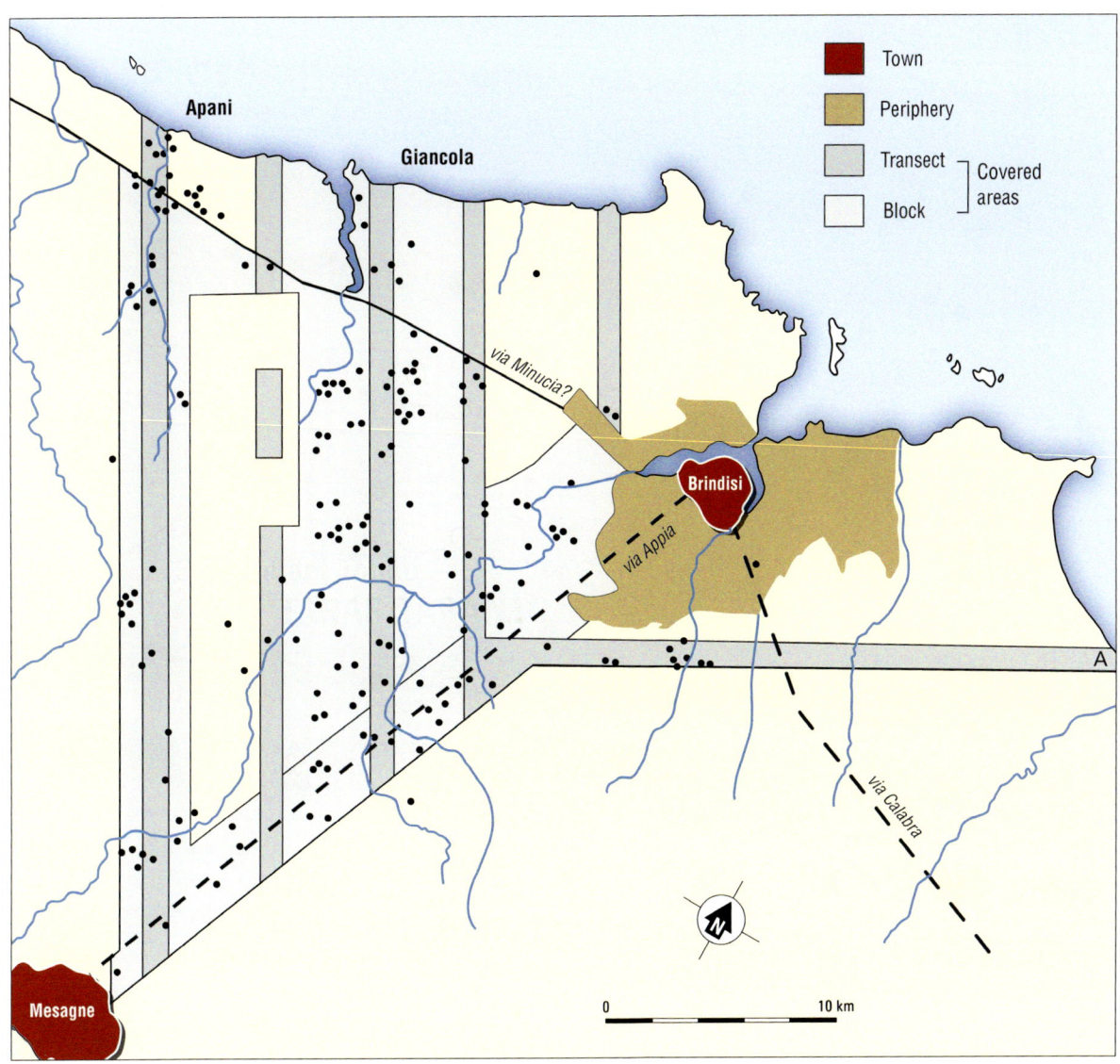

Fig. 3.5. Areas surveyed and sites recorded in the early 1990s by the University of Siena in the Brindisino (after: Cambi 2000, fig. 18.1).

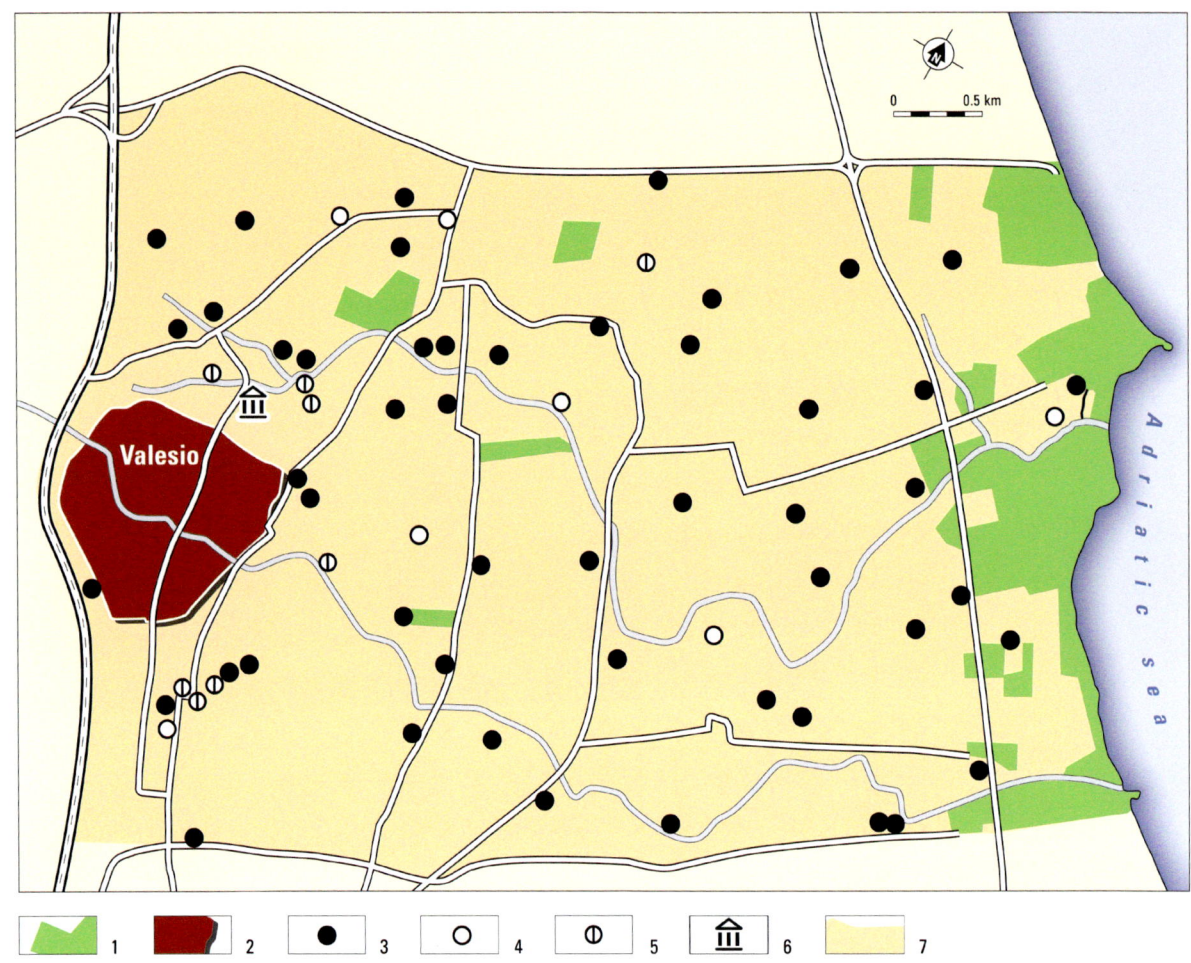

Fig. 3.6. Distribution of sites in the Valesio field survey area with artefacts dating between the late 4th century and the middle of the 2nd century BC. 1 inaccessible areas, 2 walled site of Valesio, 3 farm sites, 4 probable farm sites, 5 scatters consisting of tile and amphora only, 6 sanctuary site, 7 surveyed area.

Fig. 3.7. View across the Adriatic coastal plain towards the Murge tableland near Ostuni (photo: G.-J. Burgers, ACVU).

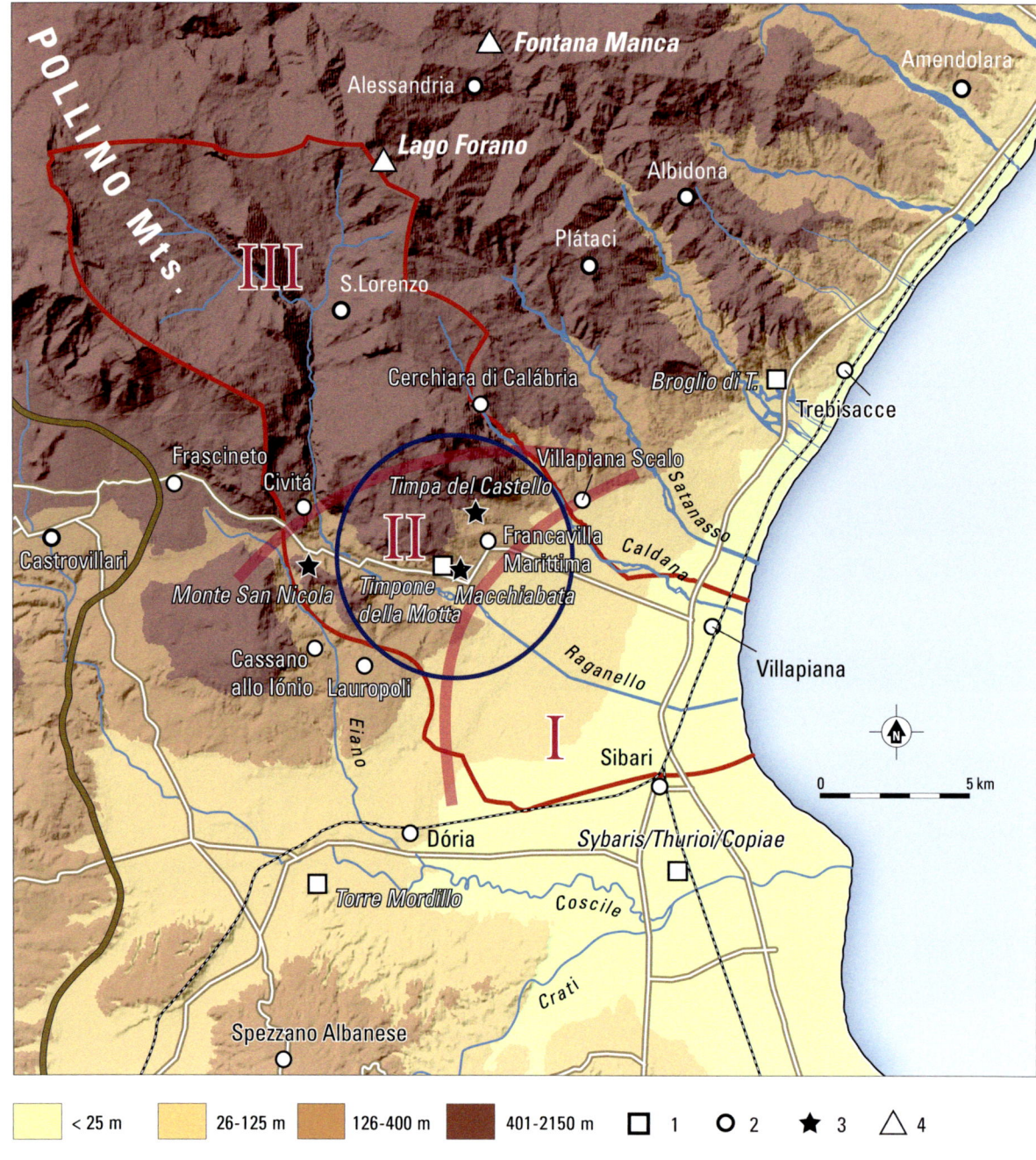

Fig. 4.1. Main features of the Raganello Archaeological Project study area. Main landscape zones: I coastal plain, II foothills, III mountains. 1 main protohistorical sites, with 5km radius catchment of the Timpone della Motta; 2 modern towns; 3 other archaeological sites mentioned in the text; 4 locations of pollen cores.

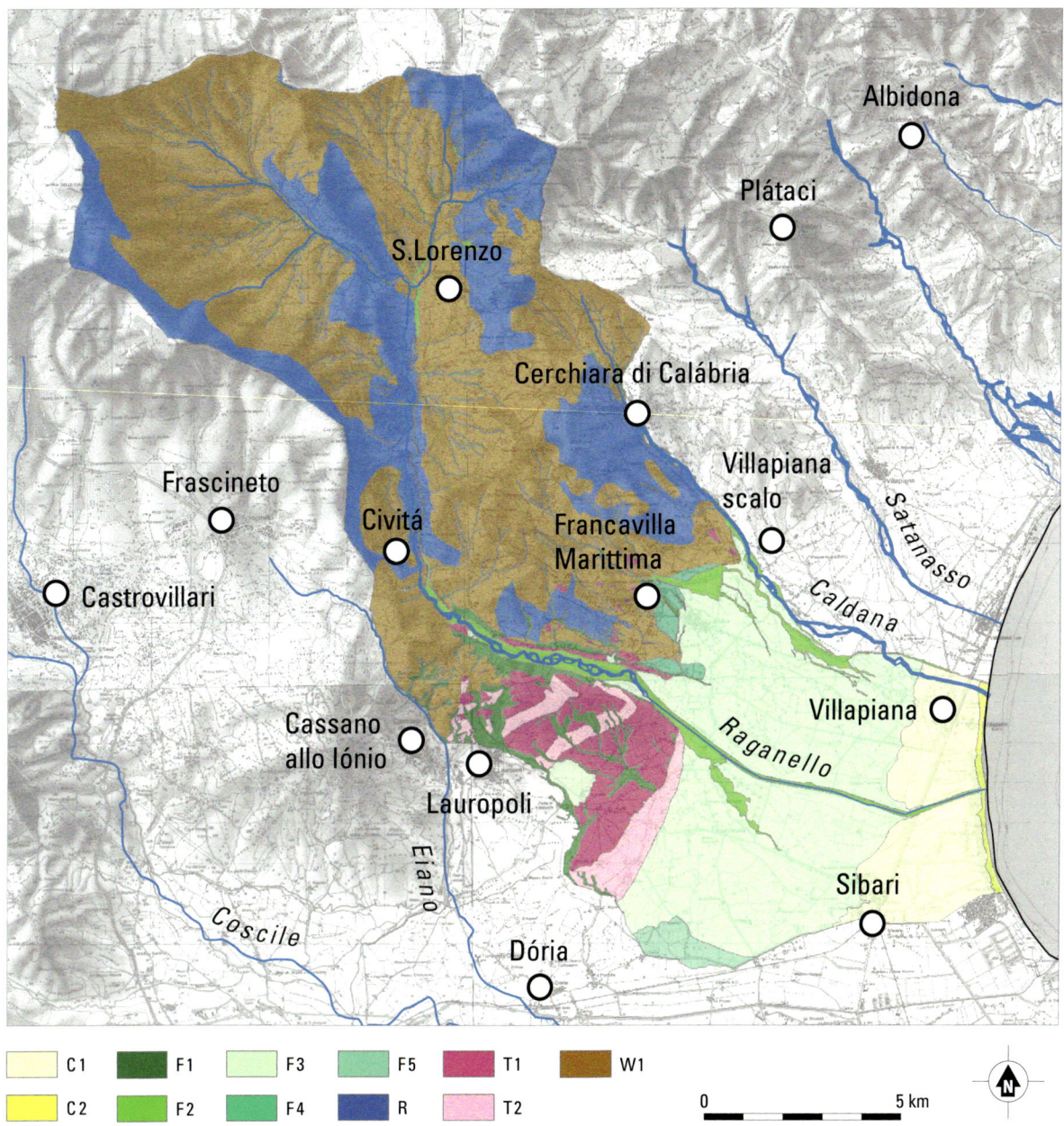

Fig. 4.2. Landscape classification map of the RAP study area. C recent coastal land units with (C2) and without relief (C1); F fluvial land units, ranging from incised gullies (F1) and broader valleys with braided (F2) or meandering (F5) streams to old (F3) and more recent (F4) alluvial fans; T ancient marine cliffs (T2) and terraces (T1); R hard rocks (limestones), forming steep slopes with little soil or vegetation; W1 weak rocks (marls, schists and shales), forming an irregular but gentle topography.

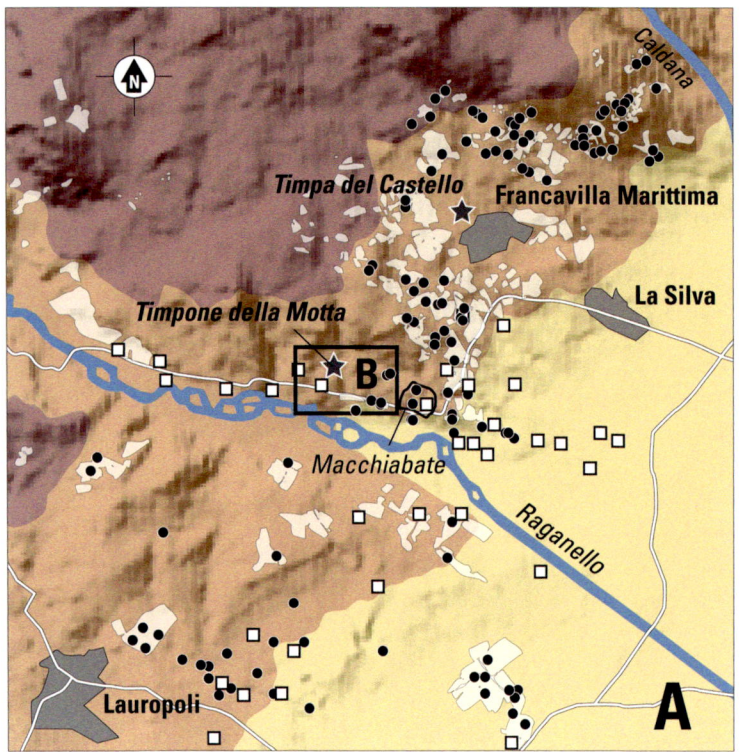
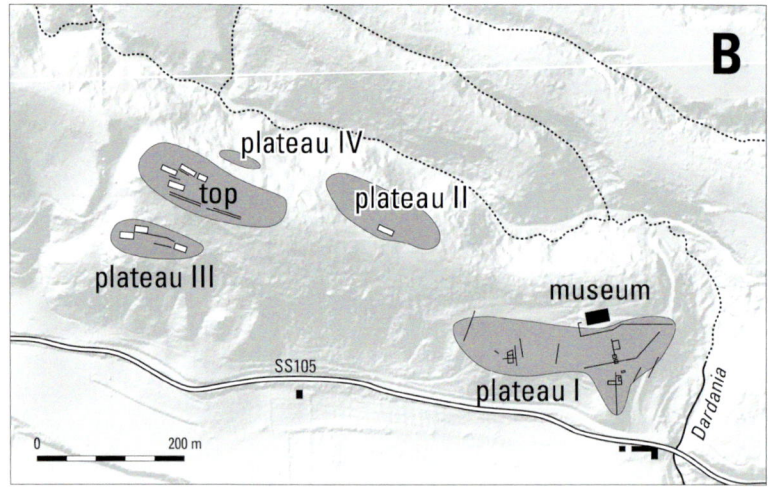

Fig. 4.6. GIA research on and around the Timpone della Motta. A: Areas surveyed intensively in the Timpone della Motta catchment area, with sites recorded in the 1960s (squares) and since 2000 (dots). B: plateaux, trenches and structures on the Timpone della Motta itself.

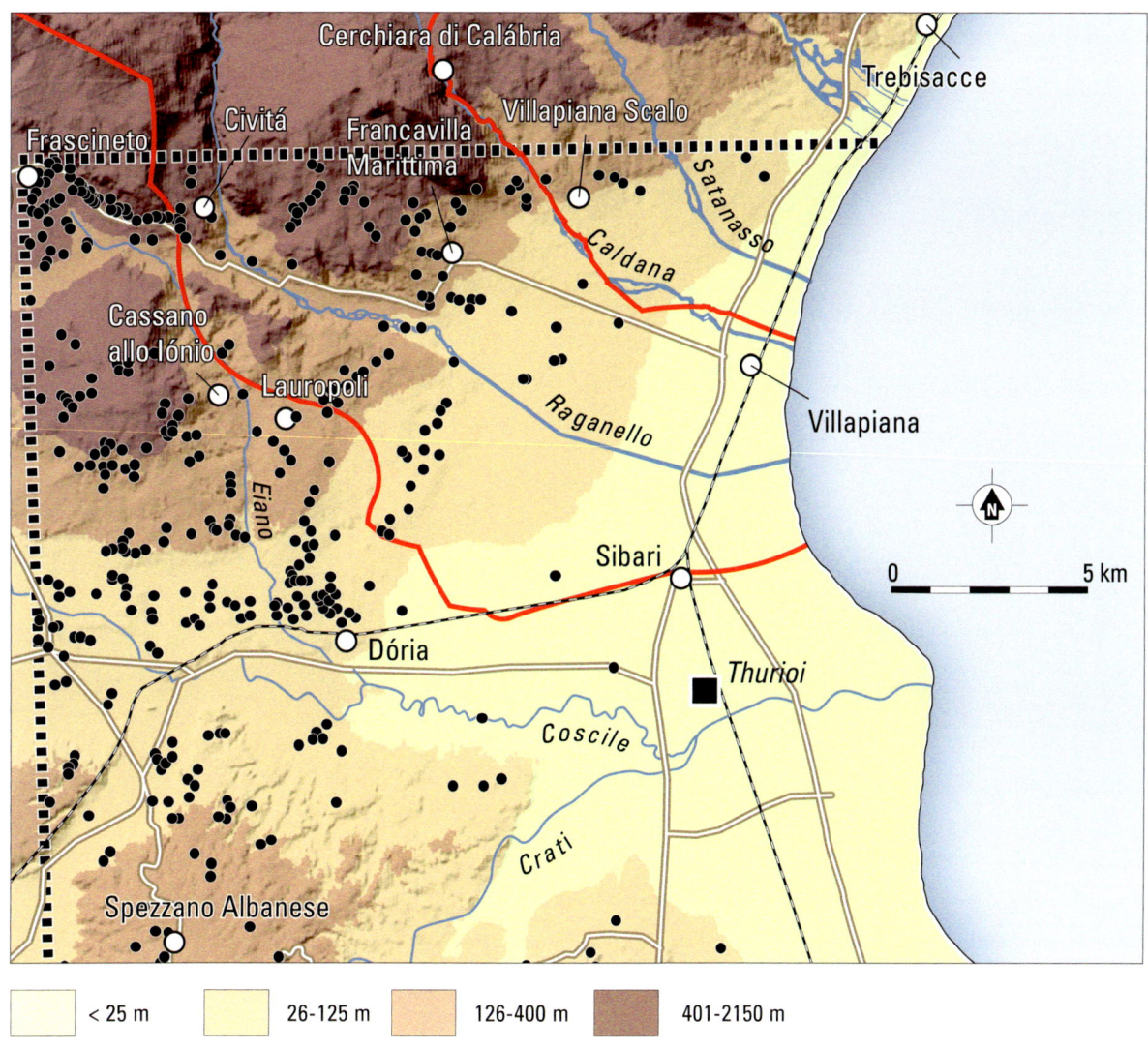

Fig. 4.9. Distribution of rural Hellenistic sites in the central Sibaritide (map compiled from site data published by De Rossi *et al.* 1969; their study area includes the foothill zone but not the mountain area). The outline of the RAP study area is added for orientation.

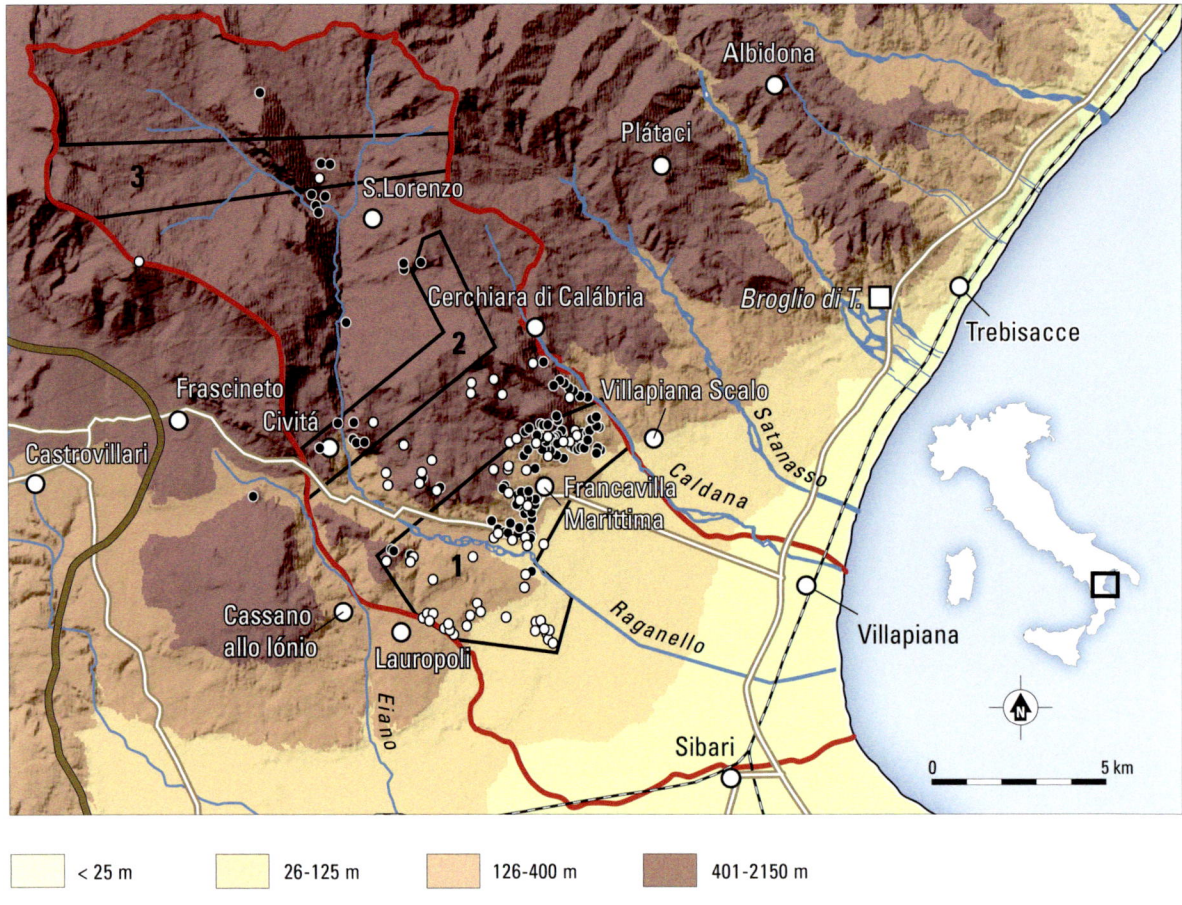

Fig. 4.10. Distribution of archaeological sites recorded by the GIA as part of the Raganello Archaeological Project (situation 2008). Black dots: protohistoric sites, white dots: Hellenistic to late antique sites. Intensive and systematic investigations have mainly taken place in the research transects.

Fig. 4.11. View from the Monte Sellaro toward the south across the Sibaritide coastal plain. The bed of the Raganello river can be seen in the middle distance (photo Nick Ryan, GIA 2000).

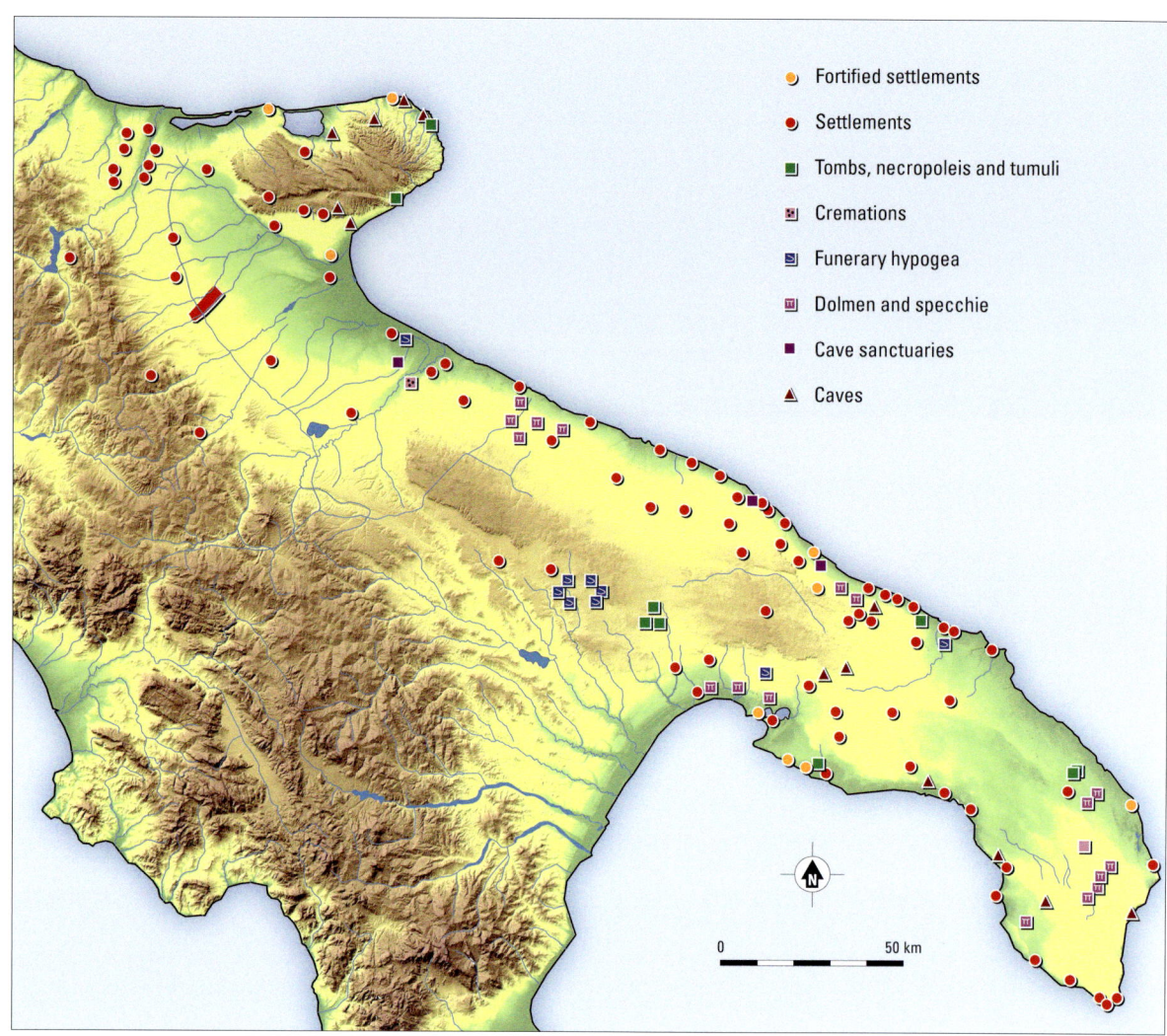

Fig. 5.1. Bronze Age sites in Apulia (after Recchia / Ruggini 2009, fig. 1).

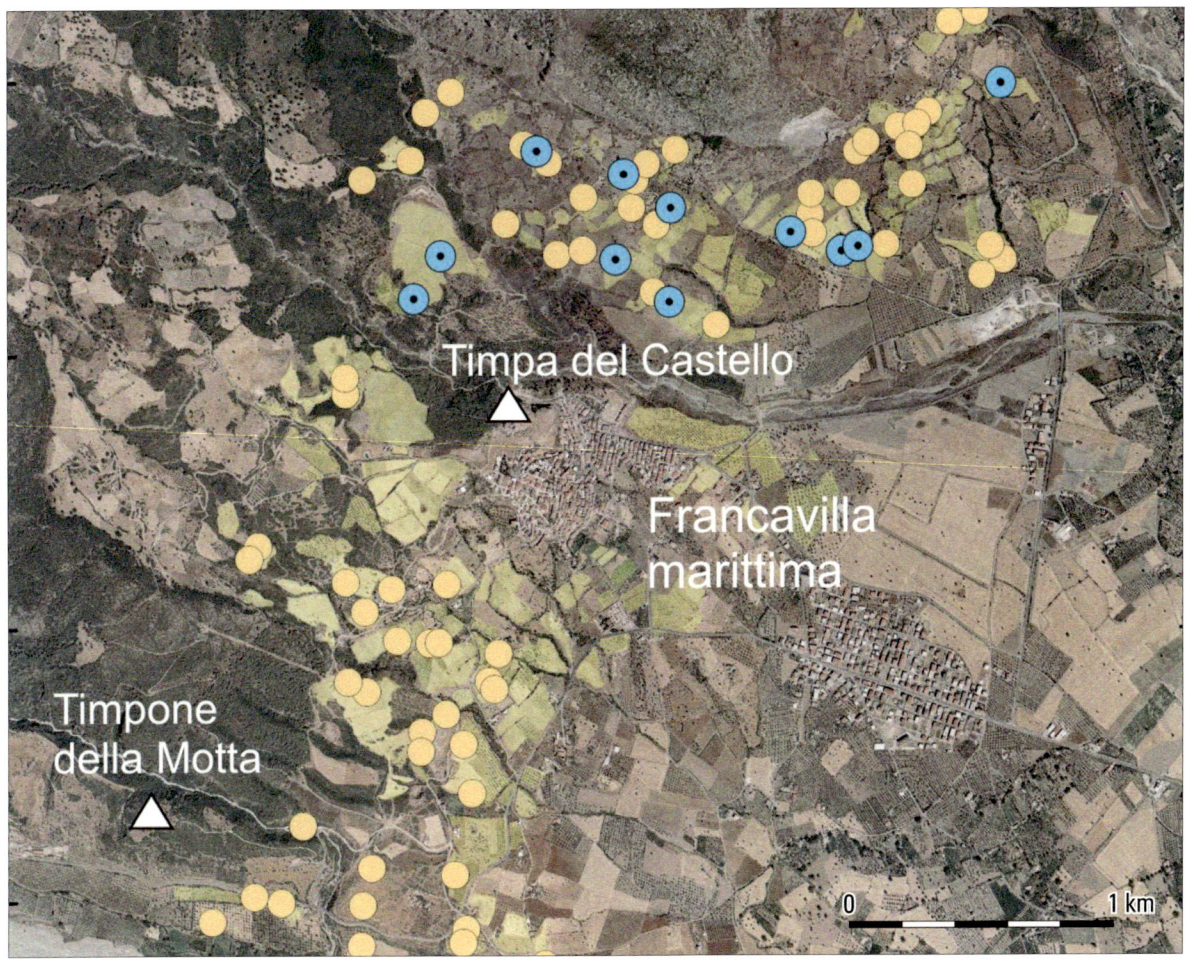

Fig. 5.4. Many of the protohistoric find spots (yellow dots) recorded by the Raganello Archaeological Project in the foothills between the Raganello and Caldana rivers have yielded sherds of Final Bronze Age *dolii a cordoni e fasce* in recent years (blue dots). The wide distribution appears to contradict Peroni's model of central management of olive oil consumption.

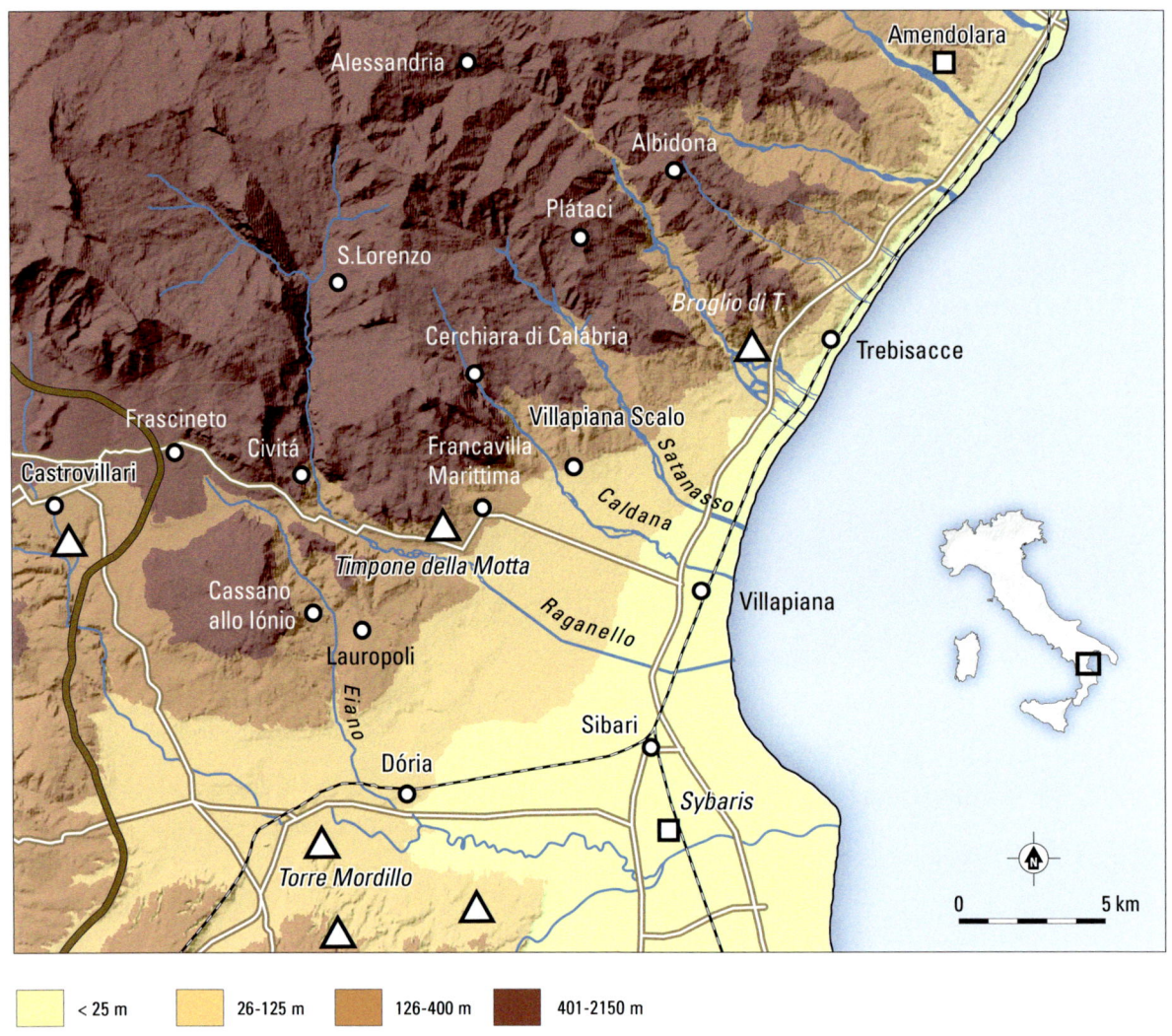

Fig. 6.1. Major Archaic sites of the Sibaritide (triangles; after Vanzetti 2002, fig. 7).

Fig. 6.2. Topography of the Taranto area, with major sites mentioned in the text.

Fig. 6.3. Photo and line drawing of stele from the Archaic necropolis of L'Amastuola (Crispiano, TA).

Fig. 6.5. Bird's-eye view of the archaeological site and masseria of L'Amastuola, with ACVU trenches visible to the left of centre (photo by permission of Mr. Giuseppe Montanaro).

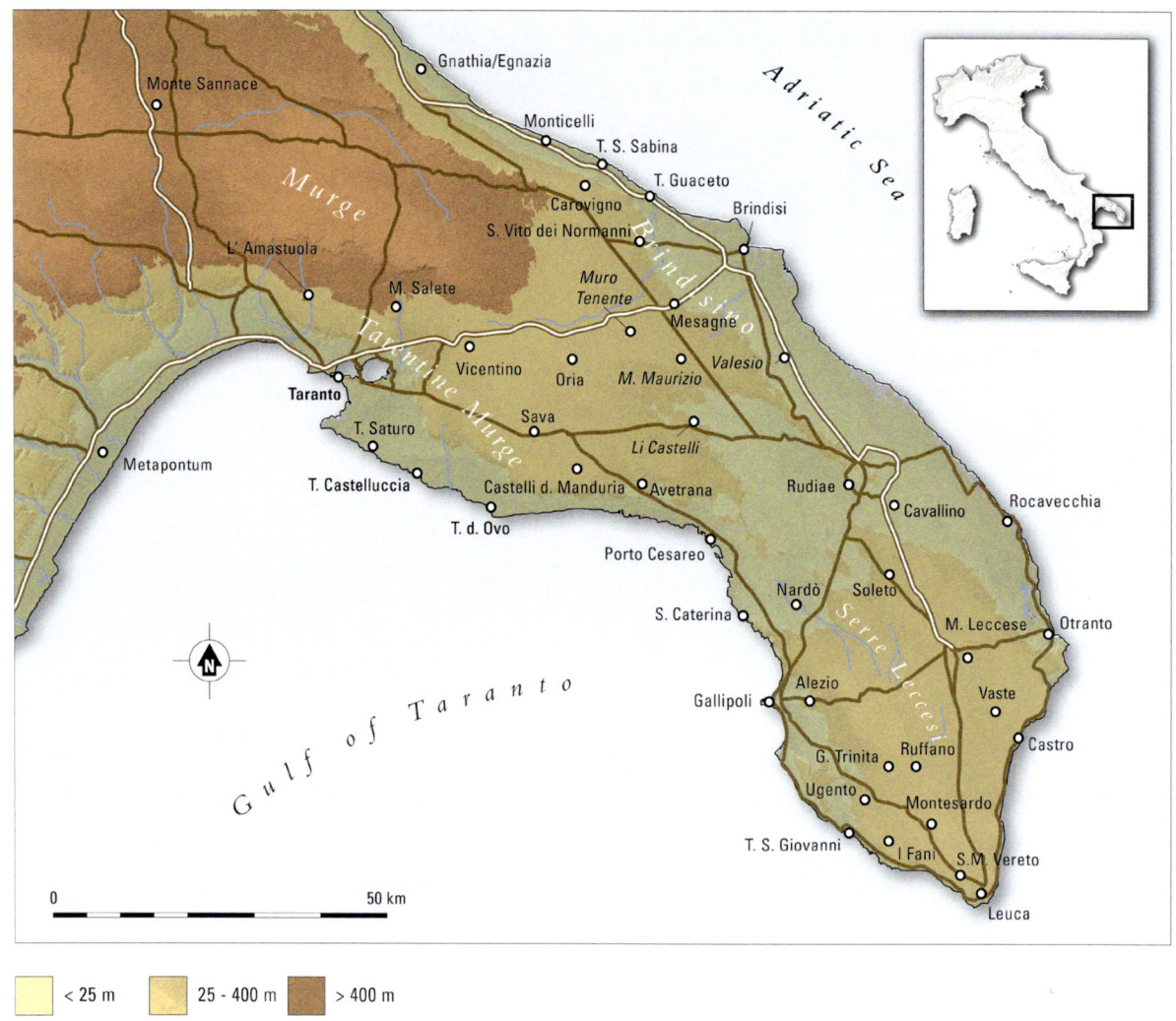

Fig. 7.1. Archaic sites of the Salento (after Semeraro 1998, 6).

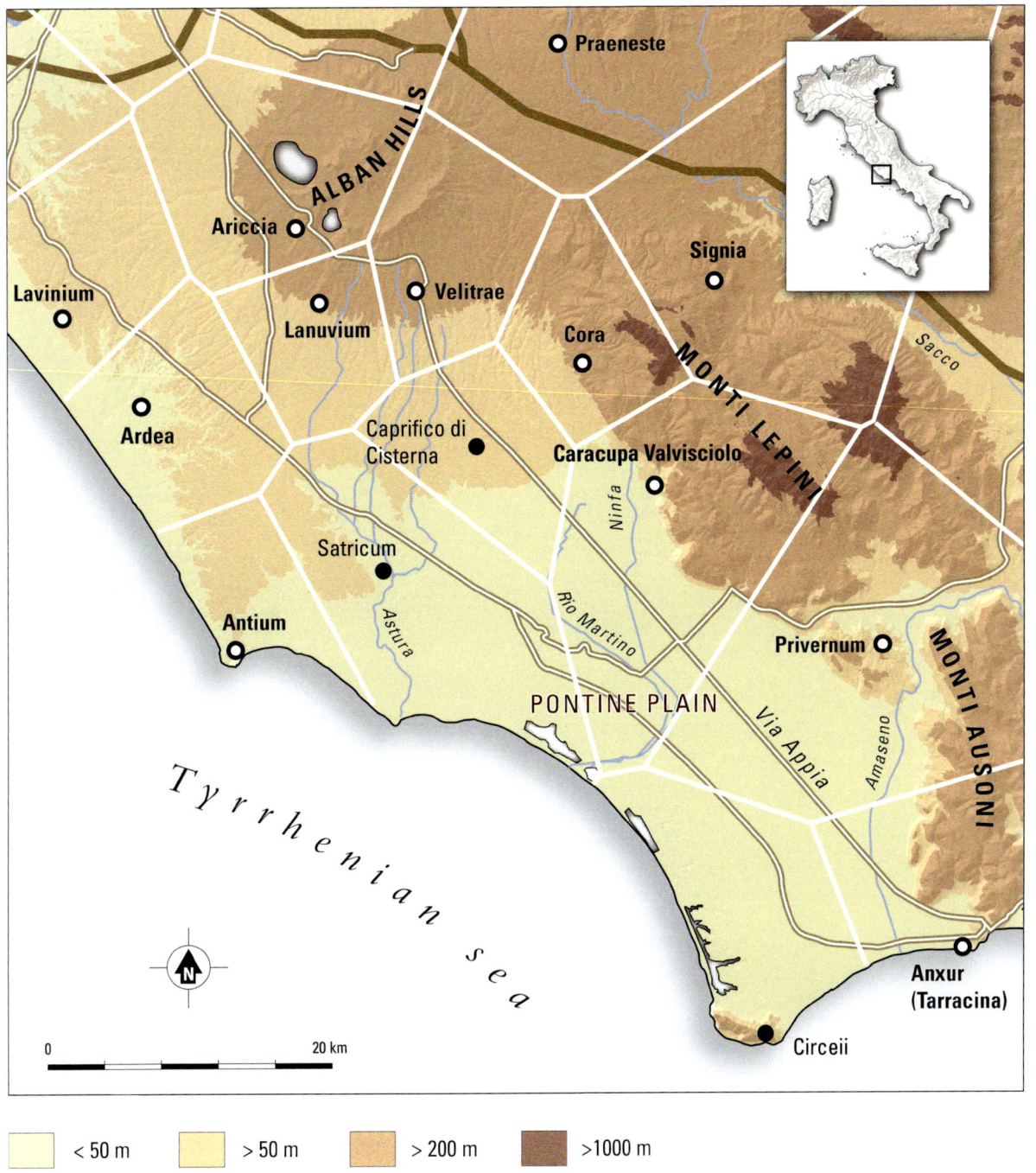

Fig. 7.2. Archaic proto-urban sites in south Lazio, with hypothetical territorial boundaries based on Thiessen polygons (T. de Haas, GIA).

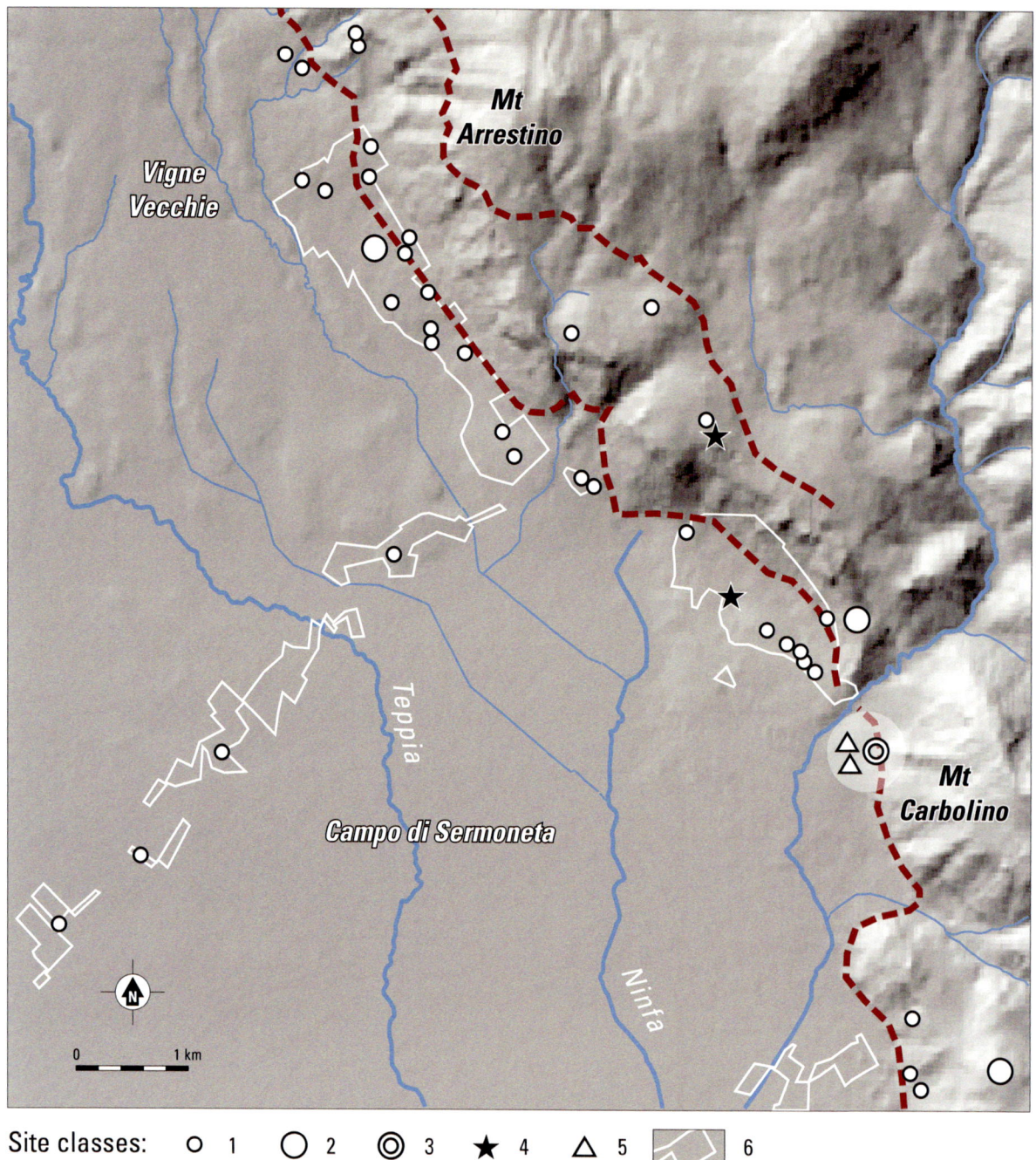

Fig. 7.3. Archaic settlement on the Lepine margins near Norba (compilation of survey results of the Pontine Region Project and sites published in the literature; after Van Leusen *et al.* 2005, fig. 7). 1. small sites, 2. large sites, 3. proto-urban site, 4. cult site, 5. graves, 6. intensively surveyed areas. Dashed lines: probable routes along the Lepine scarp.

Fig. 8.2. Artist's reconstruction of the early Hellenistic fortified site of Muro Tenente (Mesagne, BR), based on excavations and field surveys (drawing by mr. V. Camassa).

Fig. 8.3. Dispersed settlement pattern in the Murge countryside (photo G.-J. Burgers, ACVU).

Fig. 8.4. Hellenistic fortifications of the Apulian coastal town of Egnazia (Fasano, BR; photo: ACVU-archive).